CENTRAL AMERICA

Historical Perspectives on the Contemporary Crises

Edited by
Ralph Lee Woodward, Jr.

Contributions to the Study of World History,
Number 10

Greenwood Press
New York • Westport, Connecticut • London

Library of Congress Cataloging-in-Publication Data

Central America : historical perspectives on the
contemporary crises.

(Contributions to the study of world history,
ISSN 0885-9159 ; no. 10)
   Includes bibliographies and index.
   1. Central America—History—1951-
2. Central America—History—1821-1951.   3. Central
America—Foreign relations.   4. Geopolitics—Central
America.   5. Social conflict—Central America.
I. Woodward, Ralph Lee.   II. Series.
F1439.C36   1988   972.8 '05   88-208
ISBN 0-313-25938-0 (lib. bdg. : alk. paper)

British Library Cataloguing in Publication Data is available.

Library of Congress Catalog Card Number: 88-208
ISBN: 0-313-25938-0
ISSN: 0885-9159

First published in 1988

Greenwood Press, Inc.
88 Post Road West, Westport, Connecticut 06881

Printed in the United States of America

The paper used in this book complies with the
Permanent Paper Standard issued by the National
Information Standards Organization (Z39.48-1984).

10 9 8 7 6 5 4 3 2 1

8-2-90

CENTRAL AMERICA

Recent Titles in
Contributions to the Study of World History

The Myth of the Revolution: Hero Cults and the Institutionalization
of the Mexican State, 1920-1940
Ilene V. O'Malley

Accommodation and Resistance: The French Left, Indochina and the
Cold War, 1944-1954
Edward Rice-Maximin

Genocide and the Modern Age: Etiology and Case Studies of Mass Death
Isidor Wallimann and Michael N. Dobkowski, editors

Because They Were Jews: A History of Antisemitism
Meyer Weinberg

Societies in Upheaval: Insurrections in France, Hungary, and Spain in the
Early Eighteenth Century
Linda Frey and Marsha Frey

The Practical Revolutionaries: A New Interpretation of the French
Anarchosyndicalists
Barbara Mitchell

The Dragon and the Wild Goose: China and India
Jay Taylor

Land and Freedom: The Origins of Russian Terrorism, 1876-1879
Deborah Hardy

Young Guard! The Communist Youth League, Petrograd 1917-1920
Isabel A. Tirado

Engine of Mischief: An Analytical Biography of Karl Radek
Jim Tuck

Acknowledgments

The editor and contributors wish gratefully to acknowledge the assistance in the preparation of this volume of the National Endowment for the Humanities; of Thomas Niehaus and his staff of the Latin American Library of Tulane University, especially Cecilia Montenegro de Teague, Martha Robertson, and Ruth Olivera; and of Bill Meneray and his staff in the Manuscripts and Rare Books Division of the Howard-Tilton Memorial Library at Tulane, especially Guillermo Náñez, Eric Palladini, and Sue McGrady Woodward.

Contents

Central America and Historical Perspective

Ralph Lee Woodward, Jr.

During the past decade Central America has become the focus of a great deal of attention from the major powers, the international press, scholars in many disciplines, and the general public. Revolution and political change; confrontation of the superpowers; social and economic disparity and under-development; and diversity of conditions and problems in the city-states of the isthmus are themes that have been pursued in a veritable explosion of works about Central America. Much of this literature has shed new light on the region's problems and their origins. Much of it has been highly polemical, motivated by special interest or passion in the heat of the conflicts there. Still more reflects an appalling ignorance of the region's culture and history, as many outsiders have sought to place Central America in the context of world development without sufficient attention to its unique culture and history.

This volume seeks to contribute to a deeper understanding of the Central American crises by looking at several aspects of the region's historical development. It is the product of a 1986 summer seminar, "The Central American Crises in Historical Perspective," sponsored by the National Endowment for the Humanities at Tulane University under the direction of the editor of this volume. The twelve participants in this volume who participated in the seminar engaged in intensive research and discussion of Central American history and culture. In many cases, they brought years of earlier research in and about Central America with them. In other cases, they brought fresh insights While the majority were historians, the seminar included two anthropologists, a political scientist, and a literature specialist. This diversity gave the seminar a distinctly interdisciplinary quality.

Although these papers do not pretend to embrace the entire history of Central America nor even all the historical aspects of the present crises, they do highlight several themes central to understanding the problems faced on the isthmus today. One is the continuing role of major outside forces on isthmian development. Nearly all of the essays reflect this presence and suggest a number of distinct effects. In the twentieth century, of course, the United States has been the major outside force in the region, and North American hegemony is a subject touched upon in various ways by nearly all the contributors.

A second common theme is the importance of native culture to the region, even though there is considerable diversity among the cultural patterns of the Central American states. This includes not only attention to indigenous and folk cultural patterns in several states but also to broader Central American cultural institutions, notably the Roman Catholic Church, with its powerful influence on politics and behavior. Several essays also address the strong class conflicts that have developed between entrenched elites dating from the colonial period and the emerging middle and working classes who have begun to organize and speak out in the twentieth century.

Although these essays focus on individual states, with the exception of the first two, collectively they reflect one of the strongest themes in isthmian history and one of the most important sources of the present conflicts: the failure of the region to reunify following the disruption of the Central American federation in 1840. Powerful local interests in each state have emphasized their diversity and asserted their defense of class privileges that might be submerged in a national union. Thus most of these essays, as with Central American studies in general, continue to focus on the individual city-states — in reality antinational units — since that is where the power structure and control of these societies continue to reside.

The first two essays are broad overviews of the powerful influence of outside political and economic forces. Thomas Leonard traces U.S. policy, stressing North American fear of European encroachment as the central theme in U.S. attitudes toward Central America, from the American Revolution to the present. Thomas Schoonover, on the other hand, is more impressed by the economic motivation of the major powers. In the second essay, he traces the important rivalry between the United States, Germany, and France in the nineteenth and early twentieth centuries, as all three sought to dislodge the British from their predominant position in Central American commerce. Both essays document the ultimate establishment of U.S. hegemony on the isthmus — a hegemony which incited the contemporary demands for independence in Central America, as well as the potential challenge of a new external force, the USSR.

The next three essays focus on modern Guatemala. Larry Yates looks at the origins of the current insurgency in Guatemala, paying particular attention to U.S. military involvement in the counterinsurgency efforts of the 1960s. His essay, based in part on recently declassified diplomatic and defense records, is highly illuminating regarding U.S. policy and action in Central America during the period just prior to the contemporary crises. As such, it sheds much light on the mentality and operations surrounding present U.S. military assistance programs in Central America.

Marilyn Moors shifts the focus from external forces to the plight of the indigenous population of Guatemala; yet her analysis of the threats to traditional Mayan community life does not ignore the impact of foreign economic pressures. She emphasizes that the growth of agro-export economies has increased the demand for Indian labor, encroached upon the Indians' traditio-nal land system, and forced the Indians into Western economic patterns, usually in a highly disadvantageous way. Relying on sixty years of U.S. anthropological research among the Guatemalan Indians, Moors demonstrates that modernization in Guatemala has contributed to the poverty and misery of a substantial portion of the rural population. Hubert Miller looks at a very different aspect of Guatemalan history, that of church-state relations during the revolutionary administration of Juan José Arévalo (1945-1951). Miller demonstrates how the ecclesiastical hierarchy played a major role in opposing the Guatemalan Revolution's social and political goals, attacking them as "communist," and in the process supporting the counter-revolution that eventually regained control of the country in 1954. His essay has particular relevance for the present situation in Central America, where the church is intimately involved in the revolutionary struggles in Nicaragua, El Salvador, Honduras, and Guatemala.

Donna and Edward Brett also investigate the role of the Catholic Church, but in neighboring Honduras, with particular reference to the important role of the clergy in mobilizing social consciousness among the working classes. Reflecting extensive research in Honduras as well as in this country, their essay demonstrates the dramatic changes occuring among the Central American clergy during the past few decades. Their analysis helps explain why Honduras has not experienced major social revolutions like other Central American states but also suggests that Honduras is certainly not immune from such social and political upheaval.

Three essays deal with aspects of Nicaraguan cultural history, all having direct relevance to the Sandinista revolution. Anthropologist George Castile traces the history and modern problems of the Miskito Indians of eastern Nicaragua, explaining their stubborn resistance to "Spanish" or "Nicaraguan" domination. Castile underscores one of the major problem areas of the new Sandinista government and also the existence of strong ethnic and cultural diversity even within a single Central American state. John Heyl, by contrast, looks at mainstream Nicaraguan cultural life and considers the extraordinary role that poetry has played in Nicaraguan political culture in this century. He focuses especially on death imagery in the works of Rubén Darío, José Coronel Urtecho, Pablo Antonio Cuadra, and Ernesto Cardenal in a penetrating analysis of the relation between culture, national identity, and political revolt in Nicaragua. David Whisnant, using the methodology developed in his study of cultural identity and policy in Appalachia, examines Sandinista cultural policy in its historical context. In the process, Whisnant clearly drives home the national cultural resentment that U.S. presence in Nicaragua has engendered over the past century, relating it to the argument that the Sandinista revolution is primarily a demand for national independence.

The last three essays in this volume deal with foreign policy questions, especially relative to Central American revolutionary governments and other regional actors. Kai Schoenhals shows how right-wing repression led to left-wing takeover in Grenada, while maintenance of the British parliamentary system in Belize kept moderate governments in power there. He also provides an interesting commentary on the peculiar friendship of Belize's relatively conservative government under George Price with revolutionary governments in Guatemala in the 1950s and in Nicaragua in the 1980s. Hugh Campbell examines the influence that Mexico has tried to exert in Central America in the twentieth century, with particular reference to its involvement in Nicaraguan revolutions (including that of the Sandinistas). Mexico's position as a rival of the United States for influence in Central America is a powerful conditioning element in its policy. Campbell argues persuasively that Mexico's present attitude toward the Sandinistas is consistent with its earlier policy. In the final essay, Frank Kendrick analyzes Costa Rica's efforts to stay neutral in the conflicts around her and maintain her non military tradition. Kendrick makes clear that this policy has become increasingly difficult under the pressure of the Reagan administration to isolate Nicaragua and to mobilize the other four Central American states in support of the Contras.

These twelve essays suggest the complexity of Central America's historical development and that the present crises are much more than simply a confrontation between capitalist and communist empires. Together, they deepen our understanding of the complexities and the powerful strains that modernization has placed on traditional Central American life.

CHAPTER 1

"Keeping the Europeans Out": The United States and Central America since 1823

Thomas M. Leonard

In May 1826, three years after the United States had extended recognition to the United Provinces of Central America, John Williams arrived in Guatemala City as U.S. envoy to the new nation. Although this "South American" republic was in a "position of highest geographical importance," Williams was the first of only five of the twelve U.S. diplomats assigned to Central America to actually reach their posts between 1823 and 1839, when the federation collapsed. According to one historian, this effort was one of "diplomatic futility" (Lockey 1930).

However, this was not a period of diplomatic futility. While the new nation was not confronted with a serious European threat, the instructions given each of the twelve diplomats and the 1825 treaty between the United States and the United Provinces of Central America reflected long-standing principles of American foreign policy. The instructions sought to limit the extent of European penetration into the region. The British colonies at Belize and on the Bay Islands were of primary concern. Subsequently, French and Dutch interest in transisthmian canal projects merited attention. At the insistence of Secretary of State Henry Clay, the 1825 Treaty of Peace, Amity, and Commerce detailed neutral rights with respect to blockades, search, and contraband (Stansifer forthcoming; Manning 1925, 1933). Washington officials clearly wanted to avoid European entanglements and were fearful of intrusions that might stir up problems that had occurred in the Caribbean in the early nineteenth century.

The principles of U.S. policy toward the region developed during the forty-year period between the establishment of U.S. independence (1783) and Central American independence (1823). While North Americans dreamed of exporting their wares to Central American markets — a dream never fully realized — the fundamental objective of U.S. diplomacy was the elimination of European influence in the region. As early as 1775, revolutionary pamphleteer Tom Paine advocated the avoidance of Europe, a thought echoed by George Washington in 1796 and Thomas Jefferson in 1801. Noninvolvement in European affairs meant security for the United States, and if Europe were removed from the Western Hemisphere, a greater degree of security would be achieved.

In the years following independence, U.S. contacts in the Caribbean were predicated upon the vicissitudes of European events. Pending European alliances, U.S. vessels and their crews were at the mercy of the British, French, or Spanish. Neutral rights were violated. On the northern fringes of the Caribbean, French and Spanish influence in Louisiana and the Floridas threatened the nation's borders, a threat that motivated the acquisition of these territories by the United States and led to the 1811 congressional "no-transfer" resolution. During the Spanish-American independence movements, the United States worried about growing British influence at the expense of a weakened Spain, particularly in Cuba. Jefferson's Cabinet concluded that the United States was persuaded by "the strongest repugnance to see [Cuba] under British or French subordination." In 1822, when President James Monroe notified Congress that he had extended recognition to Mexico, he explained that it would help prevent that country from becoming a dupe of European policy. A year later, in December 1823, Monroe's warning to Europe not to extend its influence to the Western Hemisphere climaxed forty years of foreign policy expressions (Bemis 1943, chaps. 2-4; Graebner 1985, chaps. 1-6; Jones 1985, chaps. 1-5).

Thus, by the time Williams arrived in Guatemala City in 1826, the fundamental tenets of U.S. policy toward Central America were dictated by the larger Caribbean policy: the Europeans must be kept out.

The Nineteenth Century

Not until the 1840s did the United States move its Central American policy from the proverbial back burner. Manifest Destiny, discovery of gold in California, and victory in the Mexican War caused Americans to look southward in anticipation of a transisthmian canal. This heightened interest coincided with British imperial designs, which caused consul Henry Savage on May 2, 1848 to warn that Nicaragua needed protection against British expansion.

British interests in Central America dated back to at least 1670, when it gained privileges at the mouth of the Belize River from Spain. In several agreements from 1786 to 1814, Spain acknowledged British rights of settlement, but not sovereignty. Interest in the settlement lagged until the 1820s when Belizean residents, seeking new woodlands, moved southward to Nicaragua's coast. In 1841 the British extended their protectorate over the Mosquito Coast to San Juan del Norte on the Nicaraguan-Costa Rican border. Hoisting the Union Jack, the British renamed the little port "Greytown".

Elijah Hise, who served briefly as special U.S. envoy to Central America in 1848 and 1849, and his successor E. George Squier, reflected the American resolve to check British expansion. Hise arrived in Guatemala City "determined to resist...European influence," while Squier believed that the British "must be driven from this part of the continent," because its agents were responsible for the turmoil in Central America (Manning 1933, 3:286). Squier butted heads with Frederick Chatfield, the British consul general in Guatemala City. Since his appointment in 1834, Chatfield had aggressively sought to protect British interests throughout Central America. The climax of their confrontation came in October 1849, when Chatfield instructed a British naval squadron to seize Tigre Island in the Gulf of Fonseca, near the probable western terminus of the anticipated Nicaraguan Canal, on the pretext of collecting unpaid debts. The real reason for Chatfield's unauthorized action was the treaty Squier had negotiated with Honduras which granted the United States the right to occupy the island.

As tempers flared in Central America, cooler heads prevailed in Washington and London. Both the United States and Great Britain wanted a solution to the problem, which came with the Clayton-Bulwer Treaty, signed in Washington on April 19, 1850. Article 1 of the treaty provided that neither the United States or Britain would obtain or maintain for itself any transisthmian canal, "or occupy, or fortify, or colonize, or assume or exercise any dominion over Nicaragua, Costa Rica, the Mosquito Coast, or any part of Central America," except the British colony at Belize. The U.S. Senate ratified the treaty only after Secretary of State John M. Clayton convinced the opposition that the treaty was a practical application of the Monroe Doctrine and that it required the British to abandon its protectorate over the Mosquito Coast (Naylor 1960; Rodríguez Beteta 1963; Rodríguez 1964; Squier 1850; Howe 1937).

Despite later charges of ambiguity, the Clayton-Bulwer Treaty appeared to satisfy a fundamental demand of U.S. policy toward Central America: preventing European expansion. The British were to retreat from "seized" territory. Unable to undertake a canal project itself, the United States was satisfied to prevent the most likely candidate from pursuing that task.

The ink barely dried on the Clayton-Bulwer Treaty before differences in interpretation surfaced. The controversy was sparked by the conversion in 1851 of Punta Arenas, on the Nicaraguan Caribbean coast, into a prosperous American colony by Cornelius Vanderbilt at the expense of Greytown. The British, who claimed governing rights over the entire coastal area under Clayton-Bulwer, demanded payment of port fees from Vanderbilt's ships. Secretary of State Daniel Webster asserted that the British action not only violated the 1850 treaty, but also the Monroe Doctrine.

Tensions increased the following year when the British seized Roatán and other islands in the Gulf of Honduras. The Senate Foreign Relations Committee understood the islands' strategic significance, and saw the British seizure not only as a violation of Clayton-Bulwer and the Monroe Doctrine, but also of Honduran territory. The committee asserted that the British claim to rights in Central America were void because their agreements with Spain for occupation had terminated with Central American independence.

From 1853 until 1859 the two nations struggled diplomatically with the problem. The Americans were adamant: the British must go. The British, who would not "give three coppers to retain any post on the Central American territory," sought an honorable, face-saving solution. Only when the British suggested abrogating the Clayton-Bulwer Treaty in 1858, did the American position soften. Secretary of State Lewis Cass indicated that the United States wished only to secure the trade routes to a transisthmian canal, projected to pass through Nicaragua. The British then agreed to settle the Belizean boundary in return for the right to build a road from Guatemala City to the Caribban; leave the Bay Islands to Honduras provided that they were not turned over to a third party; and relinquish its protectorate over the Mosquito Coast (Van Alstyne 1939; Dozier 1985, chap. 4; Jones 1974; Kortge 1973; Moore 1911, vols. 9-11). Unaware of British motivations, Americans rejoiced at the British exit from Central America. The jubilation was short-lived because of the onset of the Civil War and the subsequent agony of Reconstruction. Not until the 1880s did the Americans again look outward, at which time Central America again became a focal point of foreign policy.

Three motivating factors dovetailed in the 1880s and 1890s to thrust the United States into world affairs: economics, naval expansion, and a missionary desire to uplift inferior peoples. Well into the 1880s, manufacturers were cognizant of the need to develop foreign markets for their goods. Anticipated markets were in Asia and along the west coast of Latin America, not particularly in Central America. The maritime route to Asia and Latin America's west coast, along with the Pacific coast of the United States, however, was across the Central American isthmus. The need for markets was supported by those advocating an expanded navy, such as Admiral Alfred T. Mahan, Henry Cabot Lodge, and Theodore Roosevelt. Coaling stations would be needed at distant points from the United States, and to reach those in the Pacific, a transisthmian canal was essential. An American canal through a region plagued with political turmoil would be subject to foreign intrigue. To secure the region from that possibility, the inferior local inhabitants would have to be uplifted by the implementation of democracy (Beisner 1975; Hagan 1973; Hofstadter 1959; LaFeber 1963; Langley 1976; Westcott 1941).

In Central America, chief competitors were the British, Germans, and French. British and Germans had expanded their commercial interests in the region, while French activity in Mexico and Panama were sources of concern. Journalist John A. Kasson understood the issue at hand. Writing in the December 1881 issue of the *North American Review*, he noted that the Europeans, failing to respect "our demand for non-interference in the internal affairs of the hemisphere..., have forced us to vigilance." While the Europeans had the right to make treaties and engage in war with the American states, if their actions interfered with U.S. interests, America had every right to take defensive action. More important, Kasson argued, was the weak condition of the Central American states that invited European interference, and directly challenged U.S. interests: "It means a flanking position, a military and naval rendezvous in time of war and an exclusive commercial position in time of peace." This threat, Kasson warned, was especially significant because of the anticipated construction of a transisthmian canal. The canal, Kasson opined, should not be under European control: "No chance should be left to convert a weak Central American state into another distracted Egypt by means of foreign possessory rights in another isthmian canal" (Kasson 1881, 523).

Kasson's demand that a transisthmian canal be controlled by the United States was not new. Until the end of the Civil War, the U.S. canal policy was defensive. Doubting that it could build and maintain a canal on its own, the U.S. government deferred to the private sector, both at home and abroad, provided that any canal be open upon "equal rights" to all nations as against "exclusive control" by any one nation. Therefore, the United States was willing to stand with Britain or any other nation in "joint protection" of the route.

This attitude changed after the Civil War. President Ulysses S. Grant determined in 1869 that the United States should build a transisthmian canal. He was willing to forego the canal provisions of the Clayton-Bulwer Treaty and apply only the noncolonization principles. Cognizant of Grant's position, outgoing Secretary of State William H. Seward reflected this view when announcing that henceforth the United States would be "unwilling to enter into an entangling alliance with other nations for the construction and maintenance of a passage" across the isthmus (U.S. Congress 1901, vol. 1:37). At the same time, the U.S. Minister to Costa Rica, Charles N. Riotte, cautioned that if the United States did not build a transisthmian waterway, either the British or French would.

No canal effort was undertaken until 1879, when Frenchman Ferdinand deLesseps contracted with Colombia to build a canal through its province at Panama. Given the threat of new European expansion into the Western Hemisphere, the U.S. reaction was swift. President Rutherford B. Hayes asserted that his country would never accept a transisthmian canal under non-American control. Secretary of State William B. Evarts claimed that if deLesseps completed the project, the United States had the right to construct fortifications at each terminus. Former Civil War General Ambrose E. Burnside, now a senator, sponsored a resolution stating that the United States could not accept European control or protection over any portion of the isthmus because it violated the Monroe Doctrine. Subsequently, Secretary of State James G. Blaine advocated abrogating the Clayton-Bulwer Treaty so that the United States could build the canal itself.

Wracked with corruption, the deLesseps company failed in 1889, but U.S. interest in a transisthmian canal did not diminish. The Spanish-American War and subsequent acquisition of Caribbean and Pacific territories accelerated the demand for a canal. In the face of rising German power, Great Britain was casting about for friends at the century's end. Looking to the United States, the British willingly abrogated the Clayton-Bulwer Treaty in 1901. Until this time, the Nicaraguan route was most favored, but in the Senate debates from 1898 to 1901, Panama, from both engineering and economic standpoints, emerged as the most feasible site. After diplomacy failed, as President Teddy Roosevelt later acknowledged, the U.S. "took" Panama in 1903 (Howarth 1966; Mack 1944; McCullough 1977; Parks 1935). The Americans would finally have their canal.

The 1898 Peace of Paris that ended the Spanish-American War, the 1901 Platt Amendment which was added to the Cuban constitution under pressure from Washington, and the 1903 Hay-Bunau-Varilla Treaty by which Panama obtained its independence and the Americans the right to build their canal, represented both the culmination of nineteenth-century security thinking and a harbinger of future U.S. policy toward Central America. Under U.S. supervision, the conditions that might cause European intervention—political and financial instability—were to be corrected. The foreign policy of each nation was restricted to conform with United States aspirations, while defense provisions made the United States the sole guarantor of military security.

Removing The External Threat: 1900 to 1945

During the first fifteen years of the twentieth century, presidential policies toward Central America varied, but all had the same objective: to keep the region secure from foreign intrusion. Teddy Roosevelt expressed these sentiments in his instructions to the U.S. delegation attending the Second International Conference of American States meeting in Mexico City in October 1901. Roosevelt asserted that every political, economic, and social failure on the part of the Central Americans that menaced their stability or invited foreign interference "would be a misfortune for us." Roosevelt was more emphatic in his annual message to Congress on December 6, 1904:

> Chronic wrongdoing...may...ultimately require intervention by some civilized nation, and in the Western Hemisphere the adherence to the Monroe Doctrine may force the United States, however reluctantly, in flagrant cases of such wrongdoing or impotence, to the exercise of an international police power. (*Congressional Record* 1905, 39:19)

For its own security, the United States assumed the right to intervene, as an international policeman, in another's internal affairs. Thus the Roosevelt Corollary to the Monroe Doctrine was pronounced.

President William Howard Taft, who succeeded Roosevelt, accepted the advice of his secretary of state, Philander C. Knox, who advocated refinancing debts and customs receiverships to "render their Governments stable and keep them from foreign intervention" (*FRUS* 1919:1091). In short, "dollar diplomacy" replaced the "big stick."

Although Woodrow Wilson came to the White House as an outspoken foe of imperialism, he eventually carried out more interventions in Latin America than any of his predecessors. He explained that just government rested upon consent of the governed, and that law and order must be based upon the public conscience and approval. The United States, Wilson asserted, had "no sympathy with those who seek to seize the power of government to advance their personal interest." While Wilson's moral crusade paralleled that of his immediate predecessors, the outbreak of World War I introduced a new dimension. Secretary of State Robert Lansing called for a reaffirmation of the Monroe Doctrine to protect the Panama Canal from foreign—particularly German—interlopers. German influence, Lansing charged, in any Caribbean nation would not be tolerated (Baker 1961; Beale 1956; Cooper 1983; Marks 1979; Scholes & Scholes 1970).

In light of these broad declarations, U.S. policy toward Central America during the early twentieth century is understandable. In 1907 the U.S. sponsored a Central American conference in Washington following the eruption of war between El Salvador and Nicaragua, a conflict that threatened to spread throughout the isthmus. The United States assumed that this conflict, like previous ones, was based upon mutual jealousies, revolutionary governments, and blatant disregard for Honduran neutrality. Political instability invited foreign intervention. The results of this conference reflected these assumptions. Honduran neutrality was guaranteed; a Central American Court was established to settle disputes; revolutionaries were banned from basing their operations in neighboring countries; and recognition was to be withheld from unconstitutional governments. The search for orderly government became the justification for direct U.S. military intervention in Nicaragua beginning in 1909, and in Honduras in 1911. Refinancing and a customs receivership, in order to forestall intervention from foreign creditors, were part of the financial plans imposed upon Nicaragua beginning in 1911 and unsuccessfully sought for Guatemala and Honduras.

Although the United States had secured the Panama Canal route, and commenced construction in 1904, consideration of the Nicaraguan route continued. In 1908 rumors circulated that President José Santos Zelaya attempted to interest the Japanese in a transisthmian canal. Two years later, the British were reportedly offered the Corn Islands, near the Caribbean terminus of the proposed canal route, in return for debt cancellation. Subsequently, reports of German and Canadian interest circulated. With the Nicaraguan route open to possible intrigue, the United States concluded the Chamorro-Weitzel Treaty in 1913, only to have the Senate refuse its consideration. Secretary of State William Jennings Bryan renegotiated a treaty more to the Senate's liking in 1914, and a year later it was ratified. Giving the United States exclusive rights to the Nicaragua route, another opportunity for foreign intervention was eliminated (Bailey 1936; Berman 1986, chap. 9; Calcott 1942; Langley 1980, chaps. 1-3; Munro [1964] 1980; *FRUS* 1910, 2:601-728).

While U.S. policy after 1900 has been a reaction to anticipated causes of intervention, the United States had no coherent defense policy for the Caribbean when World War I erupted in August 1914. Until the U.S. entry into the war in 1917, the Central American states maintained a pro-Allied neutral stance. Following the American intervention, all but El Salvador declared war on Germany and, at the encouragement of the United States, took steps to curtail German activities within their borders. But the United States did not consider the German threat to Central America serious, as witnessed in the continued nonrecognition of the Federico Tinoco administration in Costa Rica. President Wilson determined that Tinoco had seized power in violation of the 1907 Washington treaties, and despite his pro-Allied declarations, restrictions upon Germans in Costa Rica, and warnings that German plots were being organized there, Wilson held firm (Baker 1964; Dinwoodie 1966, chap. 6; Martin 1925, 2:491-504; Murillo-Jiménez 1978; *FRUS* 1917, Supp. 1:222, 236-38, 259, 290-92, 309-12; *FRUS* 1918, Supp. 2:89, 371-96).

For fifteen years following World War I, U.S. policy toward Central America was at crosscurrents. There was a continuation of previous intervention practices, while at the same time there was a movement toward noninter-vention.

The interventionist policy in Central America emerged in 1923 when the United States, in response to a possible isthmian war, convened another Central American conference in Washington. The resulting agreements were considered an advance over those reached in 1907. A new Central American Court was established; unconstitutional governments unworthy of recognition were more sharply defined; and steps were taken to limit arms. Arms limitation was a new concept designed to remove the military as a source of political power. Secretary of State Charles Evans Hughes was satisfied with the treaties because to "a remarkable degree these treaties conserved the best interest of the Central American Republics...as well as those peculiar to the United States" (Hughes, n.d.:1-2). The treaties, however, failed to bring political stability to Central America. Before the decade was out, the United States again found itself directly intervening in Honduras and Nicaragua to achieve that goal. In Guatemala, Minister Sheldon Whitehouse brokered for the eventual presidential election of Jorge Ubico in 1934. The U.S. withheld recognition of Salvadoran dictator Maximiliano Hernández Martínez on the grounds that his 1931 fraudulent electoral victory violated the 1923 treaties. Influenced by Central America's recognition of Hernández Martínez, and as an application of the Good Neighbor policy, the United States eventually extended recognition in 1935.

Nor were the arms limitations agreements successful. Except for Costa Rica, military expenditures remained at approximately 25 percent of national budgets. The suggestion that a National Guard be established to replace highly politicized armies was accepted only by Nicaragua. Like the armies in Guatemala, El Salvador, and Honduras, the Nicaraguan Guard, however, remained a major player in national politics. Finally, in pursuit of national order, U.S. Marines spent considerable time chasing Nicaraguan rebel Augusto C. Sandino around the countryside, until their withdrawal in 1933, as an application of the Good Neighbor policy (Grieb 1970; Grieb 1971; Hackett 1924; Kamman 1968; Leonard 1982a; Macaulay 1967; Munro 1974).

The origins of the Good Neighbor policy can be traced to the early 1920s. World War I had temporarily eliminated the European threat to the Western Hemisphere, thus reducing the need for an aggressive defense policy. At the same time, there was growing opposition to intervention among U.S. policymakers, who came to recognize that intervention failed to bring political stability. Assistant Chief of the State Department's Latin American Affairs Division, Stokeley W. Morgan, noted in 1926 that revolutions in Central America were the only means to bring about government change. Because of U.S. intervention, there was a more vociferous "anti-Yanqui" sentiment in Latin America that impressed U.S. policymakers. Successive heads of the State Department's Latin American Affairs Division, Leo S. Rowe, Francis G. White, and Edwin C. Wilson, believed it was no longer necessary to extend unwelcome protection, or to meddle in Central American affairs. In 1928, Franklin D. Roosevelt wrote the same in *Foreign Affairs*, and immediately after his election, Herbert Hoover went on a goodwill tour of Latin America, including a Central American stop. Subsequently, the Clark Memorandum repudiated the Roosevelt Corollary.

Thus, when Franklin D. Roosevelt announced the Good Neighbor policy in his 1933 presidential inaugural address, he summarized over a decade's worth of thought. At the Seventh International Conference of American States in 1933 at Montevideo, the Latin Americans were told that this meant nonintervention in their internal affairs: U.S. Marines would be withdrawn, elections would not be supervised, and recognition would not be withheld in order to force conformity to U.S. objectives. Withdrawal of the Marines from Nicaragua was an application of the new policy in Central America, as was the resistance to overtures between 1934 and 1936 from all sides to prevent Anastasio Somoza from moving into the presidential palace on January 1, 1937. The constitutional maneuverings by Hernández Martínez, Somoza, Carías, and Ubico to extend their presidencies were scorned by U.S. officials as extralegal devices, but there was no discussion of withholding recognition (Clark 1930; DeConde 1951; Grieb 1977; Leonard 1985; Roosevelt 1928; Wood 1961).

More important were the war clouds rising over Asia and Europe, which diverted U.S. attention from Central American politics to hemispheric defense. From 1936 to 1940, U.S. policymakers became increasingly concerned with the German trade effort in Central America; the professed admiration for Mussolini, and to a lesser degree Hitler, by Ubico and Hernández Martínez; and the potential for sabotage by Germans residing in Central America.

The German trade offensive of the 1930s centered around the *Aski* system, under which Germany bought Central American foodstuffs and raw materials with *Aski* marks. These marks remained in Germany for the purchase of machinery, metal goods, coal, chemicals, and the like. By 1938, Germany had replaced Britain as the chief supplier of goods in many countries. In Central America, the gains were most notable in Guatemala and El Salvador.

As admirers of fascist principles, both Ubico and Hernández Martínez looked favorably upon Mussolini's personal and political style. The spread of fascist principles to the officer corps came through the German military missions attached to military schools in Guatemala and El Salvador. The pro-

German sentiment was not confined to Guatemala and El Salvador. The German legation in Guatemala City was a regional distribution center for Nazi propaganda. Even Costa Rican President León Cortés was suspected of harboring German sympathies. The large German colony that permeated the Guatemalan economy was considered a potential nucleus of subversive activities. The smaller German colonies in El Salvador, Honduras, and Nicaragua were also viewed with suspicion.

Following the German invasion of Poland on September 1, 1939, Central American leaders began to line up behind the United States. All five presidents pledged sympathy and support to the Allied cause. They also supported the U.S. call for a 300-mile security belt around the Americas south of Canada, with a warning that belligerents refrain from warlike activities within the area. The pro-Allied expressions of sympathy, however, did not put a halt to rumors that German submarines were refueling from bases in Central America. But all five states did increase their vigilance. El Salvador, for example, dismissed the German director of its *Escuela Militar* and the German head of the state-run Mortgage Bank, who also served as German consul and local Nazi leader. Before Pearl Harbor, all Axis military personnel were sent home and replaced by U.S. military missions. Guatemala prepared for naval patrols of its coast.

Following the fall of France in June 1940, the United States determined its Western Hemispheric defense policy, which did not call for the use of Latin American forces in combat abroad. Rather, the Latin Americans were to be supplied with enough arms to ward off an external attack until U.S. forces arrived. Military staff agreements were completed to provide for interchange of security information, development of a secret service to keep aliens and subversive groups under surveillance, and elimination of Axis propaganda. To meet military needs, some $400 million in Lend-Lease aid was to be made available. Before Pearl Harbor, a Lend-Lease agreement was reached with Nicaragua, and after December 7, 1941, with the other Central American states. Because of wartime demands elsewhere, and a shortage of materiel in the United States, Lend-Lease supplies did not begin to flow in earnest until 1943, long after the German threat had receded.

In addition to these agreements, the Central American states cooperated with the United States in other ways to meet the Axis threat. Following the Pearl Harbor attack, they all declared war on the Axis and signed the United Nations Declaration in January 1942. Guatemala agreed not to press its claim to Belize during the war. Ubico also shut down the German legation and deported German nationals to the United States for internment during the war. Guatemala, Honduras, Nicaragua, and Costa Rica signed defense agreements that permitted U.S. air and naval forces to use necessary facilities to guard the Panama Canal approaches and Caribbean sea lanes. This was important, for during 1942 the Germans sunk 336 ships in the Caribbean. To adjust for the economic dislocations caused by Central America's cooperation against black-listed German firms, the U.S. increased its share of imports from the republics, so that by the war's end it accounted for over 70 percent of the region's exports.

As the Axis threat to the Western Hemisphere decreased in 1943, so too did U.S. Lend-Lease and economic assistance. Until that time, the thrust of American policy was designed to secure the region from an external attack and protect it from subversive movements. The United States was not interested in the domestic political challenges confronting the dictators. For example, Lend-Lease requests from Hernández Martínez and Somoza were turned down, because, as Chief of the State Department American Republics Affairs Division John C. Cabot observed, "these lethal toys [are] more likely to be used for a very different purpose than they were intended" (Astilla 1976; Conn & Fairchild 1960; Freye 1967; Gellman 1979; Grieb 1979; Haglund 1984; Humphries 1981; Trueblood 1937). U.S. policy toward Central America during World War II, then, was a continuation of that at the start of the century. Its objective was to prevent European penetration of the region.

Subversion: The Challenge Since 1945

As the threat of war receded from Central America in 1943, internal threats to the dictators began to surface. Within a year both Ubico and Hernández Martínez were forced from office, and Somoza gave the appearance of abdicating power by stepping aside from the presidency (he remained head of the National Guard). Only Tiburcio Carías weathered the storm. The pressure for change came from the middle sector group that had been developing since the 1920s. Comprised of professionals, white-collar managers, small businessmen, and intellectuals, they demanded political participation for themselves, but not the lower socioeconomic groups. Costa Rica's 1948 civil war was interpreted in a similar light. Although the country was long portrayed as a democracy, politics were dominated by a landed aristocracy, which José Figueres ousted. For its part, the United States merely observed these events because it perceived no external threat (Bell 1971; English 1971; Leonard 1984; Woodward 1976, chap. 8).

Influenced by Asian and European affairs, U.S. global strategy sought to contain the expansion of communism after World War II. In the Western Hemisphere, preparations were made for a possible external attack. The inter-American system was brought into the struggle against external aggression. By the Act of Chapultepec adopted at Mexico City in 1945, the American republics agreed to consult before taking action against an external attack upon any one of them. Two years later, at Rio de Janeiro, at which time the United States had more sharply defined its policy against the Soviet Union, the American republics agreed to provide assistance against aggressors prior to consultation. At Bogotá in 1948, the Inter-American Defense Board was charged with developing hemispheric defense plans. Finally, in 1951 Congress approved the $51 million Mutual Security Act for direct military assistance to Latin America. The initial Military Assistance Program to Central America emphasized security of the Panama Canal, the Caribbean sea lanes, and Mexican and Venezuelan oil, not an international communist threat (Bailey 1967; Burr 1967; Hayes 1984; Mecham 1963).

Diplomats in Central America, however, consistently cautioned that mass poverty throughout the region was a breeding ground for communist exploitation. Based on World War II cooperation against German subversion, the U.S. sought postwar Latin American cooperation against Soviet-sponsored subversion. The American republics agreed at Rio de Janeiro in 1947 to consult with each other in case of subversion. By the end of the Truman administration, the threat of communist subversion appeared real, particularly in Guatemala although there was no evidence of a Soviet connection. The programs of Presidents Juan José Arévalo and Jacobo Arbenz appealed to the lower socioeconomic groups at the expense of the traditional landed aristocracy and the United Fruit Company. Such appeals paralleled the communist paths in Eastern Europe and China.

To the Eisenhower administration, communism or anything resembling it was a threat to the United States, and would not be tolerated in the Caribbean region. Communists, however identified, were considered agents of the Soviet Union, and therefore linked to an international conspiracy against the United States. Perceiving a Soviet threat, at the tenth Inter-American Conference of American States in Caracas in March 1954, Secretary of State John Foster Dulles sponsored a resolution asserting that any American nation subjected to communist political control was considered foreign intervention and a threat to the Western Hemisphere. Accordingly, decisive action was called for, presumably under the 1947 Rio Treaty. Not known at the time was the U.S. intention to remove Arbenz from power. Given the conspiracy thesis, and the Arbenz land reform program, the Eisenhower-Dulles team justified its sponsorship of Carlos Castillo Armas in June 1954 in ousting Arbenz from office. International communism, the American people were told, was removed from the hemisphere. Military assistance for the remainder of the decade contributed to the facade of stability. With the exception of Costa Rica, Central American governments failed to address the social and political issues facing them. Neither did the United States, for the communist threat supposedly was removed (Immerman 1982; Schlesinger & Kinzer 1982; *Tenth Inter-American Conference* 1954; U.S. Department of State 1954).

Fidel Castro's victory in Cuba (1959) brought the consequences of social and economic disparities and political repression to the forefront, and caused President-elect John F. Kennedy to warn that it was "one minute to midnight" in Latin America. Kennedy personally — and through his spokesmen, Adolf A. Berle, Adlai Stevenson, and Edward M. Martin — expressed a willingness to accept moderately leftist governments meeting the demands for economic, political, and social reform. In fact, the administration was intolerant of military coups against such governments, as illustrated by the withholding of recognition of the Oswaldo López Arellano junta in Honduras in November 1963. Aid was halted and all military advisers were withdrawn.

The 1961 Foreign Assistance Act replaced the Mutual Security Program. The new program provided military aid to stymie both internal and external aggression. The Central American military was now prepared for internal security, and at the same time engaged in civic action programs — construction of roads, schools, hospitals, and the like — to improve its image.

The centerpiece of Kennedy's Latin American program was the Alliance for Progress, which along with the Peace Corps and Food for Peace Program gave promise for improvement of the region's social and economic problems and for broadening the base of political participation. Some $644 million was pumped into the five Central American republics. The objective was to remove the causes of potential communist subversion.

The effect of these programs is difficult to judge, however, because of Kennedy's assassination in November 1963. His successor, Lyndon Johnson, and Assistant Secretary of State for Latin American Affairs Thomas C. Mann emphasized national security and protection of U.S. investments while giving only verbal assurances of economic, political, and social reform. In practice, the policy shift meant that the Central American military and police received intensified training to deal with internal subversion. Application of this policy was best seen in Guatemala, where massive amounts of military assistance was provided to suppress a guerrilla movement, whose leadership dated from the 1950s (Alba 1965; Berle 1961; Davis 1975; Martin 1963; Mann 1964; Morrison 1962; Walton 1972; National Security Council 1964).

Central America was ignored in U.S. policy by the mid-1960s because of Vietnam and domestic crisis. The Central American economies were never vitally important to the United States, and the threat of communism was viewed as minimal. After 1964, Communist parties in all Central American countries were outlawed, and local militia and civil authorities controlled the small clandestine groups advocating insurgency. Until Jimmy Carter moved into the White House in 1977, Central America was again placed on the proverbial back burner. During the Nixon-Ford years, economic assistance was slashed by 50 percent. Only Nicaragua, because of its devastating 1972 earthquake, received substantial assistance. Congressional cuts in military aid were not restored until 1974-1976, when insurgent movements again emerged (Cochrane 1972; Gil 1976; Silvert et al. 1975; Stephansky 1975).

Central America was on the verge of eruption when Carter became president in January 1977. At first, he appeared to understand the legitimacy of local leftist reform movements. This understanding was most evident in the 1977 Panama Canal Treaties. Subsequent decisions failed to demonstrate an understanding of Central American realities. The requirement to improve human rights violations as a precondition for U.S. economic and social assistance resulted in the severance of military aid to Guatemala and El Salvador in 1977, but the cuts failed to end human rights violations, which continued and even worsened by 1980. Carter's Nicaraguan policy was equally ineffective. Last-minute efforts to interpose a post-Somoza government to prevent a Sandinista takeover left deep scars on U.S.-Nicaraguan relations. Still, Carter was willing to extend $75 million for postwar reconstruction, and another $100 million in long-term assistance.

The problems in El Salvador threatened to make it "another Nicaragua" in the eyes of many Americans. To stem the tide, the Carter administration pursued a dual policy of military and economic assistance. If the tide was not stemmed in El Salvador, Guatemala and Honduras would soon be victimized. Before leaving office, Carter's Central American policy drifted toward a military solution. Honduras became the lynch-pin because the October 1979 coup in El Salvador gave hope for a moderate solution there, while the military in Guatemala remained stridently opposed to any change. Honduras was encouraged to officially end the 1969 Soccer War with El Salvador and to resume its association with the Central American Defense Council (CONDECA). In the final year of his administration, Carter sent ten helicopters and a military mission to Honduras (Booth 1982; Brown & MacLean, 1979; Findling 1987; Millett 1980; Montgomery 1982; Nelson 1980; Schoultz 1981; Valenta 1981; Pastor 1987).

If Carter appeared hesitant, not so Ronald Reagan. He was convinced that Central America had to be saved from Soviet-Cuban expansionism. Reagan's determination came from two sources: (1) the belief that Carter had been too tolerant of leftist regimes which permitted communist influence to spread; and (2) the convictions of the Defense Department and the intelligence community that U.S. supremacy should be reasserted in the region. Failure to act close to home, in the administration's view, only encouraged the Soviets to seek advances elsewhere. The Reagan administration sought to rid Nicaragua of the Sandinista regime and the Soviet-Cuban connection. A program of economic destabilization was undertaken; training and support of a counter-revolutionary group, the Contras, followed; and Guatemala and Honduras were accorded military assistance. El Salvador, already involved in internal conflict, received special assistance. Tiny Costa Rica, burdened with a huge foreign debt, had difficulty resisting U.S. pressure to join the struggle against the Sandinistas, at least to the point of allowing the Contras to use its territory. While there was a dramatic increase in economic assistance to Nicaragua's neighboring republics over the preceding years, the policy focus remained military (Ashby 1987; Blachman et al. 1986; Dickey 1983; Feinberg 1982; Hayes 1982; Leiken, ed. 1984; Molineu 1986, chap. 8; Muravchik 1987; Reagan 1983; U.S. Department of State 1981).

Reagan's policy was an extension of that practiced since 1945. The nature of the European threat had changed from direct intervention to subversion. Correct or not, the postwar administrations linked local communist movements to an international communist conspiracy that had to be contained. Except for the Alliance for Progress, the U.S. response was consistently a military one. Reagan, however, was more direct. Believing he needed to reassert U.S. prestige following nearly a decade of retreat, following Vietnam, he made a bold initiative in a region where the United States has had its way since 1900.

Summary

The United States determined its Central American policy by the time the United Provinces of Central America had achieved independence in 1823.

Based upon its own colonial experiences as well as those in the Caribbean after 1800, the United States resolved that the Europeans must be kept from the region. Until the end of the nineteenth century, the British were the major threat, followed by the Germans and French. The need to keep Europeans out of Central America intensified with the construction of the Panama Canal. The fear that local financial and political instability invited European intrusions led the United States to intervene in the Central American republics from 1907 through 1933 in an unsuccessful effort to create stable conditions.

World War II introduced a new fear — subversion. Vigilance was needed to prevent the German "colonies" throughout Central America from subverting governments and conducting acts of sabotage. At the same time, steps were taken to defend the region against external attack.

After World War II, the fear of external aggression remained, which caused the United States to direct the militarization of the inter-American system. At the same time, the United States assumed that Central American Communist parties were being directed by the Soviet Union to destabilize local governments by capitalizing upon regional socioeconomic and political problems. This perception resulted in efforts to remove communism from Central America. With the exception of the Alliance for Progress, the means to that end has been military.

Often without regard for the impact of its policy upon Central America, the United States has consistently sought to exclude European influences from the region. In so doing, U.S. policy often contributed to the exacerbation of regional adversities, which are addressed in other chapters in this volume.

CHAPTER 2

Metropole Rivalry in Central America, 1820s-1929: An Overview

Thomas Schoonover

Central America attracted the attention of the metropole states as a vital point for expansion into the Pacific basin in the nineteenth and early twentieth centuries.[1] As modern capitalism expanded the world market, competition became so multifaceted and pervasive as to form the major perspective of the nineteenth and twentieth centuries. In addition to a struggle among the metropole states for large shares in the distribution of security and well-being, laissez-faire competition existed between firms and sectors of national economies, between permutations of metropole and peripheral land, labor, and capital, and other combinations which rose from urges to survive and prosper in a dynamic situation. The world system penetrated new areas, tying older areas into the system with new threads, and reweaving old areas with new linkages and bonds, thus ever broadening the competitive nature of the world system. Any aspiring metropole state had to involve itself in the economics and geography of the Central American isthmus, or risk being eliminated from the immense material accumulation which Pacific demographics and geography promised. Great Britain enjoyed early superiority in the region, but U.S., French, and German competition soon challenged British hegemony. (Braudel 1979; Wallerstein, 1974-1980; Williams 1966; Wehler 1983; Cardoso & Faletto 1979; Frank 1969).

This chapter describes the rivalry which grew out of the internationalization of laissez-faire competition and suggests some of the problems which this competition created for peripheral areas like the Central American states. International competition was common in the mercantilist age, but most states had attempted to limit it through imperial law and custom. The decline of mercantilism and the rise of laissez-faire societies in the eighteenth and early nineteenth centuries shifted competition into the international sphere. The inability of laissez-faire systems to deal with the grave internal and external economic crises of 1873-1898 and the stronger interrelationships of the world system in the late nineteenth century magnified world economic problems (Rosenbert 1967; Wehler 1974, 24-36). The political units in this greatly disturbed world economy sought to alleviate internal socioeconomic problems which posed a threat to internal security by social imperialism (i.e., using external relations to solve internal problems).

The first response was to heal the malfunctioning laissez-faire system by expanding it onto a world scale, evident in British free trade policies, the U.S. open door policy, and President Woodrow Wilson's fourteen points (points 2-6 described a freer world trade system). Unleashing laissez-faire in the world system, where the mechanisms of political and social control were weaker than within the nation states, underscored the attempt to resolve internal problems by exploiting growth and capital accumulation possibilities in peripheral areas. Since it was thought that security and well-being were threatened by the internal economic woes of the metropole states, the metropole leadership intended only modest control over the entrepreneurs who went abroad. Competition among the metropoles in peripheral areas like Central America became quite fierce. The sovereignty and well-being of the peripheral states was inevitably subordinated to metropole needs because they could not be allowed to stand in the way of necessary capital accumulation and transfer. Such subordination was evident with regard to transit, internal and external communications, capital access, and cultural and military affairs, where Central American states were at best only marginally involved in the major decisions regarding the disposition of their wealth and rights.

Although in the nineteenth century the Central American states repeatedly tried to play one metropole state off against another, this strategy was seldom successful and became increasingly less so in the twentieth century. The Central American states resisted playing the metropoles against each other with diplomatic maneuvers. Opposition caused metropole use of force. Since use of force reduced the ability of the metropole to create and extract accumulation, the metropoles sought to build comprador groups (individuals in peripheral or semiperipheral societies who are persuaded, induced, or co-opted to serve metropole ends) which would allow foreign interests to maximize wealth production and encourage dependency. Social imperialism, which defined metropole well-being and security in terms of external factors, intensified metropole competition which, in turn, stimulated the resistance of peripheral Central American societies to exploitation. The greater the resistance, the greater the need to restrict the sovereignty and independence of Central American states, that is, to establish dependency, because these areas were defined as solutions to metropole well-being and security.

The United States experienced various transformations in the international competitive imperialism of the nineteenth and twentieth centuries. From the 1820s to the 1860s, a bitter contest developed between the remnants of a paternalistic, mercantilistic agrarian order and the more laissez-faire, industrial capitalism emerging in the United States. Only the most advanced sectors — communications, some elements of raw material acquisition, and a few advanced industrial sectors (textiles and some processed food stuffs) — sought external expansion with any urgency. The modest export capital went into market expansion-oriented communications projects (e.g., Panama railroad, Nicaragua transit, steamship lines).

Internal tension in the United States between mercantilist and laissez-faire advocates spilled over into the Caribbean as the defeated faction sought to salvage its deteriorating position by directing attention abroad. The rising industrial system's leadership would not permit the alienation of the mercantilist sections because the larger market area promised ideological and material well-being and security. Security and well-being required internal unification and integration of peripheral regions with the metropole's social, economic, and political realities and dreams. Britain voluntarily, if reluctantly, decided not to challenge rising U.S. political expectations. The Clayton-Bulwer Treaty (1850) spelled out the terms of Britain's retreat, which allowed Britain to retain its colonial hold on Belize and the Mosquito Coast with access to the Central American economy and transit routes. The 1850 treaty conceded the upstart United States equal status with the established and powerful British Empire in Central America (LaFeber 1983, 5-83; Nouailhat 1982; Rodríguez 1964; Schoonover 1973, 152-54).

From the 1860s to the 1890s, the United States implemented, with expedient and politically necessary limitations, laissez-faire as the national program of development. The U.S. communications net developed to facilitate the internal market, but the search for markets to feed the growth mentality so central to Liberalism expanded beyond national borders into Mexico and Central America. Profits from the U.S. domestic order remained high due to falling staple and raw material prices and friendly government, courts, and police. Rising capital accumulation created pressure to facilitate capital export opportunities. The search for such opportunities revived the dormant Monroe Doctrine, Pan-Americanism, and hypersensitivity to European presence in the New World. Britain continued its political retreat by negotiating treaties (which reduced its responsibilities and role in Central America) with Honduras, Nicaragua, and Guatemala in consultation with the U.S. government. British merchant and shipping interests slowly declined as Britain's political role diminished (Rubinson 1978, 39-71; Bourne 1967; Smith 1979b).

Beginning in the 1890s, multinational corporations became common and increasingly important devices for U.S. penetration. The 1873-1898 economic world crisis revealed to U.S. business elites that the modified laissez-faire system produced too much uncertainty and a dangerous social crisis, and threatened profits, capital accumulation, and the preservation of class, prestige, and power. Major U.S. enclave developments in Central America began during these years, accompanied by moves to foster a comprador elite which would facilitate the use of even more metropole power. Foreign influence in Central American educational, professional, and military institutions, and in public administration, and the urban infrastructure became widespread in these years. On Nicaragua's north coast and in Panama, Britain decided not to resist U.S. determination, evident in the Roosevelt and Lodge Corollaries, to restrict foreign access to Central America and the Caribbean (Cardoso & Pérez Brignoli 1977; LaFeber 1963; Woodward 1985, 149-223; Wilkins 1970; Schoonover 1983, 48-50).

Since the early twentieth century, the United States has sought to incorporate Central America into its economic and cultural orb of well-being and security. Through the Central American treaties of 1906 and 1923, expanding multinationalization of economic activity, enclaves, and cultural, scientific and military agencies, the United States tried to stabilize its hegemonic position. The British role in Central America deteriorated further. In the early 1920s, the British government withheld support from capital interests negotiating for petroleum concessions when U.S. officials raised the specter of British challenges to vital U.S. security interests. Rising German presence in Central America also challenged Britain's role (LaFeber 1983, 85-144; Schoonover 1983, 50-51).

The German states, disunited until 1871, quickly established ties with independent Central America. During the early nineteenth century, the Hansa states sought commercial opportunity, while the Prussian and Austrian governments sustained the principle of legitimacy and preservation of monarchical institutions. When the Central American states threatened to cut off trade with nations that did not extend them recognition, the Hansa cities negotiated commercial agreements. Prussia knew it could not win the support of the Hansa cities and the industrializing states to a *kleindeutsch* (German unification without Austria) resolution to a splintered Germany unless it could offer them access to world trade routes. Eventually, in 1845 Prussia appointed a consul general in Central America who immediately complained that indirect trade left the expansion of sales of German products at the mercy of foreigners (Halborn 1959-1969, vols. 2, 3; Henderson 1975; Wehler 1972, 71-92; Kossok 1964; Dane 1971, 5-6, 56, 78-79, 148-50; DZM, Lang, decree, n.d. [1845], AA II, Rep. 6, Nr. 3518).

Even as it competed with Austria for leadership of a unified Germany, Prussia drifted into the imperial competition between Britain and the United States, seeking to maximize its rights to transit over the Middle American isthmus. After the grave internal crisis of the 1848 revolution and Frankfurter Parliament, Prussia sought to regain lost prestige, to use the Zollverein (Customs Union) to facilitate its supremacy in Germany, to prevent Austrian predominance in Germany, to attract the Hansa cities and the industrial areas of Germany, and to fortify — yet subordinate — German nationalism to the Prussian monarchy. Such far-reaching objectives pressured Prussia to adopt international policies within the context of German unification, while strengthening German power and prestige. Thus, in 1850 Prussia named Privy Councilor Franz Hugo Hesse to head a mission to acquire trade and colonization concessions and to develop German transit possibilities. Hesse's dispatches invariably returned to the central theme of nineteenth-century imperial relations with Central America—the quest for transit and communication routes. He observed that the United States had gained domination of Panama, Tehuantepec, and Nicaragua, a domination which signified a defeat for England and a shifting of great advantages to U.S. navigation and trade in the Pacific basin. Prussia had to keep a close eye on isthmian affairs to prevent either Britain or the United States from excluding or curtailing German commerce. Aware of the difficulties involved in renewing the Customs Union compact, Hesse speculated that prospective agreements with El Salvador and other Middle American states might persuade the German states of the value of the Customs Union, thereby strengthening Prussia against Austria in the German political sphere (Hausherr 1966; Schoonover 1985, 393-422; DZM, Franz Hugo Hesse to Otto von Manteuffel, 30 Aug. 1854, 2. 4. 1., Abt II, Nr 638 [AA II, Rep. 6, Nr 3529], and 5 Nov. 1854, 2. 4. 1., Nr. 7943 [AA, Z. B., Nr 924]; Hesse to von Manteuffel and August von de Heydt, 29 July 1852, 2. 4. 1., Abt. II, Nr. 5198 [AA II, Rep. 6, Nr 1581]; Bayerisches Hauptstaatsarchiv, Never to Ministerium des öniglichen Hauses and des Aussern, 5 Feb. 1854, Abteilung II, Geheimes Staatsarchiv, M. A. 80041.)

Prussia experienced social transformations associated with industrialism, expanded communications, urbanization, and the flow of internal migration from agrarian areas to the growing urban centers. The late nineteenth-century crises—deep depressions in a generally expanding productivity—were normally interpreted as overproduction phases. Dynamic growth produced internal migration and shifted wealth from rural, aristocratic groups to urban industrial and finance bourgeoisies. Fortunate German entrepreneurs used some excess accumulation as risk or venture capital (Rosenberg 1967; Braun et al. 1972; Engelsing 1973).

Besides trade, other early German activities involved colonization schemes in Santo Tomás, Guatemala, and on the Mosquito Coast. The early stages of German industrialization were accompanied by rapid population increases and a decline in the quantity and quality of labor that the political economy could gainfully employ. Unemployed Germans emigrated in large numbers in the mid-nineteenth century, attracted by Central America's virgin lands. More than half the 850 settlers in 1846 in the Belgian colony at Santo Tomás were German. In 1844-1846, Prince Carl of Prussia, the brother of King Frederick William IV, became a partner in a contract with the Mosquito king to settle a large area in the Mosquito kingdom. The Prussian government followed this development with great interest because it involved the Prussian royal family and threatened possible confrontation with the British until it failed in 1852. The Prussian government recognized that continued German colonization on the frontiers of the New World portended difficulties with both the United States and Great Britain (Schultz 1843, 5, 29-36; DZM, Niebuhr, "Pro Memoria über die Stellung Preussens zu den deutschen Auswanderen namentlichen Rand-Amerika," 17 Feb. 1845, Alexander von Bülow to Eichorn, 10 Mar. 1845, Rep. 76 II, Section 1, Gen. b, No. 98, "Gründung einer deutschen Colonie auf der Mosquito Küste," AA, 2. 4. 1. II, No. 5245; Fröschle 1979, 566-638 *passim*; Henderson 1944, 257-71).

In the early 1850s, public meetings and colonization clubs viewed Nicaragua and Costa Rica as the best areas for German colonization, especially Baron Alexander von Bülow's colonization project in Costa Rica. Carl Scherzer reminded the German Bundestag of "the advantages which the German nation, German industry, and German commerce would derive from colonizing Central America with Germans," yet his huge colonization project failed to obtain support from either Austria or Prussia. In the 1840s and during Hesse's eight-year mission, various treaties were negotiated and several contracts were signed, with perhaps two thousand colonists migrating. In the 1860s, German settlers continued to arrive, building clubs and schools as well as engaging in agricultural, commercial, and financial affairs, thus permanently establishing German interests and culture in Central America (Published materials on colonization organizations in GSPK, I Hauptabteilung, Preussisches Staatsministerium [Rep. 90], Nr. 232; Jahresberichte des Hamburger Colonisationsvereins, 1851-1855, Akten des Bundestages, DB/28, vol. 1, Bundesarchiv, Aussenstelle Frankfurt; DZM, Hesse to von Manteuffel, 30 Dec. 1852, 2. 4. 1., Abt. II, Nr 5246 [AA III, Rep. 14, Nr 534]; Castellanos 1977a; Schottelius 1939).

Prussia's internal army and constitutional crisis in the late 1850s and the subsequent wars of unification in the 1860s briefly diverted German attention to questions closer to home. In the Caribbean, the Germans sought to use local economies as sponges for small, but growing, surpluses in textiles, iron wares, capital, and population, and as suppliers of additional raw materials and new products to satisfy demands for an improved life-style. While some of these "advances" had long been pushed by Hansa, Rhine, and Ruhr entrepreneurs, elements of the traditional ruling aristocratic, military, and bureaucratic classes joined in seeing useful aids to the problems of an industrializing economy via foreign commercial and capital expansion. Social imperialism generated support to pay for the army and to reduce the threat of liberalization of German politics. A host of problems — the breakdown of guilds, migration to urban areas, the chronic high unemployment, the growing socialist or activist labor groups, and rising crime rates — lent themselves to amelioration via social imperialism (Wehler 1972; Winckler 1964).

By the late 1860s, the Prussians were searching for naval stations in Asia, the Pacific, and the New World. In mid-1866, Bismarck was attracted to the scheme of U.S. politician, Civil War general, and speculator John C. Fremont who had obtained a Costa Rican governmental contract to build a railroad from Puerto Limón to the Pacific. He then proposed to sell his "rights" to either Prussia or the United States. Fremont offered the Prussian government bonds in his company, employment for German labor, and a choice location for a naval station in Puerto Limón as compensation for capital participation. A Prussian naval squadron conducted a charting cruise along the Atlantic coast of Central America in 1868. The squadron's commander, Captain Friedrich Wilhelm Franz Kinderling made the difficult overland trip to San José, where he encountered strong resistance to his inquiry about a possible transfer of rights over Puerto Limón to Prussia. The Costa Rican foreign minister refused to make any exclusive promise, and instead suggested that a private company should manage Prussian interests near Puerto Limón. Kinderling reported that Costa Rica welcomed the prospect of German rather than North American immigration. When an unspecified source leaked the mission's objectives, Bismarck disavowed Kinderling's activity in Costa Rica. Tulio von Bülow has convincingly argued, however, that Kinderling was Bismarck's confidential agent, floating a trial balloon. Kinderling's promotions in 1871 and 1878 hint at service to, rather than hindrance of, Bismarck's objectives. Kinderling's report to the Prussian Naval High Command confirmed he was, indeed, a special, confidential agent (DZM, Eduard Delius to the Foreign Ministry, 6 Aug. 1866, Rep. 77, Tit. 226, Nr. 118, Bd. 2; von Bülow 1973, 147-49; Arthur Morrell to Seward, 8 May 1868, Lahmann to Julio Volio, 1 May 1868, Volio to Lahmann, 6 May 1868, *FRUS*, 1868, pt. 2; DZM, F. W. F. Kinderling to Royal Navy High Command, 22 May 1868, 2. 4. 1. Abt. II, Nr. 644 [AA II Rep. 6, Nr. 3573]).[2]

After 1870 Prussian rule within the unified German Empire appeared settled. Growing German capital, the expanded consumer market, the extension of a uniform tariff, and increased security played important roles in the subsequent economic expansion of the German Empire. The German economy had to integrate more thoroughly into the world economic system in order to fulfill the rising expectations of materialistic-oriented German bourgeoisie, nobility, and prosperous elements of the working class. Security became identified with the opportunities won from the competitive struggle for protectorates, naval and military stations, and agreements to assure access to the world system. German officials and businessmen assigned Central America significance as a transit area, market, and source of products which the new German life-style and capital accumulation demanded (Spree 1977; Castellanos 1977b).

Germany upgraded its representation in Central America as trade and investment expanded there after 1860. As German "excess capital" and displaced labor entered Central America, especially Guatemala, U.S. agents became apprehensive about the expanding wealth and influence of the German colony. In 1877, U.S. Minister George Williamson asserted: "The Germans and not the British are our real competition for the trade of the whole of Spanish America." In 1880, U.S. Minister Cornelius Logan agreed that German competition was economically and strategic-politically threatening (USNA, Williamson to Evarts, 24 Sept. 1877, DD, CA: 14 [M 219/r 33]; Cornelius Logan to Evarts, 14 April 1879, 14 May 1880, DD, CA: 16 [M 219/r 35]).

Siemens, Krupp, Deutsche Bank, Überseebank, Kosmos, Hamburg-Amerika-Passagier-Aktien-Gesellschaft (HAPAG), and a myriad smaller German enterprises increased Germany's military and economic role in Central America, but produced jealous confrontations with the Monroe Doctrine. In the early 1880s, German Minister Werner von Bergen accused the United States of imperial ambitions. During a dinner attended by U.S. and Central American officials, von Bergen asked Salvadoran Foreign Minister Gallegos how long he believed Salvador could retain her freedom and autonomy. When Gallegos asked for an explanation, von Bergen mentioned the U.S. intention to absorb the Central American states. Von Bergen noted that the dinner celebrated the opening of the Guatemala Central Railway, built by Yankee concessionaires. This railroad, he warned, would bring a flood of Yankee immigrants to the Central American states. Von Bergen labored to build "a better relationship between Guatemala and Mexico...[to] prevent the United States from using the discord between the two countries to win a dominating influence in Central America, which would directly harm the considerable German material interests." Thus, in the late nineteenth-century contacts in Middle America contributed to the economic rivalry between Germany and the United States (USNA, Evarts to Andrew White, 6 Aug. 1880, RG 59, DI, Germany: 16 [M 77/r 67]; Logan to Evarts, 14 Oct. 1880, 7 Jan., 1 Feb. 1881, RG 59, DD, CA: 17 [M 219/r 37]; PAAA, von Bergen to Bismarck, 22 Sep. 1888, Abt. IA, Mexiko 2, Bd. 2).

The world economic crisis of 1873-1898 compelled each Middle American country to devalue sharply its silver, often forcing the use of paper currency. In 1891 foreign merchants and diplomats vigorously protested the Guatemalan law forcing acceptance of the paper currency instead of silver coins. The law threatened to ruin German businesses which had achieved preeminent positions in Guatemalan economic life. In 1898, foreign office economic specialist von Eckert detailed German economic activity and investment in Guatemala where Germans owned 50 central merchant locations with 18 branches and 64 million marks of rural and 600,000 marks of urban real estate which represented a total of 2725 square kilometers, including 17.7 million coffee trees and 14.3 square kilometers of sugar plantings. There were no German banking firms nor any German investment in mining and only minimum investment in railroads. German working capital in Guatemala totaled 183.5 million marks. Considerable German economic participation took place in other Central American countries. In 1899, Berlin estimated the gross profit of German firms trading in Nicaragua at 1.8 million marks and German investment in Nicaragua at 14 million marks (PAAA, Von Bergen to Leo von Caprivi, 10 Apr. 1891, IA, Guatemala 1, Bd. 3; SH, von Eckert report of 1897/1898, alte P-II-8/97, P. Metternich to Dr. Carl Burchard, 12 June 1899, Bestand: Senatskommission für die Reichs- und auswärtigen Angelegenheiten, neu A III, c.22). This extensive German investment and trade in Central America faced major losses if currency devaluation were to occur.

When national capital for the Guatemalan National Railroad dried up, von Eckert reported the new government intended to finish the project with foreign capital. He preferred German capital, for "scarcely anywhere else in the exterior would a German rail-line find a rear area where so many German interests exist in so small a space, where a larger part of the land belongs to Germans, another part is mortgaged to Germans, where two-thirds of the exports go to Germany and almost one-fourth of the imports come from Germany." Resident German trade and agricultural circles were interested in completing the Atlantic railroad because thirty-five to forty million marks of goods moved annually between Guatemala and Germany around the Magellan Straits or over the Panama Railroad and Pacific Mail (SB, Enclosure with Reichards to Bremen Senate, 28 Apr. 1898, A. 3. C. 1., Nr. 85).

By the end of the nineteenth century, the German economy, straining to continue rapid growth, pushed for vital world markets, investment opportunities, raw materials, and naval support points. Albert Ballin, director of the HAPAG, claimed that a Panama canal would be a powerful weapon in North American hands. A Ballin associate reflected upon the "unhealthy consequences [which sole U.S. control over the canal] would have for German trade and navigation and even for its position in East Asia." The Panama Canal Company scandals negated any possibility of raising funds in France, and Ballin became convinced that "success [with German financial circles] was unthinkable without effective support from the Imperial government." He trusted that the German foreign minister recognized that positive action to retain an internationally neutral canal, not merely passive protection, was needed to safeguard endangered German interests (PAAA, Albert Ballin to Bernard von Bülow, 2 Sep. 1899, enclosing Koch to Ballin, 30 Aug. 1899, IA, Amerika Generalia, Nr. 12, Bd. 1).

Ballin's concern about the Panama Canal falling under sole U.S. control stimulated Admiral Alfred von Tirpitz to argue that the fighting navy and merchant marine shared interests in a shortened route from Europe to the Pacific Ocean because of Germany's "varied economic relations with Latin America and the Pacific." Von Tirpitz warned that a canal closed in wartime posed a major obstacle to Germany. The German navy planned a strategic offensive which required a campaign to seize the closed canal (meaning war with the United States), or, alternately, to use the slow and costly Magellan Straits and the Suez Canal. He emphasized "the significance of such a connection will increase steadily in the future because our growing foreign interests will constantly compel us to increase our occupation of foreign stations." Berlin's oldest merchant organization maintained that "a serious disturbance of our foreign trade relations would be very disadvantageous not only for the circles immediately effected, but would indeed have ominous consequences for almost the whole population." If Germany could not obtain a favored position with regard to the future canal, von Tirpitz wanted assurance of the canal's international character. Few informed German groups presumed Germany could withdraw from Latin America, particularly Middle America and the Caribbean, and still experience a fruitful economic future (PAAA, Alfred von Tirpitz to Foreign Ministry, 29 Oct. 1899, IA, Amerika Generalia Nr. 12, Bd. 1; GSPK, *Denkschrift* 1901, I Hauptabteilung, Rep. 108, Nr. 5104).

German firms were seeking to extend rather than limit their involvement in Central America. In 1900, Siemens's subsidiary, Empresa Eléctrica de Guatemala, which invested about 3,400,000 marks in the electrification of that country after 1890, offered to pay the outstanding debt related to the electrical works and to purchase the Guatemalan president's 13 shares of Empresa stock at about 13 times their market value, in exchange for doubling the duration of its concession and the right to convert to a German corporation. When Guatemalan President Manuel Estrada Cabrera broke off negotiations, the

German chargé intervened immediately. Siemens officials believed that a subsequent attack upon this chargé represented a response to his protection of Empresa. In mid-1901, under pressure from the German government, the Guatemalan government began repaying its debt to the Siemens subsidiary, yet continuing to deny Empresa the right to become a foreign corporation as long as a Guatemalan owned one share of stock (PAAA, Report on Empresa Eléctrica de Guatemala, Oct. 1900, Tonio Bodiker to the Foreign Ministry, 29 Oct. 1900, IA, Guatemala 1, Bd. 4; WSIGHS, Bodiker to Oswald von Richtoven, 26 Oct. 1900, Bodiker to [?], 31 July 1901, 25/Lt. 201).

In late 1903 the Germans and Americans twice rejected the Guatemalan government's request to construct a pavilion for an annual Minerva festival, a popular celebration consisting of music, dancing, and free drinks. While reporting Empresa Eléctrica's moral victory in the Minerva affair, the firm's manager explained how he had deceived the Guatemalan government about price and profit in a clever manner which would facilitate continued deception regarding price and profit in the future. After the deception, he calculated the Empresa's gross profit amounted to 40 percent of total revenue (WSIGHS, Ernest Greve to Siemens & Halske, 9, 29 Sep., 16 Dec. 1903, Greve to Transportation Minister, 13 Sep. 1903, Siemens to Empresa Eléctrica, Nov. 7, 1903, 25/L1 449).

In mid-1905, Captain Paul Behneke, commander of the German naval vessel *Falke*, summarized German business, settler, and cultural activity in Central America for the German government. He estimated 55 Germans had collectively invested about 1/2 million marks in Panama. In Costa Rica, Germans had invested 15 million marks in 9 large German businesses, about 7 million marks in land, and 3 million in credit. He estimated German investment in Nicaragua at 24 million marks, divided into 12 million in trade and 6 million each in land and credit which he believed was slightly larger than the North American investment. Although 19 German business houses operated in Nicaragua, trade flowed strongly to the United States. Behneke estimated that German investment in Guatemala had reached about 300 million marks: 150 to 160 million in land, 110 million in credit, 30 million in trade, and 10 million in enterprises, about 2 1/2 times the total value of all other foreign investment. Germans owned 60 percent of Guatemala's coffee plantations. German interests and investments in El Salvador, worth about 30 million marks, ranked behind North American and French investments. There were 176 German residents and 4 clubs, but no German school in Costa Rica. About 400 Germans resided in Nicaragua, supporting 3 clubs. Behneke described a large German community in Guatemala which supported 5 clubs and a German school. El Salvador had few German residents and no clubs (BMF, Paul Behneke to Emperor William, 24 Apr. 1905, RM 5/v. 5428, and 18 May 1905, RM 5/v. 5401, and 18 May 1905, Von Ammon to Emperor William, 3 Feb. 1906, RM 5/v. 5402, Behneke to Emperor William, 18 May 1905, RM 5/v. 5412, and 18 May 5/v. 5432).

In the early twentieth century, German influence was on the rise in Central America, but was confronting mounting U.S. political opposition. Behneke expected the U.S. assumption of authority over the Panama Railroad in April 1905 would aid the Kosmos line in conjunction with HAPAG to extend operations into the Pacific. He lamented that, although "there is no foreign land in whose economy Germany is so strongly participating and on whose development, therefore, Germany is so interested, as Guatemala....The North American influence dominates here also." The Guatemalan minister of war regretted that "an active [German] officer will scarcely be allowed to enter into the Guatemalan army given the jealousy and suspicion of the United States and the harassment of its press." Nicaraguan President José Santos Zelaya endured, the German consul at Managua pointed out, because "his weapon" was his army, which had been reorganized with German aid and supported through a cadet school under German direction. "Germany had in any case no grounds to be unsatisfied with the continuation of his rule," the consul observed, since Zelaya had been "generally friendly toward German interests, and, in any event, a strong government like his offered the best guarantee against American intervention" (DZP, Heyer to Bülow, 23 Jan. 1906, 09.01, Nr. 12494; BK, von Seefried to von Bülow, 27 Sep. 1905, R 85/2852). Throughout Central America, the German government competed chiefly with France and the United States to supply military missions. All three governments expected these missions to parlay into increased home country trade and security.

In addition to clashes in Samoa, the Philippines, China, the Congo, and over pork sales, the United States and Germany competed for access to the canal, naval stations, investment, commerce, and political influence. A North American syndicate negotiated a loan contract with Guatemala, asking for land and mineral rights rather than customs revenue as security. The German minister predicted that mining activity, which paid higher wages and offered year-round employment, would undermine the hiring of agricultural labor for the numerous German coffee plantations. He argued that the U.S. economic conquest of Guatemala through railroads and banana plantations "should not occur at the expense of 160 million marks of German money invested in land, of 30 million marks invested in German trading firms, nor of German credit establishments which preserve the market here for German industry." Traveling through Guatemala, he observed, left the impression of traveling through a German colony, but he lamented that young Germans were tempted to opt for U.S. citizenship because Germany lacked political influence in Guatemala. About 1912, a bitter struggle developed between United Fruit and a HAPAG-Atlas-Atlantic Fruit combination. If Atlantic Fruit "fell under United Fruit control," German diplomat Seelinger warned, "United Fruit would achieve a power which would make it very difficult, if not eternally impossible, for Germany to penetrate further that business and to continue our shipping lines." Ultimately, Atlantic Fruit collapsed, disrupted by World War I and United Fruit hostility. The Middle American states generally welcomed German capital, given their apprehension that U.S. economic penetration would lead to political domination (DZM, Bonin to von Bülow, 1 July 1909, Rep. 120, C XIII, 16 < a >, No. 4, Bd. 2; BK, Seelinger to Foreign Ministry, 1 Aug. 1912,

R 85/134; SH, Gnet to Imperial Chancellor, 12 Dep. 1912, Bestand: Senatskommission für die Reichs- und auswärtigen Angelegenheiten, neu C. I. d. 164).

Persistent German attempts to promote the open door in Central America represented an unexpected challenge to the United States. U.S. policy generally denied foreign bases in commercial or strategic key areas. German maritime firms needed to secure West Coast American harbors, however, if they intended to use the Panama Canal to participate in the West Coast's economic upswing which offered a rich field for German capital and entrepreneurial spirit. The Henry Cabot Lodge Corollary to the Monroe Doctrine, Seelinger noted, threatened any foreign acquisitions near the canal zone. He observed: "The Americans have followed essentially their own interests in deciding questions related to the canal...and they have proceeded thereby with absolute ruthlessness." He expected the opening of the Panama canal to "create a situation which will lead the industrial and maritime states into a great struggle to open economically still undeveloped lands and to shape new communications routes and new consumer markets" (PAAA, von Seefried to von Bülow, 4 Apr. 1906, IA, Costarica 1, Bd. 3, Seelinger to Foreign Minister, 11 Sep. 1912, IA, Amerika Generalia, Nr. 12, Bd. 10). The U.S. open door policy (proclaiming equal access to trade and investment), however, so vital to American governmental and business circles, excluded Latin America, because the Monroe Doctrine of the twentieth century assured U.S. priority in that region.

Prior to U.S. entry in the Great War, German officials wondered how they might hinder U.S. economic activity, if that should become necessary, while the United States sought to reduce German influence in Central America. The Germans did well initially in the propaganda contest with Britain and France during World War I because of the strong German role in Central American society. When the Guatemalan German colony quickly exhausted its resources subsidizing three Guatemalan newspapers, the German foreign ministry assumed the subsidy until the war's end. In Honduras, where two papers published information from Germany, two German priests labeled the funds raised an example of the potential political "side-benefits" from cultural influence. The United States, after entering the war, wanted to replace German investments in Central American coffee, marketing, shipping, communications, and energy technology. Ultimately, the propaganda assault of the United States, Britain, and France prevailed, leading to sequestration of German property and the jailing or exile of many German businessmen. After the Great War, the German Foreign Institute acted to undo the damage done by the Allied propaganda, so Germans could successfully reenter Latin American social and economic activity (Small 1972, 252-70; Doerries 1973, 62-77; PAAA, Lehmann to Theobald von Bethmann Hollweg, 8 Sep., 5 Oct., 2 Nov. 1914, 28 Mar. 1915, IA, Guat. 5, Bd. 1, Nicolaus Cornelsen to von Bethmann Hollweg, 28 Dec. 1914, IA, Hond. 2; AMAE, French Minister to MAE, 22 Nov. 1914, CP 1918, Guat., Negociations et affairs commerciales; BK, materials in Deutsches Auslandsinstitut, R57/DAI 413).

In April 1918, the Hamburg government and merchants, persuaded that Germany would lose the war, argued in a confidential report that the foreign service of Germany, a world power, had to eschew its passive role of protection and adopt more aggressive ones. To achieve these goals, Hamburg urged the foreign ministry to establish a political reputation to match Germany's military and commercial position. The Hamburg Chamber of Commerce argued that Germany's foreign service required reliable bureaucrats who would draw commercial groups into the decision-making process. The German naval staff responded that only older men, preferably with military experience, should be selected for the consular and diplomatic corps. With capital and other resources short, Germany struggled to reestablish its economic and political ties with Central America. The post-World War I German government reaffirmed its confidence in colonization, investment, trade, and culture to generate the conditions to expand German economic activity and to enrich the local German population, transient merchants, and the firms, banks, and investors from Germany (BMF, "Hamburger Vorschläge zur Neugestaltung des deutschen Auslandsdienstes," Apr. 1918, "Stellungnahme von A I to A IV [Hamburger Vorschläge zur Neugestaltung des deutschen Auslandsdienstes]," 8 May 1918, RM 3/4382; IHK Dortmund, annual report, Hamburg Chamber of Commerce, 1918, S 6, Nr. 991; Schoonover 1983, 49-51).

The Germans regained their position in Central America so quickly in the 1920s that they aroused the jealousy and suspicion of U.S., British, and French officials. Some Central Americans viewed the German revival as an opportunity to use German capital, colonists, and trade to restrict aggressive "Yankee imperialism." Germany's commercial recovery was measured in its use of the Panama Canal: Germany was thirteenth in 1921, sixth in 1922, fifth in 1923, and fourth in 1924, and in its revived purchases of Salvadoran coffee, Germany was sixth in 1923, second in 1924, and first in 1925 and 1926. After recovering in shipping and access to raw materials, the difficult task was creating market opportunities for German products (Handelskammer Hamburg 1926; SH, *Hamburger Nachrichten* 21 Nov. 1925, Senatskommission für die Reichs- und auswärtigen Angelegenheiten, N.R., III, B 94; PAAA, Richard Kühlmann to AA, 25 May 1926, 11 Mar., 31 Dec., 1927, 12 Nov. 1929, III, S. Salvador, Wirtschaft I).

In the 1920s, new German elements, such as Allgemeine Elektricitäts-Gesellschaft (AEG), Walter Sprung in Costa Rica, Wayss-Freitag in Salvador and Costa Rica, and old firms like Siemens competed for road, city sanitation, engineering, urban transportation, and public utilities concessions. In 1924, the U.S. minister intervened twice in contract matters on behalf of Westinghouse, but AEG obtained both contracts, one of which was worth $3,000,000. The German consul in Honduras helped an AEG engineer to bid on an electric light and power contract for Tegucigalpa after a North American firm seemed to have secured the contract. Despite the U.S. minister's intervention to prevent the contract, Honduran officials signed a purchase agreement for AEG equipment. The German consul hoped that further contracts would follow this project. AEG's success in Guatemala and Honduras pointed to the rapid recovery of powerful German influence (AMEF, Revelli to MAE, 27 Jan. 1924, F < 30 > 1956: Guat.; AMAE, Revelli to MAE, 6 Oct. 1924, Amer. 1918-40, C. A., num. 22; PAAA, Cornelsen to Kühlmann, 4 Dec. 1928, III, Hond., Industrie 10).

Costa Rican President Ricardo Jiménez, concerned about growing U.S. influence in his country, asked German engineer Walter Sprung to supervise engineering and construction contracts. Sprung quietly favored German firms which, however, occasionally competed bitterly with each other. AEG and Siemens blocked each other's contracts in Costa Rica. The German minister, incensed, pleaded that once a contract was let, the unsuccessful German competitors should not interfere. The squabbling discredited German business and pushed concessions to other countries. In early 1929, after winning a fierce competition with North American firms for a $600,000 contract to pave the streets of San José, Costa Rica, Wayss & Freytag of Frankfurt reported intrigues jeopardized the contract. The German foreign ministry worked behind the scenes to undermine the intrigues directed against Wayss in order to help German firms compete against the United States elsewhere in Central America (PAAA, III, C. R., Industrie 30; Kühlmann to AA, 11 Jan. 1928, Lentz to AA, 23 July 1928, III, C. R., Handel 30, Nr. 1, de Haas to Germ. Leg. Guat., 17 Jan. 1929, Kühlmann to AA, 29 Aug. 1929, Wayss & Freytag, 14 Oct. 1929, III, C. R., Industrie 3).

As German economic activity in Central America accelerated after the mid-1920s, the Berlin government selected Gustav Noske, later minister president [*Oberpräsident*] of Hannover, to make an extensive trip through Latin America to investigate German activity. Another sign of the importance of Central America to German foreign policy was the appointment of Richard von Kühlmann as minister in 1926. Kühlmann had served with distinction in the foreign service and in the kaiser's personal service from the 1880s until Wilhelm II abdicated. Noske reported the Germans occupied powerful economic positions in Costa Rica and Guatemala, but were much influential in Guatemala. He valued the observation of a German consul and large plantation owner in Guatemala who said: "We [Germans] play about the same role in Guatemala as the anti-Semitics allege against the Jews in Germany. As economic exploiters of the country, we are every bit as loved [by the Guatemalans] as the Jews are loved normally by us in the homeland." He recalled that most German emigrés wanted to make a fortune in Guatemala and return to Germany. This expatriated capital did not benefit the masses in Guatemala, he noted, as it might have done in the hands of a domestic capitalist elite. He overlooked the fact that domestic capitalists might invest in foreign countries. Various German residents warned that Guatemala would not tolerate this huge capital loss forever. The matter was made worse because the capital accumulators paid almost no taxes. He observed that in the long run, white nations could not rule Latin America. The Guatemalan Indian inevitably compared the exalted life-style of the German to his own wretched existence and hard labor. Until the Indians or black groups finally asserted themselves, however, Germans should conduct business because the United States would continue to invest, trade, and extract profits (PAAA, Noske to Preussischer Minister des Innern, 28 June 1927, III, M.-Amer., Pol. 15, AA to Noske, [15 Dec. 1926], III, M.-Amer., Verkehrswesen 12; Kühlmann 1948).

The German foreign minister pointed out in 1928 that foreign investment and the expansive business phase in Germany meant that future market growth must be found outside Germany. Germany's rebuilt economy had saturated domestic consumer capacity. He concluded that "in the future everything must be done to penetrate foreign markets for German industry. It was the German government's job to assure that this did not occur under the appearance of crisis signals" (BK, Reichswirtschaftsminister to Reichskanzlei, 16 Feb. 1928, R431/1175). Thus, in 1928 just as with the Hesse mission in 1850, Germany's political and economic leadership had assumed that more intimate ties with Central America would alleviate some of Germany's internal socioeconomic ailments and that this contact would facilitate German security and prosperity.

The domestic German economy from the mid-nineteenth through the early twentieth centuries experienced sporadic, indeterminable economic cycles which raised a host of problems that the leaders of Germany's political economy sought to alleviate abroad. When German interests involved such a key area of the world economic system as the Central American isthmus, they encountered other nations' businessmen whose corrupted laissez-faire ideology — evident in open-door and free-trade rhetoric covering government supported multinational business ventures — generated intense competition clothed in strategic, political, social, and cultural language to reinforce the home countries' determination to assure minimum access to the capacity of Central American transit to generate wealth and security by linking the Atlantic and Pacific worlds. These understandable German aspirations confronted similar perspectives from the leadership of the United States, Britain, and France in the nineteenth and early twentieth centuries.

France's relationship with Central America changed considerably over the years. In the early decades after Central America's independence, French trade remained appreciable and French ideas, language, and culture were highly valued. French industrial progress and capital accumulation during the nineteenth century was less spectacular than that of Britain, the United States, or Germany. France's slowness in recognizing the independence of the new republics, its small merchant marine, its cautious bankers, the French preference to produce luxury goods, Britain's quickness in obtaining favorable commercial treaties with Latin America, and the effectiveness of British consuls explain the decline in France's trading position in Latin America (Asselain 1984; Caron 1979; Bouvier, 1974).

French observers recognized the need to preserve France's commercial position in Central America. A French admiral advised studying the little-known Central American countries to determine where one could best open new roads for French commerce. He used a French war vessel to aid a French company on the Central American coast because he recognized that increasing markets for French industry and commerce required naval power to balance overbearing British naval interference. He proposed combining Martinique, Guadeloupe, the Belgian settlements of Santo Tomás and Río Dulce, and the Franco-Colombia canal company to build solid French resistance to further British encroachment. A French promoter argued that either a railroad or a canal at Panama would strengthen France's commercial competitors, especially the United States and Britain. He foresaw that the United States would ultimately dominate any canal for geopolitical reasons. He believed roads to link the isthmian rivers that flowed into the Atlantic and Pacific offered France a chance to extend its markets, merchant marine, and "manufactures" throughout Latin America (AN, Ludovic Joseph Alfred de Moges to Min. Marine, 10 Apr., 25 June, 24 Oct., 7 Dec. 1842, Marine, BB < 4 > 613; AMAE, de Moges to Min. Marine, 21 Aug. 1843, CP 1871, Amér. cent., v. 6; Denain 1845, 18-21, 66-69, 190-99, 211).

After the bloodless coup of 1848 stabilized France, French interests reentered the quagmire of Central America. With prestige, security, markets, and investment opportunities in the balance, the United States and most European commercial nations sent agents to prevent any power or group of powers from acquiring exclusive access to the Pacific basin trading area. France considered naval bases, colonies, trade treaties, protectorates, and cultural ties to secure its influence in Central America. The French chargé believed the small states of Central America which generally favored France over its rival, Great Britain, would offer "all of the advantages of a colony without any of the inconveniences" (Schoonover 1983; AAM, Capt. Comte Louis Henri de Gueydon to Adm. Le Goarant de Tromelin, 29 Apr. 1848, BB < 4 > 1596). French leaders believed its liberal and civilizing reputation would carry great weight. In fact, with Central America conservatives often sympathetic toward Britain, both France and the United States found the Central American liberal factions friendly.

In 1848, the French minister terminated relations with the Guatemalan government, urging France to use the rupture to seize Santo Tomás as a base for a French colony in Central America. Determined action at Santo Tomás, he assumed, would persuade Nicaraguans to seek French protection for the projected San Juan del Norte Canal. In the fall of 1848, he warned that, given the disturbed conditions in Central America, if a great European nation rooted in Roman tradition and Catholicism did not build a "dam [in Middle America] against the...Anglo-Saxon race and the Protestant nations," the United States would "extend the stars and stripes over the two Americas" (AMAE, Charles Alexander de Challeye to MAE, 22 June, 1 July 1848, CP 1871, Amér. cent., v. 7, de Challeye to MAE, 18 Nov. 1848, CP 1871, Amér. cent., v. 8). France's economic and cultural prospects in Central America required considered, purposeful plans to oppose U.S. penetration.

Various French interests expressed concern over the impact of British and U.S. negotiations over Central American transit in 1849 and 1850 upon French trade. The French minister found France's role in Central America exasperating: "We watch the English and the Americans act and maneuver freely, with our hands in our pockets," even though Guatemala constantly signaled for French protection. Rebuilding France's reputation would require naval vessels, firm demands regarding reclamations, and an agent with authority to act when necessary. He welcomed confidential negotiations to undermine U.S. penetration by means of a "hidden intervention in the pacific form of colonization." He recommended that France should use Belgium as a surrogate to block British and U.S. ambitions. A French diplomat judged that the selection of Santo Tomás as Guatemala's principal port would offer excellent opportunities for French commerce (AMAE, Alfred de Valois to MAE, 10 Feb., 21 Apr. 1849, CP 1871, Amér. cent., t. 8, Fourcade to MAE, 22 Jan. 1850, CCC, Guat., v. 4).

Under the visions of Gabriel Lafond du Lurcy and Félix Belly, the French sought colonization and transit rights in Costa Rica, Nicaragua, and Panama from 1850 to 1870. In 1850, the foreign minister assured Lafond, serving as Costa Rica's consul general in France, of France's assistance "to the limit of international law" for an extensive colonization and development concession from the Costa Rican government which Lafond envisioned would encourage French commerce in Middle America. Lafond perceived that the Gulf of Dulce was destined to become the best entrepôt for French marketing in California, "Polynesia, Australia, Malaysia, China and India." Lafond's project received widespread approval from French political and entrepreneurial circles (Scheips 1956; AMAE, Gabriel Lafond du Lurcy to Napoleon, 9 May 1850, MAE to Lafond, 31 May 1850, CP 1871, Amér. cent., v. 9; Lafond 1856).

Many Europeans believed that the United States intended to use the Crimean War to cover expansion in Panama and in Central America. Belly described how the United States exploited this crisis in Nicaragua. The United States alleged British violations of U.S. neutrality, yet it sold arms to Russia and allowed men, materials, and funds to be raised for filibustering in Central America. In his view, the weaker Latin American states looked to Europe, especially France, to aid the Latin race in resisting Anglo-American absorption. Nicaragua was ready, Belly insisted, to grant transit concessions if Europe could assure its independence (Allen 1967; Belly 1858, 121-57; Pincetl 1968).

The Lafond and Belly ventures were related to Napoleon III's intervention in Mexico and his emphasis on shared "Latin American" values to hinder U.S. expansion southward. U.S. projects to colonize freed blacks in Central America revealed that North American expansionism was not being held back by the Civil War. As a countermeasure, Napoleon III's government contacted Belgium and Guatemala about reorganizing the old Belgian Santo Tomás company with French capital and colonists. Santo Tomás' harbor would become a powerful auxiliary French military point in the Gulf of Mexico. Since French economic and military resources were often limited, the French government encouraged the use of colonization and other cultural tools, such as honors and awards, in an effort to develop alternative sources of influence to accomplish its objectives. La Compagnie Internationale pour l'exécution du Canal Maritime de Nicaragua wanted a French war vessel to carry the

Legion of Honor for Nicaragua's President and decorations for seven other Nicaraguans. The French cabinet feared that French medals would lose value if so distributed and that a war vessel might provoke a new U.S. invasion since the company's project would appear to be under French protection (Kuhn 1969; AMAE, Hardy to MAE, 1 May 1862, CCC, Guat., vol. 7, unsigned report, 24 Feb. 1863, Affaires divers politiques, carton 2, folder, Affaires coloniales Belgiques; Edward Loos to Napoleón III, 18 June 1863, analysis of Loos dispatch, July 1863, Mémoires et Documents, Amér., vol. 68).

Competition between firms often assumed a national character. In the late summer of 1873, the Panama Railroad Company rescheduled its Pacific steamers out of synchronization with the French steamers on the Atlantic coast. The French consul in Costa Rica complained: "The change of dates...has been done with the objective of attempting to eliminate at least one of their numerous competitors," and not because the company was responding to local needs. A year later, the Transatlantique Company's steamer service to Middle America was in a precarious situation (AMAE, Edouard Carpentier to MAE, 19 Aug. 1873, CCC, San José de C. R., vol. 1, Gustave Langlade to MAE, 22 Oct. 1877, CCC, Guat., vol. 9; AAM, to Admiral commanding Pacific Division, 23 Jan. 1874, BB < 4 > 1596).

The economic burden of reparations and the need to redefine its role in Europe after the defeat of 1871 induced France to reduce its role in Central America. Ferdinand de Lesseps' canal venture in the 1878-1889 years can be easily misinterpreted. It appeared to signal a continued French interest in Central American transit and world trade, an outlet for French capital, and a revived nationalism as France's best engineer undertook a second "impossible" project to benefit mankind, trade, and France. De Lesseps' project, however, was less a sign of powerful French interest in Middle America than of French confidence in de Lesseps. The interoceanic canal was expected to allow lagging French trade to capture an appreciable share of the Pacific and Central American trade (AAM, Correspondence for June 1871 to Feb. 1872, in BB < 4 > 942, Capt. Parizot, renseignements *Hussard*, Jan. 1880 [2 reports], BB < 4 > 1397, Parizot to de Petit-Thouars, 22 Feb. 1880, BB < 4 > 1596; Rowley 1982).

When the Panama Canal was completed, the French chargé suspected naval stations on the Pacific side would become more valuable, adding that the British and Germans sought stations. The French naval ministry rejected three islands in Fonseca Bay because it expected that acquisition would generate problems with Nicaragua, Honduras, El Salvador, and the United States. While rejecting the islands in Fonseca Bay, France examined the Galapagos Islands, Costa Rica's Cocos Island, and Clipperton Island as possible naval support points (AAM, MAE to Min. Marine, 28 Oct. 1886, BB < 4 > 1391, Aube [du Seignlay?] to Capt. la Guerre, 17 Feb. 1887, BB < 4 > 1199, La Guerre to Min. Marine, 29 April, 15 May 1887, BB < 4 > 1204, Adm. Jules Charles August Lefèvre to Min. Marine, 20 Feb. 1889, BB < 4 > 1229, Min. Marine to MAE, 30 Sep. 1886, BB < 4 > 1357; AMAE, Correspondence in CP 1896, Amér. cent., vol. 28).

The Panama Canal Company's failure was traumatic in France, but left a multitude of Frenchmen who found other tasks or activities in Central America. An earlier French Guatemala City-Atlantic coast railroad concession which promised much for French interests in Guatemala floundered and then stalled. Later, a syndicate headed by the former administrator of the Suez Canal, Henri de Cottu, bid $3,750,000 to purchase the Guatemalan Central Railroad. In early 1889, a Cottu-led group obtained the $10,000,000 project to build the Guatemala-Atlantic railroad. The railroad project would bolster French influence where German and U.S. traders and investors were most visible. The U.S. minister acknowledged that the Atlantic railroad would have great value to the United States even though a French loan would displace the United States which had supplied most of Guatemalan railroad capital in the 1880s. The French were favored, U.S. diplomats noted, because the Church party, returning to power throughout Central America, was intensely anti-American and sympathetic to European powers. Several years later Cottu withdrew from his contract (USNA, Hosmer to Wharton, 9 Sep. 1889, CD, Guat.: vol. 7 [M 337/r 7]; AMAE, L. Reynaud to MAE, 24 Apr. 1889, 25 Oct. 1892, CP 1896, Guat., Travaux publiques, chemins de fer, navigation, N. S. vol. 8, Reynaud to MAE, 5 Oct. 1889, Affaires divers commerciales, carton 543 [copy in AN, Commerce, F < 12 > 7054]; Reynaud to MAE, 8 Oct. 1889, CP 1896, Amér. cent., vol. 29; AAM J. Gaillard to Min. Marine, 10 Mar., 1 Apr. 1890, BB < 4 > 1237; USNA, Lansing B. Mizner to James G. Blaine, 7 Mar. 1890, DD, CA: 32 [M 219/r. 52]).

The French viewed language and culture as foundation stones for building influence in foreign areas. In the early 1890s, France created the Alliance Française to propagate French language and culture. The French chargé believed the five Central American states recognized that France would guide them to progress and civilization. French diplomats reported upon the instruction of French. In Costa Rica's program, every primary and six-year secondary school required two years of French. Eight Guatemalan and four Nicaraguan secondary schools offered French. El Salvador had two schools for girls, both with French women as directors, and six for boys which offered French. The French consul in San José surmised that, despite moral sympathy for France in Costa Rica, the commercial preponderance of the British and North Americans lent English preference over French. French officials lamented the inadequate support for the French language through the Alliance Française (AMAE, George Ritt to MAE, 15 Nov. 1893, enclosing "Note sur l'instruction publique et l'enseignement du française au Costa Rica," Série C, Administratives, dossier #135, Alliance Française, Costa Rica, J. Begueries to MAE, 26 June, 24 & 26 July 1893, A. Charpentier to MAE, 19 Jan. 1894, Série C, Administratives, dossier #138, Alliance Française, Guat., Ritt to MAE, 3 Mar. 1895, CCC, San José de C. R., vol. 1, Emile Joré to MAE, 1 May, 1 & 10 July 1898, Affaires divers commerciales, carton 220, Enseignement du français en Amérique Latine, folder Cent. Amér.).

In early 1895, the French agent in Guatemala observed that the Northern Railroad would allow European products to reach Guatemalan markets.

Guatemalan Minister Múñoz welcomed more French capital and engineers to counter German and North American influence. The French chargé believed French imports stagnated in Guatemala while German imports increased yearly because the Germans had built a market for their inferior goods, and because the colossal German merchant houses extended special facilities to their clients. The French chargé hoped French commercial institutions would learn from the Germans who had acquired Guatemala's military supply contracts, created credit establishments, drew large profits, and established trading houses which exchanged coffee and sugar for German manufactures via two German shipping firms. French capital had stagnated at home, but French capitalists were presented another opportunity to participate in the Northern Guatemala Railroad, which would compete capably with the completed Panama Canal (AMAE, Casimir Challet to MAE, 18 Mar., 20 Aug., 4 Sep., 12 Nov. 1895, Min. Commerce to MAE, 12 Oct., 9 Dec. 1895, MAE to Challet, 28 Dec. 1895, Guat., Finances Publiques, Emprunts, vol. 1, N. S. 6).

Around the turn of the century, the French military industry challenged Germany's leading role in Central America. In early 1891, Guatemala requested a fourteen-man French military mission to serve as instructors. After an apparent agreement, a French diplomat advised withholding the mission because poor administration had produced a bad economic situation in Guatemala. In 1898 France contracted to send a small military mission to Guatemala. The mission remained until the early 1930s. From 1896 to 1901, a French military mission in El Salvador influenced acquisitions of weapons and military supplies. In mid-1899, when French officials assumed the Nicaraguan request for a six-man military mission would strengthen French prestige in Central America, an anonymous, confidential warning (perhaps from Guatemala) created reservations. The successful French mission in Guatemala helped persuade Honduras to solicit a French officer to organize its army staff (AMAE, MAE to Guat. chargé, 19 Jan. 1891, Paul Louis Reynaud to MAE, 23 & 25 Jan., 3 June 1891, CP 1896, Amér. cent., vol. 30, Min. Guerre to MAE, 17 Jan. 1896, CP 1918, San Salv., Politique extérieure, N. S. 2, Jean Jerôme Cazard to MAE, 15 May 1899, Pourtales Gorgier to MAE, 30 July 1900, Affaires divers commerciales, cartons 305 and 306, Joré to MAE, 9 Oct., 19 Nov. 1899, 2 Jan., 4 & 16 Mar. 1900, CCC, San José de C. R., vol. 2, Louis Jean Clément Lévesque l'Avril to MAE, 2 Feb. 1914, CP 1918, Hond., pol. intérieure, chemins de fer, N. S. 1).

While Guatemala had traditionally purchased its military supplies from the German Krupp firm, in the early twentieth century it began purchasing from France due to the initiative of the well-liked head of the military mission. In 1911, Krupp's agent revived a challenge — unsuccessfully — for Guatemala's artillery order. In 1917, Guatemala turned to France, not the United States, to modernize its army for a possible call to Europe (AMAE, Auguste Jean Marc Rigoreau to MAE, 5 Aug. 1911, Min. Guerre to MAE, 18 Sep. 1911, Min. Finances to MAE, 6 Oct., 24 Nov. 1911, de Arce to MAE, 11 Oct. 1911, CP 1918, Guat., Défense nationale, II, N. S. 3, Fabre to MAE, 15 Oct. 1912, José Lardizabal to MAE, 13 Oct. 1917, 26 Mar. 1918, Min. Guerre to MAE,

9 Dec. 1917, CP 1918, Guat., Dfense nationale, II, N. S. 4, contract, 23 Nov. 1920, Amér., 1918-40, C. A., Num. 33).

While acknowledging U.S. supremacy in Middle America, many Frenchmen believed France had some influence because of the thousands who died pursuing de Lesseps' dream. In mid-1909, a French foreign ministry memorandum observed that an estimated 1.5 billion francs had wandered to the New World. France's large investments throughout Latin America underscored French interest in New World affairs. At the turn of the century, French investment in Central America, exclusive of about 225 million francs in the Panama Canal and a large sum in Honduran railroad bonds of questionable value, amounted to about 47 million francs. The total surpassed 300 million francs. This sum fell to 88 million on the eve of World War I, because of the sale of French Panama Canal interests, and rose again to 250 million by the mid-1930s (AMAE, Unsigned, "Note par M. le Rapporteur de la Commission de Budget," 27 July 1909, Mémoires et Documents, Amér., vol. 67; Levy 1897; La fortune française 1902; Rippy 1948; Eusebe 1972). France's role as a significant investor revitalized in the post-World War I years.

French desires to expand its investment role in Central America, however, inevitably caught the worried attention of the U.S. government. When Nicaragua inquired in mid-1909 about floating a loan on the Paris stock exchange, the French foreign minister consulted the U.S. secretary of state who suggested that the French might inform the Nicaraguan agent that a loan would be conditional upon arranging its affairs so that France would not be in an adversary role toward the United States. Accepting the secretary of state's suggestion, France was willing to squeeze Nicaragua, but not the United States. The French consul in Costa Rica warned that the State Department considered José Santos Zelaya "the cause of all the unrest which blocks the material and political progress of Central America." When France misread the hypocrisy behind the apparent U.S. willingness to allow a loan to Nicaragua and prepared to allow the loan to float in Paris, the secretary of state claimed the funds would strengthen "Zelaya in his hostility to peace and progress in Central America." Under this direct pressure, France withdrew permission for the loan. In the early twentieth century, France was prepared to sacrifice its expectations in Central America because it desired U.S. goodwill in the intensifying struggle with the central powers in Europe (AMAE, MAE to Jean Jules Jusserand, 17 & 24 May, 4 June 1909, Jusserand to MAE, 22 May, 1 July 1909, Henry White to Stephen Pinchon, 28 May 1909, Min. Finances to MAE, 29 May 1909, MAE to Min. Finances, 2 July 1909, CP 1918, Nic., Finances, Emprunts, N. S. 3 [copies in AMEF, F < 30 > 393 < 1 > : folder Nic.]; AMEF, MAE to Min. Finances, 3 May, 2 & 17 July, 3 Aug. 1909, enclosing U.S. min. in C. R. to Francis Huntington Wilson, 19 June 1909, Pinchon to Min. Finances, 3 June 1909, F < 30 > 393 < 2 > : folder Nic.).

French banks, interested in a fifty million franc loan to El Salvador in 1911, consulted the French finance and foreign ministries. The finance minister saw political advantage in cooperation with North American banks only if North Americans purchased and held bonds. The foreign minister suspected certain clauses in the Salvadoran loan contract might produce tension with the United States. The French consul general in New York doubted whether U.S. banks should be invited to join the French creditors because he suspected Salvador preferred financial aid which would not threaten its independence. Sole French financial aid, he argued, should augment French prestige within Salvador, where French investments had reached twenty million francs (AMAE, French consul general to Jusserand, 14 Dec. 1911, CP 1918, San Salv., Finances, N. S. 4; AMEF Min. Finances to MAE, 13 Nov. 1911, MAE to Min. Finances, 23 Nov. 1911, F < 30 > 393 < 2 > : folder San Salv.).

The French consul warned that Europe unwisely expected the U.S. "pax americana" and economic development in Central America to benefit the Old World. Central Americans, however, recognized that North American preeminence produced advantages for Yankee enterprise and little for other countries. For example, the United States used minor incidents which occurred in Nicaragua in 1912 to consolidate its position on the mixed customs commission to the detriment of Germany, Britain, and France (AMAE, Fabre to MAE, 3 & 17 Nov. 1912, CP 1918, Nic., Pol. intérieure, affaires commerciales, N. S. 1, Fabre to MAE, 29 Dec. 1912, MAE to Jusserand, 25 Feb. 1913, Ed. Perelti de la Rocca to Pinchon, 23 Aug. 1913, enclosing memorandum of U.S. reply, 21 Aug. 1913, CP 1918. Nic., Pol. étrangère, N. S. 2).

During the Great War years, the French perceived an opportunity to acquire Germany's plantations, shipping lines, and trade establishments in Middle America. The French government launched a program to undermine German interests, but its deteriorated economic position did not permit it to take advantage of the German weakness. On the contrary, the modest French interests were under assault from U.S. agents who sought French and British holdings at bargain prices. The post-World War I French economy allowed no speedy rebuilding of its position in Central America. Moreover, the French were dismayed to discover U.S. enterprises using German firms seized during the war, like Bayer, to push French products out of the Central American pharmaceutical market (Plauchut 1930; Kemp 1972; AN, Min. in Cent. Amer. to MAE, 23 Feb., 5 Aug. 1915, MAE to Min. Commerce, Oct. 20, 1915, Commerce, F < 12 > 8944, de Larroque to Director, National Office of Foreign Commerce, 12 Oct. 1914, Commerce, F < 12 > 7226, Fr. Minister to MAE, 19 Sep. 1919, F < 12 > 7222, Cent. Amer. et Chile).

At times the French blatantly used honors as bribes. In the fall of 1918, France awarded Guatemalan President Estrada Cabrera the Grand Croix de la Légion d'Honneur. The French minister repeatedly reminded Estrada Cabrera of the need to act vigorously against the Germans in Guatemala, but by the winter of 1918, the French agents were convinced that Estrada Cabrera was unreliable and dishonorable because he did not meet the understood commitment toward the Germans which was the price for his Légion d'Honneur (AMAE, Pinchon to Min. Guat., 7 Sep. 1918, Chayet to MAE, 19 Sep. 1918, Amér. 1918-40, C. A. [Guat.], num. 20, Chayet to MAE, 30 Nov. 1918, CP 1918, Amér. cent., II, N. S. 2, MAE).

In the summer of 1921, French war hero General Charles Mangin and Naval Lieutenant Lecoq undertook a five-month mission to Latin America to study French economic and political interests. Mangin reported that the Guatemalan president desired closer economic and political relations between the two countries. France needed to profit from sympathy and favorable conditions to obtain an advantageous commercial treaty. Mangin contended that the black laborers imported to work on banana plantations and railroads had boosted English past French as the first foreign language learned in Guatemala. The Guatemalans, who detested U.S. control of the railroads, Puerto Barrios, the banana plantations, and the iron mines, preferred a French company for the petroleum concession. He hoped French businesses would pursue coffee production, which was not under contract. Inadequate communications, unfortunately, forced France to use Dutch or British lines. He urged the French government to alert the business community of the need for credit and direct mail and freight service, if it wished to compete adequately with German firms (AMAE, Charles Mangin to MAE, 20 July 1921, Amér. 1918-40, C. A., num. 21; AAT, "Amérique du Sud," 8 Sep. 1923, 7N3374, dossier 2; AAM, Lecoq, "Guatemala du 5 au 8 Juillet 1921: Renseignements politiques," 2 Sep. 1921, I BB < 3 > 6, dossier 1921; Herwig & Heyman 1982, 239-40).

After World War I, France remained a spiritual center for Latin American intellectuals. Mangin recommended awarding Madame Antoine Peyre, head of the girls school and the Alliance Française in Guatemala, the "palmes académiques" for excellent work in spreading French influence in the school system, particularly the better lycées. While the French colony in Panama was not imposing, he saw the basis for an improved French cultural position. The 1928 Levy-Bruhl mission produced educational or university exchanges with Guatemala, Costa Rica, and El Salvador (AAT, Mangin to MAE, 20 & 21 July 1921, 7N3378, Mission Mangin, dossier 3; AMAE, Henri Eugène Aymé-Martin to MAE, 26 Oct. 1928, Amér. 1918-40, C. A., num. 7, Fernand Pila to Sébastian Charlety, 3 Nov. 1928, Amér. 1918-40, C. A., num. 30, Aymé-Martin to MAE, 8 Nov. 1928, Amér. 1918-40, C. A., num. 45).

French economic and strategic interests faced a strengthened U.S. position after World War I. U.S. intention to dominate Nicaragua's canal route was evident, in Mangin's view, in the Bryan-Chamorro Treaty, the U.S. Receiver General of Customs, the U.S. Marines, and U.S.-occupied Nicaragua's refusal to sign the Central America Union pact. He recommended establishing a legation to reward Panama's loyalty to France during the Great War. Panama could be extremely useful as the commercial distributing center for a large area in which France must develop its interests (LaFeber 1978; AAT, Mangin to MAE, 21 July 1921, 7N3378, Mission Mangin, dossier 3, Mangin to MAE, July 1921, 7N3376, dossier 4 [Nic.]; AAM, Lecoq, "Panama Renseignements politiques," July 1921, I, BB < 4 >, dossier 1921).

U.S. preeminence troubled Middle American societies, which in turn created opportunities for French and other foreign interests. Colombia preferred granting a petroleum prospecting concession to France, Lecoq reported, but no French group signaled an interest. The United States rejected force in the Costa Rican-Panamanian border dispute, he suspected, in order to create a deal involving petroleum. Costa Rica would give preference to Standard Oil over the British Amory firm for a disputed petroleum concession, and, in return, the United States would support Costa Rica in its border dispute with Panama. Then any oil in the disputed region would fall to an American firm. Lecoq overlooked the fact that United Fruit, with major interests in the disputed region, probably preferred Costa Rican control because of its powerful influence in that country. Latin Americans, in his estimation, sympathized with Panama out of a racial-cultural antipathy toward absorption by a powerful Anglo-Saxon power (Salisbury 1984; AAM, Lecoq, "Panama: Renseignements politiques," July 1921, I, BB < 4 > 6, dossier 1921).

Despite a persistent challenge from North America in the post-World War I years, the French military missions continued to receive sympathetic reception in Guatemala. In the fall of 1922, French diplomat Revelli claimed that the two senior officers of the oft-praised French military mission in Guatemala lacked the requisite qualities to advance the mission. He persuaded Guatemala's president not to accept a U.S. military mission to replace the French, even though U.S. officers would have received less pay. He speculated that the U.S. minister would be livid when Guatemala ordered military materials from France with funds borrowed in New York. Despite opposition, the French military mission was extended into the 1930s (AMAE, Albert Antoine Revelli to MAE, 4 & 19 Sep., 22 Dec. 1922, Amér. 1918-40, C. A., num. 58, Revelli to MAE, 31 July 1924, Adrian Recinos to MAE, 3 Dec. 1924, José Matos to MAE, 5 Jan. 1929, Amér. 1918-40, C. A., num. 34).

In the 1920s, French officials dreamed of rebuilding France's financial role in Central America. Revelli wanted North American and Guatemalan capital for a central bank provided "the direction would remain essentially French" so that the bank could serve French economic penetration of Central America. The finance minister warned that Revelli's bank could place France in opposition to U.S. policy in Central America. He agreed, however, to inform private French banks of the Guatemalan opportunity. Although the new commercial treaty might increase French trade with Guatemala, the French finance minister judged the lack of direct communications would hamper commercial expansion (AMAE, MAE to Delaye, 16 July 1923, Delaye to MAE, 27 Aug. 1923, Amér. 1918-40, C. A., num. 87).

While the study of Central America's relations with the world in the nineteenth and early twentieth centuries has understandably focused upon Britain and the United States, it has overlooked a host of other significant relationships. The British began a retreat in Central America with the Clayton-Bulwer Treaty of 1850, expanded in the 1890s Nicaragua-Mosquito Coast agreement and 1901 Hay-Pauncefote agreement to allow U.S. militarization of any canal, and broadened again with the British decision not to challenge the United States for petroleum exploration rights in Central America in the 1920s. The French role declined, less willingly, for the most part. The Germans represented a growing and persistent challenge to North American geopolitical and economic interests in Middle America. Despite Britain's slow retreat, competition—real and imaginary—remained central to understanding foreign metropole intrusions of Middle America.

Prussia was an early defender of German interests on the Middle American isthmus. The 1850s mission encouraged levels of German activity which called forth warning signals from U.S., British, and French diplomats in the 1860s and 1870s. In the 1880s, German entrepreneurs were heavily involved in coffee, merchant activity, and shipping. By the early twentieth century, German entrepreneurs were scurrying to introduce the technological products of Siemens, AEG, and other firms. German banks financed coffee trade and utilities investments.

France certainly interacted in important ways both with other metropole powers and with the Central American societies. Early French interests in independent Central America eroded in the middle and late nineteenth century until the de Lesseps project revitalized French capital, trade, culture, and residents in Central America. U.S. policy in the early twentieth century, which urged replacement of non-U.S. interests in the transit area, destroyed any lingering impact of de Lesseps' project. At the turn of the century, French military missions were common in Central America. Post-World War I France struggled to retain cultural influence and hoped to revive broader economic ties through financial activity.

The burgeoning U.S. political economy used the World War I era as an excuse to undermine German, French, and British activity in Central America. Although German entrepreneurs made considerable recovery in the 1920s, French efforts to assert a financial role in Central America's development proved unsuccessful. U.S. hegemony in Central America seemed secure in the 1930s, but the contradictory and unstable nature of organized capitalism (a combination of laissez-faire ideology with bureaucratic-corporatist structures) allowed little room for self-confidence in a competitive world system.

World War I and its aftermath disrupted and destroyed Europe's presence in Central America. The war underscored the maturing of the U.S. political economy which had incorporated the West, thirty million European immigrants, and much of the Caribbean region into its expanding production system. Essentially isolated from the European war, elements of the U.S. political economy secured formal political and strategic and informal economic power in the whole Caribbean and Central American area. U.S. efforts to transform its bastardized free market system via the open door policy and President Woodrow Wilson's peace program magnified U.S. interests on the isthmian transit, a key to the expected material flourishing of the rejuvenated world economy. The United States had initiated its interventionism in the decade before World War I and would continue this aggressive policy throughout the 1920s. The weakened European powers wished to reenter this vital area, but lacked the material or political capacity to force equal opportunity in the region, so they had to settle for whatever crumbs the United States allowed to fall from the table.

The United States and Germany pursued social imperialism in their relations with Central America. Both states manipulated their Central American policies in response to domestic economic and political problems. The dissemination of laissez-faire convictions and the nineteenth- and twentieth-century projects to internationalize laissez-faire — British free trade, the open door, Wilson's fourteen points — represented the frustration of faltering and bastardized, domestic laissez-faire systems. The metropoles believed salvation could be achieved through expanding market competition to a world scale. The consequence was intensified competition with few mechanisms to control the abuses and excesses because of the weak institutions of international law and order in the nineteenth and early twentieth centuries. This competition intimidated Central American states, because they were pressured to pick sides in metropole conflicts such as World War I, but also on smaller scales in regard to concessions for canals, steamship lines, loans, and so forth.

The Central American states also suffered restricted sovereignty. For example, the United States insisted that its Monroe Doctrine forbade Costa Rica, Nicaragua, Honduras, or El Salvador to sell islands in their possession to non-New World states. In the late nineteenth century, the Central American states were already swamped with metropole agents pushing developmental schemes. Soon the peripheral Central American states had surrendered major control over their internal communications, public utilities, national debt, currency, state revenue, and other economic activity which made up the gross national product to foreign metropole interests. The Central American states and societies struggled to find a secure role in the revised world order. The huge power imbalances between the metropoles and themselves largely determined their success. The peripheral Central American states were incorporated by bits and pieces into the broadening market-exploitation system. Metropole rivalry was rooted in home country internal disorders, implemented on a worldwide, highly competitive economic and strategic battlefield, yet unquestionably had a profound, lasting, and transforming impact on Central America.

NOTES

1. Briefly, metropole states are those political units which create and/or control the factors of production in their political economy, land, labor, capital, and the distribution of goods, services, and capital. Unsatisfied with their political economies, the metropoles incorporate external factors of production.

2. Polakowsky (1943, 56–65) denies that Bismarck approved Kinderling's proposal.

CHAPTER 3

The United States and Rural Insurgency in Guatemala, 1960-1970: An Inter-American "Success Story"?

Lawrence A. Yates

The telegram arrived at the State Department shortly after noon on November 13, 1960. Its message, while disquieting, sought to be reassuring. "Some kind of uprising Guatemala City aborted early this morning," began the U.S. ambassador to Guatemala, John J. Muccio. He then relayed in sketchy terms reports indicating that at least two officers at a military installation on the outskirts of the capital had been killed by an "unidentified group...who escaped with some military vehicles." Loyal Guatemalan military and police units had been placed on alert, President Miguel Ydígoras Fuentes had returned to the city, and the situation was "apparently under control" (Telegram No. 222, Muccio to Sec. of State, Nov. 13, 1960, *DDRS* #71C 1976; Sereseres 1971, 44).

Subsequent events belied Muccio's cautious optimism. The "uprising" constituted nothing less than an attempt by a disaffected portion of the Guatemalan armed forces to overthrow the Ydígoras regime. When a nearby unit failed to join the revolt at Fort Matamoros, the installation outside the capital to which Muccio referred, the rebel troops fled eastward and seized a military base in the department of Zacapa. Other rebel units occupied the key city of Puerto Barrios on the Atlantic coast. In the confusion, reports that unknown numbers of soldiers were defecting to the rebel ranks lent an air of increasing urgency to the crisis. President Ydígoras, blaming the coup attempt on Guatemalan leftists backed by the revolutionary government of Cuba's Fidel Castro, declared a state of siege.

By the morning of November 14, top foreign policy officials in Washington had concluded that the turmoil in Guatemala required U.S. action. Although President Dwight D. Eisenhower complained of receiving incorrect intelligence on the situation, he and his advisers could not rule out Cuban involvement in the affair even though, as the State Department would later concede, they lacked "hard proof" of Castro's intentions. Most alarming

Cuban involvement in the affair even though, as the State Department would later concede, they lacked "hard proof" of Castro's intentions. Most alarming was Ydígoras' assertion that Cuba would send arms or intervene directly in Guatemala. Lending credibility to this charge was the fighting already taking place in Nicaragua against a rebel band, presumed to be Cuban-sponsored, that had invaded from Costa Rica only two days prior to the Guatemalan uprising. Muccio's assessment on the evening of the 14th—that logic militated against interpreting the revolt in Guatemala as being "Communist-Castro inspired"—did not allay Washington's worst fears. For as the ambassador himself went on to warn (in terms similar to those the United States would use to justify intervention in the Dominican Republic in 1965), it mattered little who was responsible for the revolt; the situation was "of course ideal for exploitation by extremists both right and left." These considerations, plus the Eisenhower administration's perception of Cuba as a promoter of leftist revolution in Latin America, provided few reasons for Washington to define the attempted coup as a strictly Guatemalan affair. U.S. officials could have waited for additional information on the situation, but inaction seemed too risky given what was at stake (Memorandum of Telephone Conversation with the President, Nov. 14, 1960, microfilm reel no. 11, in Kesaris & Gibson 1980; Intelligence Items Reported to the President, Nov. 14, 1960, *DDRS* #1682 1986; Telegram No. 223, Muccio to Sec. of State, Nov. 14, 1960, *DDRS* #71E 1976; *New York Times*, Nov. 15, 1960, 1, 17, Nov. 18, 1960, 3).

What *was* at stake, besides the usual adverse repercussions that Washington perceived would accompany the downfall of any Central American ally, was the security of an enterprise Eisenhower had sanctioned earlier in the year: the training of Cuban exiles by the CIA to invade Cuba and overthrow the Castro regime. Ydígoras had provided the exiles a training site in Guatemala. Originally shrouded in secrecy, the existence of the camp soon became common knowledge within his government and throughout much of the countryside. Statements from Havana left little doubt that Castro also knew what was going on, and Washington could not rule out a preemptive move by the Cuban leader to remove the threat to his regime. Cuban assistance to the Guatemalan rebels or the landing of Cuban forces in Guatemala could jeopardize the success of the proposed U.S. enterprise. That, Eisenhower determined, must not be allowed to happen. The immediate question, then, quickly narrowed to what the United States could do, short of military intervention in Guatemala, to restore stability to that country while protecting it from an overtly hostile move from Cuba.

Eisenhower, who was in Augusta, Georgia, conferred by telephone with Secretary of State Christian Herter mid-morning on the 14th. Herter had already discussed with key State, Pentagon, and CIA officials the possibility of moving U.S. air and naval forces closer to Central America to provide surveillance and, if necessary, to interdict any movement of Cuban arms or men into the area. Should the president approve, the secretary would instruct the American ambassadors in Guatemala, Nicaragua, and Costa Rica to ask each of those governments to make a formal request for such assistance.

Eisenhower agreed to the proposal, adding that the requests should also be submitted through the Organization of American States (OAS) and that they would be "much stronger" if "each country says there is external aggression." Guatemala and Nicaragua delivered their formal requests two days later. Costa Rica demurred on the grounds that surveillance was no longer necessary. With five American ships, including an aircraft carrier with a Marine amphibious group aboard, having already arrived in Central American waters, the White House announced the interdiction decision on November 17 (Memorandum of Telephone Conversation with the President, Nov. 14, 1960, and Memorandum of Telephone Conversation with Sec. [of Defense] Gates, Nov. 14, 1960, microfilm reel no. 11, in Kesaris & Gibson 1980; Memorandum for the President [from Sec. Herter], Nov. 16, 1960, *DDRS* #1747 1984; *New York Times*, Nov. 15, 1960, 1, 17, Nov. 18, 1960, 1, 3).[1]

In the meantime, efforts to suppress the military revolt in Guatemala proceeded on a sporadic basis. Muccio reported on the 14th that the Guatemalan air force was strafing Puerto Barrios and Zacapa and airlifting troops into the area. Later that evening, though, he expressed concern because the revolt had not yet been crushed. Government troops had not landed at the port or moved against Zacapa, where, from both places, he had received reports of rebels "handing out arms wholesale to civilians." Muccio attributed the military's inaction to dissension within the air force and to the unwillingness of loyal military officers to fight brother officers or to believe Ydígoras' charges that the rebels were Castro's agents (Telegram No. 226, Muccio to Sec. of State, *DDRS* #71C 1976).

Perhaps sensing that he could not count exclusively on his own military to put down the revolt, Ydígoras called upon the Cuban exiles training in Guatemala to mount an airborne assault against Puerto Barrios. Washington gave its permission, but when the operation was called off en route because of erroneous reports that the rebels had fled the port, Secretary Herter sent instructions to Muccio that the trainees, once back in camp, were to remain there unless they received word from Washington to the contrary. From the CIA base, Ydígoras did receive two transport planes for airlifting Guatemalan troops to the port.[2] On November 17, with U.S. naval units operating in Central American waters, he declared the revolt defeated. Puerto Barrios, the last rebel stronghold, had fallen to government forces the previous day amidst reports that "casualties had been heavy and the populace had suffered extreme hardships" (Telegram No. 239, Muccio to Sec. of State, Nov. 16, 1960, *DDRS* #71G 1976; *New York Times*, Nov. 16, 1960, 4, Nov. 17, 1960, 4, Nov. 18, 1960, 3).

As the fighting ended, Ydígoras attempted to censor reports that the revolt was simply the consequence of military dissatisfaction with his regime and not communist inspired (Telegram No. 250, Muccio to Sec. of State, Nov. 19, 1960, *DDRS* #72B 1976; Telegram No. 252, Muccio to Sec. of State, Nov. 21, 1960, *DDRS* #72C 1976; Dispatch No. 270, Nov. 25, 1960, *DDRS* #72F 1976). In hindsight, there is little doubt that the November uprising was indeed an internal matter prompted by grievances within the armed forces against Ydígoras' incompetence and corruption and his political interference in military affairs, especially promotions. Perhaps the sorest point, particularly among the younger men within Guatemala's fiercely nationalistic officer corps, was the president's apparent willingness to subordinate Guatemalan interests to those of the United States. This touched a sensitive nerve that had first been exposed in 1954, when Guatemalan officers allowed a U.S.-sponsored coup to topple the reformist — some believed communist — government of Jacobo Arbenz Guzmán, only to have the United States virtually dictate to them an unacceptable successor to Arbenz, Colonel Carlos Castillo Armas. From that point on, the regular military viewed the United States with ambivalence. Guatemalan officers wanted U.S. arms and training, but resented the political and military dependency such arrangements entailed.

When Ydígoras became president in 1958, he, too, shared this ambivalence. Initially regarded by Washington as a friend, his sporadic anti-American outbursts, together with an increase in communist influence among Guatemalan workers, became unsettling to U.S. diplomats. As one State Department staff study concluded, "we consider it a possibility that Ydígoras might attempt to garner nationalistic support by presenting himself as the defender of Guatemala's sovereignty against U.S. incursions." A similar study charged that, as an integral part of some political maneuver, the conservative president was subsidizing left-wing groups (Handy 1984, 151-52, 230-31; Jonas & Tobis 1974, 177-79; Interviews by author with Guatemalan officers).[3]

Whatever Ydígoras' true political intentions or feelings toward the U.S., he could not turn down the CIA's lucrative offer for a site on which to train a brigade of Cuban exiles. When acceptance of this offer became an open secret, up to 150 Guatemalan officers began to plot against him, some because they had been cut out of the deal, others because they could not abide this latest manifestation of American domination. When the revolt broke out on November 13, however, most of the plotters "chickened out," leaving only 45 officers and the enlisted men who joined them to attempt the coup. Defeat was inevitable.[4]

Although the November uprising was put down four days after it began, it opened a new chapter in Guatemalan history: it stands as the seminal event leading to the creation of an insurgency that, in spite of several serious setbacks, still exists (Gott 1971, 47-57; Jonas & Tobis 1974, 179-81; Handy 1984, 231-32; Gilly 1965; Howard 1966). Ydígoras himself helped write the first paragraph of that chapter when he initially decided to pardon only the enlisted men who had taken part in the revolt, thus forcing rebel officers to flee into Mexico, Honduras, and El Salvador. Some would return later, after the president had softened his hard-line position; others returned under the general amnesty declared after the military deposed Ydígoras in a bloodless coup in 1963. By this time, however, a handful of the rebel leaders had become converts to leftist revolutionary ideas of one form or another. When they returned to Guatemala, it was not to accept amnesty but to continue their struggle against the government.

Foremost among the converts were Lieutenants Marco Antonio Yon Sosa and Luis Augusto Turcios Lima, who at the time of the November revolt were twenty-two and nineteen years old, respectively. In 1960, neither officer embraced a coherent political philosophy aside from the intense nationalism prevalent within the military. But once in exile, both men encountered peasants sympathetic to their cause. These experiences, together with talks they held with various political organizations and army officers during surreptitious forays into Guatemala City, gradually turned them into revolutionaries. Of the people and groups they consulted, the communist *Partido Guatemalteco del Trabajo* (PGT) showed itself the most receptive to their desire to overthrow Ydígoras. Turcios later attributed this response to the PGT's being the only political organization that "really cared about the people" (Gott 1971, 50). In fact, expediency more than lofty goals dictated the Communists' encouragement. Despite the lip service it paid to armed struggle as "the main road of the Guatemalan revolution," the Moscow-oriented PGT was accustomed to concentrating on "electoral and union politics" and hoped to use what military activity the rebel officers could direct against bear upon the government mainly as a "pressure tactic within the existing system of bourgeois politics" (Jonas & Tobis 1974, 180).

In July 1961, at the time the talks with the PGT were taking place, the capture and execution of Alejandro de León, another unrepentant rebel leader, ended any doubts in the minds of Yon Sosa and Turcios Lima about launching a guerrilla war against the government. In a statement issued from a hide-out they had set up in the Sierra de las Minas in Guatemala's eastern department of Izabal, the two rebels called for a democratic Guatemala, to be achieved by overthrowing Ydígoras and setting up a government "which respects human rights, seeks ways and means to save our country from its hardships, and pursues a serious self-respecting foreign policy" (Gott 1971, 52). Despite their drift leftward on the political spectrum, neither man at this point espoused the need for social revolution. Indeed, each still hoped that, despite Ydígoras' efforts to appease the military after the November uprising, a new insurrection would win support from "old comrades" (Jonas & Tobis 1974, 179) in the Guatemalan armed forces. Turcios and Yon Sosa were willing to accept PGT support for their insurgency, but an ideological chasm separated the party and the fledgling guerrillas.

The guerrilla offensive opened in February 1962. With a meager force estimated at between fifty and a hundred PGT cadre and peasants under their command, Yon Sosa and Turcios Lima, who as army officers had learned the finer techniques of insurgency in U.S. military schools, launched attacks on a United Fruit Company office and two military outposts in Izabal. Although the attacks failed militarily, they won more peasants to the movement. They did not, as hoped, attract widespread support from within the armed forces. In fact, the army virtually destroyed two other guerrilla columns that Yon Sosa and Turcios had helped form. Furthermore, when the insurgent attacks triggered student and labor demonstrations in Guatemala City, the army put down the strikes and riots with sufficient force to produce several hundred casualties. To prevent a recurrence of such demonstrations, Ydígoras reorganized his cabinet, a move that virtually turned power over to the military .

These events in the spring of 1962 left the guerrilla movement demoralized but still functioning. As Jonas and Tobis point out, "this had been the first meeting between the new armed movement, the mass movement, and the political organizations; it made possible a consolidation of several heterogeneous groups and different conceptions of armed struggle – differences which had contributed to some of the early setbacks" (p. 180). Consolidation became even more likely after Turcios, Yon Sosa, and their colleague, Luis Trejo Esquivel, visited Cuba in September and received instructions from Ernesto "Che" Guevara to work directly with the PGT in expanding the guerrilla struggle (Johnson 1973, 62). The desired union was consummated in December 1962, with the establishment of the *Fuerzas Armadas Rebeldes* (FAR), which included Yon Sosa's and Turcios Lima's *Movimiento Revolucionario 13 de Noviembre* (MR 13) as the major group. FAR was to provide the military arm of the struggle against the government; the *Frente Unido de Resistencia* (FUR), organized by the PGT and deliberately excluding guerrilla membership, would provide the political arm.

Loosely following the "foco" theories of Guevara and Régis Debray, FAR abandoned hopes for a quick military victory, began to talk of social revolution, and concentrated on a long-term strategy for creating revolutionary conditions in the country through a combination of small-scale guerrilla actions and more vigorous efforts to win peasant support. The organization decided to establish three military fronts, all in eastern Guatemala: two would operate out of Zacapa, with Turcios and Trejo each in command of one, while the third under Yon Sosa would operate out of Izabal. Ideological unity between FAR and FUR – even within FAR itself – proved elusive, but in December 1962, that potentially divisive condition seemed less important than the fact that opposition to the Guatemalan government had survived and now seemed better organized for waging a political/military struggle.

The incipient insurgency in Guatemala did not escape the notice of Eisenhower's successor in the White House. President John F. Kennedy believed that unconventional guerrilla warfare represented the most dangerous communist threat to American security interests in a world in which "the sweep of nationalism" presented "the most potent factor in foreign affairs today" (Schlesinger 1978, 418). A visit to Vietnam in 1951 had convinced him that subversion and insurgency were the Communists' preferred methods of expansion. Castro's victory in Cuba in 1959 reinforced this conviction; so, too, did a speech made by Nikita Khrushchev on January 6, 1961, just two weeks prior to Kennedy's inauguration, in which the Russian premier proclaimed Soviet support for "wars of national liberation" in Asia, Africa, and Latin America.

Taking Khrushchev at his word, Kennedy and several of the civilian foreign policy advisers he brought into his administration imagined dire consequences should they ignore the Kremlin's "challenge." Consequently, the concept of *counterinsurgency* acquired special prominence within the strategy of flexible response the Kennedy people devised for containing communist expansion across the spectrum of conflict from subversion to nuclear war (Gaddis 1982, 198-236).[5] As originally conceived, counterinsurgency encompassed a variety of programs that would allow third world nationalists to realize their aspirations for social and economic change not through violent revolution but through a process of peaceful evolution. What the Kennedy administration sought was to channel the forces for progressive change into a middle course wide enough to accommodate diversity, but insulated from both reactionary dictatorship on the Right, which through its repressive methods in support of the status quo could open the door to insurgent movements, and revolutionary upheaval and communist totalitarianism on the Left.

In theory, the process by which underdeveloped countries of the Third World could evolve into productive, stable nations while staving off communist insurgencies sounded deceptively simple (Blaufarb 1977, chap. 3; Schlesinger 1978, 417-42, 460-67; Child 1980, 143-87; and a variety of declassified documents from the *DDRS*, too numerous to list here). Extensive aid from international sources, both private and public, together with structural reforms and better management of resources within recipient countries, would pave the way for economic development, social progress, and, in those countries where it did not already exist, political democracy. To protect this process of peaceful development from communist subversion and insurgency, the United States would encourage a government's military forces to work alongside the people in civic action programs designed to improve the economic and social conditions of the poor and disadvantaged. Through this civilian-military interaction, the armed forces would come to understand better the aspirations of the people, while the people would learn to trust the military and support the government it represented. When necessary, indigenous police and military forces, in addition to supporting those reforms and civic action programs that would deny the guerrillas essential popular support in the cities and countryside, would take military action against hard-core insurgents whose ideological fervor prevented them from accepting the peaceful reformist approach to modernization and stability.

Counterinsurgency, in its broadest sense, then, encompassed a wide range of economic, social, political, psychological, and military activities that required the assistance and expertise of various instruments of the U.S. government. The Agency for International Development (AID), for example, would oversee economic assistance, while its Office of Public Safety would train indigenous police forces in methods of interrogation and riot control. The United States Information Agency (USIA) would help vulnerable governments improve their image at home and abroad, while the CIA would engage in intelligence, covert, and paramilitary activities. U.S. military missions would provide advice, training, and supplies to the armed forces of recipient countries. In this, they would be assisted when necessary by small Mobile Training Teams (MTTs) of U.S. Special Forces (the Green Berets).[6] Within a threatened country, the American ambassador would manage the counterinsurgency effort through the mechanism of the Country Team. In Washington, a Special Group (Counterinsurgency) established by Kennedy in early 1962 would oversee U.S. counterinsurgency programs around the world.

During the Kennedy administration, the Special Group (CI) focused most of its attention on the Western Hemisphere. Kennedy himself observed that "the most critical spot on the globe nowadays was Latin America, where the situation seemed made-to-order for the communists" (Memorandum of Conversation, Feb. 15, 1963, *DDRS* #2563 1985). The cornerstone of Kennedy's hopes for the peaceful development of Latin America was the Alliance for Progress, a program that, as in the case of many New Frontier initiatives in the hemisphere, had its seeds planted in the latter days of the Eisenhower administration and, in this case, owed much to the tenacity of President Juscelino Kubitschek of Brazil (Memorandum of Conference with the President, May 13, 1960, *DDRS* #2473 1982). Through a program of massive economic aid from internal and external, public and private sources and through the enactment by the recipient governments of fundamental socioeconomic reforms, the Alliance hoped to eliminate poverty, social inequities, and repression — the perceived causes of communist revolution — and place Latin American economies on a self-sustaining basis by the end of the decade.

Kennedy and those advisers who ran the Alliance programs preferred to work through Latin American governments in which democratic parties of the Center or Left held power. The prospect that these governments might succumb to military coups could not be discounted given the power and the traditional role played in politics by Latin American military establishments. But many of the president's advisers embraced a then popular thesis that younger officers within these establishments had by the early 1960s become more professional and technically skilled and would not only accept civilian democracy but would also serve as willing agents of the reform-development process (Barber & Ronning 1966). If in some countries Latin officers lacked experience in civic action and other counterinsurgency programs, they could receive the necessary training, often in military schools in the United States or at the U.S. Army's School of the Americas in the Panama Canal Zone.

There was more to American military support than formal schooling. A Military Assistance Program (MAP) for Latin America, passed by Congress during the Korean War, prompted a series of bilateral treaties under which the United States provided arms, supplies, training, and advice to all Latin American countries except Mexico and Argentina. The American government also sent military missions to eighteen of the treaty countries, including Guatemala. The original rationale for MAP had been hemispheric defense, but a 1959 study of the program recommended a greater emphasis on internal security. The Kennedy administration accepted this new rationale, reflecting as it did the president's predilection for civic action and counterinsurgency.

Further evidence of the administration's preoccupation with Latin America took the form of increased MAP funding and the creation of three military organizations: the *Consejo de Defensa Centroamericano* (CONDECA), the Southern Command (SOUTHCOM), and the Special Action Force (SAF). Established in 1963, CONDECA was headquartered in Guatemala City and provided a regional structure for sharing intelligence, setting up communication networks, holding multilateral military exercises, and providing a forum for U.S.-Central American military exchanges. SOUTHCOM was activated that same year in the Canal Zone, thereby upgrading the U.S. Army's Caribbean Command for Central and South America to the status of a unified (more than one service) command. A 1500-man Special Forces Group (designated the Eighth Special Forces Group in 1963) augmented by detachments skilled in civil affairs, psychological operations, engineering and construction, medicine, intelligence, interrogation, riot control, and electronic security composed the SAF. SAF was located at Fort Gulick in the Canal Zone; prior to 1961 no Special Forces had been specifically designated for operations in Latin America (Child 1980, 117-27, 154-68; U.S. Joint Chiefs of Staff 1977, 24; Simpson 1983, 69-70; Eighth Special Forces Group n.d.[7]).

Military power and hyperbolic rhetoric could not guarantee success for the Alliance for Progress. Even before Kennedy's assassination in November 1963, that part of the program stressing structural change had run into serious trouble. The Alliance had promised more than it could ever deliver considering: (1) the resistance or lukewarm support of Congress, U.S. government bureaucrats, American businessmen and financiers, Latin American oligarchs, conservative campesinos, and even the allegedly "progressive" elements (i.e., the military and middle class) in Latin American society; (2) the population explosion in Latin America; (3) the use of aid to repay existing debts or to expand the oligarchs' entrepreneurial horizons; (4) North American ethnocentrism and lack of technical expertise; and (5) the tenacity with which the ancien regime held on to power and wealth, often under the guise of democracy and reform. The list goes on (Levinson & Onís 1972; Schlesinger 1975; LaFeber 1982).[8]

Lyndon B. Johnson gave little thought to Latin America, save for a symbolic nod or two toward the Alliance and in 1965, the intervention of U.S. troops in the Dominican Republic under the "No More Cubas" policy. Preoccupied at first with the Great Society at home and then with the Vietnam War, the president, with the acquiescence of his secretary of state, left Latin American affairs in the hands of Assistant Secretary of State for Inter-American Affairs Thomas Mann, a conservative Texan. Under Mann, the Alliance's original emphasis on structural reform and political democracy gave way to a concern with economic development and protection of American economic and security interests. As a result of this new orientation, the military and paramilitary aspects of the Alliance would continue and, in many cases, expand. Nowhere was this more true than in Guatemala, where fundamental changes involving land reform or the redistribution of wealth were virtually nonexistent, although civic action and counterguerrilla assistance flourished.

The failure of the Alliance for Progress and the subsequent militariza-tion of counterinsurgency programs was far from apparent in 1962, the year that the Special Group (CI) included Guatemala among the list of nations that, because of the existing insurgency, required Washington's special atten-tion. The view from Guatemala was somewhat different. As previously indi-cated, 1962 had not been a productive year for the guerrillas in terms of military operations. So insignificant did the insurgent threat seem in 1962 that U.S. Ambassador John Bell debated whether to query Washington about such a threat. He was reluctant to take that approach, however, because Washington's request for an Internal Defense Plan offered an opportunity to get U.S. policy for Guatemala reviewed and revised. Consequently, Bell sub-mitted a plan that emphasized the need to attack the social and economic problems that fueled insurgencies. His primary recommendation was to in-crease the Guatemalan military's involvement in civic action programs. In line with Washington's directive, however, Bell also called for more "in-country advisory assistance in the field of security and intelligence" and "counterguer-rilla training within all echelons of the armed forces" (Interview with Bell, Nov. 6, 1986; McLintock 1985, 37). Some of the programs called for in the In-ternal Defense Plan had been in operation even before Bell made his recom-mendations. Others would be enacted or expanded in the early 1960s, thanks to Washington's concern over the situation in Guatemala.

In terms of economic development—the presumed key to social and political progress—the Guatemalan GNP showed one of the highest growth rates in Central America. But the figures were misleading. The growth rate, while impressive, was erratic and did not reflect the devastatingly unequal dis-tribution of wealth in the country. An estimated 50 percent of the population did not participate in the money economy, while a small oligarchy controlled much of the country's real wealth (Dombrowski et al. 1970, 219-20). Despite the rhetoric and aid associated with the Alliance for Progress, fundamental reforms did not take place under Ydígoras, the military government that replaced him, or the "Third Revolution" government of Julio César Méndez Montenegro elected in 1966. In the latter case, Méndez' commitment to demonstrating that a civilian president could serve a full four-year term precluded the enactment of reforms that might prompt the military and the oligarchy to attempt a coup against him.

The absence of political support for structural reform in Guatemala and growing concern in Washington about the insurgency during the 1960s meant that what changes did take place resulted primarily from the involve-ment of the Guatemalan army and paramilitary forces in internal security programs, mostly U.S.-sponsored. Quantitatively, this military emphasis is reflected in the continuously increasing size of the Guatemalan army, in the figures for U.S. MAP and Public Safety Program assistance, and in the num-ber of U.S. MTTs operating in the country.

Information pieced together from declassified documents and other sources indicates that in several important counterinsurgency programs in Guatemala, U.S. advisers encountered both success and frustration. In the field of civic action, piecemeal projects undertaken in the 1950s gave way to a more systematic approach when the U.S. Army established a formal civic action program in May 1960. Intending to create a model for Latin America in general, a Civic Action MTT arrived in Guatemala on November 26, 1960, to survey the country and recommend a wide range of projects that the Guatemalan military might initiate to improve socioeconomic conditions and, as a consequence, military-civilian relations.[10]

A lack of funding held up meaningful activity for two years, but by the mid-1960s U.S. aid was helping to sponsor hot lunches for school children, well digging, road building and other construction efforts, medical care, youth camp and community development experiments, and literacy and education programs. Civic action projects existed in all of Guatemala's twenty-two departments. In each program, U.S. advisers maintained a low profile, and in each, initial goals were usually exceeded, met, or nearly met (Interview with Ambassador John Bell; and documents from Combined Arms Research Library, U.S. Army Command and General Staff College, Fort Leavenworth, Ks.)[11] More might have been accomplished but for shortages in funding and trained personnel, problems with the maintenance of essential equipment, bureaucratic inertia, and the difficulty in overcoming the population's traditional distrust of the military. Most important, the improvements civic action programs achieved paled alongside the enormous and ingrained socioeconomic problems that plagued the country.

The same mixture of success and frustration characterized U.S.-sponsored programs to improve the military capabilities of the Guatemalan armed forces, paramilitary units, and irregular militia to deal with the insurgent threat (Except as otherwise noted, this account of U.S.-supported military programs in Guatemala is based on Jenkins & Sereseres 1977; McClintock 1985; English 1984, 253-67; U.S. Army Mission to Guatemala, *U.S. Army Mission Program Reports*, 15 Jan. 1965 and 15 July 1964). According to Sereseres and Jenkins, the Guatemalan armed forces in the early 1960s consisted of under-strength brigades, battalions, and companies scattered throughout the country and lacking centralized direction. To correct these deficiencies, MAP focused on upgrading four infantry battalions and one engineer battalion, creating an elite rifle company (airborne) and a special force company, and, in general, improving military training, leadership, communications, transportation, intelligence, and logistics. Many of the programs proved marginally or highly successful.

The First Rifle Company (Airborne) became the best unit in the army, geared to counterinsurgency tasks. The two MAP-supported battalions in Guatemala City became fully supplied by the mid-1960s, and the engineer battalion completed several important construction projects. Training programs became standardized, a non-commissioned officers program filled a critical void, and U.S.-supplied communications, transportation equipment, and transport and combat aircraft (including helicopters) improved the scope and mobility of combat operations. A complex logistical system began to function, and the establishment of a Central Maintenance Center and a Central Recruit

Training Center provided a degree of centralization to other military functions. An Army Command Center, charged with integrating police and military forces into an effective organization capable of carrying out search-and-destroy missions against the guerrillas, was set up in the strategic Zacapa department. Finally, enlisted men received better living facilities along with more intensive anticommunist indoctrination.

Detracting from these considerable accomplishments were the entrenched military patterns that continually frustrated American advisers. The lack of General Staff coordination and the latitude given brigade commanders in the various departments militated against achieving the level of centralized control desired by MAP representatives. The establishment of a coordinated intelligence system proved particularly difficult, given organizational and personal rivalries. Police training did little to improve the quality of the National Police, an effort hindered further by the military's fear that the police might become a serious competitor for political power.

U.S. officers were especially critical of the command structure of the Guatemalan army—largely the result of Ydígoras' promotion policies—in which full colonels served on battalion staffs and colonels and lieutenant colonels commanded infantry companies. Senior officers often lacked adequate training or dedication, a condition that did not prevent them from frustrating the efforts of those well-trained younger officers who managed to find assignments in various units. The MAP-supported battalion in Zacapa suffered from a succession of poor brigade commanders who devoted more time and personnel to guard duty than to counterguerrilla operations. Particularly unsettling was the extreme nationalism of the military. Colonel Enrique Peralta Azurdia, who became "chief of state" following Ydígoras' overthrow in 1963, used American aid to expand Guatemala's internal security system, but resisted several U.S. programs and, in a practice emulated by departmental commanders, often kept U.S. advisers in the dark as to the intentions of the Guatemalan military. One American colonel, the head of the military mission in 1966, complained that "Peralta had restricted the number of Guatemalan officers permitted to participate in U.S.-sponsored training programs in the U.S. and the Canal Zone" and that the chief-of-state had instructed Guatemalan officers to withhold information from the American mission because it and "'the U.S. already know too much'" (Jonas & Tobis 1974, 195).

The greatest irritant to U.S. advisers was Peralta's refusal to take decisive action against the insurgents. Alarmed by an upswing in guerrilla activities in 1965, many American officials became exasperated over the colonel's persistence in dismissing the guerrillas as "bandits." In putting pressure on Peralta to mount a counterinsurgency campaign, the Americans betrayed a scant appreciation of the colonel's precarious political position. The military-controlled government over which he presided was, as Sereseres has noted, "in actuality a coalition of senior officers, economic interests, and technicians/administrators." Among both military and civilian officials, factions had emerged, in part over whether to counter the insurgency with reforms or with bullets. Occupying a middle position, Peralta played the broker whose "political survival...depended on his not losing his balance by attacking the guerrillas" (Sereseres 1971, 58-69).

By the time Méndez Montenegro became president in July 1966, as the result of a "relatively honest" election, the situation had changed so dramatically that a counterinsurgency operation was all but inevitable. There were several reasons for this, U.S. pressure being perhaps the least among them. For one, as a part of the upswing in guerrilla activity in the countryside, Turcios Lima had ambushed an army patrol, wounding one officer and killing eleven soldiers. A survivor told how Turcios himself had executed the wounded officer, a former classmate. The shocking news stunned the Guatemalan officer corps, which regardless of the issues that divided it into various factions, exhibited a tremendous bond of personal loyalty when it came to the institution itself. The killing of a brother officer in some internecine conflict often strained that bond; the deliberate execution of one's own classmate broke it and, with it, the reluctance on the part of many officers to take up arms against the rebels (author's interview with Guatemalan officers). As it turned out, Turcios escaped retribution, but not death. An automobile crash in September 1966 took the life of the guerrillas' most charismatic and effective leader.

The increase in guerrilla activity in 1965 and 1966 also hit urban areas, where it took the form of blackmail and kidnappings —which added payoffs and ransom money to the insurgents' coffers —and the killing of several persons considered dangerous enemies of the revolution. The response to these terror tactics was quick and brutal. Frustrated by what they considered the inadequacies of the judicial system, some army officers and national policemen, together with right-wing zealots associated with the *Movimiento de Liberación Nacional* (MLN), formed a counterterror death squad, MANO Blanca, that turned terror tactics, often indiscriminately, against the guerrillas and anyone suspected of sympathizing with them, meaning anyone suspected of holding "progressive" views. The methods, applied with a vengeance, included kidnapping, torture, and summary executions.[12]

Méndez could not control the escalating counterterror, at least initially, but neither could he ignore the threat it posed to his regime. Receiving a plurality in the March 1966 elections primarily because the military had split its vote between two candidates, Méndez assumed the presidency only after agreeing to certain conditions dictated to him by the army. One condition was that the military have a free hand in conducting counterinsurgency operations. Regarded as a reformist member of the *Partido Revolucionario* (PR), Méndez presumably remarked that Guatemala had two presidents, himself and the defense minister who "kept threatening me with a machine gun" (Millett 1986, 413). Any attempt by the elected president to assert his independence could mean a military/right-wing coup against his government. Thus, he rarely spoke out against the counterterror, even when members of his own party became its targets. What he did do, however, was approve plans for a counterinsurgency campaign against the guerrillas in Zacapa and Izabal. Such a campaign would establish his anticommunist credentials with the Right, keep the army occupied in the east, and strengthen U.S. support for his government.

The counterinsurgency campaign against the guerrillas operating in the rural areas of the Oriente began to take shape with the appointment of Colonel Carlos Arana Osorio as departmental commander in Zacapa in July 1966. Here was the kind of hard-crusted officer the Americans had been looking for in Zacapa for several years. Arana brought in Green Berets to provide further training for the MAP-supported brigade in the department and for reinforcements from the capital.[13] The crack First Rifle Company (Airborne) arrived ready to take to the field. Arana also employed reserve forces in the area, the *comisionados militares*, comprised of former soldiers, ladino farm owners, farm administrators, and their representatives whose duties had come to include gathering intelligence on the guerrillas and their sympathizers. The *comisionados* received Arana's authorization to organize and arm a 2000-man civilian militia. To this organization could also be added rural right-wing terrorist groups such as they *Consejo Anti-Comunista de Guatemala* (CADEG), created by landowners to protect their holdings from troublemakers. Many members of the reserve and paramilitary units belonged to the MLN. According to Sereseres, "during the rural pacification campaign, the army and the MLN formed an alliance against the guerrillas which later led to a political partnership aimed at carrying Colonel Arana, with MLN support, to the presidency."[14]

With this force at his disposal, Arana launched a campaign in which regular military units would go after an estimated 200 to 400 guerrillas, while the militia and other groups would concentrate on providing local security and destroying the guerrilla infrastructure. Arana kept five regular 171-men infantry companies in the field at all times during the first part of the campaign. Their objectives were to secure the important all-weather highway that ran parallel to the Sierra de las Minas, then use it for mobility and logistical support in running the guerrillas to ground. The operation took time but worked as planned: by early 1968, the guerrilla fronts in Zacapa and Izabal had been destroyed. A wounded Yon Sosa took refuge in Mexico (where he was later killed in a fight with a Mexican patrol), while other survivors fled to the capital or the hinterland. Meanwhile, the paramilitary and vigilante groups, with the sanction of the army, systematically swept the towns and villages, identifying and dealing with known guerrilla sympathizers. The process of identification, however, was indiscriminate, and 4000 or more innocent peasants lost their lives in what often became an excuse to eliminate any "leftists" (including PR members) in the area or to settle old political or personal feuds. By the time regular army units arrived in the towns and villages to continue a massive civic action program for the area, they confronted the difficult task of overcoming the enormous bitterness and suspicion aroused by those who had preceded them. The civic action campaign ultimately won over a number of peasants, but Arana himself never shed the sobriquet, "Jackal of Zacapa" (Collazo-Dávila 1980, 112, 115-17, 121-22; Etchison 1975, 15).

Operation Zacapa gutted the rural insurgency that had arisen in Guatemala during the early 1960s. For a brief time, there was some concern that the guerrillas might regroup and, from bases in several of the more isolated areas of the country, mount a campaign on so many inaccessible fronts that the military would be unable to counter it. But these fears soon eased. Arana's tactics and U.S. military assistance had done too much damage. The guerrillas themselves also contributed to their demise. Always small in numbers, they had weakened what little military capability they had by failing to overcome debilitating ideological factionalism. Furthermore, they had operated in an area of the country that contained few Indians, the most numerous but most oppressed people in Guatemala, and thus a potential constituency for a guerrilla movement. (Observers in the 1960s who believed the Indians too conservative and suspicious of outsiders to join an insurgency would in the 1970s have cause to reexamine their assumptions.) Those guerrilla survivors who fled to Guatemala City did manage to regroup and take part in an escalating cycle of urban terror and counterterror that would continue into the early 1970s and witness the murder of a U.S. ambassador and his German counterpart, two U.S. military advisers, a former Miss Guatemala, and countless innocent civilians, most of the latter at the hands of right-wing death squads. A temporary halt to the urban violence occurred in 1972, after Arana, elected president in 1970, instituted even more draconian measures against the Left.

To U.S. officials at the end of the 1960s, Guatemala seemed a "success story," one among many in Latin America where every communist-inspired rural insurgency of the decade had been destroyed or rendered incapable of effective action. Success, however, proved illusory; in the mid-1970s a much more virulent strain of guerrilla warfare came to infect most of the countries considered immune only a few years earlier. Guerrillas who had survived the 1960s regrouped, learned from their mistakes, and returned to the struggle, often gaining support from segments of the population — Catholic priests imbued with Liberation Theology and, in Guatemala, various Indian groups — who had, with some exceptions, previously opposed or ignored them. Whereas in the 1960s, guerrilla bands often numbered no more than a few hundred and their supporters a few thousand, the insurgencies of the 1970s often counted thousands among the active guerrillas, several hundred thousand among their supporters.

What had happened? The answer to that question is complex enough in terms of general propositions and becomes even more so when applied to specific countries. The case of Guatemala is no exception, although the conclusion to this chapter will offer only one part of the answer, and a simplistic part at that: the 1960s "success story" in Guatemala was written primarily in military/paramilitary prose. New Frontiersmen fervently talked about structural socioeconomic and political reforms as a prerequisite for true progress and stability, but most did so from an ethnocentric perspective that in many ways equated Guatemala with America during the Great Depression or with

Europe in the aftermath of World War II (Wiarda 1984). Reforms and money had transformed the United States and Europe; it was now Guatemala's turn to be remade.

Not all U.S. officials dealing with Latin America during the 1960s failed to recognize that fundamental differences existed between the United States and Guatemala in terms of historical and cultural development; social, economic, and political institutions; and the perceptions each held of its role in domestic and regional or international affairs. But even those Americans not blinded by ethnocentrism often failed to recognize the depth and implications of these differences, or realizing both, decided that one had to settle for what one could get. Once it became apparent that certain reforms could not be made without asking the Guatemalan elite to commit political and economic suicide, many U.S. officials in the late 1960s supported or acquiesced in the military solution that counterinsurgency seemed to offer.

After the bloodletting in Guatemala during the late 1970s and early 1980s, the military renounced a program based primarily on armed force. The elected government of President Mario Vinicio Cerezo has supported a greater emphasis on civic action and reform, and Washington has concurred wholeheartedly. Yet, there is something of a familiar, hollow ring in Washington's position, however sincerely proclaimed. In Guatemala's neighbor, El Salvador, where an insurgency came close to toppling the government (or precipitating a right-wing coup) in the early 1980s, U.S. officials are again talking about a "success story." Certainly, the election of President José Napoleón Duarte as a spokesman for the middle course of democracy and reform served to fuel Washington's optimism, as did certain changes in the Salvadoran military that enabled it to take highly effective measures against the insurgents. Yet, in El Salvador today, as in Guatemala in the 1960s, fundamental changes such as land reform, essential to depriving the guerrilla movement of its supportive infrastructure, seem to be stalled, the result of internal conditions and vested interests over which the United States can exercise but limited influence. Still, because the guerrillas have been hurt militarily and are on the defensive, the talk continues of an inter-American "success story." Those who employ such rhetoric might do well to study the course of Latin American insurgencies in the 1960s, beginning, perhaps, with the "success story" in Guatemala.

NOTES

1. Costa Rican President José Figueres later criticized the U.S. naval movements for serving the interests of the Guatemalan government and the Somozas of Nicaragua (*New York Times*, Nov. 28, 1960, 9).

2. For official documents referring to the role of CIA trainees in the Guatemalan revolt, see Telephone Calls, Nov. 14, 1960, Memorandum of Telephone Conversation with Secretary Gates, Nov. 14, 1960, Kesaris & Gibson 1980; Memorandum from the Assistant to the Secretary of State, Nov. 14, 1960, *DDRS* #1384 1986; Kesaris 1981, 170. Some unofficial accounts of the

revolt argue that the CIA trainees took a much more active part in military operations against the rebels. See, for example, Gott 1971, 46-47; Prouty 1973, 41-42; Wise & Ross 1964, 33; Marchetti & Marks 1974, 298-99. The last two books claim that Cuban exiles and American pilots flew B-26 bombing and strafing raids over Puerto Barrios.

3. On the 1954 overthrow of Arbenz, see Immerman 1982; Schlesinger & Kinzer 1982. On the nationalism of the Guatemalan officer corps and its ambivalence toward the United States, see Adams 1970, 260-62. Several months after the revolt, Colonel Catalino Chávez Pérez, a former student of Ydígoras at Guatemala's military academy, charged that the younger officers involved in the revolt had had their minds "poisoned" by Marxist teachers during the Arévalo and Arbenz period. As for the older officers who took part, Chávez categorized them as "generally unstable, unduly ambitious, or 'leftists.'" U.S. Embassy Guatemala to Dept. of State, June 23, 1961, *DDRS* #73B 1976. On Washington's perceptions of Ydígoras and the changing situation in Guatemala, see Memorandum, Herter Memorandum for the President, Feb. 15, 1958, *DDRS* #176 1982; Dulles Memorandum for the President, Feb. 22, 1958, *DDRS* #71B 1976; Dept. of State, Staff Summary Supplement, Feb. 25, 1959, *DDRS* #1094, Staff Summary Supplement, Sep. 3, 1959, *DDRS* #2482, Staff Summary Supplement, Oct. 12, 1959, *DDRS* #287 1984.

4. Gott (1971, 47) gives figures for the number of plotters and those who actually went through with the revolt. Jonas & Tobis (1974, 179) cite the number of plotters as being 120 officers and 3000 soldiers, over a third of the army. They argue that the goals of the rebels were to overthrow Ydígoras and reform the army. Rebel leaders who escaped into Honduras claimed that, had they been victorious, they would have reduced the size of the armed forces and set up a coalition government headed by a junta with a civilian majority. They also "blamed their defeat in part on the 'chickening-out' of many of their comrades" (Dispatch No. 283, U.S. Embassy in Guatemala, Dec. 2, 1960, *DDRS* #72G 1976).

5. That Kennedy's civilian advisers proved more eager than their Pentagon counterparts to devise military capabilities to prevent communist insurgency or, failing that, to fight unconventional war against communist guerrillas is best documented in Krepinevich 1986, 3-127, and Bowman 1985. During the Eisenhower administration, a number of army officers, chafing under budget cuts and low manpower ceilings, protested that the president's strategy of "massive retaliation" left the United States unprepared to fight "brush-fire wars" against communist aggression. What the dissenting officers meant by "brush-fire war" was not unconventional guerrilla warfare, but the kind of conventional, limited war the United States had fought in Korea, a war in which high technology (short of nuclear weapons) and large units could be employed against the enemy. With the Kennedy administration came more money for the army, but also the requirement to develop an unconventional warfare capability. Most officers went along out of a sense of duty, but many did so reluctantly, believing that counterinsurgency was not a proper or productive role for a modern military establishment. Even Kennedy's chief military

spokesman for counterinsurgency, General Maxwell Taylor, was never an enthusiastic supporter of the concept.

6. For an insightful, albeit sympathetic account of Special Forces development and activities, see Simpson 1983.

7. The Eighth Special Forces Group was well trained in Spanish (or Portuguese) and Latin American history. While no guarantee of success, this training certainly facilitated the missions of MTTs in Latin America. On the subject of MTTs, Simpson stresses that they had to be requested by the host government and approved by the U.S. ambassador and the U.S. military mission. Approval was also required from SOUTHCOM and the Department of the Army. Once in the host country, MTTs, whose mission was to train, advise, and assist, came under the operational control of the U.S. military mission. When a conflict of interest arose over what organization would undertake a given activity (e.g., between AID and Special Forces over the training of police), the ambassador would determine who would get the mission.

8. LaFeber argues that by failing to deliver on its unrealistic promises to ameliorate unemployment, promote democracy, and bring about land reform and a redistribution of wealth and power, the Alliance helped to create a volatile situation that made the violent revolutions of the 1970s and 1980s inevitable.

9. In the early 1960s, the Guatemalan army was increased to 8000; by the the time of the counterinsurgency offensive during 1966-1968, it stood at 10,000 (English 1984, 259). Jenkins and Sereseres (1977, 578) cite MAP funds to Guatemala as $1.4 million between 1956 and 1961. During the remainder of the 60s, MAP assistance averaged about $2 million per year. McClintock (1985, 109) provides a yearly breakdown of military assistance budgets that supports the aforementioned generalization. McClintock also provides figures for the Public Safety Program, arguing that funds increased dramatically following the November 1960 revolt, the 1963 military coup, and the beginning of the counterinsurgency campaign in Zacapa (1966-1968). Historical Reports and Historical Supplements for the Special Action Force for Latin America, located at the U.S. Army Military History Institute, Carlisle Barracks, Pa., offer the following information on the number and kinds of MTTs operating in Guatemala during the 1960s: 1962 — 1 counterinsurgency MTT, 1 counterguerrilla; 1963 — 1 counterinsurgency, 1 engineer, 1 medical, 1 signal; 1964 — 1 counterguerrilla, 1 engineer (well digging), 1 marksmanship; 1965 — 2 classified, 1 military police; 1966 — 1 explosives, ordnance, demolitions, 1 intelligence, 1 marksmanship, 1 military police; 1967 — 3 MTTs, one of which dealt with armored personnel carrier tactics and maintenance; 1968 — 9 MTTs, including one 9-man MTT to train Rangers and another to survey MTT requirements. The MTTs are listed according to the year in which they returned to the Canal Zone. A declassified Historical Supplement for the 1966 Historical Report reveals that the intelligence MTT consisted of one officer who provided training and who established and operated a prototype intelligence department for the Guatemalan brigade in Zacapa. The military

police MTT consisted of 11 men who trained army personnel in riot control measures. (In a bureaucratic turf battle, AID Public Safety officials prevented this team from teaching national policemen the same techniques.) The explosives MTT taught "selected personnel how to disarm the bomb and weapons used by Guatemalan terrorists." McClintock (1985, 103) cites a declassified document that places counterinsurgency MTTs in Guatemala in 1966, the year that the counterinsurgency offensive in Zacapa began.

10. The timing of the CAMTT's arrival in Guatemala leads one to speculate that it might have been sent as a result of the November uprising. None of the documents I have seen makes this link, and given the bureaucratic red tape surrounding the dispatch of an MTT, it is likely that the paperwork for its mission to Guatemala was underway before the revolt.

11. These included a student essay by Thomas E. Rogers, "The Military and Nationbuilding in Guatemala," U.S Army War College, Carlisle Barracks, Pa., 7 April 1967, 6-11; U.S. Department of the Army, Civic Action Branch, Civil Affairs Directorate Office, Deputy Chief of Staff for Military Operations, *Military Civic Action* (n.d.), N-16359.15-A; ibid., Office of the Chief of Civil Affairs, *Report of Civic Action Team for Guatemala* (n.d.), N-17067.29; ibid., U.S. Army Mission to Guatemala, *U.S. Army Mission Program Report* 15 Jan. 1965, CONFIDENTIAL report, declassified 1971, N-18999.20; ibid., 15 July 1964, CONFIDENTIAL study, declassified 1970, N-18999.20.

12. McClintock (1985) places much of the responsibility for the counterterror on American advice, U.S. military doctrine, and the use of similar methods in Vietnam by the army and CIA. That the United States engaged in counterterror activities in Vietnam and that some U.S. advisers to Guatemala approved the tactic cannot be denied. But two points should be kept in mind when considering McClintock's argument: (1) Guatemala has a history of violence, and the country's armed forces and paramilitary units probably could have mounted a counterterror campaign without U.S. advice or encouragement; and (2) in theory, the U.S. approach to counterterror was one of discrimination, designed to "neutralize" only confirmed insurgents; in practice, both in Vietnam and Guatemala, a policy of discrimination became virtually impossible to implement. Addressing a related point, Arthur Schlesinger has noted that "instruction in methods of interrogation can easily lead enthusiasts beyond the curriculum at the Police Academy and end in the justification of torture" (Schlesinger 1975, 75).

13. Although I have seen no official documents that place Green Berets in Zacapa during the preparations and conduct of the counterinsurgency operation, other sources leave little doubt that they were there. The controversy centers around how many were present. Sources which place the number at one thousand are suspect, but cannot be disproved. But this exceedingly high number ignores the mission and methods of the Green Berets, which were to provide small-sized units and MTTs to host countries. Guatemalan soldiers trained by the Special Forces received green berets at the conclusion of their training. This could account for reports that large numbers of Green Berets were sighted in Zacapa during the operations of 1966-1968.

14. The complex nature of the relationship among the military, reserves, and paramilitary-vigilante groups in the Oriente, and between these groups and their counterparts in the capital is best described in Sereseres 1978. See also Collazo-Dávila 1980, 112, 114; Johnson 1972, 8-9; Sereseres 1971, 69; and Adams 1970, 270-73.

CHAPTER 4

Indian Labor and the Guatemalan Crisis: Evidence from History and Anthropology

Marilyn M. Moors

Involvement of Guatemalan Indians with guerrilla movements in the 1970s followed a long period of pressure and strain on traditional Indian socioeconomic structures and patterns. The trend toward increased agro-export production of coffee, sugar, and cotton over the past century and a half contributed to increased suffering among the Indian population and challenged traditional land and labor patterns in that country. Throughout the twentieth century American anthropologists have been studying many of the Indian communities of Guatemala. Collectively their work represents an important investigation of the effects of migratory labor demands on these people. This chapter reviews historical and anthropological literature for insight into the historic and devastating changes that these developments have occasioned in Guatemala.

The labor of the Indians of Guatemala has been one of the most prized possessions of the ruling elites of that country. Spanish colonial dominion was primarily that of control over the work of the Indians, Indian labor built cities and churches, transported Spanish goods and supplies, and provided for their wealth through the production of cacao and dyes as well as the mining of gold and silver. The Spaniards fought over and carefully administered this labor power, pushing it to the point of nearly eliminating the Indians. Labor was obtained by extra-economic means, and although it was occasionally compensated, it was forced through a variety of mechanisms including first the *encomienda*, and later, *repartimiento* and taxation (Sherman 1979, chaps. 7-12).

With independence in 1821, the necessity for forced labor continued. The threats of greater taxation and alienation of Indian communal lands under the early Liberal governments led to Indian support for the Conservatives behind the popular caudillo, Rafael Carrera. While Carrera, the power in

Guatemala from 1839 to 1865, did protect some Indian lands from takeover and perhaps mitigated the intensity of the pressure on Indian land and labor, he did nothing to change Indian forced labor. *Mandamiento* replaced *repartimiento*, largely in name only, and these forced labor drafts assessed against Indian communities, together with taxation and unpaid civic labor, served to keep Indians working for landowners and rulers of Guatemalan society (Castellanos 1985, chap. 8; Miceli 1974; Woodward 1979).

Coffee production began during the Carrera regime, but remained relatively insignificant until coffee planters took control of Guatemalan society under the leadership of Justo Rufino Barrios in 1871. The Liberal reforms of the period supported the expansion of coffee as a large-scale export commodity. This linked the Guatemalan growers to the capitalist markets of Europe and America without the mercantile restraints that the Conservatives had imposed. Closer ties to international capitalism, however, did not imply a shift to capitalist concepts of free labor subject to supply and demand within Guatemala. Land was taken away from Indian communities and the church, and foreign and ladino settlers were encouraged to develop coffee plantations in these areas. Planters demanded forced Indian labor to plant, tend, and harvest the coffee in ever greater amounts. Usually the Indians received compensation at low rates, but their labor was still coerced by extra-economic means, primarily the *mandamiento*. The reduction of Indian lands also served to make subsistence agriculture more precarious and thus to force Indians into labor on the *fincas* in order to survive. In addition to the harvest drafts, the landowners needed to get their harvest to port, and they pressed the Indians into transporting coffee, building roads, and working in other civil construction. The Indians considered this nonagricultural labor the most hateful of burdens, and it was often imposed as a punishment on those Indians who did not fulfill their plantation labor duties (McCreery 1986, 104-05; Castellanos 1985, 209).

The tremendous increase in forced labor which the ever growing coffee production necessitated had a telling impact on Indian communities. These communities were depleted of a large portion of their male population for several months at a time during the harvests. Ladinos expanded into Indian communities, taking over land, setting up mercantile establishments, becoming *enganchadores* for the labor drafts, and forcing direct presence and control over Indian economic affairs (Colby & van den Berghe 1969, 69). Indian communities responded in a number of ways — protesting, rebelling, fleeing — but primarily by forming what Eric Wolf called the "closed corporate community" as a way to limit the ladino penetration into their lives and the concomitant loss of their culture (Wolf 1957).[1] Establishment of this dual agricultural system in Guatemala — of large plantations growing export crops and ever smaller highland farms growing subsistence crops — assisted the landowners in another way. Landowners did not have to bear the full cost of the reproduction of their labor force, nor pay for their subsistence during the part of the year they were not needed. The profitability of this system kept capitalist relations of production from developing in the agro-export sector of the Guatemalan economy (McCreery 1986, 104).

Guatemalan history in the first part of the twentieth century is characterized by the continued expansion of coffee production. Between the 1870s and 1940, coffee production increased tenfold, much of it for European markets. Between 1900 and 1944 the United Fruit Company and its subsidiaries extracted land and other concessions from the Guatemalan government. In support of United Fruit prerogatives, the U.S. government used diplomatic pressure to unseat Guatemalan presidents. Guatemala's long-standing ties to European markets and its own nascent capitalist ventures were broken by the monopolies granted by the Guatemalan government to North American companies. The Guatemalan economy was more completely and directly linked to that of the United States (Jones 1940, 210; Handy 1984, 86-89).

Forced labor was still used to care for and harvest the coffee. Until the 1930s, debt servitude, the legally enforced collection in work of debts which were often forced upon the Indians and the extension of the fathers' debts to their sons, was the primary mechanism. It was supplemented by the *man-damiento*.

The first studies of Indian communities by anthropologists occurred during this period. Beginning with Oliver LaFarge in the 1920s, they provided important documentation of the increasingly heavy labor demands being made by the Guatemalan landholding elite, and of the threat to Indian subsistence by the abolition of Indian individual and communal landholdings. La-Farge described the operation of debt peonage and the migration to the plantations, reporting that the men often returned sick and drunk. He noted the unpaid civic labor of the Indians for the ladino leadership of the community (McNickle 1971; Blom & LaFarge 1926; LaFarge & Byers 1931; La-Farge 1947).

Ruth Bunzel, in her classic study of Chichicastenango, reported that by 1932 land for the Indians had become scarce, communal lands were gone, and many families were experiencing intergenerational conflict as fathers reached difficult decisions about dividing land among sons. Wealthier landowners, mainly ladinos but including some Indians, hired poorer or disinherited Indians for the equivalent of about seventeen cents a day. Unpaid labor was under the control of the ladino alcalde, who passed the labor demands to the Indian alcalde responsible for organizing the labor party. Bunzel also documented the growing domination of Indian labor by ladino masters and the necessity for a growing number of the Indians to work outside the community, as local ladino alcaldes connived at recruiting labor for the plantations by imprisoning Indians for minor offenses and setting high fines. The fines were paid off by an *obligador* in return for Indian labor on specified plantations (Bunzel 1972).

The regime of Jorge Ubico (1931-1944) abolished debt servitude, substituting vagrancy laws to supply labor to the plantations. Landless peasants were required to work 150 days on the coffee *fincas* or for nearby landowners, and those who owned some land, including the majority of the Indian population, had to work 100 days. Peasants had *libretos*, small books in which their work accounts were kept, which they had to produce on demand for any authority. Unpaid civic labor also continued during this period, and Ubico imposed a two-dollar road tax on all Guatemalan households. If the household could not pay the tax, it could be worked off with two weeks of unpaid labor on the roads. Since most ladinos could pay it or found a way to be exempted from it, most of this labor levy fell on the Indians. The network of roads created by Indian labor served to link Indian communities to larger cities and thus exposed many Indians to greater outside contact, pressure, and control. In consolidating his political hold over the country, Ubico also replaced all locally elected officials with *intendentes* who served as mayors of *municipios* under his control and at his pleasure (Handy 1984, 98).

Community studies during this period demonstrate these patterns of labor for several communities. *Habilitadores*, who loaned money to Indians to insure their work, signed up Indians for plantation labor at 12 to 25 cents a day. Often abusing this power and the labor laws, local *intendentes* often required unpaid labor from the Indians under their control (Wagley 1941; Siegal 1942). In Panajachel, however, Sol Tax reported that the Indians had developed a cash crop agriculture and had persuaded Ubico that the labor necessary to produce these crops was sufficient to exempt them from the vagrancy laws (Tax 1953; 1937). During the same period Charles Wisdom reported from eastern Guatemala (Jocotán) that the poorest Indians worked for ladinos, and that in addition, Indian men had to work 10 days a year without pay on the roads and give 2 weeks of unpaid militia service, neither of which was required from the ladinos (Wisdom 1940). Almost a decade later, Melvin Tumin studied another eastern Guatemalan community (San Luis Jilotepeque) and found that 90 percent of the men were *jornaleros*, day laborers without enough land to be exempted from the vagrancy laws. Indians received 10 cents a day in wages and ladinos 15 cents. In his sample, the average Indian landholding was 2.2 acres, with the majority owning less than an acre. The average ladino landholding was 31.2 acres (Tumin 1952).

Notwithstanding the valuable data and impressions of these earlier anthropologists, taken as a whole there is not much information on Indian labor on the *fincas*. For many the fieldwork period was brief, and repeated trips to the same community each summer did not reveal annual migratory labor patterns. Most conducted their field research in Spanish, relying on a few bilingual informants, usually wealthier Indians, and sometimes even ladinos.[2]

A coalition of urban middle-class groups, including students, military officers, and industrial workers, ousted Ubico in 1944. The subsequent ten-year reform period of Juan José Arévalo and Jacobo Arbenz brought many changes to Guatemala, opening political participation to many for the first time, establishing social security and labor legislation, and promoting the development of a national capitalist economy. Many of these reforms were of great benefit to the developing urban middle and working classes in Guatemala. The fully proletarianized agricultural workers on the plantations, particularly those of United Fruit, gained higher wages, better living and working conditions, and the right to organize. The gains for Indian communities were less dramatic, but clear. Forced labor ended in 1945, bringing the market relations of capitalism to the seasonal labor force of Guatemala for the first time. Unpaid road work, civic service, and militia duty also ended. The *intendentes* of the Ubico period were eliminated, as *municipios* regained the right of self-government. Some health care and education penetrated Indian communities, and Guatemalan anthropology began with the formation of the Instituto Indigenista Nacional (Silvert 1954; Davis 1983).

By the time forced labor was abolished, the Indian population of Guatemala had increased to the point at which the remaining land base of many Indian communities could no longer support a large part of its population. John Early estimated that by 1950 the Mayans comprised 56.2 percent of the population, or approximately 1,612,000 people (Early 1982). Henceforth, economic necessity would compel a certain percentage of these people to the plantations. Wages for plantation labor rose, but union organization was not allowed for seasonal workers. Indebtedness, usually in the form of wage advances, was the primary mechanism for labor recruitment, and labor contractors, both Indian and ladino, filled their quotas by making loans which were redeemed by labor on a certain finca at the appropriate time. Indians who did not fulfill their labor contracts faced jail sentences, and debilitating diseases accompanied workers back to their highland villages from the lowland plantations (Handy 1984, 124-25; Gillin 1951; Oakes 1951).[3]

Much of the anthropological work of the period centered around acculturation, modernization, and cultural change. Ethnic relationships between Indians and ladinos continued to be an important theme, perhaps echoing the internal problems of the United States with the simmering discontent of its race relations. Studies of the Indian communities show considerable changes in social and political relationships with ladinos. Political parties and local elections had challenged ladino domination in some communities. Landlessness and the aborted land reform program were a source of anger for others (Adams 1957).[4] Indian communities were more open to the outside world, more integrated into national issues and organizations, and could no longer be considered as closed corporate communities. They had grown in population and diminished in land base, and while labor was no longer forced by extra-economic means, poverty and chicanery bound many Indians to the annual cycle of plantation labor. In retrospect, Gillin's comments on San Luis Jilotepeque during the Arbenz period are of particular interest. The political turmoil and the great anger of the landless Indians in eastern Guatemala foreshadowed the guerrilla movement and the subsequent military repression of the 1960s (Gillin 1957).

In 1954 the U.S.-sponsored overthrow of the Arbenz government brought all progressive changes to a halt. The Castillo Armas regime reversed nearly all the gains of the previous decade. It banned labor and peasant organization, and rounded up moderate to leftist political activists, killing many. Former owners reclaimed land that the Arbenz government had distributed to peasants or made available for rental at reasonable rates. Corruption, graft, and inept governments eroded many of the political and economic gains of the ordinary people (Handy 1984, 150-53).

U.S. corporate and financial interests accompanied this new, safer climate in Guatemala. Money and credit were made available for the expansion of the agro-export sector of the economy. U.S. corporations took advantage of the Central American Common Market to develop and expand industrial facilities in Guatemala. After the Cuban revolution and subsequent U.S. economic embargo, Guatemala received an increase in its sugar quota. Coffee exports increased and cotton became another important export commodity.

Table 4.1

GUATEMALAN EXPORT COMMODITIES (1952-1970)
(In thousands of kilos)

Year	Coffee	Cotton	Sugar
1952	61,042	—	—
1953	56,580	—	—
1954	52,118	5,244	—
1955	59,156	6,620	—
1956	63,204	8,188	—
1957	61,824	4,222	—
1958	71,714	10,258	—
1959	85,008	10,948	—
1960	83,812	12,466	—
1961	80,960	22,402	—
1962	82,396	29,078	33,894
1963	98,237	50,416	46,674
1964	76,051	45,200	54,864
1965	95,282	70,593	31,587
1966	109,033	92,472	52,241
1967	81,295	67,052	60,918
1968	94,292	77,863	56,437
1969	99,649	84,144	46,041
1970	95,124	57,741	57,343

Source: *Boletín estadística* (Guatemala:
Banco de Guatemala, 1952-1970).

Table 4.2

GUATEMALAN EXPORT COMMODITIES (1970-1984)
(In thousands of kilos)

Year	Coffee	Cotton	Sugar
1970	95,124	57,741	57,343
1971	100,044	55,597	66,723
1972	113,689	85,066	91,173
1973	114,848	98,239	126,227
1974	121,072	126,218	134,180
1975	135,732	108,509	203,513
1976	119,075	117,816	314,152
1977	132,672	142,113	305,233
1978	132,249	142,382	153,265
1979	142,611	171,437	156,758
1980	128,343	135,044	212,057
1981	109,896	94,369	199,535
1982	141,186	65,877	127,249
1983	137,918	38,300	444,371
1984	126,120	51,585	275,979

Source: *Boletín estadística* (Guatemala:
Banco de Guatemala, 1970-1984).

All three crops called for large amounts of labor during the growing season and at harvest. Increasing numbers of impoverished workers were rounded up by the *habilitadores* for work on the coast. Wages were low, interest was charged on all loans, and workers were regularly cheated of their pay. A growing export beef industry for the U.S. fast food industry put even greater demands on the land, and the increasing use of herbicides and pesticides promoted by U.S. chemical agriculture experts meant increasing illness for Indian workers (Smith 1977, 89; Burgos-Debray 1984; Adams 1970, 375; Williams 1986).

Estimates of migratory laborers in the 3 most labor intensive crops were as follows: between 118,000 and 150,000 in cotton, between 167,000 and 237,000 in coffee, and between 17,500 and 21,000 in sugar. The departments of El Quiché and Huehuetenango provided 34 percent of this labor, while 78 percent of the total labor force came from the highlands. Cotton work paid better wages (Q0.93 to Q1.30 a day) than did coffee (Q0.57 to Q0.75 a day) or sugar (Q0.65 to Q1.00), but working conditions were the worst on the cotton plantations.[5] Half of the cotton plantations provided no corn ration for their migratory workers, 80 percent did not pay workers when ill, and only 20 percent provided any medicines. Few plantations paid workers for the seventh day, although the law stated that workers who worked 6 consecutive days should be paid for 7 days work. Few allowed workers to pick fruit growing on the plantation. Poisonings and deaths from negligent insecticide use were highest on the cotton plantations. The number of deaths reported to the Instituto Guatemalteco de Seguridad Social (IGSS) increased each year during the 1960s and many cases were not reported to the IGSS at all (Adams 1970, 369-70).

A series of studies from the mid-1960s reported rural malnutrition. It was worst in the Chiquimula-Jalapa area (May & McLellan 1972). There peasant misery and landlessness induced by cattle ranching formed a backdrop for the small guerrilla movements of the 1960s (Gilly 1965). The United States, under the Alliance for Progress, supplied counterinsurgency training and weapons as the Guatemalan army destroyed the peasant agricultural base in eastern Guatemala in its war against a handful of guerrillas.[6] The second worst area of the country for malnutrition was Quiché and Huehuetenango. Rather than consider any type of land reform which would enhance the meager holdings in and around Indian communities, the government began a colonization program in the Petén and Alta Verapaz, and hundreds of families, sometimes whole communities, moved onto these designated lands. The government assured the people that they would receive titles to their plots after they had established themselves, but subsequent investigation revealed that they often never received titles and that they had to continue to work for others (Carter 1969, 2-5).

Anthropological studies of Indian communities during this period were undertaken by Rubén Reina (1966),[7] Benjamin Colby and Pierre van den Berghe (1969),[8] Robert Hinshaw (1975),[9] Waldemar Smith (1977),[10] and William Carter (1969).[11] These studies report rapid and extensive change taking place within these communities. The civil-religious hierarchies, which had constituted the traditional Indian leadership system, were changing. Some had ended; others were modified to replace the burden of sponsorship on one person with more general community support for the celebrations of the patron saints, thus eroding the traditional routes to becoming an elder. Other religious changes included the development and growth of Catholic Action groups and the expansion of Protestant missionary activity. In effect, these changes reduced the power of the traditional elders within the villages.

There was also an increasing diversification of economic activity and economic power bases within these communities. In most, the need for land continued to outstrip availability, and people sought ways to make up the deficit between what they needed and what they could grow. Migratory labor was only one option, and was the one chosen only if there was no alternative. Marketing, cooperatives, cash crops, increased yields through the use of fertilizers,and access to tourists supplied some of the deficit for certain communities, while others had no alternative to seasonal work on the plantations. Some groups of Indians migrated to the departments of the Petén or Izabal to attempt to start over. There continued to be economic differences within Indian communities, but greater differences existed between communities and these were based on differential access to land or to cash income other than from migratory labor (Melville & Melville 1971; Hinshaw 1975; Burnett 1986).

After 1970 Guatemala saw the continuation and intensification of the patterns of the previous fifteen years. The agro-export sector of the economy continued to grow, with a large expansion of sugar production and smaller increases in coffee and cotton (See Table 4.2). There was an ever growing demand for labor to harvest these crops, yet wages for this work did not rise. Prices for corn and beans did, however, as the population continued to grow and landholdings in the highlands became smaller (Handy 1984, 205-10). Land productivity also decreased because the 1973 increase in the world market price of oil meant a concomitant rise in the price of fertilizer, putting it beyond the reach of many Indian families who had previously depended upon it (Frank & Wheaton 1984, 39). Seventy-five percent of Guatemala's children were undernourished (Handy 1984, 221-24). Furthermore, the earthquake of 1976 brought destruction to many poor communities, both shantytowns around Guatemala City and rural communities in the highlands. An estimated 22,000 people died. International relief efforts opened certain communities to outside sources of money and spurred economic development projects in a number of areas (Davis & Hodson 1982).

During this same period, the Guatemalan military establishment consolidated its control over national politics, both by manipulating existing political parties of the Right and by preventing the formation of parties in the Center-Left range. The military expanded control over the economy, developing the Bank of the Army and a large military construction business. They continued to open lands in the Petén and along the northern transversal highway, assigning the land to top military personnel after it had been cleared by peasant labor, peasants who had been led to believe that the land would be theirs before they were dispossessed. The Guatemalan military leaders did not compete directly with the established landed oligarchy of the country but sought to expand their personal and collective wealth through alternate economic development (Handy 1984, 221-24).

Despite military repression, widespread labor unrest and organization marked the period. Peasants and workers, urban and rural, protested their wages, their working conditions, and the price increases that forced them into poverty. Remnants of the 1960s insurgency reappeared during this period, growing into four major guerrilla organizations working in the cities and the countryside (Handy 1984, 228-34). Their growth parallels both the increasing army repression and the increasing economic desperation of the poor. The conflict between the guerrillas and the military reached a climax (but did not end) with the military occupation of sections of the Indian highlands in 1982.

Among the community studies of the 1970s, those by Douglas Brintnall (1979),[12] Laurel Bossen (1984),[13] Kay Warren (1976),[14] John Watanabe (1981)[15] revealed increasing stratification between communities as well as internal divisions of wealthier and poorer Indians. Some areas were facing severe misery and large-scale labor migrations. In other villages, wealthier Indians avoided plantation labor while poorer Indians continued to migrate to the coast for seasonal work. In regions where other economic options were available, most Indians found other ways to make a living and few engaged in seasonal harvest labor. Relations between Indians and ladinos on the local level continued to change, reflecting an erosion of the traditional ladino domination in economic and political matters. There were more religious options for the Indians as well, as in most areas the authority of the traditional civil-religious hierarchy was a thing of the past. Newer religious groups offered literacy and community development programs and sponsored economic projects which aided members.[16]

While the Guatemalan army had engaged in acts of violence and repression since 1954, most of these had been directed at supporters of the Arévalo/Arbenz administrations or at other urban political targets. Attacks on highland Indian communities commenced in 1975 in the Ixil triangle of northern Quiché, an area of intense poverty and one which supplied large numbers of laborers to the coast. This was also an area which the *Ejército Guerrillero Popular* (EGP) had begun to work. In July 1975, the government seized thirty-seven cooperative members and for the next two years the army, which had established a base near the town of San Juan Cotzal, sporadically occupied towns in the area, kidnapping and executing men and boys. In November 1976 Father Bill Woods, active in helping Indians resettle in the colonization projects, died in a suspicious plane crash. By 1977, sixty-eight cooperative leaders from the Ixcan region, forty community leaders from Chajul, twenty-eight from Cotzal, and thirty-two from Nebaj had been killed.

In 1978 the arrests and disappearances spread to Uspantán. An opposition party claimed that three hundred of its members had been persecuted by authorities in Quiché. Indians and peasants, now having a common language and common experiences in land and labor matters, formed the *Comité de Unidad Campesino* (CUC) to "fight for the resolution of problems that most afflict peasants: work, high prices, kidnapping, and robbery of water and forests" (Davis & Hodson 1982, 47-48). The CUC, working with trade unions and student groups, protested against this repression, sent letters to government officials, and mounted demonstrations in Guatemala City. In May 1978 the army massacred more than one hundred Kekchi Indians in Panzos, part of a group of six hundred who had marched to the town to protest land takeovers and to obtain information on the whereabouts of three community leaders who had been taken by the army. The government threatened foreign religious workers, expelling several. Military and paramilitary groups captured, tortured, and killed catechists and priests. Peasant and student leaders of the CUC were kidnapped at Los Encuentros and tortured (Ibid.).

Throughout 1979 military activity continued to be concentrated in northern Quiché. Cotzal, Chajul, and Uspantán residents experienced harassment, kidnappings, bombings, the rape of women, and the ransacking of homes by soldiers. The government created a new military zone in Cobán, Alta Verapaz, to police the northern transversal strip and provide protection for the engineering corps working on the road. A priest was expelled for protesting land takeovers in the Baja Verapaz (Davis & Hodson 1982, 48). In 1979 the National Police announced that between January and October of that year 1224 "criminals" had been killed by *El Escuadrón de la Muerte* and 3252 "subversives" by the *Ejército Secreto Anticomunista* (Nairn & Simon 1986, 15).

The pattern intensified in 1980. Government and police forces firebombed protesting Indians from Quiché in the Spanish embassy in January. The Ixil triangle was the focus of ongoing military activity and harassment. Indians from Sacapulas were kidnapped. Two more priests from Quiché were killed and the bishop of Quiché ordered the diocese closed (Davis & Hodson 1982, 49-50). In the spring, CUC and CNUS, the National Committee of Labor Unity, called a strike against the sugar and cotton plantations which brought out 75,000 workers and forced the government to announce a new daily wage rate of Q3.20. Although the payment of the wage was not enforced, this demonstration brought forth a new wave of repression against all who were suspected of CUC membership (Handy 1984, 229). In August and September, army massacres of Indians occurred in Chajul and Cotzal. In the fall, the army began operations in Chimaltenango and Sololá, and community leaders in those towns disappeared or were kidnapped. The director of the Catholic radio station in Santiago Atitlán was killed as was an American development worker, Kaiyutah Clouds (Davis & Hodson 1982, 49-50).

The violence escalated in 1981. The first half of the year saw continued attacks on Indian communities in Chimaltenango, with San Juan Comalapa and San Martín Jilotepeque experiencing the worst killings. More than 1500 Indians in the department were murdered in 2 months. Uspantán, Nebaj, and Cotzal in Quiché were also the sites of attacks. In June army units occupied 7 cooperative villages along the Usumacinta River in Petén and killed 50 people; 3500 inhabitants of these communities fled to Mexico. Mexican authorities deported them back to Guatemala in July. Emeterio Toj Medrano, a CUC leader and popular announcer on Radio Quiché, was kidnapped and tortured, but was later rescued by the EGP. Father Stan Rother, a North American priest in Santiago Atitlán, was killed by 3 masked men. In the fall, the army mounted a major offensive in Baja Verapaz, killing about 1000 in a 2-week period. The army implemented scorched earth, counterinsurgency tactics in northern Quiché, burning houses, food stores, and crops, and killing animals and residents. In November the army established a base in Chimaltenango, and General Benedicto Lucas García, commander of the army offensive in the highlands and brother of the president, announced that troop strength in the area would be increased from 5000 to 15,000 men (Davis & Hodson 1982, 50-51).[17]

According to Handy, the army's attacks on the Indian population in 1980 and 1981 are important to understanding the growth of the guerrilla movement. What had been a limited operation in the Quiché region became nationally known with the Spanish embassy massacre and, like the Panzos massacre, again brought home the lesson that there would be no justice through nonviolent means. The kidnapping of Toj Medrano was another such event and his rescue made clear the link between the EGP and the CUC. Both the EGP and ORPA (Organization of People at Arms) began to draw large numbers of recruits from the most repressed areas. In those areas where alternative economic development had freed Indians from abject poverty and migratory labor, support for the guerrilla movement was less strong, although in some of these areas church, cooperative, literacy, and development programs and personnel were attacked in a more selective fashion (Handy 1984, 247-50).

In 1982 the army, after the coup d'état that brought General Efraín Ríos Montt to the presidency, implemented a full-scale military counterinsurgency program in the highlands that General Lucas had planned. Massive killings of whole villages and a continuation of the scorched earth policy, together with the establishment of military bases in each *municipio* formed the basis of the attack. Thousands of Indians fled from Quiché, Huehuetenango, San Marcos, Chimaltenango, the Verapazes, and the Petén. They sought refuge in Mexico, in the more remote mountains or jungles, in the cities, or on the south coast. An estimated 20,000 died violently, 1,250,000 left the region, and another 50,000 are unaccounted for (Frank & Wheaton 1984, 92). The survivors were offered resettlement in strategic hamlets, model villages, or re-education camps. The military organized Indian men into civil patrols and announced military-directed work programs and development schemes.

There are several explanations for the Indian attraction to armed insurrection under the leadership of the guerrilla groups and the consequent intense repression. Among them is that offered by the Guatemalan military officers themselves. Michael Richards interviewed several military officers and soldiers stationed in the Ixil area and found that they believed that the Indians were a primitive, underdeveloped people. Outsiders, especially foreign priests and nuns, brought new ideas to these Indians and when the guerrillas contacted them, the Indians did not have enough mental capacity to understand what they should do. The officers maintained that since the Indians' existence was idyllic, they would not have been attracted to guerrilla ideas if the outside clergy had not interfered. According to the officers, the Ixiles were duped by the guerrillas, and although the violence was hard on them, they had to pay for the mistake of siding with the guerrillas. The officers also believed that centuries of backwardness and neglect would be corrected by promoting the development of the Indians through the model village program, Spanish language training, and civic re-education (Richards 1985, 101).

A more common explanation is that landlessness, overpopulation, and poverty were the major reasons for the Indians to find common cause with the guerrillas. This explanation is well expressed by the historian David McCreery:

> By the late 1970's the pattern of exploitation established after 1945 in capitalist agriculture was itself breaking down. Falling labor demand in the export sector, the result of a decline in the market for Guatemala's raw material exports together with the effects of mechanization and the substitution of chemicals such as herbicides for human labor, conflicted with the survival needs of a rural population that had continued to ex-

pand at a rapid rate and was now, given the existing distribution of resources, irremediably dependent for survival on cash earnings from the fincas. But such work was less and less to be had. Even at wages lower than subsistence levels, available labor could not be absorbed by the plantation sector, and the state showed no willingness to undertake the sort of land reform that would provide alternative opportunities for this "surplus population. Far from continuing to subsidize the export sector as a reserve-reproducer of artificially cheap labor, the villages in the 1970's became increasingly a "problem for the state by their support of revolution. (McCreery 1986, 115)

This rationale also underlies many U.S. government statements and reports on the area, including the Kissinger Commission report, and suggests that industrial development to absorb the surplus labor will relieve these problems.

Carol Smith offers an opposing hypothesis. In a provocative paper that traces the dialectical processes of class formation in Guatemala, she argues that increasing labor shortages and growing unrest among the migrant work forces was behind the government's repression of economic development alternatives in those areas which had traditionally supplied much of the plantation labor. It was this repression, she maintains, which caused the Indians to join with the guerrillas in the hope of ending the killings and securing a modicum of rights as workers and peasants. The military attack on the subsistence base for highland, Ixcán, and Petén peasants could create a pool of potential laborers for the plantations and for the development of the transversal lands that the military had taken for themselves.

Drawing upon her 1977-1978 survey of Indian male occupations in 131 rural hamlets, she found that the number of males engaged in agriculture of any type had declined from her previous studies and that more men were engaged in commerce, construction, and artisan work. Fewer were engaged in subsistence agriculture, but fewer were also going to the plantations. The deficit in Indian migratory labor was exacerbated by the economic development activities of churches and international agencies, which made subsistence farming more productive, freed more Indians from contractor debts, and made new occupations available through literacy and other training opportunities. Plantations turned to the cities for laborers and hired Salvadorans. Both groups were more fully proletarianized workers and more militant in their consciousness. The resulting work stoppages and strikes brought forth repression against labor leaders and the leaders and members of Indian self-help groups, community development programs, and cooperatives in the areas which traditionally supplied plantation labor. And it was this repression, beginning in 1977, which linked the Indians to the guerrillas (Smith 1984).

Smith delineates a labor shortage in the mid- and late 1970s for the harvesting of the agro-export crops. She hypothesizes that army repression served to strip peasants of land and thereby reduce alternate income sources so as to force another step in the proletarianization of the Guatemalan peasantry. In her account, the Indians joined the guerrillas as a result of the repression. The position taken by McCreery and others posits that the peasant rebellion stemmed from unemployment and poverty. It was this rebellion which was then repressed by the army. On the surface it would seem an easily resolvable issue to determine whether there was a job or a labor shortage on the coast at harvest time, but there is little direct evidence to support either side. Increasing populations and decreasing land availability do not automatically mean that people will take whatever work is offered, particularly if there are other options. Smith 's position finds support from several sources. The pattern of the military attacks themselves, as described above and more fully detailed in Davis and Hodson's report, presents evidence for both the geographic areas attacked and the specific people targeted. The enormous increase in the agro-export output of hand-picked crops in the 1970s (see table 4.2) would have demanded a considerably larger labor force. Declines in output after 1980 indicate the effects of terrorism directed at Indian populations and the world economic slump (Davis & Hodson 1982).

In one of the few direct studies of agro-export labor, Jude Pansini also reported labor shortages for the south coast plantations. These shortages were less severe in the areas closer to El Salvador, but were particularly hard on the coffee plantations. Cotton and sugar cane could be harvested mechanically if need be, but coffee had to be picked by hand. The coffee harvest labor shortage was quite severe in 1979 and 1980, although some planters reported that the reduction in available Indian labor began as early as the late 1960s (Pansini 1983).

The outcome of the military occupation of the northern highlands and the reorganization of Indian life in the model villages will ultimately confirm or reject Smith's thesis. The information from these areas is still sparse, as investigators are not free to travel or do research apart from what the military authorizes. In spite of these difficulties, several researchers have traveled to the area to make brief assessments of the situation, and human rights organizations have also published reports (See, e.g., Krueger and Smith 1983; or Beatriz Manz' material in Americas Watch Committee 1984a; or Krueger & Enge 1985). These accounts report that the conscription of Indian men into the civil patrols has limited their ability to move freely, to engage in commerce, to work on the coast or to work their milpas in areas away from the village. Patrol duty also takes time and energy, involves the men in construction work as well as guard duty, and is not compensated (Americas Watch Committee 1984a).

The construction of the model villages was accomplished under a food-for- work program that provided subsistence as long as the work lasted. Most of these programs have now ended. The army's ambitious and widely publicized development "poles" (plans for regional economic development) are not in evidence. There is little work available in the model villages, migration to the coast is cut short by patrol duty, and land is either unsuitable or insufficient for subsistence agriculture. An estimated three hundred thousand highland people have taken refuge in Guatemala City, where their only option will be some form of wage labor (Krueger & Enge 1985, 21). For those in the model villages, the pattern at present seems to be one of no work, little migratory labor, and no subsistence agriculture. The people are poor and hungry. There are disproportionate numbers of widows and orphans. They are still quite clearly controlled by the Guatemalan military (Interview with Chris Krueger, Washington, Nov. 1986).

The future is not clear. The outcome of the military occupation of the northern highlands will depend on the Guatemalan military, on the still active guerrilla movement, and on the tenacity and courage of the Mayan people, who are again facing a restructuring of their lives to fit the needs of the dominant classes.

NOTES

1. Carol Smith, however, argues that the closed corporate community was a construct of colonial times and was coming to an end during this period (Smith 1984).

2. This is most clearly seen in Jackson Lincoln's field notes (Lincoln n.d.). Taken by the courtesy and hospitality of the owner of the *finca* San Francisco, Lincoln quoted him extensively on matters of Indian labor. None of these anthropologists accompanied the Indian men to the plantations to observe the conditions there for themselves. For most, the focus of their work was not on labor. LaFarge and Bunzel were primarily interested in religious beliefs and practices. Tumin and Siegal, and later John Gillin, focused on ethnic relationships between Indians and ladinos. Tax and Wagley both took a more economic approach, but were largely concerned with the internal economic activities of the community or with agricultural rounds. The differences between their two communities is very instructive, because even in the 1930s it is clear that the Indians of Santiago Chimaltenango had lost considerably more land than those in Panajachel, and that the Panajacheleños had other economic options available to them, making them much less susceptible to the demands of wage labor, a pattern evident in the anthropological literature until the late 1960s.

3. Other reports from Guatemala during this period include Nash's study (1967) of the adaptation of the Indians of Cantel to a textile factory in that community and King 1974. King's otherwise complete report barely mentions the Indian labor that created the great coffee wealth of this district.

4. Adams also assessed the degree to which Indians had been affected by the "communist" agitation of the Arbenz years. See Newbold [Richard N. Adams] 1956.

5. The Guatemalan currency unit, the *Quetzal (Q)* was equal to the U.S. dollar.

6. See also Williams 1986 for an analysis of the impact of cattle ranching on eastern Guatemala and a detailed examination of the effects of the increased cotton and beef exports in Central America.

7. Reina reported a diminishing land base for Chinautla, a community near Guatemala City. During the Arbenz years, men took advantage of

government land rental programs and grew corn and beans on the coast. Under Castillo Armas, however, the rental costs of this land tripled, and the men abandoned that effort. Wage labor was available to Chinautla men in the capital, so they did not migrate to the coast.

8. Colby and van den Berghe also reported landlessness and large migrations of laborers from the Ixil villages, about 2000 leaving each month from the Nebaj labor market. As much as 40 percent of the able-bodied population might be away at any one time.

9. Hinshaw examined the cash crop agriculture of the Indians of Panajachel and compared their land base and income from cash crops to data from the earlier studies of Sol Tax. They showed no decline in land base; and some were actually intensifying production through the use of fertilizers. In comparison with other Atitlán communities, Hinshaw found that only 2.2 percent of the men from Panajachel engaged in migratory labor, while poorer communities sent 50 to 80 percent of their men.

10. Smith also undertook comparative studies in the department of San Marcos and found large differences between Indian communities in land base and in opportunities for cash income other than migratory labor. The poorest communities had little land, great dependency on the income from migratory labor, and high birth rates. Sometimes, whole families went to the coast, many working both the coffee and the cotton harvests. In others, a greater land base or opportunities for artisan or trade work reduced the necessity for migratory labor.

11. Carter investigated a community of Kekchi migrants from Alta Verapaz to the lowlands in the department of Izabal. He reported that the Indians had settled on lands which they thought were government owned and thus available for settlement, but that the lands turned out to have been under dispute. When the dispute was resolved, the Indians found themselves living either on the land of an absentee landowner who demanded work on one of his *fincas* in exchange for rent, or on land owned by the International Nickel Corporation, which assessed the *municipio* a fee for the squatters. The *municipio*, in turn, taxed the settlers and made them work off their debt if they could not pay by assigning them to *fincas* where there was a labor shortage, precisely the situation the settlers had left the highlands to avoid. This area continued to experience conflict over land, and as the government sought to open more of this area to private development these conflicts intensified, culminating in the Panzos massacre in 1978.

12. For Aguacatán, Brintnall reported that the garlic crop provided income for those who owned or could rent irrigated land and wage labor. The garlic crop widened the gap between richer and poorer Indians within the *municipio*; and for those *aldeas* where there was no irrigable land, many families went to the coast. Some Indians also became contractors for the cotton harvest, since the ladino contractors worked for specific coffee *fincas*. Both fluency in Spanish and literacy were promoted by church groups, and Indians no longer needed ladinos to deal with the outside world.

13. Bossen investigated a Mam community in the northwest highlands and reported that plantation labor was so widespread that the only time all community members were together was for the important festivals. Half of the population might be absent at any one time. Women with small children were the most reluctant to go, since the people believed that the coast killed babies. Bossen also reported that people were packed into *galeras*, dirt-floored, open sheds without water or toilet facilities.

14. Warren reported that the development of a cooperative in San Andrés Semetabaj which promoted wheat growing among the ladino land-owners provided local work options for the community's Indians. Indians could also work on the roads or in Guatemala City. The number of options open to the Indians forced the local wheat growers to raise their wages. Ladinos sought to bind Indians to them through loans or godparent relation-ships and thus insure a dependent labor force. Indians preferred to remain independent of this patron-Indian complex.

15. Watanabe reported the cash crop growing of coffee for about one-half of the Indian population in Santiago Chimaltenango. Of the households in the community, 36 percent did no plantation labor, 42 percent went for 1 or 2 months, and 22 percent went for 3 or more months. Some Indians were migrating to Mexico to pick coffee, since the wages and the working conditions were better there. Wealthier Indians often owned 2 houses, one in the town and one in the *aldea* near their coffee fields. Rural Indians from the *aldeas* were considerably poorer than those from the town.

16. The anthropological studies of this period are more diverse and go far beyond the communty studies cited here. Readers seeking a broader view of this research are urged to consult a recent bibliography on Guatemala, such as that in Nyrop 1983 or Bossen 1984. While neither is complete nor limited to anthropological works, the range of titles listed in these bibliographies demonstrates the scope of anthropological interest in Guatemalan Indians. Several of these studies reported desperate conditions in certain areas, but there is little indication of the holocaust to come.

17. Williams (1986) believes, however, that the Panzos massacre was the turning point for Indian participation with the armed resistance.

CHAPTER 5

Catholic Leaders and Spiritual Socialism during the Arévalo Administration in Guatemala, 1945-1951

Hubert J. Miller

The generation that brought about the downfall of General Jorge Ubico on July 1, 1944, and his henchman Federico Ponce Vaides on October 20, 1944, envisioned the death knell of Liberalism in Guatemala. The October 20 Revolutionaries, as they called themselves, had lost faith in Liberalism. The much heralded democracy promised by the Liberals since the 1870s had hardly been realized under Ubico's harsh dictatorship.

The generation of 1944 was not, however, eager to challenge the Liberal religious reforms embodied in the Constitution of 1879. Catholic leaders, on the other hand, saw Ubico's overthrow as an opportunity to restore the rights and privileges that the church had enjoyed before the Liberal Reform of 1871. This chapter analyzes church leaders' efforts to restore those rights and privileges as well as their positions in relation to socioeconomic problems and communism during the Arévalo administration. Peripheral issues raised by the study include the potential routes of Christian democratic and liberation theology movements.

The study is limited to an examination of the position of the hierarchy and a small group of Catholic lay leaders known as the *Secretariado Social Rerum Novarum*, who published the weekly *Acción Social Cristiana*. The vast majority of Catholic laity may not have agreed with their pronouncements, but this small Catholic core assumed the leadership role in attacking nineteenth-century Liberalism and propagating papal teachings on socioeconomic issues.

The Guatemalan church during the Ubico years was a shell of its former self. In the late eighteenth century the jurisdiction of the archdiocese of Guatemala had stretched from Chiapas to Panama with a clergy that num-

bered more than 500 (Calder 1970, 12). By the late 1940s its sphere of influence was reduced to the republic of Guatemala, and although it served
twice the population it had served at the end of the colonial period, its clerical personnel had declined to some 130 priests (*Acción Social Cristiana*, June
2, 1949, 1). The privileged position of the colonial church had been challenged
by the Liberal governments of Mariano Gálvez and Francisco Morazán in the
1830s, but the church quickly regained its lost privileges under the rule of
Rafael Carrera after 1839. In 1871 Carrera's policies were reversed with the
arrival of a new breed of Libeals and *La Reforma*.

The *Reforma*'s call for expulsion of religious congregations caused a
drastic reduction of clergy. Abolition of the tithe and state ownership of all
church property destroyed its economic power. Removal of the church from
education greatly weakened its moral power as did the government's usurpation of recording vital statistics, ownership of cemeteries, and issuing marriage
contracts. A financially weakened church concentrated more and more
resources in large urban centers and strengthened its bonds with the wealthy.
By 1944, for example, the Department of Huehuetenango had only 2 priests
for 176,000 inhabitants (Calder 1970, 19). Despite these setbacks, the church
still remained a significant moral influence in some rural areas.

Although Jorge Ubico, who came to power in 1931, took great pride in
his Liberal heritage, in many respects his was a mellowed, anticlerical
Liberalism. Ubico adopted a conciliatory policy which did not undo the
Liberal religious reforms, but permitted church liberties not allowed by the
Constitution of 1879. For instance, in 1936 he accepted an apostolic nuncio to
Guatemala. The following year the Jesuits arrived to teach in the archdiocesan
seminary, and Maryknollers, forced to leave their Chinese mission posts, came
in 1943. The only restriction the president placed on these religious orders
was that they refrain from political activities (Calder 1970, 53-54).

Nuns also benefited from Ubico's conciliatory policy. First, he renewed
the contract with the Sisters of Charity of St. Vincent de Paul, whose indispen-
sable service in the General Hospital had precluded their expulsion during
the *Reforma* of the 1870s. More significant was the arrival of a group of Belgian nuns to conduct a private school. Another group came from El Salvador
and purchased property for their Colegio de Santa Teresita. These actions, as
well as wearing religious garb in public, were clear violations of the Constitution of 1879 (Holleran 1949, 212-18).

It was also during the Ubico years that lay Catholic Action groups began
to address the clerical shortage by teaching the Indians. The lay leaders
worked under the direction of a pastor and were notably active in Momos-
tenango, Chiquiumula, and Quiché. They provided an important moral influence for the church in Indian communities (Falla 1980, 427-28).

No prelates suffered expulsion under Ubico, which had been common
in the country since independence. Ubico's relations with Archbishop
Mariano Rossell Arellano were remarkably cordial. Speculation has it that the
prelate's appointment in 1939 was approved by Ubico, but there is no proof
of this contention (Calder 1970, 177; Arévalo 1963a, 114-19).

Rossell Arellano was born in Esquipulas on June 18, 1894, educated in Guatemala, and ordained into the priesthood in 1918. Shortly thereafter he served as the private secretary to Archbishop Luis Javier Muñoz y Capurón and was exiled when that prelate was expelled in 1922. On his return he continued his pastoral work and in 1935 received the appointment of archdiocesan vicar-general, paving the way for his nomination as archbishop (*Revista del Ejército*, Dec. 1964, 7). Rossell Arellano found little to criticize in the Ubico regime, except for the fact that the church was denied its right to impart a Christian education, but even these remarks were tempered by the admonition that Christian education teaches obedience and respect for authority. In fact, the archbishop even hoped that Ubico would establish a ministry of religious education, obviously too much to expect of the president's Liberalism (Calder 1970, 177-79).

The archbishop and Ubico shared similar views on communism and General Francisco Franco of Spain. Both saw the former as an evil and a disruptive force that at all times had to be condemned. Falangism, on the other hand, was viewed as a religious and patriotic movement. The prelate's biased views were evident in his comments on the civil strife in Spain when he condemned the atrocities of the Left but minimized those of the Right (Calder 1970, 180-82). During the Ubico administration, a Spanish colony of some 1000 residents, of which probably about 600 held Falangist sympathies, was formed. The immigrants were pro-Ubico and in 1943 circulated a letter urging him to remain in power. Other evidence of Falangist influence was the number of Spanish priests who entered Guatemala at the time. Of some 273 parish priests, 1/4 were Spaniards, many of whom were engaged in nonpastoral work (Calder 1970, 184, 186).[1]

Padre Felipe Alvarez served as leader of the Falangists. Rossell Arellano contributed to their publication, *Amanecer*. The archdiocesan publication, *Verbum*, also carried articles supporting Franco, as did *Acción Social Cristiana*. Both the archbishop and the papal nuncio, Rafael Triana y Blanco, attended the celebration marking the Falangist victory at the San Francisco Church (*Amanecer* [Guatemala], Apr. 30, 1939, cited by Calder 1970, 188-90).[2] Falangists also operated the La Voz Blanca radio station, located in the Cerrito del Carmen Church under the direction of Padre Augusto F. Herrera. The station's Falangist propaganda was a factor contributing to its demise after Arévalo took office. Finally, the Falangists made inroads into educational circles. Notably, Falangist sympathizer Isidro Iriarte served as rector of the diocesan seminary, while the Spanish Marist religious order propagated Falangist propaganda in their Colegio de Infantes next to the cathedral (Calder 1970, 189-90; Frankel 1969, 191-240). Ubico benefited from the Falangist propaganda. Strong support for authoritarian government, stability, and respect for a hierarchical society fit the general's views of what a well governed Guatemala should be. The church paid a price for its close association with the Falangist cause, as many of its leaders became suspect after the dictator's overthrow.

The closing years of World War II were not auspicious ones for Central American dictators. The Atlantic Charter proclaimed democracy, liberty, and respect for human rights, which the Allied powers desired to restore in Europe and the Far East. The message had special relevance in Central America,where it served as a rationale for the removal of dictators. Opposition to the fourteen-year rule of Ubico was especially strong among university students, who received support from younger military officers and workers. Led by Mario Méndez Montenegro and Mario Efraín Nájera Farfán, leaders of the National Renovation party (PRN), they were joined by the Popular Liberation Front (FPL) and the Social Democrats (PSD), whose common purpose was to terminate the Ubico dictatorship. Ubico's last-ditch effort at wage increases failed to stave off growing urban labor support for the opposition. The murder of a young school teacher, Maria Chinchilla, on June 25 by government forces provided the opposition with a martyr. Faced with a crippling railroad strike, the dictator resigned on July 1, turned over the government to a triumvirate headed by General Federico Ponce Vaides, and left for to New Orleans, where he died two years later (Grieb 1979, 265-80).[3]

The Ponce government immediately promised to hold elections in November, enforce constitutional guarantees, and permit the existence of political and labor parties. Despite these promises, it ruled with an iron hand and repressed political campaigning, forcing a leading presidential candidate, Juan José Arévalo, to seek refuge in the Mexican embassy. Opposition to Ponce came to a head on October 1, when after Alejandro Córdova carried a story in *El Imparcial* that Ponce intended to forego the November elections and continue in power, police agents murdered the popular editor. The refusal of the presidential candidates to continue campaigning and the rebellion of young army officers, headed by Major Francisco Arana and Captain Jacobo Arbenz Guzmán, led to the overthrow of the provisional government on October 20 and the setting up of a new triumvirate, composed of Arana, Arbenz, and Jorge Toriello, a civilian from a prominent Guatemalan family (Schneider 1979, 12-14).

The revolutionary junta called for decentralization of executive power with effective separation of powers and an independent judiciary, an end to the practice of hand picking presidents, no re-election and the right to rebel if re-election were attempted, an apolitical army, university autonomy, and a new constitution that recognized democratic political parties, obligatory suffrage (including the public vote of illiterates), and recognition of citizenship of women prepared to exercise it (Guatemala, Junta Revolucionario de Gobierno. 1945b, 32-36; see also Galich 1977, 373-74; Silvert 1954, 9-10; and, for the Junta's additional instructions, Guatemala, Junta Revolucionario de Gobierno. 1945a, 4-11). These goals and others served as the revolutionary blueprint for the new Guatemala.

The legislative and presidential elections in November and December resulted in a sweeping victory for Arévalo and his United Front of Arevalist parties, which included a minority of Marxist supporters. Arévalo captured

255,000 of the 295,000 votes cast by the literate male population (Schneider 1979, 15). Other contenders in the race included Guillermo Flores Avendano of the Social Democratic party and Adrián Recinos of the National Democratic Front. The president-elect took office on March 15, when the constituent assembly completed its work on the constitution.

There is no evidence that the campaigning or overthrow of Ubico and Ponce caused any difficulties in church-state relations, yet the archbishop's close ties with the Ubico government could have been a source of embarrassment. The behavior of the prelate during Ubico's final days and the subsequent presidential campaign was noncommittal (Mejía 1949, 69). This was not the story of a broadside authored by concerned Catholics, who warned about impending dangers for the church. One compared Arévalo to Hitler in that he used all types of followers to gain power and then persecute them after attaining power (BLAC, Stella Colima, *La similtud sorprendente entre Arevalismo y Nacismo* [Guatemala, 1944], broadside no. 66). Another urged all religious sects to pray daily for protection against the impending, but undefined danger (BLAC, *Guatemaltecos: la patria está en peligro* [Guatemala, 1944], broadside no. 154). A third one supported Recinos because he and his family were Catholics and respected religious freedom (BLAC, Diario de Guatemala, *Pueblo católico de Guatemala: el licenciado Recinos respeta la libertad religiosa* [Guatemala, 1944], broadside no. 84). These unsigned propaganda sheets are anonymous, but reflect apprehensions of Catholics deeply concerned about the uncertainty of the October 20 revolution.

A quick response of Catholic leaders to the unfolding revolution was the creation of the *Secretariado Social Rerum Novarum*. Its publication, *Acción Social Cristiana*, first appeared on January 11, 1945, and carried an editorial calling for the formation of a Christian social conscience and a warning about communism. The editorial stressed that the publication was "essentially apolitical" and intent upon practicing true Christianity, which it proposed to implement by means of periodic conferences and the establishment of a library and school for workers. At all times, the *Secretariado* insisted that it would adhere to the principles stated in the *Rerum Novarum* and *Quadragesimo Ano*, which included the right to private property, good relations between capital and labor, minimum salary, and the equitable distribution of goods. A subsequent editorial argued that such Catholic socioeconomic doctrines were the best means to combat communism (*Acción Social Cristiana*, Jan. 11, 1945, 1-2; Jan. 18, 1945, 6; Jan. 25, 1945, 1).[4]

Maintaining an "essentially apolitical" position was not easy and received an immediate test during the constituent assembly debates on the new constitution. The eighty-eight-page draft, completed by January 11, 1945, outlined a socioeconomic program that increased the role of the state in the private sector and rejected the laissez-faire of the 1879 Constitution (Asociación de Abogados de Guatemala 1945).[5]

The new constitution retained the religious provisions of 1879, which (1) prohibited church ownership of property, establishment of religious congregations, public religious practices, and religious instruction in public schools; (2) guaranteed religious liberty as long as it was not used for subversive purposes; (3) provided for lay education and civil marriage; and (4) required secular status for the president, members of the national assembly, and judges (*Diario de sesiones...* 1953, 12-21). A review committee headed by Jorge García Granados found little to disapprove in the proposal, but one member, Juan Antonio Reyes Córdova, wanted the church to enjoy property rights. Clemente Marroquín Rojas supported this proposal, arguing that to deprive the church of property rights destroyed its independence. Other members insisted on retaining the articles, feeling that church ownership of property would lead to economic stagnation — the traditional Liberal rationale of "dead hands." The opposition also feared that any concession in this matter would allow the church to reclaim all the property that it had before the Liberal victory of 1871. In the end, Reyes' efforts failed (*Diario de sesiones...* 1953, 126-31).

Article 30, restricting religious exercises to the interior of churches, received considerable attention. Some members wanted the restriction removed, reasoning that it might be used to prohibit traditional religious processions. They also feared that if applied to the home, it could violate the right of private domicile. The opposition countered that processions were not affected by the restrictions because they were customs — not cults. They argued that lifting the restrictions could lead to practices detrimental to public order and peace. The brief debate shows that the attempt to remove the restrictions had little support. Of greater interest was the prohibition of religious freedom for subversive ends, reflecting the concern of the committee that religious leaders might use the uneducated masses for such purposes. García Granados reminded the church not to become involved in labor organizations because that was a task for the workers themselves. All in all the committee's debates on religious matters were neither lengthy nor acrimonious, as was the case in the drafting of the Liberal Constitution of 1879. Articles treating labor and other socioeconomic issues received much more attention than religious questions and demonstrated the direction that the new constitution was to take (*Diario de sesiones...* 1953, 123-25).

The committee's proposed constitutional provisions treating religious affairs aroused little debate in the constituent assembly's deliberations, except the provision prohibiting religious activities outside of churches. The archbishop and the bishops sent a petition to the assembly urging the members not to restrict religious freedom and to respect the church's right to hold property and operate schools, which the petition claimed was already enjoyed by Protestants. The constituent assembly, heeding nineteenth-century Liberal doctrines, disregarded the petition and approved the recommended provisions (Guatemala, Asamblea Nacional Constituyente 1951, 15-16, 230-33, 240-58, 927-28. For the final version of the constitution see Guatemala. Asamblea Nacional Constituyente 1945; see also Marroquín Rojas 1945, 22-24, 39-40, 45).

The Catholic press was active in its opposition to many of the provisions during the deliberations of the constituent assembly. Editorials in *Verbum*, the official archdiocesan mouthpiece, expressed dismay with restrictions on religious liberty, and claimed they limited Catholic Action activities and the church's teaching mission (Reprinted in *Verbum*, Mar. 12, 1950, 1, 4). More prolific were the comments of *Acción Social Cristiana*. Starting on February 1, 1945, it alerted its readers about the constitutional limitations on religious acts outside churches and prohibition of the church's owning property. It believed these restrictions tied the church's hands and were worse than those in the Constitution of 1879. The weekly carried a petition signed by ten thousand people to demonstrate popular opposition to the provisions. Particularly offensive was the prohibition of clergymen from organizing labor unions, an activity in which Catholic Action was involved. Moreover, the editor claimed that the church's teachings in defense of private property were essential in combating communist unions. *Acción Social Cristiana* also objected to the prohibition of clerics from holding public offices. The greatest mistake in the new constitution according to the weekly, however, was the failure to recognize that Guatemala was a Catholic country historically and culturally (Feb. 1-Apr. 12, 1945).

Broadsides also kept the Catholic laity informed about these issues and like *Acción Social Cristiana* were critical of the assembly's actions restricting the church's freedom and urged the public to protest actions (BLAC, *¡Alerta pueblos de Guatemala!* [Feb. 9, 1945], broadside no. 462; Acción Social Cristiana, *Para "El Imparcial"* [1945], broadside no. 459; *Carta abierta a El Libertador* [Guatemala, 1945], broadside no. 469; Manuel Coronado Aguilar, *Anticlericalismo o falsa democracia* [1945], broadside no. 475; and *¿Que es la libertad religiosa? ¿Que es lo que piden los católicos?* [Guatemala, 1945], broadside no. 518). A broadside addressed to the constituent assembly by José García Bauer summed up much of the Catholic opposition when it observed that authentic democracy must allow absolute liberty for all religious sects, except "nazifacistas." García Bauer could not understand why the new constitution had not removed the religious shackles. Particularly ironic to him were Articles 30 and 33, which promised religious liberty and the right of association, only to be denied later when the constitution prohibited the establishment of religious congregations. Such prohibitions made it impossible to have enough priests to minister to the needs of the people, especially in a time when the nation had only a hundred priests for three million Catholics. García Bauer insisted on the restoration of the church's right to teach religion in the schools and attacked the public schools as centers of atheism. He warned that if the church could not not fulfill its mission of teaching morality, the inevitable result would be chaos in public and private life (BLAC, José García Bauer, *Democracia y religión ante la honorable asamblea constituyente y pueblo de Guatemala* [Guatemala, 1945], broadside no. 492).

The constituent assembly's approval of the religious provisions did not make for an auspicious beginning in church-state relations under the Arévalo administration. Despite the much heralded "new day in Guatemala, the assembly clung to the Liberal heritage of the "Reforma. There was still fear that unrestricted liberty for the church could make it a political and economic threat to the state. The church leaders, on the other hand, felt that the conciliation initiated during the Ubico years offered an opportune time for removing the antireligious constitutional articles. In pursuing this course of action, they ignored significant socioeconomic innovations in the document. That failure gave church leadership a negative image when it came to supporting socioeconomic reforms, which the October 20 revolutionaries insisted was the essence in the creation of a "new Guatemala."

The inauguration of Arévalo brought a man of a different mold to the Guatemalan helm, for he was neither a military man nor tied to the oligarchy. He was a professor in Argentina when university students in Guatemala sent him a radiogram on July 4, 1944, asking him to be their presidential candidate. Prior to his self-imposed exile in 1936, he had served briefly as Ubico's minister of education until his disgust with the dictatorship had prompted him to leave for Argentina, where he earned a doctorate in education. His identification with educational reform and university autonomy in the early 1930s and his disdain for the Ubico dictatorship ingratiated him with the students. Rising from the middle class, he was part of the challenge to Liberalism and the search for a new Guatemala, but his long absence from the country raised questions about his familiarity with the actual problems of the country.[6]

Arévalo referred to his program as "spiritual socialism," the essentials of which he had already outlined in his campaign for the presidency. He observed that the October 20 revolutionaries had rejected nineteenth-century Liberalism and Conservatism. Although socialists, the revolutionaries were not materialists who sought the division of material goods to achieve "economic equality of men economically different." Arévalo's socialism called for the psychological and spiritual liberation of mankind, which both Conservatives and Liberals failed to achieve. He admitted that citizens need material well-being, but that this should never be the ultimate goal; man must also have dignity which only psychological and moral liberation can provide. He rejected egotistic Liberalism in favor of man in a collective setting: "Social concerns are now displacing individual concerns." He reminded his countrymen that Communists, fascists, and Nazis were socialists, who gave food with the left hand but with the right violated the "moral and civil essentials of man." These essentials included man's spiritual or religious needs, dignity, tranquillity, and culture (BLAC, *Conservadores, liberales y socialistas* [Guatemala, 1944], broadside no. 19; and Arévalo 1945d, 143-49).[7] Yet Arévalo made clear his intention to seek material improvements for his people. "It is a socialism that does not persecute," he declared, "but protects. It does not take away, but gives" (Arévalo 1945b, 17). One admirer summed up these aspirations well when she wrote, "spiritual socialism desires to liberate, protect and dignify man as well as his resources and his relations...to all material and spiritual elements that constitute the patrimony of the nation" (Dion 1958, 123).

Although a strong supporter of both freedom of press and speech, Arévalo foresaw the need for some limitations. Lies, he argued, spread among an educated citizenry ccould do little harm because such citizens were sophisticated enough to distinguish truth from falsehood. But among the uneducated, false rumors could cause violence, as happened during the presidential campaign when illiterate Indians were told by Arévalo's political opponents that he would castrate the Indians and kidnap their women (Arévalo 1945b, 11-13). Later, limitations on freedom of expression became a bone of contention between Catholic leaders and the government when it suspended publications and closed down radio stations.

Arévalo spelled out his position on church-state relations prior to assuming office. As a traditional Liberal, he distinguished between religion and the clergy, respecting the former but not the latter (Sante Arrocha 1962, 44-46; and Dion 1958, 80-81). He supported separation of church and state in the Liberal tradition because he conceived it as mutually beneficial. Thus Catholicism should not be converted into a political party, nor should it become enmeshed in socioeconomic or political controversies. Nevertheless, Arévalo urged Catholics as private citizens to work for the resolution of socioeconomic problems and to join political parties to realize their goals. He wanted no revival of the old religious controversies and foresaw no difficulties for the new constitution in matters of religion as long as those within the church did not seek to convert it into a political party and use it for subversion (1945b, 11-13). Later, in 1963, he admitted that this aspiration remained unrealized despite the fact that he sought to prevent confrontation with the clergy so as to avoid being pictured as an enemy of the church (1963b, 49).

Acción Social Cristiana initially agreed with spiritual socialism, but observed that the president sounded too "philosophical and literary" (Feb. 22, 1945, 1-2). While reiterating its opposition to religious restrictions in the constitution, on inauguration day it called on Catholics to support the new government. At the same time, it warned civil officials that Catholics owed obedience to the state only when man's laws do not contradict those of God and His church. The same issue carried a petition directed to the constituent assembly calling for the restoration of the church's rights to carry out its mission. Especially odious were Article 25, which prohibited religious associations and clergy from participating in labor organizations, and Article 27, which outlawed religious congregations (Mar. 15, 1945, 1-2, 11-12).

The archbishop's pronouncements, meanwhile, had been rather low-key, even including the petition to the constituent assembly requesting the removal of religious restrictions. This tone had prevailed in the pastoral Rossell Arellano circulated soon after the fall of Ubico, in which he called for peace and unity based on charity while warning against the excesses of liberty (Rossell Arellano 1944b). His message was the same during the presidential campaign, as he urged the clergy on November 8 to stay out of politics. Rossell Arellano offered the church's cooperation in bringing about needed reforms, but reminded the clergy that the new order must be based on morality and that there could be no complete separation between the spiritual and material realms (Rossell Arellano 1944a).

This low-key approach changed in January 1945 when the archbishop reacted to attacks leveled at the church in *Nuestro Diario*. He denied that the clergy was involved in politics or was spreading Falangist propaganda. Citing his November 8 circular to the clergy, Rossell Arellano denied that a growing distance was developing between clergy and laity. He took the occasion once more to urge respect for the church's right to perform spiritual and social action programs as guaranteed in the Atlantic Charter (Rossell Arellano 1945). Despite his failure to achieve removal of the undesirable constitutional articles, Rossell showed his good will toward the new government by attending the inauguration ceremonies (Arévalo 1945a).

The issue of communism became a key controversy in the church's relation with the government. Arévalo's commitment to a democratic society caused him to tolerate individual Communists, but not an organized communist party. In fact, he often found Communists helpful in promoting reform measures. It was in this atmosphere that Communists opened Escuela Claridad in 1945 as an indoctrination center to train labor and peasant leaders. It was not always easy to ascertain who the Communists were during the early years of the Arévalo administration. It is even doubtful that the president was fully aware that some of his young supporters were Marxists (Schneider 1979, 22-23). Yet such men as José Manuel Fortuny and Carlos Manuel Pellecer were active communist organizers. Both had served in the constituent assembly and the former became a leader in the legislature.

It was in this environment that the archbishop issued a pastoral on October 1, 1945, warning of the communist threat. The pastoral blamed the Liberal educational system for exposing Guatemala since independence to many foreign ideologies, resulting in the gradual elimination of God. Such were the consequences of the introduction of French revolutionary ideas, followed by oppressive capitalism, which created a discontented proletariat ready for violent revolution and atheistic communism. For these reasons, Rossell Arellano condemned communism for its doctrine of class hatreds and desire to eliminate private property. Warning Catholics not to be misled by the preachers of this false doctrine, the pastoral cautioned them not to join the Red Confederation of Latin American Workers (CTAL). Other warnings on the dangers of communism included the destruction of family life and a complete change in the economic order. To remove this menace, the prelate urged the rich to pay just wages and to improve the lot of their workers. Along with this admonition Rossell urged charity, but warned that improved wages and reduced working hours were not always the solution because such innovations could lead to drunkenness, gambling, and moral dissolution. The concluding message was an endorsement of the Catholic labor union, *Liga Obrera de Guatemala* (LOG), as Rossell urged Catholic entrepreneurs to Christianize the economic life. At the same time, he instructed the priests to go to the poor and warn them about agitators who exploited their miseries and promoted envy of the rich in order to convert them to communism. The pastoral did not call for substantial socioeconomic reform, and the references to the 1945 Constitution as "communistic" only added to the image that the hierarchy was reluctant to work with the October 20 revolutionaries (Rossell Arellano et al. 1945; see also BLAC, *Verbum, Obreros de Guatemala* [Guatemala, 1946], broadside no. 686; Frankel 1969, 205).

Less than two months later, another pastoral warned against the dangers of class struggle, as the archbishop defended the existing order and declared that "capital cannot exist without labor and labor cannot exist without capital." Complementary class structure was divinely ordained and should be accepted *sin molestia* (*Acción Social Cristiana*, Nov. 28, 1946, 9-10). Rossell's views coincided with those of the elite landholders and entrepreneurs, who felt threatened by a laboring class that was no longer docile nor accepted its status as divinely determined.

The battle against communism required more than pastoral pronouncements and so the archbishop called for implementation of a Catholic Action program on March 12, 1946. The shortage of priests demanded that the laity help spread the message of the gospel. Catholic Action members, well-instructed in the faith, were expected to combat the "obscene" press, champion the rights of families, educate workers, patrons, and professionals in social justice principles, raise the cultural level of the laity through conferences, publications, and artistic presentations, and, finally, help recruit more priests. In all of these activities the members were warned not to mix in politics (Rossell Arellano 1946a; *see also* Falla 1980, 427-428). The prelate was convinced that a successful Catholic Action program was the only appropriate way to resolve the growing conflicts between labor and capital. He wanted to unmask leaders who, obeying foreign designs, used the proletariat to create discord (*Verbum* editorial of Sep. 22, 1946, reprinted in *Verbum*, Mar. 12, 1950, 1-2).

Rossell Arellano's position on communism, Catholic Action, and social justice reflects the encyclicals of Popes Leo XIII and Pius XI. The failure to distinguish between communism and socialism is very evident in these pronouncements.[8] Moreover, he failed to recognize options in socialism or the possibility of the church working with socialists to achieve socioeconomic reforms. Communism and socialism were indistinguishable, monolithic, and anti-Christian; no good Catholic ought to cooperate with them.[9] In short, the archbishop adopted a defensive, status quo position that became even more obvious when he appointed José Calderón Salazar, former contributor to the Falangist *Amanecer*, to a Catholic social services agency. Salazar was the same individual who had considered Ubico too progressive when he opened schools for Indians, claiming it created agitators and lazy louts. In fact, he thought the Indians were "too fragile" to handle books (Frankel 1969, 196).

Also appointed for social service work was Juan Alberto Rosales F., director of *Acción Social Cristiana*, who was as committed to defending the status quo as was the archbishop. These leaders must have alienated many Catholics, who looked to the church for leadership in building the new Guatemala. The advice of a Guatemalan worker who urged the church to ally itself with the poor because Christ was poor fell on deaf ears (Ruiz Franco 1950, 212).[10]

The prelate's pronouncements were pale compared to the anticommunist barrage of editorials, commentaries, and news releases on the communist menace that appeared in *Acción Social Cristiana* throughout the Arévalo years. The paper blamed nineteenth-century Liberalism as the progenitor of communism with its doctrines of rationalism, self-interest, materialism, and the dream of an earthly utopia. The weekly reported an unending litany of the evils of communism, including atheism, class conflict, destruction of the spiritual and moral dignity of man, totalitarianism, destruction of family values and promotion of concubinage and illegitimacy, abolition of private property, and rejection of loyalty and obedience to the fatherland and the church (Aug. 22, 1946, 6-7; July 18, 1946, 1; Nov. 28, 1947, 8-10; Nov. 6, 1947, 1; and Oct. 13, 1949, 1). It attributed material inequities to varying individual skills and ambitions. "Misery is not the cause of communism, but communism is the source of misery" (Aug. 6, 1948, 1).

Additional warnings focused on communist efforts to implant a proletarian dictatorship, foment class conflict so that workers could seize private property, and establishment of "Red terror" government that would destroy the church (Oct. 20, 1949, 1-2). Equally dangerous was the communist threat to the army, protector of national interests, which the Communists sought to convert into an enemy of the people and use it as their agent (Nov. 24, 1949, 1). From the beginning of the Arévalo administration, *Acción Social Cristiana* alerted its readers to Communists who were "extending their tentacles within our nation," by occupying government positions (June 14, 1945, 3; July 12, 1945, 5-6; Nov. 27, 1947, 1-2; Sep. 13, 1949, 3-4). It deplored the opening of diplomatic relations with the USSR and breaking of relations with Spain in 1945, arguing that Franco was the true enemy of communism (Apr. 19, 1945, 1-2).

Acción Social Cristiana also lashed out against syndicalism, identifying virtually the entire trade union movement as an effort to establish a proletariat dictatorship. The paper continually attacked the CTAL, the Guatemalan railway workers union (SAMF), and the Guatemalan Confederation of Labor (CTG), and urged the government to repress the communist influence in these unions (Apr. 20, 1945, 8-10; June 28, 1945, 1; Sep. 6, 1945, 3; Sep. 22, 1945, 1-3, 6; Nov. 21, 1946, 1; Dec. 5, 1946, 1-2).[11]

Tied to the communist menace was Protestantism. According to *Acción Social Cristiana*, Protestant evangelical schools planted seeds of agnosticism, which served "as a bridge for communism in Hispanic America." Furthermore, the newspaper linked Protestant and communist expansion in Guatemala to conspiracies hatched by "communist" Mexico, the "Red Dean" of Canterbury, and the Russian Orthodox Church (Mar. 23, 1945, 4-6; Apr. 12, 1945, 6-7; Oct. 11, 1945, 9; Dec. 13, 1945, 2). A common practice of the publication was to reprint North American and other foreign anticommunist articles, most of which had nothing to do with Guatemala, but served the paper's anticommunist crusade (see, e.g., an article by J. Edgar Hoover, Dec. 5, 1946, 2. See also June 26, 1947; and Sep. 9, 1948, 1-2).

Scholars who have studied the Arévalo administration have not found the communist threat as dangerous as the Catholic leaders feared. Daniel James, no friend of communism, estimated that by the time of the overthrow of Jacobo Arbenz in 1954 there were only 3500 to 4000 Communists in the country (James 1954, 16; Rey 1958). Undeniably, such Marxists as Manuel

Fortuny, Víctor Manuel Gutiérrez, and Carlos Manuel Pellecer Durán, organized labor, peasant, student, youth, feminist, and peace movements. Ronald Schneider has sketched the activities of key Marxist leaders in these areas and it needs no retelling here. Marxists found it easy to move into leadership roles because Ubico had permitted no real labor movement and the elites shied away from any movements that they judged radical or inimical to their interests. Therefore, Marxists encountered little or no difficulties in moving into the vacuum despite the fact that the rank and file members did not profess Marxism or for that matter even know what it was. Church leaders who condemned any cooperation with movements involving Marxists contributed to this vacuum. Their proposed solutions were vague and outdated statements on social justice, charity obligations, and the impotent LOG and offered few alternatives for the rank and file Guatemalan workers. The inevitable consequence for the religious leaders was to stigmatize them as reactionaries opposed to the revolution—the very image they denied (Frankel 1969, 201-6; Woodward 1962).

The criticism of *arevalismo* by *Acción Social Cristiana* for a drift to the left was undoubtedly a factor in the government's closing down the publication during October and November of 1946. The frequent attempts from the Right to overthrow the government aroused fears of subversion and set the stage for the suspension. *Acción Social Cristiana* quickly denied that it carried "subversive" articles (Jan. 3, 1946, 1). Once the suspension was lifted, it insisted that it would continue to speak out on issues that affected the best interests of the church and the nation, which meant instructing Catholics in their Christian obligations and giving warnings about the communist threat (Dec. 6, 1945, 1). Suspension of the media, however, did not affect only those on the Right, for the government also ordered the communist Escuela Claridad to cease operations on January 25, 1946. Schneider believes that Arévalo took this action under the pressure of Arana, who favored the Right, but the suspension was also consistent with Arévalo's fear of organized communism (Schneider 1979, 23).

Demonstrations became another means to express opposition to the government. On August 25, 1946, Antonio Du Teil, associated with *Acción Social Cristiana*, and some sixty Catholics called for a demonstration against government acts they considered a violation of religious freedom (BLAC, Antonio Du Teil, et al., *Aclaración al pueblo de Guatemala* [Guatemala, 1946], broadside no. 577, and *¡Alerta Católicos!* [Guatemala, 1946], broadside no. 583). But a "Committee of Catholic Defense," calling themselves "authentic Catholics", countered these efforts and advised Catholics not to attend (BLAC, Comité de la Defensa Católica, *Pueblo sufrido de Guatemala* [Guatemala, 1946], broadside no. 601, and Los Auténticos Católicos, *Pueblo Católico de Guatemala* [Guatemala, 1946], broadside no. 660).[12] Faced with criticism, the archbishop issued a circular advising the clergy to remain free of politics, but he gave his blessing to the demonstrators who gathered in the central plaza in front of his residence (BLAC, *Circular* [Guatemala: Unión

Tipografía Castañeda, Avila y Cía., 1946], broadside no. 670); Holleran 1949, 216).

A counter-demonstration took place on September 8 against Falangists, whom the organizers claimed were responsible for the August 25 manifestation. They appealed to women to attend in support of women's rights and end the abuses inflicted on women by the "Judases of religion." Several broadsides carried anticlerical messages, demanding an end to Jesuits entering Guatemala because they considered them Falangists (BLAC, *¡Alerta Guatemaltecos!* [carbon copy of typescript, 1946], broadside no. 689; *Mujeres de Guatemala* [Guatemala, 1946], broadside nos. 634 and 635; El Comité Femenino Pro-Manifestación Popular, *Mujeres de Guatemala* [Guatemala, 1946], broadside no. 603; Asociación Cívica Femenina Federación Sindical de Guatemala, et al. *Las fuerzas revolucionarias, democráticas de Guatemala* [Guatemala, 1946], broadside no. 620). Anticlericalism reached its zenith with the republication of Lorenzo Montúfar's *Un dualismo imposible*, a nineteenth-century tract that argued that it was impossible for the state and church to cooperate because they were ideologically contradictory (BLAC, [Cristobal, Panama Canal Zone, 1946], broadside no. 630).

Continued antigovernment and inflammatory comments by the Catholic press and radio caused the assembly in 1947 to limit freedom of expression, noting that propagation of false reports endangering public order was a violation of Article 36 of the Constitution. The decree became the tool for closing the church's radio station in Huehuetenango, in November 1947, because of alleged dissemination of Falangist propaganda (Guatemala, Ministerio de Gobernación 1947. 23; *Diario de Centro América*, May 9, 1947, 4; Jan. 27, 1948, 1,7; Jan. 31, 1948, 1; *Acción Social Cristiana*, Jan. 8, 1948, 2; BLAC, *Protesta católica contra maniobras falangistas* [Guatemala, n.d.], broadside 1018). Vehement protests from the archbishop and the Catholic press were of no avail (BLAC, *Declaraciones de monseñor Mariano Rossell Arellano al pueblo de Guatemala* [Guatemala, 1948], broadside no. 873; *Carta Abierta [Huehuetenango, 1948], broadside no. 848; Acción Social Cristiana*, Dec. 4, 1947, 1; Jan. 15, 1948, 5; Feb. 5, 1948, 1-2).

The growing power of labor unions and their alleged ties to communism also elicited severe criticism from church leaders. The October 20 revolutionaries considered labor reforms as one of their major objectives, and they regarded the church as antilabor. This controversy became more heated with the passage of the Labor Code in February 1947. Implementing the extensive list of labor provisions in the Constitution, it provided for the right to unionize, set minimum wages and maximum hours, required a weekly day of rest, equal pay for equal work, adequate housing, medical care, workman's compensation, maternity leaves, and regulated child and female labor. Labor disputes came under the jurisdiction of specially created labor tribunals. The underlying principle of the code was that "private interest must give way to social and collective interests." Reflecting the strong influence of the Mexican Constitution of 1917, the code served as a Magna Carta for Guatemalan workers (Guatemala, Asamblea Nacional Constituyente 1945, 11-14; Bush 1950, 41-44).

Throughout the Arévalo administration the archbishop had claimed to champion the cause of labor. His remarks addressed to workers and entrepreneurs in September 1946 denied that the church was on the side of the rich—an accusation he viewed as a communist plot against the church. Rossell Arellano pointed to the church's past record of charity, defense of the Indians by Bishop Bartolomé de las Casas, and the social justice work of Cardinal Henry Edward Manning of England, Bishop Emmanuel von Kettler of Germany, and the social encyclical of Pope Leo XIII. At the same time he repeated his condemnation of socialism and class struggle, as he cited Pope Leo XIII's concerns over the miseries of the proletariat. The traditional paternalism of the Guatemalan church became evident when, in his defense of private property, Rossell observed that Divine providence allows human inequalities in order for the rich to serve as *mayordomos* for the less fortunate. He admonished both rich and poor to remember that this world is temporary and that the ultimate goal is the next life, where Christ promised eternal consolation for the oppressed. In conclusion, Rossell argued against breaking up landed estates, favoring instead "the elevation of the proletariat through a just distribution of wealth," but offered no specifics as to how to achieve this (Rossell Arellano 1946b, 3-10).[13]

Rossell elaborated on this social justice theme in a 1948 pastoral letter. After reiterating warnings about class struggle, Liberalism as the progenitor of communism, and the threat of communism, he introduced a new theme: the condemnation of speculators, whose price manipulations aggravated the miseries of the poor. Therefore, he said, they must share in the responsibility for fostering communist propaganda that blamed the church for poverty and high living costs. Rossell's social justice message called for elimination of vices such as divorce and pornography, increased contributions to church and state charitable agencies, and the payment of just wages. The fulfillment of these obligations would reduce working discontent and remove a fertile field for communist agitation. He counseled that at times it is necessary to throw the treasure overboard in order to save the sinking ship. The message was a reluctant one, for it left the impression that readers must either follow this plan or face the dire consequences of communism. Perhaps, in the prelate's mind, this was the only pragmatic solution that the conservative elite would be willing to accept (Rossell Arellano 1948a, 3-13). Despite the moderate tone of the message, the editor of the *Diario de Centro América* commended the archbishop for his attack on speculators who, in causing shortages of basic necessities, threatened political stability. He welcomed Rossell's cooperation in remedying these abuses (*Diario de Centro América*, Nov. 22, 1948, 3, 6).

Acción Social Cristiana echoed the archbishop's social justice pronouncement and called for better treatment of workers to stave off the threat of communism. While it accepted the concept of the right to strike, it emphasized that this right should be used only as a final resort and never in violation of a legal contract between employer and worker. While approving of the Labor

Code's limitations on strikes in the public sector, it was critical of the amount of power it placed in the hands of officials and judges in labor disputes. The right of the Inspector General of Labor to enter a work place to check on abuses, it declared, could easily lead to violations of inviolability of the domicile. It believed the code conferred too much arbitrary and dictatorial power on judges in assessing penalties for violations. Even worse was the stacking of the labor tribunals with persons approved by the unions. It cited the fact that since the law had been in effect, 80 percent of the decisions had gone in favor of labor and drew the conclusion that the "dictatorial code would ruin entrepreneurs" (Aug. 2, 1945, 1; Sep. 4, 1945, 2; Dec. 20, 1945, 9-10; Oct. 3, 1946, 1; July 24, 1947, 2; July 31, 1947, 2; Aug. 7, 1947, 1; Aug. 14, 1947, 3-4).

Favoritism toward the *patrón* was in evidence any number of times. The paper warned that increased wages alone could not improve the standard of living, for without increased production, higher salaries caused inflation and alcoholism. It repeatedly supported the efforts of the Planters Association and Chamber of Commerce and Industry to have the "leftist" code changed. The pro-entrepreneurial biases were consistent with the paper's paternalistic views of the working class (May 20, 1948, 1-2; Sep. 18, 1947, 1. For examples of paternalistic themes in *Acción Social Cristiana*, see Dec. 20, 1945, 3-4, and May 13, 1948, 14. See also Ordoñez Argüello 1951, 23-24). Nor can the paper's support of LOG be interpreted as prolabor. LOG, founded in 1945, was a small, impotent union whose goals included democracy, education, improved international trade, respect for private property, increased production, "gradual and systematic" improvement of purchasing power, better health and housing, cheap credit, elimination of unemployment, social security, respect for family life and rights, religious liberty, land conservation, and hydroelectric power. It was a platform attractive to *Acción Social Cristiana* that sought harmonious relations between capital and labor. Its impotence, however, was obvious to the Guatemalan worker and as such it passed into historical oblivion (May 31, 1945, 1; June 7, 1945, 11; June 14, 1945, 12; Aug. 16, 1945, 1; Aug. 23, 1945, 1; Frankel 1969, 222).

Catholic leaders claimed that their stance was apolitical, but their attacks on *arevalismo* indicate that this was an ideal not easily achieved. The editor of *Acción Social Cristiana* defended these attacks because of the leftward drift of President Arévalo and the growth of Red syndicalism. The two were so intimately related in his view that the pro-Arévalo parties were nothing more than extensions of Red syndicalism. He concluded that "yesterday, the Liberals and Masons; today, the syndicalists and communists; and it is clear that the Catholic Church is being asphyxiated under insupportable oppression" (Oct. 30, 1947, 1-2). The paper accused Arévalo of dictatorship, and claimed that he had expelled more than one hundred persons without due process — a number that exceeded those expelled during the Ubico and Ponce administrations (Jan. 1, 1948, 5). The editor judged "spiritual socialism" and democracy to be incompatible, for, in his words, "under the Arévalo regime there is no liberty or equality or fraternity, the elements without which democracy as a political and practical theory of government is inconceivable" (Jan. 8, 1948, 2).

Such criticism failed to credit the president with continuing the conciliatory policy of Ubico in church-state relations. Foreign religious orders continued to enter the country and some engaged in operating schools — all in clear violation of the Constitution. Official relations with the Vatican also continued. The *Diario de Centro América* took the occasion to remind Catholics of the government's good intentions toward the church, pointing to the reburial of the remains of Archbishop Luis Xavier Muñoz y Capurón in Guatemala in January 1958, originally interred in Colombia after his expulsion from Guatemala in 1922. The editor remarked that Ubico had served in the cabinet of the José María Orellana government, which had expelled Muñoz and his secretary, Mariano Rossell, and that now a democratic government was seeking good relations with the church (Jan. 26, 1948, 1, 3, 7).

Arévalo made every effort to maintain good relations with the church. When reminded that some clergymen engaged in politics, he answered that his government was democratic and that he would not take action against them. Rather, he lauded the recent arrival of eight Italian priests, made possible through the good offices of the papal nuncio (*Diario de Centro América*, Dec. 21, 1948, 3). In a similar conciliatory mood he quickly quashed rumors in July 1948 of the archbishop's imminent expulsion because of his pastoral letter on the obligation of voting (Acción Social Cristiana, July 29, 1948, 1, 3; *Diario de Centro América*, July 27, 1948, 3, 6).

The pastoral letter on voting obligations raised serious questions about his nonpolitical stance. It began by warning Catholics about the dangers of electing communists and urged Catholics to vote, even if there were suspicions of electoral fraud. The faithful were counseled not to vote for anyone who showed disrespect for the church's autonomy, property, its teaching mission, or the inviolability of marriage. Neither must a Catholic vote for candidates sympathetic to communism or tainted with anti-Christian ideologies, immorality, or "political Catholics" who used religion as a political lure. The pastoral called for support of social justice programs and a vote for the lesser of two evils where neither candidate was completely acceptable. In order to avoid the the latter situation, the prelate urged the faithful not to run good candidates against each other (Rossell Arellano 1948c).

The pastoral raised a storm of protest, causing Rossell to issue a clarification on August 5, in which he reiterated that he espoused no doctrines except those of the Catholic Church and that his instructions were nonpolitical. He claimed his advice to Catholics was simply to vote according to the norms of God and country, and not to vote for a Communist or for anyone espousing anti-Catholic sentiments. Basically, Rossell defended his action as advising the faithful about their moral obligations but not telling them for whom to vote. Another brief exhortation followed on October 12, in which he urged Catholics to practice charity and abstain from violence in electoral campaigns (*Acción Social Cristiana*, Aug. 12, 1948, 2; Rossell Arellano 1948b).[14]

Acción Social Cristiana realized that much more was needed to defeat *arevalismo* and communism than encouraging Catholics to vote. Repeated editorials reflected concern over lack of solidarity in opposing the *arevalistas*. As the presidential campaign of 1950 approached, these concerns became more obvious and the paper worked actively against voter apathy. The stepped-up solidarity campaign first became evident in the departmental elections during the closing months of 1948. An editorial of October 14 spoke of the need to unite forces and fight together, a theme repeated on November 18 when it urged candidates of opposition parties to renounce their candidacies in favor of one opposition candidate. The editor encouraged opposition parties to rally around a broadly based platform that included constitutional reform, reopening of Radio PAX, an end to educational secularism, labor code reforms, removal of arbitrary restrictions on religious marriages, and improved social security services (Oct. 14, 1948, 1; Nov. 18, 1848, 1-2; Dec. 9, 1848, 2-3). The paper gave its quick approval when seven candidates united to support one slate of candidates for the national assembly in the department of Guatemala. It lamented the fact that this had not occurred in four other departments. The tactic paid dividends when four opposition candidates won seats in the department of Guatemala, although the *arevalistas* still enjoyed a majority (Nov. 25, 1948, 15; Dec. 30, 1948, 15-16.[15]

The task of presenting a successful united front in the presidential election of 1950 proved to be difficult. With the assassination of Col. Francisco Arana, the inside track belonged to thirty-six-year-old Major Arbenz, then minister of defense.[16] He belonged to the Partido de la Revolución Nacional (PRN) which joined Arévalo's PAR along with the Frente Popular Libertador (FPL) and Partido de la Unión Nacional (PUN) to form the Unidad Nacional. Included in the coalition were moderates and Communists who had organized a clandestine party in 1947, but did not surface until September 1949. The following year the Communists began publication of their weekly, *Octubre*, but being realists, they knew that their continued impact on the revolution could best be achieved through the support of Arbenz (Schneider 1979, 55-122; Alexander 1967, 305-64).

In December 1949 the editor of *Acción Social Cristiana* warned the opposition not to waste time debating possible candidates, but to concentrate on forming a united opposition front (Dec. 8, 1949, 1). A month later he found it necessary to reiterate the warning when he wrote that the "revolutionary oligarchy's" victory would be assured if action were not taken quickly (Jan. 5, 1950, 1-2). Again in April he expressed dissatisfaction with the behavior of opposition parties, which were too concerned with finding an "unsurpassable candidate" (Apr. 13, 1950, 1). By the spring of 1950, however, the "unsurpassable candidate" surfaced in the person of General Miguel Ydígoras Fuentes, whom the paper found acceptable, except for his "serenade on secular education." Ydígoras soon emerged to head the conservative opposition National Redemption party and the Partido de Unificación Anticomunista (PUA) and received the paper's official endorsement (Mar. 9, 1950, 1-2; July 20, 1950, 1-2).

The endorsement of candidates by Catholic lay leaders led to new charges that the church was involved in politics. Reacting to these accusations, the archbishop, on May 25, issued a statement on the "correct position" of the church. He reminded his accusers that the church has a duty to teach morality and defend itself against attacks by Liberals, Masons, and Communists. Should a priest as a private citizen make a political observation, that is a personal matter over which the prelate has no control. Neither can the church, he continued, be held responsible for political commentaries made by publications that have a Catholic orientation. He denied that the church was partisan when it received members from different political parties, arguing that the church must be open to all political persuasions. His closing remarks noted that the church retains the right to counsel the faithful in morality, which included advising them not to vote for Communists, Liberals, or "liberalizers" (BLAC, *Aclaraciones del excmo. y revmo. sr. arzobispo metropolitano sobre la recta y firme postura de la iglesia de Guatemala con relación al presente momento político y protesta por las insidiosas calumnias del partidos políticos contra el clero de nuestra patria* [Guatemala 1950], broadside no. 1146). A final directive from the prelate's office shortly before the November elections expressed concern over the use of the name Catholic in political propaganda. He condemned the tactic and reminded the faithful of their duty to vote their conscience in accordance with Catholic doctrine (BLAC, *La curia arzobispal de Guatemala* [Guatemala, 1950], broadside no. 1058).

The opposition, of course, did not fare well in the campaign. Ydígoras, fearing for his life, left the country in July and on his return spent much time in hiding during the final month of the campaign. Government trucks during the three election days brought voters to the polls. Even had these tactics not been used, there remains little doubt about Arbenz' victory. He garnered some 267,000 votes (65 percent of the total), to a mere 74,000 for Ydígoras. Arbenz offered few specifics as to where he stood on issues confronting the nation, but *Acción Social Cristiana* was convinced that the trend toward a Soviet-type dictatorship would continue. The only way to prevent this was to develop a united rightist party committed to an ideology based on the "immutable principles of Catholic morality and social doctrine" (Dec. 14, 1950, 1-2).

As Arévalo concluded his term, the rift between church and state had widened to the point that it would take herculean efforts to close it. The point of no return may well have been reached on January 10, 1951, when the diplomatic corps honored the outgoing president and his wife. The papal nuncio and dean of the diplomatic corps, Monsignor Dr. Juan Emilio Castellani, delivered the remarks in which he lauded the president for maintaining good relations with foreign powers and the courtesies extended to the diplomatic corps. He also took the occasion to praise the president's wife for her teaching work among the Indians. But the guest list of those in attendance shows that besides the nuncio, the only other cleric present was his counselor, Mon-

signor Dr. Víctor Ugo Righi (Arévalo 1951). The absence of Archbishop Rossell Arellano, who was present for Arévalo's inauguration, symbolically indicated the rift between the two powers.

In sum, the factors leading to the rift are not difficult to find. The failure
of the *arevalistas* to remove the nineteenth-century anticlerical constitutional provisions was the beginning. The perceived leftward drift of spiritual
socialism continued to color church-state relations involving issues of freedom
of expression, labor unions, social justice, and political activities. The program
that the Catholic leaders offered to stem the perceived "leftist" tide was paternalistic, authoritarian, and supportive of rightist interests. It is ironic that the
archbishop in one of his pastorals pointed to Bishop Bartolomé de las Casas
as a model for Catholic Action. Had he heeded his own advice, he might well
have become a precursor of modern-day liberation theology.

This negative assessment of the church leaders' role in promoting social
justice must not blind us to the faint outlines of a newly developing church.
Both the episcopal pastoral letters and the pages of *Acción Social Cristiana*
are replete with social justice messages and the need for the Catholic laity to
become politically involved in order to realize the church's mission in this
area. The promotion of Catholic Action, forming a labor union, and organizing political opposition parties, all laid the groundwork for greater Catholic,
clerical, and lay involvement in working for a better life for the Guatemalans.
Viewed in this light, it signaled a new day for the Guatemalan church.

NOTES

1. This number appears high in view of the figure (130) cited earlier in
Acción Social Cristiana, June 2, 1949. The later statistic probably reflects the
exodus of Spanish clergy during the Arévalo years.

2. Subsequent Falangist writers eulogized General Franco for his
renovation of Spain in accordance with Christian social doctrines. They
predicted that "within a few years Franco will place Spain in the first rank in
Europe." See *Acción Social Cristiana*, Apr. 4, 1946, 2.

3. According to Edwin Lieuwen, the older officers supported Ponce
Vaides to prevent a social revolution, whereas younger officers opted for the
rebel cause. Included among the latter were Jacobo Arbenz and Francisco
Arana (Lieuwen 1956, 91-92).

4. Key persons included Juan Rosales Alcántara, director of the publication; Antonio Du Teil, editor; Padre Isidro Iriarte, a Jesuit priest in charge
of the seminary; and Rafael Aycinena, a member of a prominent conservative
Guatemalan family.

5. The Constitution of 1879 had been amended several times between
1885 and 1935, but this did not alter the basic ideology of the document. See
Silvert 1954, 13-14.

6. Born in the south coast municipality of Taxisco on September 10, 1904,
in a middle class farming and cattle raising family, Arévalo studied for a teach-

ing career in Guatemala. He discusses his early life in Arévalo 1963c and 1970. For additional biographical information see, Barcos Archilla 1985 and Jorge Raygada 1951. Because of his educational background, Arévalo often saw himself as a teacher. See Arévalo 1963b, 22. In addition to teaching, he did extensive writing in the field of education. His doctoral dissertation at the University of La Plata (1937) was "La pedagogía de la personalidad." See also Arévalo 1945c; 1946; and 1974.

7. For further analysis of Arévalo's spiritual socialism, see Sante Arrocha 1962, 24-37; and Dion 1958, 111-26).

8. The papal encyclicals on social justice teaching were not updated until Pope John XXIII, who realized that "signs of the time" required a new look at social justice, socialism, and communism. See Mitchell 1985, 465-81.

9. In 1949 he reminded the faithful of a decree issued by the Vatican Sacred Congregation of the Holy Office that any Catholic who joins a communist party or propagates its aims is excommunicated and that pardon was reserved for the Holy See. *Verbum*, Sep. 25, 1949, 1-2.

10. Rossell would have done well to follow the conduct of his contemporary, Archbishop Víctor Sanabria in Costa Rica, who saw no difficulties in Catholics working with Communists as long as they severed their relations with Moscow. See Leonard 1982b, 19-20.

11. The Mexican Marxist labor leader, Vicente Lombardo Toledano, was repeatedly cited as a threat to Guatemala and the rest of Latin America.

12. *Acción Social Cristiana* (Sep. 5, 1946, 3) denied the existence of groups such as the Comité de la Defensa Católica .

13. A similar message appeared in *Verbum*. See BLAC, *Obreros de Guatemala* (Guatemala, 1946), broadside no. 685.

14. *Acción Social Cristiana* reprinted the Aug. 5 clarification on 31 Mar. 1949, 3, and gave strong endorsements to the prelate's statements on voting obligations on June 17, 1948, 1; July 8, 1948, 6-7; Oct. 7, 1948, 1; May 25, 1950, 1-2.

15. The paper later sensed a similar victory of opposition candidates in Guatemala City municipal elections. See Feb. 10, 1949, 1.

16. *Acción Social Cristiana*, like many others, was highly critical of Arévalo for failing to push a more thorough investigation of this deed. See issues of Sep. 15, 1949, 1, and Sep. 29, 1949, 1.

CHAPTER 6

Facing the Challenge: The Catholic Church and Social Change in Honduras

Edward T. and Donna W. Brett

The Catholic Church in Honduras has traditionally been poorer, less influential, and less effective than in other Central American states. Geographically isolated and lacking a sufficient supply of native labor, Honduras received little attention from the Spanish crown after its shallow gold mines were exhausted early in the colonial era. Consequently, its church never acquired the vast landholdings and political power that other branches of the Spanish-American church eventually came to possess. After independence, most of the Spanish priests left, and the church had only a handful of native-born clergy. With the ascendancy of Liberalism during the presidency of Marco Aurelio Soto (1876-1883), the government expropriated what little wealth and influence the church still had. Its fortunes plummeted even further, however, during the dictatorship of Tiburcio Carías Andino (1932-1949).

When in 1933 the see of Tegucigalpa became vacant upon the death of Bishop Augustín Hombach, Carías insisted that his former teacher, Padre Ernesto Fiallos, be appointed to fill this post. But as Fiallos was in poor health and unqualified for the position, the Vatican rejected Carías' request. Unaccustomed to having his demands ignored, Carías refused to allow any other candidate to hold the see. Thus Tegucigalpa was without a bishop from 1933 until 1947, when José de la Cruz Turcios was named archbishop after the death of Fiallos (Tojeira 1986, 1-2, 5-191, 207-8; Muller 1981; Reina 1983; Becerra 1982, 75-146; R. Cardenal 1974, 16-17). He proved a poor choice, however, at least from an organizational point of view, for he paid little attention to the governance of the archdiocese, failing to supervise parish administration, promote training of the clergy, or even write pastoral letters or establish better relations with the government (White 1977, 192-195). When Turcios finally resigned in 1962, his public statement that he was forced from office for political reasons, made while he was "crying like a baby," did little to bolster the church's tarnished image.

The church fared no better in the diocese of Santa Rosa de Copán. There the bishop's see was vacant from 1924 to 1928, and the Vatican's appointment in 1952 of Carlos Luis Geromini proved so disastrous that he had to be removed from office after only six years due to incompetence and moral unfitness. It should be added, however, that although Turcios neglected his administrative duties, he spent much time in pastoral work in the small villages of southern Honduras, helping to organize rural church and civil projects. In so doing he inadvertently carved out the infrastructure that would later form the basis for a clergy-peasant alliance in Honduras. It is no accident that the churches of Choluteca and Valle provided a social model for the rest of the country throughout the 1960s and early 1970s (Tojeira 1986, 210, 242; R. Cardenal 1974, 29; White 1977, 195).

In summary, by mid-twentieth century, the Honduran church had long been in disarray. Its lack of leadership combined with other factors to make it ineffective. The quantity and quality of clergy declined sharply after 1920, and by 1950 there were only 122 priests in a country where the church estimated a need for 684 to function effectively. Many parishes were without clergy and in those where Sunday mass was regularly celebrated, less than 10 percent of the baptized populace attended. Hardly any adult males received communion (White 1977, 197-202, citing Brufau 1959).

In an effort to resolve this problem, religious orders were invited back to Honduras beginning in the 1940s to provide clergy for entire departments. U.S.-based Franciscans established themselves in Olancho in 1944, while in 1947 Jesuits from the U.S. staffed parishes in Yoro. Likewise, French-Canadian missionaries became active in southern Honduras. Later, Passionists, Capuchins, and Claretians would accept invitations to work in the country, and the U.S. Franciscans established a mission in Comayagua. These missionaries were funded by their home countries, so not only did they provide Honduras with competent, well-disciplined clergy, but with much financial help as well (White 1977, 227; Tojeira 1986, 203-4; Bacigalupo 1980, 6-14, 23-53, 114-22, 137-49, 168-70, 195-201). But, in the early 1950s, just as the foreign missionaries were beginning to rejuvenate the Honduran church with new vitality and resources, a serious new challenge, the general strike of 1954, confronted it.

On May 1, 1954, United Fruit Company (UFCO) workers began a 69-day general strike that would paralyze the whole north coast. The strike rapidly spread from UFCO to Standard Fruit Company. Soon miners, brewery, tobacco, and female textile workers joined the movement. In all, more than 35,000 workers took part in the strike. Their modest demands were certainly not revolutionary — a 50 percent wage increase (in 1954 the average worker earned $1.68 per day), better working conditions, and legal recognition of their union. Nevertheless, the U.S. fruit companies blamed the strike on communist agitators from Guatemala. The government of President Juan Gálvez Durón could ill afford to act against the interests of the powerful United Fruit

Company, but on the other hand it did not want to appear to be breaking a popularly supported strike in the upcoming October national elections. Gálvez decided to establish a government mediation commission and the workers formed a Central Strike Committee which met with company officials in San Pedro Sula on May 28. When the workers refused to agree to a settlement after several days of negotiations, the talks broke down. The Gálvez government then arrested several representatives of the Central Strike Committee, claiming that it had documented proof that they were Communists. They were soon replaced with "anti-Communists" who reached an agreement with UFCO on July 9. Not surprisingly, the workers got only a small fraction of what they had demanded. They did, however, achieve recognition of their unions by the fruit companies (MacCameron 1983; Posas 1981b; Posas 1980, 5-9; Meza 1981, 75-98).

Whether the church was fully prepared for the role or not, the 1954 strike would force it to face, for the first time, Honduras's serious social problems. Yet the church's reaction would be complicated and muted by several factors. Archbishop Turcios was more comfortable visiting the aldeas of southern Honduras and chatting with peasants than composing theoretical statements on labor problems and social unrest. It was not until a week after the prolonged strike was over that the apostolic nuncio, Antonio Taffi, finally prevailed upon the reluctant head of the Honduran church to issue a pastoral letter on the subject. Unwilling or unable to assume a position of forceful leadership, Turcios delegated the writing of the letter to a subordinate, and the statement that resulted was an unimaginative rehash of papal teachings. The fear that the seeds of communism had sprouted in Honduras during the strike haunted church officials and colored their vision of the strikers' motives and actions. Thus, the document to which Turcios finally affixed his signature, though it called for the improvement of working conditions and recognized that social unrest was the result of the unequal distribution of riches and property, nevertheless primarily stressed the horror of communism (the "fatal virus") and warned workers to beware of its clutches. So anticommunist was the pastoral letter that the banana companies actually had it republished and widely distributed throughout the north coast (R. Cardenal 1974, 23-24, 59-60; Tojeira 1986, 227-29).[1]

Although the church's relations with the Honduran government had not been smooth and the fourteen-year stalemate with Carías over appointment of the archbishop was still a fresh memory, there had been no other direct church-state confrontations, and with the succession of Gálvez to the presidency, political leaders began to perceive the church as a "potential ally" against their mutual foe of communism. Thus, President Gálvez, without any publicity or fanfare, had begun to aid the church financially. Under these circumstances, it was unlikely that the church would differ radically in its reaction to the strike from President Gálvez, who had once been a lawyer for UFCO and who had strongly opposed perceived communist influences throughout the great strike (Tojeira 1986, 240; R. Cardenal 1974, 54).

Finally, another factor in the church's approach to the strike may have been that the clergy — especially those from the U.S. — enjoyed useful privileges offered by the fruit companies, such as free passage on their railroads and steamships. Consequently, the clergy, subconsciously perhaps, came to identify the banana corporations as benefactors. Sister Mary García recalls that when she was stationed in Olanchito the UFCO gratuitously provided the missionaries with all their gasoline. She also remembers traveling to the U.S. twice on banana company ships free of charge. Bishop Nicholas D'Antonio, then a parish priest, likewise recalls that the fruit companies transported his jeep, clothes, and medicines to Honduras at no cost (Interviews with Sister Mary García and Bishop Nicholas D'Antonio, New Orleans, July 9, 1986). Fr. Guadalupe Carney's recollections are especially telling:

> The priests in Progreso did not think it was so bad to be closely identified with the officials of the big Tela Railroad Company....Ever since their arrival in Progreso the Jesuits had been friends to the general manager and other American administrators who were sent to manage the enterprise in Honduras. The administrators had offices, big houses for their families, a golf course, swimming pool, and dance hall right in the center of Progreso, exclusively for them. Various Jesuits used to like to play golf and visit with these Americans and with the top officials who were Hondurans and who also lived in this "Company Zone" in Progreso. The Jesuits, visiting the different banana camps, used to eat and sleep in the big houses of the top administrators. We also received gifts of entire wooden buildings from the Tela to be taken apart and put in the villages as churches. The parish received all its gasoline free from the company, and even a monthly donation check.[2] (Carney 1985, 117)

Thus, the north coast banana workers, never attracted to the church to begin with, emerged from the strike with a heightened sense of anticlericalism. They perceived the church as part of the power structure — along with the U.S. fruit companies and the government — which was unsympathetic to their needs. Carney, who himself traveled free of charge to and from the United States on the Great White Fleet of the United Fruit Company in his early years in Honduras, recalls that "priests went around with the soldiers and with the officials of the Tela looking for the 'communist' leaders of the strike. Even though they paternalistically helped the workers with food during the sixty days that the strike lasted, some of the worker leaders accused the 'gringo' priests of being identified with the company owners and with the army against the strike." He adds what many of his fellow missionaries came to echo in the mid-1960s:

> What a mistake of the priests to identify themselves with the gringo owners instead of with the workers, for fear of "communism"!...The Church has lost the workers....It is true that Marxist propaganda fostered this, but the priests lost their golden opportunity to win over the workers when they did not back them up in the strike, and did not openly denounce the transnational banana company for its exploitation of the workers and repression of the incipient labor union.

Instead of preaching against the injustices of the U.S. company, they preached against the dangers of communist infiltration in the unions. So once again religion served (unconsciously, perhaps) to justify the repression of the workers, to support the capitalist system of exploitation. With good reason some of the labor leaders said that the gringo priests were bought off by the company. It is very compromising for the clergy to receive gifts from the rich, especially from the bosses of their worker parishioners. (Carney 1985, 117-18, 171)

The rapprochement between the church and the Honduran government continued to thrive under President Julio Lozano, who succeeded Gálvez, but the relationship became a bit strained after the 1957 election of the Liberal Ramón Villeda Morales. For one thing, the hierarchy became agitated over the inclusion of the word *laica* in the constitution of 1957 with regard to public education (White 1977, 212-13; Tojeira 1986, 227).

But more importantly, many churchmen perceived the new president as soft on communism, a charge that is unsubstantiated by the facts (Becerra 1982, 168-74). One priest, José Carranza, representing a large group of Catholic activists, actually confronted the Honduran leader publicly with this charge, using words reminiscent of Senator Joe McCarthy: "President Dr. Ramón Villeda Morales, I have here in my pocket the names of all the members of the Communist party in your government, and I am willing to give you the list....I ask that you take action immediately to dismiss these people from your government." Nevertheless, Villeda Morales and the clergy did cooperate fully in public ceremonies, and his administration offered the church some financial assistance (White 1977, 212, 214).

Fidel Castro's revolution in Cuba furthered Honduran fears of "atheistic communism" and, combined with the church's conviction that Villeda Morales was not militant enough against communism, gave impetus to an uncompromising anticommunist pastoral letter by the bishops on September 15, 1962. They warned that international communism "like a cancer...without remedy" threatened Honduras. Characterizing its subversive activities as "well nourished and directed from outside our boundaries," the bishops further cautioned that in a communist state, "the old, the sick and the useless are eliminated," and "children...are torn away from their parents at a tender age." Workers, students, and peasants were singled out as the preferred targets of communist propaganda. The bishops admonished the Honduran laborer not to listen to those who teach hatred, violence and sabotage, or who paint a glorious picture of Russia; and they exhorted students to beware of student impostors who were actually agents of the odious ideology. But the bishops reserved their most explicit warnings for the peasants. While they acknowledged that the majority of rural Hondurans did not even have enough land to satisfy their own families' needs and that a few greedy landowners were trying to extend their holdings, they cautioned that the Communists would try to exploit this situation to encourage peasants to seize land violently and illegally. They called on "our campesinos to remember that usurpation is never a legitimate title of natural possession. For there exists the right to ownership whose violation is forbidden by the seventh commandment." They instructed the peasants to resist those who urged them to violence or forceful occupation of the land. The bishops were also suspicious of Villeda Morales's agrarian reform law. While they supported it insofar as it reflected divine and natural law, they noted that the complexities of the land problem had been overlooked and that in the long run the peasant may simply become a tenant of another proprietor — the state: "The Church condemns, in this regard, every collective system that smacks of communism" (CENSA 1962).[3]

Communism, however, was not the only threat the Honduran Catholic Church faced, for U.S.-based Protestantism was also making inroads there. By 1957 there were about 355 Protestant missionaries in the country, more than twice the number of Catholic priests. Although the number of Protestant converts was insignificant, the Catholic clergy resented their virtually unlimited financial resources that were in large part being used to serve the needs of the lower classes through schools and medical clinics. Such social service made the negligence of the Catholic Church in this area most glaring (White 1977, 206). The bishops were also irritated that Villeda Morales, in true Liberal fashion, treated these Protestants with the same graciousness he bestowed on the Catholic church (R. Cardenal 1974, 54).

Thus, Catholic leaders concluded that in order to counteract the still small, but growing, influence of communism, and, to a lesser degree, Protestantism, before they became serious competitors, they would have to become more aggressive, more committed to the needs of Hondurans. Perhaps more important, the church realized that it had become a near nonentity in Honduran society. With the post-World War II social and technological developments in the country, the church was rapidly becoming anachronistic. It was being viewed as an irrelevancy, a part of the past with little if any significance in modern society. The Honduran elite, long wedded to the dogmas of Liberalism, was consumed with transforming the economy into the modern agro-export type that had already been created in much of the rest of Central America. At best they tolerated the church as they would a doting grandfather. Intellectuals, students, and labor leaders, for their part, had long placed no faith in the church, but many of them were now becoming infatuated with Marxism and saw the Cuban revolution as the model for the future. Only in the rural areas did the people still feel some sense of identification with Catholicism, albeit more often than not they practiced a religion steeped in superstition and folklore. But even here the church was beginning to face a Protestant challenge.

Behind the new, revitalized leadership of Héctor Santos, soon to become archbishop, and with an influx of foreign priests and nuns equipped with valuable material resources from North America and Europe, the church began a process of resurrecting itself. In May 1961 the *Comité Coordinador de Organizaciones Democráticas de Honduras* (CORDEH) was formed to promote democracy based on Christian values; but in its early years such promotion consisted of exposing the "evils of communism." Two years later, however, when lawyer-economist Fernando Montes became its director,

CORDEH de-emphasized its anticommunist orientation and became a support structure for the new Christian social movement. At the Universidad Nacional, CORDEH captured control of the United Democratic University Front (FUUD), a student political group. Soon, under the able leadership of John Fisher, a U.S. Jesuit, FUUD members were introduced to the ideology of the Christian Democratic party (PDC). Eventually, Fisher's group formed a new student political organization, the *Frente Revolucionario Estudiantil Social Cristiano* (FRESC), whose members soon began to spread the ideology of the PDC to campesino groups (White 1977, 208, 246-47; Tojeira 1986, 214-15). This, in turn, led to formation in early 1964 of the *Asociacíon Campesina Social Cristiana de Honduras*, which would later evolve into the important *Unión Nacional de Campesinos* (UNC) in 1970 (Posas 1981a, 16-18).

According to Guadalupe Carney, Fisher "was one of the two priests whose work did most to cause the rejuvenation of the Catholic Church in Honduras that was so notable in the decade 1965-75." When Fisher went to Venezuela for a short course on Christian social doctrine, Carney recalls, he brought back to Honduras a team of Venezuelans, who gave the same course to the group of Catholic students that Fisher had formed. Fisher and his group started giving this class to many other Hondurans. Carney took the course in 1964, practically his "first introduction to an economic-social analysis of the Honduran reality (although it was not a revolutionary, but a reformist analysis)." These Venezuelan Christian Democrats later interested Fisher's group in organizing a Christian Democratic party in Honduras (PDCH) (Carney 1985, 125-26).

The church also attempted to make inroads in the rural communities and eventually its work there would intertwine with that of the PDCH-oriented activities of the urban-centered followers of Fisher and Montes. Evelio Domínguez, prior to being named auxiliary bishop of Tegucigalpa in 1957, introduced the *Caballeros de Cristo Rey*, a lay organization, into his parish. Soon the movement spread throughout south-central Honduras. In the 1950s the French-Canadian clergy formed the Apostleship of Prayer in southern Honduras, while the secular clergy did likewise in the west. Meanwhile, the Jesuits in Yoro and the Franciscans in their jurisdictions began the Legion of Mary. These associations basically had the same goals: the moral conversion of the campesinos, their instruction in the Catholic faith, and their attendance at weekly prayer services. Members were to bring others to conversion and fill in for the priest when there was none available (Carney 1985, 133-34; White 1977, 230-32; R. Cardenal 1974, 71-72; Tojeira 1986, 211).

The church went much further, however, in reaching out to the peasants. At the instigation of Bishop Domínguez, it created *Radio Católica* in 1959 and the following year launched a radio school program. With Domínguez as its driving force, by 1964 it was serving 14,624 students. The radio schools taught the campesinos reading, writing, arithmetic, health care, agriculture, and religion. Each community had a monitor who was trained to supervise the classes and recruit students. Monitors were provided with radios and classes were often held at their homes. Texts, notebooks, and pencils were provided to the students at no cost. At the end of the year the pupils took an examination that was brought to the central office and was graded on a pass-fail basis. The French-Canadian and U.S. missionaries were especially enthusiastic about the radio schools. They encouraged their parishioners to join the program and allowed their parish buildings to be used as administrative centers. For their part, members of the *Caballeros de Cristo Rey*, the Apostleship of Prayer, and the Legion of Mary provided lay leadership for the program (R. Cardenal 1974, 5, 50, 64; White 1977, 234-38; Carney 1985, 196-97).

Since the church lacked the financial resources to cover the cost of the expanding radio schools, they were placed under the *Acción Cultural Popular Hondureña* (ACPH), an urban-based nonprofit group with connections needed to get funds from governmental and private sources. At first the Honduran government supported the church's new social involvement, so much so that in 1963, at the urging of President Villeda Morales, the national congress voted unanimously to provide 30,000 *lempiras* annually to the radio schools (White 1977, 241). But even prior to this, the government was beginning to view the new religious organizations and projects with suspicion. The successful participation of the *Caballeros* and other popular lay groups in the radio school program produced a new sense of pride and optimism in the campesinos. With the enthusiastic support of their priests, local improvement projects were undertaken and an emphasis was placed on developing social awareness.

This new attitude of the rural poor almost immediately created opposition from the local political elites, who saw the campesino leaders as a threat to their own power. Accusing members of the peasant organizations and their clerical supporters of being Communists (and sometimes even Protestants), they bitterly complained to the national government and the church hierarchy. Confronted by such hostility, peasant leaders searched for a political ideology that would be meaningful to them, while also allowing them independence from the traditional party structures. They found it in the incipient Christian Democratic ideology which had come to dominate the thinking of FRESC and CORDEH. Soon CORDEH was offering courses in rural parishes in which the precepts of Christian social democracy were taught; by 1964 agrarian associations were being formed (White 1977, 231, n. 12).

As early as 1963 the traditional Liberal and National Parties began to move against the PDCH-oriented peasant movement and its affiliates in Tegucigalpa. Rodolfo Cardenal's description of persecution of the *Caballeros de Cristo Rey* applies as well to the other campesino religious organizations:

> The government of Dr. Ramón Villeda Morales was fearful when it saw the strength that this organization [*Caballeros*] had. The *comandantes* began to see the churches full of men and the enthusiastic attendance at gatherings....They became aware that this was a powerful threat. They jailed some of the leaders of the *Caballeros de Cristo Rey* accused of listening to Radio Havana and possessing communist propaganda. Bishop Domínguez had to stand up for them on repeated occasions so that they

would not be molested. During this period, Bishop Domínguez was alone; he did not find support in the hierarchy or in the clergy. No one wanted to collaborate closely with him, fearing the consequences that organizing the peasantry would draw. (R. Cardenal 1974, 72; Tojeira 1986, 211)

This vacillation of the bishops and clergy explains why in 1964, when leaders of the Liberal and Nationalist parties complained to Archbishop Santos of the activities of Fr. John Fisher, accusing him of teaching communism, the archbishop forbade Fisher to continue his work at the university (Carney 1985, 126). Such complaints were also in part responsible for Santos' removal of French-Canadian Fr. Pablo Guillet as director of the radio schools (White 1977, 270).

Thus the new social awareness which the Honduran church had done so much to foster was by 1964 opposed by the country's traditional power structure. Consequently, with the notable exception of Bishop Domínguez, the Catholic hierarchy and much of the clergy began to backtrack. Perhaps the "anti-communist" church would have divorced itself completely from the "monster" it had created had it not been for a monumental development in the international Catholic Church, namely the Second Vatican Council (1962-1965).

In 1959 Pope John XXIII (1958-1963) announced plans for a general council to renew and modernize the Catholic church. His two encyclicals, *Mater et Magistra* (1961) and *Pacem in Terris* (1963), set the tone by calling on the well-nourished to feed the hungry of the world, while warning against colonialism and new forms of imperialism. From a third world perspective, the most important document of the council was *Gaudium et Spes*. In no uncertain terms it condemned the hoarding of wealth and power for the benefit of a small segment of society. It further stipulated that everyone is entitled to the basic necessities of life. Therefore, if an individual is in extreme need, he or she is morally justified in taking from the excessive wealth of others. Perhaps as important as its contents, *Gaudium et Spes* introduced a radically new methodology to Catholic theologians. As Edward Cleary notes, "Instead of proceeding in the time-honored fashion, discussing theological or biblical principles and then applying them to a present-day situation, *Gaudium et Spes* reverses the process: it begins with a careful analysis of the *de facto* situation, then turns to sacred scripture and theology for reflecting on that situation, and finally, as a third step, makes pastoral applications. Theological reflection thus becomes the second, not the first, step" (Cleary 1985, 59-61; Brett & Brett 1988). Moreover, *Gaudium et Spes* went beyond the traditional philosophical and theological approach, employing the social and behavioral sciences.

The Honduran bishops, like the Latin American hierarchy in general, did not play a leading role in Vatican II. They did learn much from it, however, and returned to their dioceses with a new awareness of the Christian commitment to social justice. Bishop Nicholas D'Antonio, a North American who was appointed to head the Olancho prelacy in 1963 after nearly two decades of work in Honduras, recalls how the council affected him:

I administered the Sacrament of Confirmation mostly to large numbers of baptized infants. This was my pastoral duty and, at the time, it satisfied me that I was doing something. Then came the invitation by the Holy See for me to attend the second half of Vatican II Council (1964-1965). I found myself in St. Peter's Basilica in a totally new world....When I got back to my Prelacy after my first session at Vatican II, I found trouble. A group of my best laymen were in jail accused of Communism....Because of my authority and personal friendship with the Military Major, I was able to convince him that these men were in no way Communist agitators. He freed them, but fined each $7.50! This was my first serious encounter with military authority.

In 1965, I was back at Vatican II Council and this time much more alert as to what was happening around me. I returned to my Prelacy determined to put into practice what the Holy Spirit wanted of the Catholic Church, a house-cleaning, an up-dating. This meant no more triumphalism...and an open door for the involvement of [lay]men and women in the building up of the Body of Christ, the People of God....

To begin with, I got rid of the episcopal throne in the Cathedral and stepped down to become one among equals....I invited my clergy to study together the Vatican II documents, in order to learn how to set up a Pastoral program. (D'Antonio n.d., 1-3)

A Latin American Conference of Bishops at Medellín, Colombia, in 1968 began to implement the results of Vatican II. Using the methodology of *Gaudium et Spes*, it changed the direction of the Latin American church from one involved at least indirectly with the power structure to one that sided with the poor and oppressed. As Cleary explains:

The final document would say, in brief, that the church is a sinful church in a sinful (unjust) society, one marked by structured inequalities. Latin America, it went on, is a region suffering from two massive evils: external dominance and internal colonialism. Change was obviously called for and the church wished to take part in the change. The church chose the side of the poor. It must reach out to them, and to the whole continent. This would be accomplished through evangelization and lay participation(*pastoral de conjunto*) from which grassroots communities (*comunidades de base*) would emerge. (Cleary 1985, 42)

Medellín's impact on the Honduran hierarchy and clergy was immediately apparent. On January 13, 1969, the Episcopal Conference issued a press release, in which they outlined numerous projects and tasks for the Honduran church: the work of the radio schools would be intensified; laypeople would be trained as community leaders in *institutos para la capacitación*; courses in individual and social awareness would be offered; and a Commission of Justice and Peace would be formed. Moreover, the church would foster and continue the attempts it had already made to reach out to the Honduran people by encouraging lay participation in church work and by "giving official, united support to the active minorities (union and cooperative leaders, etc.)." In general, the church's task would be "to denounce with energy and prudence at the same time, the injustices and abuses of power; to defend firmly the rights of the human person" (Tojeira 1986, 215).

In fact, between Vatican II and Medellín, the Honduran church had already made great strides in committing itself to the poor. In 1965 Honduras became the first Central American country to make use of an innovative form of liturgy, when the Celebration of the Word was inaugurated in the prelacy of Choluteca and, to a lesser extent, in Yoro. The celebration was a Sunday religious service led by a church-trained lay delegate of the Word (Carney 1985, 164-65; Alvarez 1986). By 1971 there were more than five thousand delegates in Honduras, alleviating the acute shortage of priests. But the delegates did more than just lead Sunday liturgical services; they also spearheaded the formation of the Christian base community. Delegates organized small groups of campesinos for Bible study and prayer. Biblical passages would be read and the group would reflect on them, relating them to the actualities of their own everyday lives. In this manner the campesinos in the *comunidades de base* went through a process of consciousness-raising.

But the renovation of the Honduran church after Vatican II went much further. In 1966 Fernando Montes became director of ACPH, the board in charge of the radio schools. He quickly convinced Bishop Marcelo Gerin to recall Padre Guillet, who had been dismissed from his radio school position in 1964. Benefiting from the open atmosphere generated by Vatican II, Guillet opened the La Colmena leadership training center in Choluteca in 1967. The following year, Montes hired a North American nun, Sor Crista, to set up an ACPH-directed department to promote the much heralded consciousness-raising methods of Paulo Freire. Trained in these techniques, the staff of La Colmena taught potential campesino leaders how to analyze the problems of their local areas and organize their fellow peasants for change. So successful was La Colmena that Montes easily convinced other bishops to allow him to set up similar centers throughout Honduras. By 1969 centers were also functioning in Olancho, Yoro, Santa Barbara, Comayagua, Santa Rosa de Copán, and Ocotepeque. Meanwhile, in 1967 Archbishop Santos appointed Padre Guillermo Arsenault, a French-Canadian, to establish a Honduran branch of the International Confederation of Catholic Organizations for Charitable and Social Action (CARITAS). He and his staff, however, resolved to make CARITAS more than a dispenser of food to the needy; they saw its primary goal as changing the unjust structures in Honduran society that cause poverty. The church also helped set up rural credit unions, cooperatives, and women's organizations (White 1977, 277-83).

Thus, by 1970 the church in Honduras had developed a highly successful program of social action, which could have served as a model for other third world nations. The social commitment of the hierarchy and clergy had come a long way since the early 1960s. The profound influences of Vatican II and Medellín are immediately obvious in the bishops' pastoral of January 8, 1970. The contrast between this more sophisticated and compassionate analysis of campesino struggles and the bishops' agitated letter of 1962 that focused on the imminent threat of communism is remarkable. In the 1970 letter, the hierarchy recognizes that there are two sides to the agrarian problem: on the one hand, some landholders are greedily exploiting and hoarding land, while on the other, some campesinos are violating private property in land occupations. But the bishops' sympathy for the campesinos who live in "conditions of poverty and misery" is strong. Quoting Popes John XXIII and Paul VI and the documents produced by the Medellín conference, the letter emphasizes the yearning of the campesino for "adequate shelter, medical attention, educational opportunities for his children, land from which to live and, above all...to see himself really integrated into the progress and development of our society."

Aware of the fact that there has been some violence on the part of campesinos, the letter also points out that the peasants' search for ways out of their state of marginalization and their frustration at inadequate application of land reform laws are often to blame for their excesses. Nowhere can there be found the previous clarion call to campesinos to be wary of those who would organize them to demand their rights lest they be caught in the snares of communism. Instead, the bishops insist on the campesinos' right to unite and organize, to express themselves and to make collective decisions about their future. When the bishops do find it necessary to offer some prophetic advice, it is directed no only to campesinos, but also to political leaders and the elite. Campesinos are warned to avoid violence for it simply generates new injustices and misery; whereas the powerful in Honduran society are admonished not to fear the campesino associations, or worse yet, keep them from organizing, for "repression — whether obvious or veiled — would retard the process of change, but will not impede it."

On the touchy subject of campesino occupation of unproductive land (land recuperations), which the bishops had strongly opposed in 1962, there is now a different emphasis. Citing various ecclesiastical texts, the letter maintains that private property, a God-given right, is not meant to be monopolized by the few, no matter how much this is sanctioned by law, since this is actually a contradiction of the natural right of all social classes to own property — a right which must be extended to those that do not now enjoy it. The bishops still maintain that the church in no way "is able to sponsor the invasions of land and illegal attempts against property as a normal means for solving the problem of our peasantry"; nevertheless, they recognize that "if the [agrarian] problem is not attended to fully and with great sincerity [by the state], very serious conflicts of violence can arise" (CEH 1970b, 3-10). Thus, not only the influence of Vatican II and Medellín, but also the Honduran clergy's immersion in campesino life during the 1960s is evident in the sympathetic tone of this pastoral letter.

While the church involved itself in rural social activism in the 1960s, an unforeseen socioeconomic change was taking place in the countryside that would affect the church immensely. Before 1960 there was no serious land shortage in Honduras, but the growing international market for certain agricultural products encouraged expansion of agro-exports. Consequently, owners of large commercial estates began to absorb the *ejido* (communal) and public lands around them. *Ejido* land declined by 39 percent between 1952 and 1965. Large estates often extended their boundaries simply by enclosing common land, thereby denying *ejido* members access to land their families had worked for generations (Volk 1981, 13-14).

What especially upset the peasant leaders was that a 1962 agrarian reform law had promised to take unproductive public lands and turn them over to campesinos. The government had even established a National Agrarian Institute (INA) to supervise land reform. Government neglect of the agrarian reform law infuriated the peasants; instead of getting land as promised, they were actually losing much of what they had. But now, unlike in the past, the campesinos were no longer passive when confronted by the power structure, their consciousness having been raised in large part by the various church-related programs. Equally important, because of the shortage of priests, the church's social projects had passed from clerical control into the hands of competent lay leaders. Whereas the clergy had tended toward moderation and steered clear of politics, the church lay leaders had a well-defined social ideology based on the tenets of the Christian Democratic movement. Faced with what they perceived to be an unjust land situation, they had no qualms about organizing the campesinos to fight back. In August 1969, backed by the staff at La Colmena, six hundred peasant men and women who had been evicted from public or *ejido* lands in Choluteca, occupied land in the Namasigue area. Other peasants began similar occupations. Many of the leaders of the land recuperations, as the campesinos called them, were Delegates of the Word who had been organized by the Christian Democratic-oriented National Federation of Farm Workers (FENTCH), which in April 1970 would become the National Campesino Union (UNC).

Furious at the audacity of the long docile peasants, the large landowners of Choluteca accused the clergy of instigating the land "seizures" (the term they preferred to use). But in reality most of the rural clergy actually had reservations about such "radical" actions and a few conservative priests even openly condemned them. As the situation became more tense, both the campesino leaders and the large landowners demanded that Bishop Gerin and the clergy take a stand. Finally, in December 1969 Bishop Gerin publicly declared that in cases of extreme necessity the landless campesinos had the right to occupy national or *ejido* lands. Going further, he accused the large landowners of caring more for their cattle than for the rural poor (White 1977, 288).

By the early 1970s, the UNC had spread to the isolated department of Olancho and gained the sympathy of its bishop, Nicholas D'Antonio. The way had been paved for the union by D'Antonio's commitment to "human promotion." Using La Colmena as a model, in 1969 he had converted a school building into a *centro de capacitación*, in which peasants learned everything from farming and nursing to the church's social doctrine, and organized themselves into cooperatives, radio schools, and Bible circles. As in other rural areas of Honduras, the educational projects combined community development with spiritual enrichment and consciousness-raising. Although wealthy ranchers in the area had also been invited to participate in program discussions, the bishop was aware of their antagonism to the church's efforts from the outset: "Some would visit our Center only to look for slogans or other material and quote them out of context. Soon we were labeled Communists and foreign agitators. Threats were made against our lives, especially 'yours truly' and I earned two nice titles, 'The Mad Communist Bishop' and 'The Hangman of Olancho'" (D'Antonio n.d., 4-5). Not only the bishop, but priests and campesino leaders in Olancho were subjected to rumors, threats of assassination, public denunciations, and investigations because of their efforts in human promotion. Thus, when the campesinos, their consciousness awakened by the church in Olancho, began to organize themselves into the UNC, they were met with ready-made hostility from the elite landowners. In 1972 this hostility erupted into bloodshed on a piece of land called *La Talanquera* (Henao 1972).

On February 15, 1972, the local director of the INA, supported by Honduran land reform laws, gave the go-ahead to a group of organized campesinos to occupy *La Talanquera*. Bishop D'Antonio, who calls the INA official "an opportunist who attempted to please both the rich and the poor," describes the mayhem that ensued:

> Euphoric with the good news, forty adult men, with their wives and children, settled themselves in the area and immediately began to prepare the soil for planting in time for the rainy season....The "owner" of La Talanquera complained to the police...and prevailed upon the [local] director of the INA to petition soldiers from the capital to get the "invaders" off the property. The troops arrived, 95 men strong, armed with automatic weapons. On February 18, at 2 P.M., shots were heard; six campesinos were brutally murdered while their companions, wives and children scattered in panic to save their lives and lost themselves in the wooded mountains. Four others were seriously injured and two taken prisoner after a cruel beating.

One sergeant was also killed, apparently shot in the back by one of his own men. Bishop D'Antonio's deacon, Luis Henao, wrote a long description of the atrocity, which was published in one of the nation's principal newspapers along with D'Antonio's authenticating signature (D'Antonio n.d., 6-7; Henao 1972).

Henao's public denunciation of the events caused a furor all over Honduras. Most Hondurans were outraged by the massacre, but a national association of landowners and cattlemen began a media attack on the bishop, claiming that he had promoted land "invasions" and was the source of the conflict. D'Antonio denied that he had in any way supported the occupation, but acknowledged that he had not "openly condemned the invasions," since he had been told by the leaders of the campesinos and the office of the INA that the land "recuperations" were legal. "The law was plain," he insisted. "If property wasn't serving a social function and the owner could not prove his legal right to it, then the peasants could take it" (D'Antonio n.d., 9).

Seeing one of their bishops caught in the vortex of controversy, the *Consejo Presbiterial*, which included Archbishop Santos, Bishop Domínguez, and eleven priests, issued a powerful declaration of support for D'Antonio. They emphasized the responsibility of the church for protection of the poor and denounced the "wave of calumnies and lies against the evangelizing action of the Church" that the Olancho bloodshed had unleashed. The document revealed the revolution that had occurred since Vatican II in the thinking of the Honduran clergy as it committed itself "to the integral liberation of man here on earth." Since "the Christian message of love and justice has to manifest itself concretely in the action of the Church to help sow justice in the world,...the Church has the right, even more, the duty, to proclaim justice in the social, national, and international fields as well as to denounce the situations of injustice," and, therefore, the Honduran church had "committed itself...to the search for the full liberation of the Honduran man....Its *centros de capacitación*, whether [in Olancho or elsewhere], have not been centers of 'subversion,'...but centers of consciousness awakening, which have helped the Honduran peasant become aware of his dignity as a man and as a person." In closing, the council implored that "our brother priests of Olancho and their bishop Nicholas D'Antonio, who find themselves actually nailed with Christ on the cross of suffering for love of their brothers, receive our unconditional support in the present circumstances, since for us they are not 'foreigners' but beloved brothers in the struggle for the complete liberation of mankind" (Amador 1975, 43-47).

The letter from the *Consejo Presbiterial* was perhaps the most outspoken defense of the oppressed campesino ever produced by the Honduran church. Yet even before it was issued, bishops and priests had begun to separate themselves from the activist peasant organizations, though they may still have sympathized with their cause. This disassociation was apparent in both Choluteca and Olancho. After Bishop Gerin's December 1969 statement in support of campesino land recuperations, the rural elite had reacted with a scurrilous radio and newspaper campaign against the "foreign clergy." In October 1970, a bill was even introduced into the national congress demanding that all French-Canadian missionaries be deported. Although the bill failed, it caused all foreign churchpeople in Honduras to come to terms with the tenuous nature of their position. Their insecurity was intensified further when the head of the Nationalist party accused French-Canadian "foreigners" of meddling in Honduran politics by supporting the Christian Democratic party and threatened to force them out of the country if they continued their "political" involvement. Concluding that all their missionary accomplishments would be eradicated if they were deported, they began to back off in their public support of land occupations (White 1977, 288-89).

D'Antonio himself took measures to curb the excessive political zeal of his lay workers, acknowledging that "some of the leaders began to place too much emphasis on the social aspect, so that prayer and especially the Eucharist were not always given their proper place." He therefore "had to exhort these well-intentioned men not to instrumentalize the parish centers and pastoral movements to gain followers for partisan purposes." He likewise pointed out that the church hierarchy could in no way favor a particular political party. To prevent the Olanchan church from seeming to give this false image, he symbolically sold the *centro de capacitación* to the workers' organization, so that they could better manage their own affairs and be free to join the party of their choice (D'Antonio n.d., 9).

Various statements of the hierarchy reflect the church's more defensive stance. As early as January 1, 1970, Archbishop Santos felt compelled to deny that the church was using its religious associations for political ends (CEH 1970a). On a less public level, however, innuendoes and accusations directed against the church were beginning to take their toll and precipitated intense internal debate among bishops and clergy. The discussions focused on the church's ties with incipient Christian Democracy, the proliferation of community development projects in which the church was involved, and whether the church was neglecting its spiritual mission (Tojeira 1986, 219-20).

In October 1971, the bishops called on those laypeople who were fostering the development of a political party from their executive posts within church-affiliated organizations "in the name of God" to renounce their positions (CEH 1971). These concerns took a back seat in the immediate aftermath of the massacre at *La Talanquera*, but within two months, the Episcopal Conference was again compelled to defend itself: "The Church is not the incubator, nor the sponsor, of any political party, specifically of Christian Democracy" (CEH 1972). That accusations of subversion and tensions over the church's social commitment were on the rise is evident from the fact that the bishops found it necessary to state at this time that the church had not allied itself to communism — an ironic turnabout, considering that only a decade earlier the hierarchy had been denouncing civil authorities for not attacking that dreaded "cancer" fiercely enough. Finally, in April 1974 the church withdrew all its organizations from the Council for Coordination of Development (CONCORDE), a national association of Christian activist groups that had been formed in 1971 and was controlled by Christian Democrats. The church was therefore well on its way to disassociating itself from more than a decade of intense social commitment, when its most fearful nightmare became a reality at a ranch called *Los Horcones* in Olancho (White 1977, 296).

On June 25, 1975, the UNC with the backing of the PDCH planned a nationwide "hunger march" on Tegucigalpa to protest governmental delay in implementing the land reform law. In Juticalpa, Olancho, the marchers set out in the morning and were halted a few hours later by the military; no one was injured. But back in Juticalpa several hours after the marchers had left, soldiers in league with large landowners broke into the *Instituto de 18 Febrero*, the peasants' *centro de capacitación*, where they murdered five campesinos and arrested several others. Later five who had been taken prisoner, along with two women and two priests — the Colombian Iván Betancur and American Casimir Cypher — were viciously tortured, executed, and buried in a well on *Los Horcones* ranch, owned by Manuel Zelaya, one of the largest landowners in the department. Plans had been made to kill Bishop D'Antonio and his residence was ransacked. He survived because he had left the country a few days earlier to attend a church conference in the U.S. Union members and clergy in other parts of the country were also attacked but none were killed. Marchers from northern and western Honduras were stopped by soldiers; their march ended when their leaders were beaten and arrested. The Jesuit *La Fragua centro de capacitación* in El Progreso was ravaged and Fr. Stephen Gross was arrested; those in the *Centro Loyola* in Tegucigalpa were also harassed as were those in the French-Canadian centers in Choluteca. Scores of foreign priests and nuns, including all the foreigners in Olancho, were arrested and brought to Tegucigalpa to await deportation, but were released after a vehement outcry from university students, churchpeople, and various organizations throughout the country and abroad (Becerra 1982, 207-8; Tojeira 1986, 245-51; D'Antonio n.d., 14-20; Maurer 1976, 266-69; Meza 1982, 39-47, 83-85; interviews with Sister Mary García, New Orleans, Mar. 14, 1984, and July 9, 1986; interview with Nicholas D'Antonio, New Orleans, July 9, 1986; Brett & Brett 1988).

Although initial ecclesiastical reaction to the Olancho horrors was outspoken and firmly on the side of the "most abandoned and oppressed," this massacre represents a major turning point in the recent history of the Honduran church, for since then the Honduran Bishops' Conference has attempted to depoliticize its activities as much as possible and has severed its relationship with many of the rural development programs. Except for the efforts of a few priests, the focus has returned to pastoral activities (CEH 1975a, 1975b; White 1977, 297).

In September the government allowed the missionaries to return to Olancho. Thirteen priests, twelve of them foreigners, did so, along with close to twenty nuns. The Vatican decided that Bishop D'Antonio should stay out of the country until tensions eased. Within a short time, only two elderly priests remained in the prelacy. D'Antonio was reassigned to the archdiocese of New Orleans where he remains today, along with Sister Mary García and Fr. Luis Henao. Several priests and nuns eventually left because they feared for their safety. In 1983 Padre Bernard Boulang was expelled from the country after being accused of guerrilla activities, a charge he hotly denied (Bacigalupo 1980, 404; Mission Letter 1986, 1; CDH 1985). Several missionaries, like Fr. Richard Preston, quit their posts out of frustration when the hierarchy forced them to abandon all work which might be construed as social activism (Preston, telephone interview, May 1986).

In 1984 Maurice Muldoon, a U.S. Franciscan, became bishop of Olancho. Probably the most conservative current member of the Honduran episcopacy, he refuses to tolerate anything but pastoral work from his clergy. When drunken soldiers murdered several peasants in Campamento, for instance, two friars attempted to get his support in demanding that the murderers be arrested, but he refused to "get involved" (Interview with Fr. Ron Roll, Comayagüela, Honduras, Aug. 1986). Moreover, when Bishop D'Antonio returned to Juticalpa in 1984 for a brief visit, he was not permitted by Muldoon to preach at mass (Interviews with several priests and nuns who wish to remain anonymous, confirmed in interview with D'Antonio, July 9, 1986). *Los Horcones*, according to Honduran Bishop Luis Santos, was most important because it intimidated the clergy and prevented those who remained from continuing their social work effectively. "It didn't really matter to them if they killed any particular priests," he said in 1984, "They killed the priests in hate to repress the church, to make them an example." The result was that the "cooperatives and humanitarian promotion work and social service work done by the church...all stopped." In Santos' view, "There was a close relation between the church and the Christian Democratic party in social promotion work; they were very involved in Olancho....It is clear that what happened in Olancho was a defense of the rights of the landlords and cattle ranchers against the work of the church with the peasants" (Street & Peckenham 1984, 6-8).

The Olancho murders also affected the rest of the Honduran church. Carney testified that the Catholic hierarchy and the majority of the priests and laymen in Honduras "retreated from any social commitment and became non-political and very anti-communist." Following the lead of their bishop, "many Canadian priests of the departments of Choluteca and Valle drew back from the line of liberation theology and of helping the popular organizations" (Carney 1985, 347). Several foreign priests and nuns in Tegucigalpa and Comayagüela indicated that after 1975 many missionaries hesitated to involve themselves more forcefully in social activism because to do so might mean deportation. They concluded that it was better to stay in Honduras even if it meant laboring under severe restrictions (Interviews with three nuns and four priests, Tegucigalpa, Aug. 1986).

From the above it would seem easy to dismiss the church's withdrawal from activism as resulting from their fear of the Honduran power structure. To a degree, this is probably true. But the full reality of the situation is far more complex and cannot be understood without reference to a new player on the Honduran scene: Protestant fundamentalism. Prior to 1970 there were about twenty Protestant sects in Honduras; by mid-1980 there were more than fifty. Most of these were evangelical, fundamentalist, or Pentecostal, and often millennarian. Their successful proselytizing has been viewed with alarm and a certain frustration by the Catholic clergy and religious. Accustomed to working with mainline Protestant groups ever since Vatican II, churchpeople in Honduras have on occasion attempted to collaborate with the new sects in the slums of Tegucigalpa, only to find cooperation impossible in the face of unveiled anti-Catholicism. Among other things, many of the fundamentalist sects accuse the Catholics of idolizing images of the Virgin and saints and identify the pope — and Catholicism in general — with the beast of the Apocalypse. For their part, the Catholic clergy and religious give grudging credit to the Protestants' ability to pack their churches, but criticize them for taking advantage of Hondurans' poverty by using material assistance to attract converts ([Tojeira] 1985, 179-92; interview with Franciscan sisters, Colonia San Francisco, Comayagüela, Aug. 1986).[4]

But differences between Protestant fundamentalists and Catholics extend beyond the realm of religious beliefs and practices. Often financed from bases in California and the Bible Belt, most Protestant sects are politically conservative and support U.S. military involvement in Central America because it is "anticommunist." In fact, they view Catholicism and communism as their main enemies in the region, often equating the two. Emphasizing personal salvation above all, they are deeply critical of social activism and do not hesitate to point out that the Catholic Church has a propensity for "mixing itself up with politics." Because of their anticommunism and refusal to denounce social injustices, the fundamentalists have been favored by the Honduran government, particularly in the tense area bordering El Salvador where refugees have gathered. According to Jesuit José Tojeira, "while Catholic priests have encountered difficulties just visiting their parishioners, some new sects have a clear, open road for building their chapels or setting up children's food centers in the most isolated border towns." Nor are they limited to aiding the refugees, for they disseminate an ideology that is more than religious. It is, in fact, obviously political ([Tojeira] 1985, 185-86; CNP 1982, 5, 16-17).

At a pastoral conference in October 1982, devoted entirely to the Protestant challenge to the Catholic Church, the report of the diocese of Choluteca includes a reference to the sects' political implications in Honduras: "There is no doubt that this Protestant advance is well planned on the Central America level and that it is responding to the preoccupation of various North American business leaders with neutralizing the influence of a Catholic church that is committed to and is raising the consciousness of the people." Whether or not this is true is debatable, but it is significant that such a perception holds sway among Catholic churchpeople in Honduras. The report of the prelacy of Olancho, where so much conflict and repression occurred, is especially revealing. In response to the question, "What is the attitude of the Protestant fundamentalists toward the Catholic church?" the report states:

— They say that the priests are responsible for the land invasions.
— They say that in the Catholic church there is more talk about material welfare than spiritual.
— They say that they [the Protestants] do not have problems with the authorities. The head of the DIN [security police] in Catacamas confirmed...that Protestant pastors have denounced priests and Delegates of the Word [to him].
— The Protestants take advantage of the fact that the Church of Olancho was persecuted.

With regard to the content of the fundamentalist sermons, the report continues: "They prohibit the faithful from participating in the popular organizations....They do not like to participate in community efforts." And finally, the report states that one reason some Catholics in Olancho convert to Protestantism is that "no Protestant sect is persecuted as much by the authorities as the Catholic religion" (CNP 1982, 14-18).

The influx of fundamentalist Protestants into Honduras placed the Catholic Church in a dilemma. The perpetual scarcity of clergy had always hindered its ability to serve the populace in spiritual matters. Now it faced conservative religious adversaries who depicted priests as diabolical and communist. Since around 80 percent of the Catholic clergy and nuns were foreigners, they risked expulsion if they acted in ways that the government perceived as "political." Already hard pressed to compete with the well-financed and "politically acceptable" fundamentalists, the Catholic Church must have felt the field would be wide open to these rivals if the governmental authorities made good on their threat to deport foreign clergy. Faced with the growth of fundamentalism on one hand and governmental repression on the other, the episcopacy felt it had no choice. Priests and nuns were henceforth to restrict themselves to pastoral concerns.

Priests who felt such limitations were intolerable usually left the country, but a few stayed and continued their activism. Guadalupe Carney was one of these and, although he had become a naturalized Honduran citizen, in 1979 he was arrested without being criminally charged and deported. Such action was illegal, but Archbishop Santos chose not to risk the wrath of the power structure by bringing the matter to the courts (Carney 1985, 423).[5]

The Catholic Church continued this quietist approach until mid-1980. Then, on May 14, the heinous Río Sumpul massacre of Salvadoran refugees occurred. When Padre Fausto Milla, a priest in this remote and inaccessible area, publicly denounced the massacre, a spokesman for the Organization of American States replied that he had "no knowledge" of such an occurrence. This prompted Bishop Carranza—the same churchman who had earlier charged Villeda Morales with having Communists in his government—and thirty-eight priests and religious of his diocese to issue the following pronouncement on June 19:

> Since last January a large number of Salvadorans, mostly women, children, and old people, have sought refuge in our country. The Salvadoran Guard has systematically harassed them as they flee.
>
> An outstanding example of harassment and cruelty occurred on May 14, 1980. The previous day, trucks and other vehicles filled with soldiers from the Honduran army arrived in Guarita....They continued...to the Sumpul River, the frontier between Honduras and El Salvador. They cordoned off the left bank....
>
> At about 7 a.m. on May 14, the massacre began in the Salvadoran village of La Arada. Two helicopters, the [Salvadoran] National Guard, soldiers and men from ORDEN began firing at the defenseless people. Women were tortured before being killed; babies were tossed into the air for target practice. Those people lucky enough to cross the river were met by the Honduran soldiers who returned them to the scene of the slaughter. By afternoon the genocide ceased, leaving a minimum of 600 dead. (CDH n.d., 36-40)

The bishop, clergy, and religious of Santa Rosa de Copán also cited the Honduran press' claim that a few days prior to the massacre, high military officers from Honduras, Salvador, and Guatemala met secretly in Ocotepeque, thereby insinuating that the massacre had been prearranged. This was particularly embarrassing to the Honduran government since it had completely broken diplomatic relations with El Salvador after the 1969 "Soccer" War. Thus, on June 24 an "official declaration of the government and armed forces of

Honduras" was issued calling the above pronouncement "calumnious, ir-responsible, and criminal," as well as "absolutely false and reckless." It pointed out "that the great majority of the priests and religious signing the statement [were] foreigners" and accused them of being "international conspirators" linked with Salvadoran communist priests in a guerrilla movement "to bloody all of Central America" (CDH n.d., 40-42). Three days later the Honduran Episcopal Conference responded by noting that several news sources as well as the clinics which treated the survivors provided corroborating proof of the massacre. In a conciliatory tone, however, it stated that the church had a pas-toral obligation to report mistreatment of Salvadoran refugees and that it "does not wish to clash with the state" (CEH 1981).

But clashes were inevitable as Honduras became more deeply embroiled in the international tensions of the region. Soon twenty-five thousand Salvadoran refugees had crossed into the primitive area of the Santa Rosa de Copán diocese. An additional two thousand Guatemalan Indians also fled into Honduras, to be followed later by about forty thousand Nicaraguan refugees (Rodríguez 1986, 93-94). As U.S. military and economic aid in-creased, so did the presence of U.S. armed forces, with their large-scale build-ing projects and joint maneuvers. Nicaraguan Contras likewise entrenched themselves along the southern border, which became a war zone. These opera-tions displaced thousands of native Hondurans. When the Catholic Church attempted to aid the displaced foreign and Honduran population, it came into conflict with governmental and military authorities, especially in the northwest where the Salvadoran refugees were located. CARITAS offices were vandalized and priests, nuns, and layworkers were routinely stopped and searched as they attempted to carry out their ministry. In 1981, a CARITAS worker was murdered by soldiers. Fr. Earl Gallagher was shot at as he aided refugees crossing the Lempa River. Padre Fausto Milla fled the country in 1982 after escaping several assassination attempts. Various priests and semi-narians were arrested, the number of *desaparecidos* increased, and clandes-tine cemeteries were discovered (Funes de Torres 1984; CDH n.d.).

Faced with escalating violence, the Episcopal Conference gradually began to speak more forcefully. After several rather timid letters calling for an end to violence, it issued a seventeen-page study on October 22, 1982. "Ter-rorism, disappearances, mysterious discoveries of cadavers, assaults, rob-beries, kidnapings, and insecurity both individual and collective appear to have increased in the last two years," the bishops noted. "Subversives" must not only be the ones to say no to violence; those who run the country must likewise do so. The newly created civil defense committees were condemned as having enormous potential for repression: We "do not know of them being organized in any country that boasted of being democratic." The bishops chided the government for corruption and warned that unfulfilled promises to the people would lead to disillusionment and further turbulence. "There is a general feeling of more fear and less liberty" throughout the country, the episcopacy added, but especially in the border zones; concern was also ex-pressed over the escalating regional arms build-up and predictions of future war with Nicaragua. "War with our neighbors is no solution," they concluded, for only through dialogue can regional problems be resolved (CEH 1982, 1-15).

Several additional episcopal statements were released after October 1982 reiterating many points in the above letter. When Sister Marina Esverry was arrested in Colón and deported on March 12, 1985, the bishops issued a press release stating that they considered the government's action "an offense not only to Sister Marina but also to our church and all our faithful," adding that the charges against her were groundless (CEH 1985a). A second release condemned the continued persecution of church pastoral agents, especially in Colón, and announced that the bishops' conference had decided to create a *Servicio Jurídico* to help protect its workers and to "intervene...in favor of human rights" (CEH 1985b). But harassment continued. In August 1985, U.S. Jesuit John Donald was arrested after criticizing U.S.-Honduran military maneuvers in his sermons. After an international outcry he was released (Francis 1985, 5). When Padre Eduardo Méndez, who worked with campesino cooperative members near Comayagua, was arrested by the antiterrorist "Cobra" police in December 1985, his bishop, Gerald Scarpone, secured his release by calling a press conference (Sheehan 1986, 11).

The most outspoken statement of the Honduran church, however, was made by the Jesuits on March 12, 1984, in a document signed by thirty-eight of their members. They charged that the government was ignoring the peasants' need for land and credit and told of how the poor among whom they worked were often treated as "communists" or "subversives" when they tried to organize in order to demand their rights. "They are imprisoned without reason. They are made to feel fear so that they won't protest. The threat of 'informants' and growing police control produce insecurity...in the judicial system." They noted the disappearances and assassinations of labor leaders, "without the guilty parties being found or justly punished," creating a climate where those who "work for good and justice feel threatened and intimidated." After criticizing the growing militarization of Honduras, "the permanent presence of troops and war material from the United States," Honduran support of Nicaraguan counter-revolutionaries, and the "training of Salvadoran troops in national territory," the communiqué concluded with the statement that "Our experience confirms the fear of our bishops [expressed] in their pastoral letter of October 22, 1982" (Peckenham & Street 1985, 174-76).

But the Catholic Church, or more specifically the bishops, had certainly not recommitted themselves totally to the activism which had been terminated in 1975. When, for instance, in 1980 the Conference of Religious invited Enrique Dussel, the well-known historian of the liberation theology movement, to speak at their annual assembly, the episcopacy refused to allow it (Carney 1985, 239). Likewise, when 150 North American religious women asked the bishops to endorse their plan to fly to Honduras to protest U.S. military involvement in Central America, the Episcopal Conference not only denied their request but publicly termed their plan "inadequate and counterproductive." Going further, they betrayed uncharacteristic anger in the tone of their letter; "the 'religious women' as they call themselves," should realize that God will hear their prayers just as well if they come from their own churches in the U.S.; and furthermore, the money such a trip will cost could be better used in helping refugees and the displaced (CEH 1984, 2). Finally, when military officials told the bishops that they considered a Franciscan priest "suspect" because he said mass on the anniversary of Archbishop Oscar Romero's death for a group called *Cristianos Hondureños por la Paz*, the bishops privately chided the priest to cease being "political" (Interview with two priests who wish to remain anonymous, Comayagüela, Aug. 1986).[6]

From these examples one can assume that church leaders had not returned to their more activist commitment of the 1960s and early 1970s but still held to their more recent policy of divorcing their priests and religious from anything that might be construed by the Honduran elite as political. Violence, repression, and suffering, however, had so intensified in their country in recent years, partly as a result of the escalation of regional tensions, that church leaders had no choice but to speak out not as activists but from a more defensive pastoral concern. Thus, to the bishops at least, their recent, more forceful approach is not contradictory to their decision of 1975 to withdraw from social activism.

In conclusion, then, it can be seen that the Catholic Church in Honduras developed rapidly from its obsessive anticommunism of the 1950s and early 1960s. Spurred on by a desire to have some relevance in Honduran society, it developed its strongest ties with the large campesino class, and these bonds were reinforced by the powerful thrusts of Vatican II and Medellín toward the dispossessed of the world. The outspoken pronouncements of the Honduran episcopacy and the social activism of the clergy and religious continued for about a decade, until finally the fear generated by the repression at *La Talanquera* and *Los Horcones* caught up with the church's own internal disagreement about its involvement in the social and political spheres. This caused it to become much more cautious, aware that its predominantly foreign clergy was subject to the whims of civil authority and could be expelled with ease, leaving the rapidly expanding Protestant sects a wide open field.

Having now committed itself to the poor, the church is unlikely to return to its earlier days of oblivion to the Honduran reality. The tragic conflicts of the 1980s forced it to speak out once again, albeit somewhat defensively and at times timidly. Nevertheless, although the church itself has drawn a fine line between "pastoral concerns" and "political activism," it is not at all clear that Honduran authorities honor the same fine line. No matter how cautiously the Honduran church treads, smooth church-state relations will remain unattainable while tensions persist in the region.

NOTES

1. This was not the first time the Hondurasn hierarchy had spoken out against communism. See, for example, Episcopado de Honduras 1933.

2. The church's ties to UFCO were similar throughout Central America. See, for example, the report of Fr. Clement Procopio on the U.S. Franciscan mission in Guatemala in the 1950s in Bacigalupo 1980, 160-61.

3. So "alarmist" is this document that Tojeira 1986, 229, suggests a possible relationship between it and the coup d'état that toppled the Villeda Morales government a year later.

4. The authors experienced some of this antagonism firsthand: On a bus from Choluteca to Tegucigalpa, a young Honduran harangued everyone on board for an hour with a heated sermon; he made a point of emphasizing the "lies of the diabolical priests" for his captive audience. After the impromptu sermon, he joined a youth group in the back of the bus that began to sing a song with the refrain "Say *adiós* to your *santos*" (CNP 1982, 13, 18).

5. Later Carney would enter the country with a guerrilla band as their chaplain. Although his body has never been found, he was probably captured and executed by the military (Brett & Brett 1988).

6. When the authors related this episode to a Jesuit in Honduras he sarcastically replied, "Now it's even a political act to say mass."

CHAPTER 7

The Miskito and the "Spanish": A Historical Perspective on the Ethnogenes and Persistence of a People

George P. Castile

There has been considerable debate among concerned scholars since the 1979 revolution as to the nature of the relationship between the Sandinista government of Nicaragua and the Miskito peoples of Nicaragua's Atlantic coast. A number of observers have been strongly critical of official Nicaraguan policy and its administration, especially the first two years of the Sandinista regime (Adams 1981a; Dennis 1981; Nietschmann 1984; Ohland & Schneider 1983; Soustelle 1982; Wilde 1981). Looking at the same policies and events, others have taken a more sympathetic view, suggesting at worst a mixture of sometimes mistaken intentions and honest errors on the part of the government while shifting the blame for major problems to the activities of outside forces (Bourgois 1985a; Grunberg 1981; Instituto Histórico Centroamericano 1986; Ortiz 1984).

Whatever one's interpretation, no one denies a series of facts which illustrate that the relationship has indeed been difficult and fraught with error and misunderstanding on all sides, facts which even Sandinista spokesmen freely admit (Borge 1985; Hooker 1985; Cabezas 1985a). The unhappy reality is that, since the Sandinista revolution, large numbers of Miskito have fled the country and many more have been involuntarily relocated internally. A great many Miskito have joined military forces in outright rebellion against the Sandinista regime and between these and the Nicaraguan army a state of war exists with all the human suffering which that implies. Apart from military violence, outside humanitarian agencies have generally reported little tangible evidence to support the extreme charges made by some of massive terror and genocide, but under the turbulent conditions on the Atlantic coast numerous individual instances of harsh governmental action in their dealings with the Miskito have been noted (Organization of American States 1984: Americas Watch Committee 1982, 1984b).

Why this conflict between the people of an economically disadvantaged indigenous sector of Nicaragua and a revolutionary government whose announced program stresses the need to redress past wrongs done to the poor, peasants, and Indians? Given the political and armed struggle that is being waged between the Sandinista government and its opponents, internal and external, there are inevitably two opposed polemical positions around which most commentators tend to rally: 1) that the Miskito are the dupes and victims of *Somocistas* and imperialists who would seek to overthrow the Sandinista regime; and 2) that the Miskito are rightly rebellious against a totalitarian and oppressive communist regime. Neither such simplistic, myopic, "rotten man" approach to history is very satisfying. This chapter offers a tentative suggestion that the conflict is very rooted in the historical experience of the Nicaraguan peoples and that its resolution is likely to be lengthy and complex.

Mary Helms observed in 1971 that "for all practical purposes, the Miskito Coast is not and never has been part of the effective National territory of Nicaragua and Honduras" (Helms 1971, 11). In part this essay explores this proposition and argues that in the present conflict the pertinent historical issue is the existence (or non-existence) of a separate cultural and/or "national" identity for the Miskito region, and its recognition or suppression by the national government of Nicaragua. The facts suggest that a pattern of cultural difference, separation, and conflict between the Atlantic coastal peoples and those of the Pacific side stretches back beyond the emergence to power of the Sandinistas in 1979, indeed, beyond Nicaraguan national existence in 1822, and even beyond the four hundred years of Spanish colonial dominance into the haze of the archaeological record.

Although any "revolutionary" government will predictably wish to claim to have started all of its programs afresh and to distance itself from discredited regimes of the past, no such separation of a people's present from its past is possible. From an examination of events and the public pronouncements of their spokesmen, it seems clear (but not apparently obvious) that the Sandinista leadership brought with them in their approach to the problem of the Miskito the explicit and unspoken assumptions of not one but two separate historical traditions – the Nicaraguan national experience and the more theoretical tradition of Marxist-Leninist thought on the "national question." There is a need to examine the extent to which in both of these lies an inclination or even a necessity to contest the separate identity of the peoples of the Atlantic region.

In the brief historical analysis that follows we shall explore the idea that since the seventeenth century the question of the integration of the Atlantic coastal region has so challenged and shaken the claims to sovereignty of every Spanish colonial and Nicaraguan national government that its resolution has become critical to Nicaraguan national identity. Yet out of that same period of conflict, and perhaps as the opposite side of the same processual coin, we shall suggest that a "people" was created whose identity depends on the denial of inclusion or integration in the larger Nicaraguan identity system.

I have written elsewhere of the problem of the "persistent" or "enduring people" themes first developed by Spicer (Castile & Kushner 1981; Spicer 1980). The process of building modern nation-states has often involved the incorporation and subordination of many formerly independent social groups. In some cases, however, the peoples continue a separate existence within the fabric of the state, adapting to the of incorporation and persisting over long periods of time. In his analysis of the archetypical enduring people, the Yaqui, Spicer examined comparatively a list of nine such peoples — Basques, Catalans, Welsh, Irish, Jews, Cherokees, Hopis, Seneca, and Maya — observing that they were "peoples who, despite seeing their language subordinated or even eliminated, despite being coerced in various ways to renounce their identity as a people and be absorbed in the dominant people, have somehow persisted through all such conditions, continuing to regard themselves with pride and maintaining awareness of a distinctive historical experience on which they place high value" (Spicer 1980, 339). The Miskito are to be included in any such listing of enduring peoples.

Although we shall not argue the theoretical case for the enduring peoples concept, we need to draw attention to Spicer's notion that the ethnogenesis and persistence of such peoples lie in an "oppositional process," "a continued conflict between these peoples and the controllers of the surrounding state apparatus" (Spicer 1971, 797). Whatever the nature of such peoples before being engulfed by expanding states, this position argues that what they become has much to do with the necessities of maintaining themselves in the face of assimilative opposition, defining who they are, at least in part, by stressing who they are not. They become essentially cultural redoubts specifically adapted to survive under such conditions, converting the external assimilative forces into a centripetal force by which they are strengthened rather than weakened. In understanding the consequences of the contact between the Miskito and the peoples they continue to this day to call "the Spanish," such a model seems to fit the data well.

Thus far the pre-Columbian archaeological record for Nicaragua as a whole and the Miskito Coast in particular is scanty (Magnus 1974; Lange & Stone 1984; Healy 1980). There has, however, been long-standing general agreement among observers that the Atlantic coastal region was not part of the Mesoamerican cultural area but had closer ties to the South American and the "Circum-Caribbean" spheres (Steward 1948). The numerous peoples of the Pacific region, principally the Chorotegans and Pipil-Nicarao, were classic Mesoamerican village agriculturists dependent on the trinity of corn/beans/squash and with nucleated populations focused on town-temple complexes. The sparse populations of the less fertile coast appear to have been semisedentary peoples combining marine-oriented hunting and gathering with the cultivation of root crops such as manioc. Among these many small and independent Chibchan-speaking peoples, one or more of them was to become the dominant coastal group we now know as the Miskito.

In early colonial sources, the peoples of the Pacific coast are better known than the Miskito, since, while the cities of León and Granada were founded in that region by 1524, the Spanish did not even make a traverse down the San Juan to the Caribbean until 1539 and never established a permanent presence there (Fowler 1985). Tragically, because of introduced disease and a vigorous slave trade, the peoples of the Pacific coast virtually ceased to exist as a distinct culture and population by the middle of the sixteenth century. From a population, estimated by some to be as large as one million at contact, there was a reduction to as low as eight thousand by 1578 (Radell 1976; Newson 1982; Stanislawski 1983). As the population rebounded it developed a relatively homogeneous mestizo character, genetically and ethnically. Those surviving modern groups, such as the people of Monimbó, (sometimes referred to as "Indian" in Sandinista official literature and which seemingly formed the basis of policy expectations for indigenous peoples), are as one author noted, "only subtly different from the dominant national group" (Ortiz 1984, 191).

Fortunately for the peoples of the eastern coast, the lack of significant exploitable resources such as precious metals, the unsuitability for Spanish agriculture, the sparse and scattered populations, and the distance from major centers of Spanish settlement made the coastal plain the sort of zone some have called a "region of refuge," no more attractive to Spanish settlement than it had been to the Mesoamericans (Aguirre-Beltrán 1967). Here the indigenous populations were not eliminated presumably because of limited contact and because epidemic disease tends to have a lesser impact on dispersed mobile populations. The devastation of slave raiding was also limited since it could produce only a meagre harvest for the effort. No substantial of hispanization of these peoples occurred, and to the extent that they were witnesses to the genocide taking place in the west, one can assume an initial climate of fear and distrust was created, the beginning of enduring opposition to the "Spanish." Whatever might eventually have become of the Spanish-Atlantic coast relation was short-circuited almost immediately by events with their causality far removed from the Caribbean.

The entire Atlantic coast Central America became the focus of a long-term struggle between Spanish and British imperial interests; and that opposition contributed fundamentally to the emerging structural "opposition" of the Miskito and the peoples of western Nicaragua. The antipathy between the British "shoremen" and the "Spanish" merged with the preexisting condition of hostility prevailing on the coast, with the native peoples rapidly becoming willing allies of the British. The Anglo-Spanish conflict itself is a complex matter beyond the limits of this current paper, but the details of its impact on the "Mosquito" shore have been reviewed (Floyd 1967; Dozier 1985). Anthropologist Mary Helms has done extensive work in exploring the record of the rise of the Miskito people in this period and this essay relies heavily on her research (Helms 1986; 1983; 1978; 1977; 1971; 1969). Recently other authors have had occasion to review the events of this period with specific reference to the "kingship" established among the Miskito and provide still further useful historical insight (Dennis & Olien 1984; Olien 1983, 1985).

British corsairs were raiding in the region as early as 1558 and began to enlist Miskito allies in their raids on the Spanish settlements at some undocumented point in time (Floyd 1967). However, the first sustained contact between the British and the Miskito came after the settling of Providence Island in 1630 and the establishment of coastal woodcutting camps shortly thereafter. In fact, in this early period not one but two new cultural elements arrived more or less simultaneously on the shore. African slaves escaping from the developing British settlements began at this point to take refuge on the coast, as they would do for many years, and one or more entire slaving ships may have been wrecked there by 1640, inaugurating the linkage of Miskito culture to a wider Afro-Caribbean matrix (Holm 1978). Some of the peoples of the coast interacted with and freely interbred with the newcomers while others maintained a greater degree of isolation.

Helms and others suggest that the Miskito were a "new" ethnic group in the sense they were composed of those among the coastal peoples who embraced the new ways and through their success came to dominate the coast and eventually to displace the more conservative (the Sumu) to the interior (Helms 1971, 18). The mixture of African and native American genes became sufficiently marked, or politically significant, to cause the Spanish to label these peoples "Zambos" and commonly refer to them by the combined term, *Zambo Mosquitos* (Helms 1977,162). Helms observes that Spanish commentators have placed far greater pejorative emphasis on the "Negro" racial character of the Miskito than have the British, presumably as an expression of the growing hostility between themselves and this newly developing people (Helms 1977). Some current Sandinista pronouncements, while specifically abjuring racism, place considerable emphasis on this same theme of "non-native" racial character and curiously suggest that Miskito separatism is itself a form of racism (Carrión 1982, 238-39).

Whether or not a new genetic "race" emerged in this era, clearly a new way of life came into being and the new "people" coalesced around it. Unfortunately, from the Spanish point of view, this new way was founded on a predatory adaptation as raiders and slave traders. The Miskito became a scourge, raiding not only their own neighbors, but also ranging far afield into Spanish settlements. Helms argues that from their initial role as providers and helpers to the British buccaneers, the Miskito rapidly became effective raiders on their own account, trading captives to the British at a time when labor demands had not yet been satisfied by African slavery (Helms 1978, 1983). In 1787 when the British, as a result of a treaty, withdrew their settlements from the shore entirely, the unaided Miskito forces were able to expel the attempt at colonization by the Spanish (Dozier 1985, 29). European goods, particularly the muskets which may have given the Miskito their name, were the obvious motivation for their raiding and trading, but Helms suggests that it was part of a more comprehensive ecological readjustment in the area, including new agricultural techniques and even kin and settlement patterns (Helms 1983, 187).

There is no question that the Miskito developed more elaborate political and social forms during this ethnogenesis, but there is considerable question as to the precise form of the early "state" and even more debate as to its sources of inspiration (Helms 1986; Olien 1983; Dennis & Olien 1984). The British first took note of a Miskito "king" and kingdom in 1687, when "Jeremy I" made contact with the governor of Jamaica, but the accounts of his visit suggest an origin some fifty years earlier (Olien 1983, 201). Whatever its precise nature, a political organization with a chief-king at its head wielded some degree of unifying control over the Miskito for over two hundred years until extinguished by Nicaragua in 1894. Although Helms and Dennis/Olien disagree over the extent to which this kingship had an indigenous basis or was derived from African or British stimulus, as well as over the extent of the power and authority of the title holder, they are agreed in crediting the Miskito political leadership with greater significance than has been historically customary.

Past commentators generally felt called upon to deride the Miskito political reality as nothing more than that of primitive and ludicrously pretentious puppet creations of the British. Dozier and Floyd both follow this path to an unfortunate extent and portray the kings as strictly British creations, repeating the long-cited anecdotes which show them as "crowned" (the word always in quotes) with mock ceremony and much given to foolish and drunken display (Dozier 1985, 15-16, 331-34; Floyd 1967, 62). Olien has persuasively argued that this image of the Miskito owes much to the mid-nineteenth-century writings of E. G. Squier who portrayed the Miskito in terms very much reminiscent of Evelyn Waugh's novel *Black Mischief* (Olien 1985; Squier 1852).

Squier was writing as an active U.S. agent at a time of intense American rivalry with the British for influence in Central America, and Olien raises the interesting issue of why such explicitly racist anti-British/British ally propaganda has so long been accepted and repeated as a standard scholarly account. While there is no question that the Miskito kings owed much of their power to British support, Olien and Dennis argue persuasively for the orderly succession rather than capricious British appointment of the kings, that they were by no means simple puppets (Olien 1983; Dennis & Olien 1984). While Helms has taken exception to Olien and Dennis' tendency toward rather sweeping revision of the character of the Miskito rulers, she has endorsed their work as bringing "useful correctives and better balance" to that of Squier (Helms 1986, 506).

Leaving aside the opposing interpretations of the Miskito political structure, the kingship has come to have an important "symbolic" quality regardless of its arguable historical reality. On the nature of enduring peoples and their histories, Spicer observes that "a given event exists in quite distinct fields of meaning for any two people experiencing it....The persistence of a people rests on a set of meanings about actual events of history, as uniquely experienced by the people....So long as the common understandings of what has been experienced in relations with other peoples are known and felt, a people will persist" (Spicer 1980, 347). The critical fact of Miskito kingship may be the opposing meanings that it has come to have for the Nicaraguan and Miskito national identity systems.

Olien and Dennis maintain that the kings were important figures in the lives of the Miskito themselves, above and beyond their significance in British schemes. The kingship technically came to an end in 1894 with the Nicaraguan takeover, but the theme of the king seems to have become by then an important element in the stock of symbols by which the Miskito define themselves. Helms's description of ritual life in Asang and later observations of Dennis both indicate that the "king" is an important element in myth and ceremony to the present day, particularly as manifest in the celebration of "Kings Day," formalized by Moravian missionaries at the time of the takeover (Helms 1971, chap. 6; Dennis 1982).

While the mestizo peoples of the Pacific coast inevitably developed their own variant of Latin American Catholicism as part of their Spanish heritage, the Miskito generated a unique religious system. The principal ingredient added to the existing indigenous elements was not Catholicism but a form of Protestantism introduced by German and American Moravian Missionaries beginning in 1849. Although Helms has made a beginning, no specific study has been made of the resultant symbolic ritual matrix for elements of self-definition in the way that Spicer has exhaustively examined Yaqui "Kohtumbre" (Helms 1971; Spicer 1980). Still, it is obvious that in this mytho-poetic scheme of things, to the Miskito, the days of the kings are remembered positively as part of their "distinctive historical experience." As Dennis notes, "for them, the king play, like school history books and patriotic celebrations in other societies, helps maintain a positive and flattering version of their past" (Dennis 1982, 395).

By the end of the nineteenth century, the "Nicaraguan" view of the Miskito and their government, and other events of the British-influenced era of Miskito history, had inevitably come to far less flattering conclusions. Throughout the Spanish colonial era, there was a consistent refusal to recognize either an independent Miskito regime or British claims to the area and an understandable tendency to deride the dignity and legitimacy of either (Floyd 1967; Gámez 1939). If things British had come to have a positive symbolic value for the Miskito, the independent Nicaraguan national governments continued in this negative Spanish tradition of Anglophobia. However, by 1860 British interest in the area was waning and, in the treaty of Managua, they yielded their role of "protector" of the Miskito kingdom, granting recognition for the first time of a limited degree of Nicaraguan sovereignty over the coastal region but still providing guarantees of continued Miskito autonomy (Dozier 1985, 141).

The attitude of the Nicaraguans toward the Miskito was revealed in such statements as those they submitted in 1878 for arbitration by the Austrian emperor of their continuing disputes with the British over Miskito sovereignty and autonomy. In their pleading they observed, "the tribe of Mosquito Indians is an exhausted and degenerate race, incapable of education and development, and that therefore the talents and presumptions required for self government are lacking" (Great Britain, F.O. 1881, 24). In their obvious racism and implied social Darwinism they were, of course, only reflecting the "positivist" philosophy that dominated this era of the quest for "progress" in Central America (Burns 1980, 19). Ironically, when they made appeal to the precedent set by the "dependent domestic nations" status of the Indian peoples in the United States, they found themselves in turn racially denigrated. Their attempt at justification by comparison was rejected since in the U.S. there is an "immense and unmixed white population that overwhelms them" (the native peoples) while Nicaragua itself "has but a feeble and mixed population." (Great Britain, F.O. 1881, 25). The arbitration found against the Nicaraguan claims and the Miskito "reservation" retained its autonomy with British support until 1894, symbolically a standing affront to the dignity of the Nicaraguan government.

Declining British involvement in the Anglo-Miskito world was gradually replaced, not by stronger Spanish-Nicaraguan influence, but by an increasing Anglo-American presence. Both Britain and the United States had a concern with the promotion of interoceanic travel across Central America and by the middle of the nineteenth century found themselves rivals. It was in this context that E. G. Squire, for the United States, generated his propaganda about the Miskito. In 1850 the Clayton-Bulwer Treaty partially quieted this conflict by assuring that neither nation would seek exclusive undue influence in the area. The continued British protectorate over the Miskito area, however, remained offensive to the United States as a violation of this agreement, and the relinquishment of it under the treaty of Managua in 1860 was more a reflection of growing U.S. influence than a recognition of Nicaraguan dignity.

To a considerable extent the inability of Nicaragua to establish influence on the coast was a result of its own internal disarray. Like most other Central American countries, after independence in 1822 the political history of Nicaragua was a turbulent record of struggle – often armed struggle – between Liberal and Conservative elites (Woodward 1985). The decade of 1850 to 1860 was particularly chaotic, including the so-called "Walker affair," when American filibusters called in by Liberals momentarily seized the government for themselves, an event which has become an important "anti-Gringo" symbol for the Sandinistas. For the Miskito shore, however, this was a period of considerable prosperity and the beginning of a cycle of boom and bust economies dependent on American entrepreneurs. In 1851 one of most flamboyant of these, Cornelius Vanderbilt, opened a route to the gold fields of California across Nicaragua with a large base at Greytown, in the Miskito reserve. Walker's war, however, led to the virtual abandonment of the route by 1857 and the decline of the boom it created, making Walker perhaps one of the few symbolic villains that Miskitos and Nicaraguans could agree upon (Dozier 1985, chap. 4).

With the completion of a railway across Panama in 1857, Central American trade, became increasingly funneled by that route to Pacific ports and interest in the Atlantic shore declined. Dozier suggests that the guarantee of continued autonomy of the Miskito region by Austrian arbitration was a major factor in encouraging the revival of American interest in the 1880s (Dozier 1985, 121). The banana market developed by Minor Keith in Costa Rica led to the establishment of plantations in Nicaragua, but equally important was the resurgence of canal interest, with work begun in 1887 on a Nicaraguan canal by the Maritime Canal Company. By the end of the nineteenth century, a substantial American business enclave had developed, based principally on mahogany, and the bananas. It continued to prosper after the canal work came to an end in 1892.

Echoing the standard historical view and without offering any specific evidence of its failings, Dozier offers a gratuitous observation about the Miskito government: "Because of its incompetence and strongly anti-Nicaraguan feeling, this government aided Americans in their business conquest" (Dozier 1985, 142). Anti-Nicaraguan it surely was, inasmuch as it sought to avoid absorption by that nation, but it is scarcely evidence of incompetence that it encouraged foreign investment as did every other Central American government.

This brief period of increasing American influence on the coast came to a temporary halt in 1894 when the Nicaragua government, newly seized by the "liberal" President José Santos Zelaya after some thirty years of conservative rule, invaded the Miskito Coast. Zelaya contended that the government was not in the hands of the Miskito but of Jamaican blacks and thus in violation of prior treaties (Olien 1983, 235). Although there was a period of turmoil, including a temporary reseizure of power by the Miskito, the political annexation of the area as the "Department of Zelaya" was successful. A critical factor was American diplomatic pressure which discouraged active British support for the Miskito, despite the strong pro-Miskito stance of resident American businessmen. Of this exception to the concept of "dollar diplomacy" one scholar has remarked, "thus passed into history one of the few conflicts between United States governmental policy and United States businessmen" (R. L. Morrow, quoted in Dozier 1985, 157).

The event and Zelaya are, of course, heroic in the national mythology of Nicaragua which in the "reincorporation" incorporated the coast for the first time. It was an important, but tragic, event in the history of the Miskito. Like the Nicaraguans, past and present, Dozier seems to stress more than is warranted a separation between the Afro-Caribbean element on the coast and their Miskito brethren and suggests that it was only the "Jamaicans" that protested the annexation. One can scarcely imagine any Miskito expressing a view much at variance with that which he quotes for the "long resident Jamaicans":

The Nicaraguans have no sympathy for the inhabitants of the Mosquito Reserve. They are jealous of the prosperity of the reserve. We do not speak the same language, we do not profess the same religion and our institutions and laws and manners and customs are not agreeable to them, and their manner of life and mode of government are obnoxious to us; and both Indians and foreigners within the Mosquito Reservation are unwilling that these men shall have the rule over us. (Dozier 1985, 152)

Dozier is also impossibly credulous in his assessment of the vote by which the Miskito "voluntarily" joined Nicaragua.

According to the Treaty of Managua, incorporation could occur when-ever the inhabitants of the Reserve freely chose it, and there was little doubt that the Indians, with whom the Nicaraguan government dealt, were ready to choose it. They had long been dissatisfied with the cor-rupt, self serving Mosquito government from which they had been vir-tually excluded. Accordingly, delegates from all the native tribes in the Reserve attended a convention and by unanimous consent declared for incorporation. (Dozier 1985, 155)

There is absolutely nothing in the long history of the Miskito to make this statement believable. A far more likely appraisal is that of Ortiz: "The Mis-kitu King was deposed, and Miskitu authorities were forced to sign a declara-tion of allegiance to the Republic of Nicaragua, called *La Carta de Adhesión de la Mosquita a la República de Nicaragua,* a historical event bitterly resented by indigenous coastal people, particularly the Miskitu" (Ortiz 1984, 209). Note also this observation by Dennis: "The general attitude about the incorpora-tion among Miskito people has been that they were tricked into giving up their 'independence' (as represented by the king) and forced to swear allegiance to a country they disliked" (Dennis 1981, 281). A part of the current Sandinista problem is the inevitable tendency of a government to believe its own propaganda; but why a historian should do so is far less understandable.

Until 1894 the Miskito "endured" as a people under many pressures and through wide swings of circumstance but always as a distinct society—not as a fragment of a larger entity. With annexation, the Miskito for the first time lost their independent political identity and become — at least technically — a segment of the Nicaraguan state. They confronted, therefore, far more inten-sely the problem of maintaining their cultural boundaries against assimilative pressures from a dominant people. However, even the farcical voluntary agreement allowed them a considerable degree of structural autonomy, in-cluding guarantees of land tenure, and exemption from military service and certain taxes (Olien 1983, 236). The threat of assimilation, in fact, turned out to be more symbolic than real since the assumption of Nicaraguan authority did not "take."

Zelaya's government initially threatened to have a heavy impact since it vigorously asserted Nicaraguan authority on the coast in the regulation of com-merce (e.g., granting and revoking monopolies). The monopolies and a wide range of tariffs and taxes caused considerable grievance among Miskito and foreigners alike. A clear harbinger of ultimate plans of assimilation was the insistence that the schools run by the Moravians be operated exclusively in Spanish (Dozier 1985, 161). However, the program was not pursued for long as troubles with the conservative neighboring governments and antagonisms with the U.S. over its decision to locate its canal in Panama led to increased international pressure on Zelaya.

In 1909 rebellion broke out on the coast led by Zelaya's own Liberal governor who raised the banner of Conservatism and gained support not only from neighboring Conservatives, but a rather favorable "neutrality" from the U.S. (Dozier 1985, 182). Zelaya resigned in an attempt to defuse U.S. pressures, but the Liberal government fell in 1910, and with it the only active and aggressive effort to assimilate the coast until 1979.

Thomas Walker's popular history reflects the current Nicaraguan view of the period from 1912, when President Adolfo Díaz called for U.S. troops, to 1934 when the last of the troops withdrew as a period of "occupation" by "imperialists" and the forces which were in arms against the government as a heroic "resistance" (Walker 1986). Richard Millett has produced a valuable study of U.S. involvement in the training of the Nicaraguan National Guard, which probably comes as close as any to an "objective" outline of the strictly military events (Millett 1977).

By the end of the nineteenth century, the Miskito had ceased to be raiders and traders and had to depend on wage labor with a base of subsistence agriculture to carry them through the bust cycles. Helms points out that their matri-local pattern of residence allowed for considerable cultural stability, the women maintaining the subsistence garden plots and a conservative "miskito" family base throughout the ever changing cycles of foreign enterprises. While men would range out from this base to work in the non-Miskito marketplace, "there was always a solid base of Miskitoness firmly established in the early years of village life" (Helms 1971, 24). Helms roughly diagrams the duration of various "booms" of rubber, mahogany, bananas, gold, and pine to 1960, and Nietschmann has described in considerable detail the most recent "turtle" boom (Helms 1971, 29; Nietschmann 1974, 1980).

In the twentieth century the Miskito Coast has been consistently "exploited" by American business interests through a series of strictly extractive enterprises. Certainly the Sandinista government takes the view that this was an era of exploitative imperialism from which the revolution has liberated the costeños (Carrión 1981; Wheelock 1974; Ortiz 1984). However, those who have worked closely with the Miskito consistently report that they regard these as good times and the exploiters as their friends (Helms 1971; Dennis 1981; Nietschmann 1980). Helms notes that an "enthusiasm for Americans and their culture is predicated on the attitude that it is the Americans who are concerned with the welfare of the Miskito, replacing the earlier British in this respect. Americans have owned and operated the various lumbering, mining and banana enterprises that have offered the Miskito jobs and cash" (Helms 1971, 221). Dennis says that "far from feeling exploited by Standard Fruit, the Miskito were delighted to have a market for their products and a chance to buy consumer goods in the company commissary." (Dennis 1981, 284).

The discrepancy between the two peoples' view of their "shared" history can be no more dramatic than in the matter of Augusto Sandino. Any examination of current Nicaraguan governmental statements shows him to be a central heroic figure in Sandinista cosmology whose name is invoked on any and all important questions and occasions. To the Marines of Chesty Puller's day, he was a "bandit" and that view is much closer to the one held by the Miskito. Both Dennis and Helms note that Sandino was primarily remembered the his attacks on Standard Fruit installations in what Helms says her informants called "the time of bandits" (Dennis 1981, 284; Helms 1971, 112). Indeed, in the late 1960s Helms suggests that memories of this era contributed to what now appears to have been a sort of prescience, saying, "There are constant rumors floating from village to village that 'bandits' were seen upriver, or that there is a new war involving the United States which will result in bombing or invasion of the river at any time" (Helms 1971, 41).

The Somoza family, which ruled from 1935 until 1979, is of course the centerpiece of the Sandinista demonology. As often as Sandino is mentioned positively, the Somozas are spoken of negatively. It is from the exploitation and oppression of the last Somoza, Anastasio, Jr., that the Sandinistas set out to free the people of Nicaragua, including those of the coast. What, then, of the Miskito view? As perhaps the ultimate irony some observers suggest that Anastasio Somoza, Jr., actually stood somewhat higher in Miskito eyes than the "Spanish" rulers (Adams 1981a; Nietschmann 1984; Dennis 1981). They suggest that to the Miskito he may have seemed notably less "Spanish" since, like themselves, Somoza was Anglicized, educated in the United States and married to an American. He was fluent in English and addressed the Miskito in that language; he was also an enthusiastic and vocal supporter of the United States, the source of many of the employment-producing enterprises on the coast.

Dennis also suggests that "there was relatively little interference in local affairs in this isolated area" as a factor in Somoza's relative "popularity" (Dennis 1981, 262). However, outside of the Sandino period, the Nicaraguan impact after Zelaya (and indeed up until 1979) was always very limited, so much so one is tempted to use the discredited phrase *benign neglect* to characterize the relationship. Of the contact between the villagers of Asang and the state Helms notes: "The desire to avoid contact is mutual" and "the state generally keeps out of village affairs" (Helms 1971, 174). Until 1979 the central government did little for the Miskito region by way of schools or medical facilities, but it was also "notable for its absence, a situation which suited the local population" (Bourgois 1985a, 32).

The individual self-governing village was the basic unit of political organization that remained under the control of the Miskito themselves after incorporation, but the Moravian Church came to provide a degree of pan-Miskito structural unity since most Miskito were members and the lay pastors were largely Miskito (Helms 1971). Partially on the the basis of the church structure a new form of Miskito political organization began to emerge in the coastal area in the last days of the Somoza regime — ALPROMISU (Alianza Para el Desarrollo Miskito y Sumu). was basically a lobbyist mechanism for Miskito causes and was actually encouraged and funded by Somoza (Adams

1981b; Dennis 1981). Dennis notes, however, that "some older Miskito men in the villages mistakenly thought ALPROMISU was trying once more to establish an independent Miskito nation to drive out the 'Spaniards' and return to the legendary days of Miskito dominance" (Dennis 1981, 285) — a mistake apparently made by the Sandinistas as well.

The Miskito appear to have taken little or no part in the struggles against the Somoza regime that resulted in its collapse and overthrow in 1979. Bourgois suggests that "they heard about the brutal fighting and repression on the radio but never saw it or felt it" (Bourgois 1985a, 32). Given the often chaotic political history of Nicaragua and the distance the Miskito have maintained from it, Bourgois is probably quite accurate when he adds: "The initial reaction of the Costeños was to treat the revolution as just another incomprehensible power struggle between two equally dangerous armed factions of 'Spaniards'" (Bourgois 1985a, 32). Aware of their own history, they had every right to believe that this new "revolution," would at best have no impact on their well-being and might well be dangerous to their interests. Promises of benefits and change had always been made during such transitions.

Sandinista leaders were reasonably aware of this same history. What sort of approaches might any new government, seeking more complete political and economic integration of the Atlantic coastal region, have considered, given an awareness of "opposition" as a central theme in that history? How might they have best proceeded to implement them?

In the face of the long-standing tension and suspicion between peoples, there was above all a need to proceed slowly. A people used to benign neglect should not have a massive "foreign" presence imposed upon them suddenly and without adequate preparation. Equally obvious, given language and cultural barriers, cadres moving into the area would need to be carefully selected and specially trained, and preferably recruited from among those members of the FSLN from or familiar with the region.

Any program of change would have to start from "where the people are." Given their ethnic insularity, it would be reasonable to make at least initial public concessions to "autonomy" and some sort of guarantees of continued territorial integrity. The things the Miskito demonstrably always wanted or feared most would have to be addressed in some reasonably conciliatory and reassuring form. Existing leadership and organizations, ALPROMISU, and at least the Miskito lay Moravian clergy, would have to be drawn in at least at the beginning stage to provide some continuity.

There is little point in pursuing this list of "reasonable" programmatic suggestions since what in fact happened had little resemblance to any such utopian scheme. Yet, the actions of the new regime, the Sandinistas, were probably as understandable from a reading of Nicaraguan history as was their inappropriateness to winning the "hearts and minds" of the Miskito. That this was a "revolutionary" socialist government, which one might expect would alter any such historical continuity, in some ways even more certainly guaranteed confusion.

Consider that any new government, "Nicaraguan" or not, could have been expected to be suspicious of, and deal harshly with, any elements thought to be loyal to the previous regime. As we have discussed at length, any "Nicaraguan" government, in the light of its history, as a matter of national identity, would necessarily be expected to insist categorically and unwaveringly on their sovereignty over the coast. On the same historical basis, they could certainly be expected to react strongly to any suggestion of the threat of a separatist movement, particularly one with the appearance of foreign, especially Anglo-foreign, backing. Given their long history of antagonism, the "Spanish" cadres could be expected to be just as suspicious and hostile toward the Miskito as the Miskito were toward them and both would be equally ignorant of each other's ways.

Bourgois has a graphic description of the realities of the first contacts: "The Sandinista fighters, for their part, were also profoundly baffled by what they found: an apathetic, if not openly hostile, population who 'refused' to understand that they were the victims of imperialism or that General Sandino was a heroic figure....A series of local crises erupted exacerbating the mutual misperception the ethnic minorities and the Sandinistas had of each other" (Bourgois 1985a, 32). In the midst of clouds of mutual suspicion the inexperienced cadres arrested the ALPROMISU leadership on the grounds of Somocista and/or separatist plottings. When Sandinista national leadership in the person of Daniel Ortega finally arrived to clarify the situation and transmute the discredited ALPROMISU into a new indigenous organization, MISURASATA, the speech making, as reported by Adams, was anything but conciliatory to notions of autonomy (Adams 1981b, 15).

A perusal of the speeches and writings of the Sandinista leadership, before, during, and after the revolution, suggests a clear set of assumptions in their revolutionary program that they brought with them to the coast (Ohland & Schneider 1983; Marcus 1985). As Bourgois notes, they expected the peoples of the coast, like the people of the rest of Nicaragua, to see themselves as the victims of imperialism, even "superexploited." In addition to their resentment over economic imperialism the minority peoples of the coast should have been resentful of the "racism" practiced by the exploiters. Apparently unaware of the peculiar subsistence/wage economy of the region, the reform model they brought to the coast was that appropriate to land hungry peasants—perhaps the people of Monimbó who seem to have formed much of the Sandinista rhetoric about "Indians." Overall one suspects they saw these peoples as just another group of downtrodden campesinos, exploited and denied their chance for integration. Given the chance for development, participation, and integration they would, of course, welcome it.

A certain set of expectations has apparently been induced by the Marxist-Leninist tendency of many of the Sandinistas (Castile In progress). As both Marxists and Nicaraguans, the Sandinistas inherited a tendency to see the ethnic identity of the Miskito as something foisted upon them by capitalist outsiders and, therefore, undesirable and destined to vanish under improved conditions.

Marx himself had little to say on the national question but what he did say suggests it as a form of false consciousness, destined to whither away under socialism: "National differences and antagonisms between peoples are daily more and more vanishing....The supremacy of the proletariat will cause them to vanish still faster" (Karl Marx, "Manifesto of the Communist party," in Tucker 1978, 498). The delayed vanishing of peoples and the emergence of a new "socialist" man are questions with which Lenin and Stalin wrestled mightily and which the Soviet state has by no means resolved (Lenin 1979; Stalin 1979, Carrère d'Encausse 1978). The Nicaraguans are not alone in their dilemma in this hemisphere since Latin American Marxist regimes in general have shown considerable ambivalence in coming to terms with *indigenismo* in its various forms (Bollinger & Lund 1982).

Ortega's first speech to the Miskito, as reported by Adams, reveals this tendency: "His talk emphasized that the Miskito and Sumu should not think of themselves as Indians. They were among the poor of the world. The revolution was not made just for Indians, but to help all the poor. Also, they should first identify themselves as Nicaraguans, for the revolution was for all Nicaraguans" (Adams 1981a, 15). His speech made perfect Marxist and Nicaraguan nationalist sense, but was wildly inappropriate to the ears of his Miskito audience. To their credit, after the initial collision of cultures and perhaps after recovering from having been swept away by their own rhetoric, the Sandinistas have backpedalled furiously to redeem the situation. Tomás Borge, now responsible for the area notes: "Without giving much thought to the consequences, we wanted to develop on the Atlantic Coast structures and projects similar to those on the Pacific....We had difficulty in grasping the ethnic character of the Miskito problem" (Borge 1985, 348). But as a Nicaraguan nationalist, Borge cannot refrain from insisting on "connecting and linking the Atlantic coast to the Nicaraguan identity" (Borge 1985, 351).

In view of this historical opposition, probably the most realistic and meaningful response the Sandinistas have made to the ethnic reality is the so-called "autonomy" project begun in 1984. An "autonomy document" was circulated for discussion in 1985 titled, "Principles and Policies for the Exercise of the Right to Autonomy by the Indigenous Peoples and Communities of the Atlantic Coast" (Ortiz 1986, 1). It is not clear just what "autonomy" might mean at this stage, but the mere suggestion of some degree of self-government inherent in the word is a step toward accommodating Miskito realities. As William Ramírez commented, "We were terrified to speak of autonomy because we did not understand it. And we didn't understand because no one understood the Atlantic Coast. Today we speak of this naturally" (W. Ramírez 1985, 392). It is perhaps inevitable that what it most certainly does not mean is an acceptance of any degree of "separatism." Note, for example, the a priori insistence in the autonomy document that "the indigenous peoples and other communities of the Atlantic Coast are an indissoluble part of the Nicaraguan people" (Ortiz 1986, 2).

Some steps toward "autonomy" have apparently been taken in the Miskito community of Yulu but, again, it is not at all clear what that means beyond a "hands-off" state of local truce ("A Year of Peace in Yulu," *Barricada Internacional*, May 29, 1986, 6). In all likelihood no resolution of the situation can occur so long as a state of war exists in the area involving significant numbers of Miskito. The Sandinistas are certainly the first Nicaraguan government to make even symbolic concessions to the national existence of the Miskito and that may argue a more hopeful future than current chaos suggests. The resolution will not be complete the moment a Nicaraguan government "triumphs" in the ongoing war. The welding together of two peoples who largely define themselves in "opposition" will not occur overnight, no matter who is in Managua.

CHAPTER 8

"¡Patria Libre o Muerte!" Death Imagery and the Poetry of Revolt in Nicaragua, 1900-1985

John D. Heyl

> *Sorrows of my land,*
> *death rattle of the*
> *great*
> *established*
> *silence,*
> *long-suffering people,*
> *slender waist of tears.*
> —Pablo Neruda, "Central America"
> (Aldaraca, et al. 1980, 21)

From its beginning, with the bloody overthrow of Anastasio Somoza Debayle in July 1979, the Sandinista revolution in Nicaragua has been a "cultural revolution." Poetry, in particular, has played a striking role in many aspects of the revolutionary process.[1] This important role for the poet and for "poetry of the people" as voices of the revolution was not invented by the Sandinistas but was rather an extension of a historical tradition in Nicaragua that has given unusual status to the poet's art. This chapter discusses that tradition by focusing on the use of death imagery in the work of four leading national figures— Rubén Darío, José Coronel Urtecho, Pablo Antonio Cuadra, and Ernesto Cardenal. What have been the poetic visions of death in Nicaragua? To what extent have these visions been "politicized" by the recurrent crises and human catastrophes experienced by the Nicaraguan people? And how do these visions reflect continuing tensions within Nicaraguan culture today?

In an important sense, all of these poets were in revolt against their society and against their era. They were, as Eric Hoffer once characterized many revolutionary intellectuals, "men of words with a grievance" (Hoffer 1951, 119). Theirs was thus a revolt in words. But these were not isolated, symbolic revolts. They were tied together in their shared national roots, even (in the case of Coronel, Cuadra, and Cardenal) by shared family ties. But, above all, they participated in—were decisive shapers of—a national cultural idiom of revolt. This chapter will present the evolution of that cultural idiom in the context of the poet's double vision of life and art. Each of these poets, as the leader of a revolutionary project, faced the concrete choices of all revolutionary movements: Which aspects of the inherited idiom of revolt should be embraced? Which should be ignored? Which should be condemned? As Theda Skocpol has recently suggested, such "intentional and self-conscious [choices]...ultimately constitute the ideology of the revolutionary movement" (Skocpol 1985; Sewell 1985). That such choices, ultimately *ideological* choices, have included the role of poetry in the revolutionary process is one of the distinctive features of the Nicaraguan experience in this century.

In view of the frequent use of death imagery in Central American poetry, it is surprising that so little has been written on this theme. To be sure, to focus on a single theme is to isolate what cannot in truth be isolated from the poetic matrix of a single writer, period, or movement, much less that of a national culture (Ellis 1974, 66-75). But in order to gain a manageable grip on the uses of poetry in this century, an appropriate theme can provide much needed leverage. Moreover, the events of the century recommend this particular choice. From devastating earthquakes to foreign interventions, state terrorism, and popular insurrections, the Nicaraguans have experienced more death than is common even in a bloody century and a strife-torn region. The earthquake of March 1931, while President Moncada's forces (with U.S. military support) were trying to suppress the guerrilla general Augusto César Sandino, claimed as many as fifteen hundred lives and destroyed thirty blocks in the capital city of Managua.[2] In December 1972, an even more devastating quake leveled some six hundred blocks of the capital, and many have been responsible for as many as fifteen thousand deaths. One comparison should be of special significance for North Americans: The anti-Somoza insurrection of 1977-1979 cost as many Nicaraguan lives (as a percentage of the total population of the country) as did the United States' most bloody conflict, the Civil War. To these catastrophic events one must add the historically high homicide and mortality rates.[3] Death has indeed stalked both the personal and national experience of Nicaragua in this century.

To be sure, one should not expect a one-to-one correspondence between the experience of illiterate campesinos and the art of an educated elite. In fact, there is no such correspondence. And yet, there is a response. "How could you write those beautiful poems about ceiba trees," Grace Schulman asked Pablo Antonio Cuadra in 1979, "when your city was burning?" "What else is a man to do?" responded Cuadra. Cuadra, chief editor of the conservative anti-Somoza newspaper *La Prensa* and celebrated poet of the *Vanguardista* generation of the 1930s, revealed here the "double vision of human concern and aesthetic commitment" characteristic of Nicaraguan poets (White 1982, iv). What is this "double vision"? Broadly speaking, the double vision, as Schulman suggests, moves between dual concerns for political engagement and artistic integrity. Seen in these terms, this duality is scarcely unique to Nicaraguan letters. There are a number of specific characteristics in the Nicaraguan case, however, that appear to distinguish it from other national variants and to offer a framework in which to ground an understanding of the historical evolution of one of its themes.

The poles of poetic dualism in the treatment of death may be thought of as the mystical, fatalistic acceptance of death on the one hand and a politically engaged rejection of suffering and death on the other. While in the gravitational field of the first pole, the poet understands death as part of a cosmic unity — the inevitable end to the human cycle of life, and the beginning of another cycle on another level; while under the influence of the second pole, the poet considers death to be a contingent experience, determined by concrete circumstances, part of a historical unity that joins past and future. In the course of the Somoza era in Nicaraguan history, her leading poets increasingly moved into this second field. Moreover, they strengthened its pull on other writers by embracing various mystical/Christian/utopian possibilities of victory over death through love and/or social reconstruction. Nicaraguan poetry, then, in both its aesthetic and ideological dimensions, reflects this bipolar movement in its death imagery. What are the historical roots of this literary matrix?

Darío's Versatile Lyre: Death as Medusa and Siren

Any discussion of Nicaraguan poetry in the twentieth century (indeed, of Nicaraguan poetry in the entire modern era) must begin with the work of Rubén Darío (1867-1916) (Anderson-Imbert 1969, 348-54; Brotherston 1975, 56-76; Torres 1952; Watland 1965; Rama 1973; Darío 1967; Darío, 1977; Ellis 1974, 3-24). Darío's legacy looms over the arts in Nicaragua in a unique way. His literary corpus was so extensive and creative, in so many different modes, and recognized so widely in Hispanic letters that all Nicaraguan governments (and those of many other countries) have done homage to *el gran Rubén*. Poets and literary critics alike have confirmed Darío as the outstanding Central American poet.

A generation ago, a reviewer of a fine analysis of Darío's poetry claimed that, except for the Argentinian Domingo Sarmiento and the Cuban José Martí, no other writer in Hispanic America had been so written about (González, 1949). At the centenary of his birth, Darío was called the leader of the entire modernist movement in Spanish literature and one of "four or five poets who linked up the great chain that had come apart at the end of the seventeenth century" (Darío 1965, 8). Recently Ernesto Cardenal, the Sandinista Minister of Culture, recalled his father's reverent readings of Darío, and acknowledged that he discovered through Darío "the magic of words" (Randall 1984). In addition to conveying a broad legitimacy to the making of poetry, then, Darío has since his death been a true begetter of poets.

Moreover, Darío was an intellectual revolutionary who was very conscious of his mission to reshape literature written in Spanish, to transform the language itself, to bring it in touch with modern human experience (Pearsall 1984, 66-98). In this important sense, he was in revolt against received canons of Spanish poetry and prose his entire life. He traveled, founded literary magazines, wrote poetry, essays, and novels, and gave speeches on behalf of his revolution. His was a "symbolic revolt" (Franco 1970, chap. 1), but it opened the range of expression so widely that it had implications far outside the circle of writers he directly affected.

The importance of the theme of death in the work of Darío has long been recognized by literary critics and historians. It may be thought of as a key sub-theme to the dominant issue in Darío's poetry: anguished eroticism (Salinas 1948; Enguidanos 1970, 14). In fact, a biographical approach to Darío's treatment of death reveals a complex evolution of numerous meanings and uses, from the conventional Christian views of his adolescence to a Pythagorean fascination with death as part of a cosmic unity, with a recurrent fear of death as real, yet ultimately mysterious and unknowable.[4] Darío's versatile lyre, writes Julio Ycaza Tigerino, permitted him "to attack all the poetic registers of death" (Ycaza Tigerino 1961, 132). Anderson-Imbert concurs: "[Darío] not only got every musical possibility out of a word, but he used the right instrument for every nuance of mood. To read him is to improve one's ear; as it improves it can perceive new registers of sound in the recitation" (Anderson-Imbert 1969, 354). But the weight of his poetry falls within the polar field of a mystical view of death as ultimately unknowable, strangely beautiful, and terrifying — as Paz has said, both Medusa and siren (Darío 1965, 17; Feustle 1976). Paradigmatic for this attitude toward death are two poems from his mature writings — "Lo Fatal" (*Cantos de vida y esperanza*, 1905) and "Poema del Otoño" (*Poema del otoño y otros poemas*, 1910).

"Lo Fatal," one of Darío's most important poems from a stylistic point of view, is a sonnet (minus the fourteenth line.) addressing the fundamental anguish of human existence in the face of the certain knowledge of death.

> The tree is happy because it is scarcely sentient;
> the hard rock is happier still, it feels nothing:
> there is no pain as great as being alive,
> no burden heavier than that of conscious life.
>
> To be, and to know nothing, and to lack a way,
> and the dread of having been, and future terrors...
> And the sure terror of being dead tomorrow,
> and to suffer all through life and through the darkness,
>
> and through what we do not know and hardly suspect . . .
> And the flesh that tempts us with bunches of cool grapes,
> and the tomb that awaits us with its funeral sprays,
> and not to know where we go,
>
> nor whence we came!...[5]

The "sure terror of being dead tomorrow" is heightened yet further by the ultimate failure to know one's place in the universe — "and not to know where we go, / nor whence we came!..." As Darío himself wrote of his poem: "In 'Lo Fatal,' against my deep-rooted religion, and despite myself, a phantasm of desolation and doubt rises like a fearful shadow. Certainly, there has existed in me, from the beginning of my life, a profound preoccupation with the end of existence...." (Enguidanos 1970, 23, quoting Darío, *Historia de mis libros* 1909). "Lo Fatal" is fundamentally a poem about mortality. If there is a suggestion of the transmigration of souls ("and the dread of having been, and future terrors..."), this possibility of past and future existence is even more reason to regret one's fate.

In "Poema del Otoño," Darío again confronts the issue of mortality, but in a somewhat different spirit (Darío 1967, 771-76; Darío 1965, 113-16). "Otoño" is a celebration of life, especially its sensual possibilities, *despite* the certainty of death.

. . .   . . .

Gozad de la tierra, que un bien cierto encierra;	Enjoy the earth, that proffers us its blessings;
gozad, porque no estáis aún bajo la tierra.	enjoy it, for you soon will lie beneath it.

Apartad el temor que os hiela y que os restringe	Forget the fear that cramps and chills your heart;
la paloma de Venus vuela sobre la Esfinge....	the dove of Venus is flying over the Sphinx....

There is, indeed, possible victory over death ("Lovers can conquer death and time and fate, / enjoying roses and myrtles in the tomb"). Darío's emphasis, however, remains on the earthly travail ("The heart of heaven is aching for the triumph of life on earth, which is struggle and is glory. / We grieve and suffer, we quail at the blows of fate"). Again, there is the Pythagorean faith in the cosmic unity of life's forces ("the very sap of the universe flows within us"), but the famous final line

¡Vamos el reino de la Muerte	Let us travel to the land of Death
por el camino de Amor!	by the path of Love!

exalts living life, not triumph over death.[6]

To be sure, on occasion Darío's treatment of death ranged far beyond the mystical/erotic/stoical outlook of "Lo Fatal" and "Poema del Otoño." In other poems he extended his treatment to include nature as killer ("Earthquake," in "Nicaraguan Triptych," 1912) (Darío 1967, 1062; Darío 1965, 132), a recurrent theme in Central American poetry. In his most frequently quoted "political" poem ("To Roosevelt," 1904), Darío paints an image of man as hunter and victim:

Se necesitaría, Roosevelt, ser	Roosevelt, you must become,
por Dios mismo,	by God's own will,
el Riflero, terrible y fuerte	the deadly Rifleman and the dreadful
Cazador.	Hunter
para poder ternernos en	before you can clutch us
vuestras férreas garras.	in your iron claws. (Darío 1965, 70)
(Darío 1967, 641	

Finally, there is the related theme of fratricide. Here Darío cries out at the failures of Hispanic America—failure to stem the tide of the Anglo-Saxons, failure to reach a truce among brothers. Here one thinks of "To Columbus" (1892) and "Song of the Blood" (1896) (Darío 1967, 595-96, 703-4). These (and other) poetic images of death represent additional dimensions of Darío's critique of his society, its culture and politics (Enguidanos 1970, 27-29). This critique, though often wrapped in irony and contradicted by occasional opportunism, justified inclusion of his "Por que?" in a collection of revolutionary poetry in the late 1960s and an early Sandinista-sponsored edition following the overthrow of Somoza (FSLN 1968, 109-10; see also Mejía Sánchez 1980). Most recently, President Daniel Ortega, leader of the San-dinista National Directorate — and a poet himself — declared: "The Sandinis-ta front is the anti-imperial stance and social advocacy of Rubén Darío" (Speech of 17 July 1984, in Marcus 1985, 309; see also Balladares 1982, 97; Kinzer 1987, 3). Despite these important departures into social/political themes of death, Darío remained centrally concerned with death as an existential/mystical problem, that is to say, he remained within the pull of the field on the first pole of interpretations of death outlined at the outset of this chapter.

Coronel Urtecho and the *Vanguardistas*:   From Surrealistic Death to National Humiliation

Despite his enormous literary output, Darío did not found a "school" of poetry as such. He produced instead countless imitators. These versifiers continued to refine Darío's idiom on philosophical themes. A trio of León-born poets — Azarías H. Pallais, Alfonso Cortés, and Salomón de la Selva — offered new alternatives, but de la Selva, for instance, lived most of his life outside Nicaragua (Gutiérrez 1970, x).[7] The revolt against the lifeless imitation of Darío, as it turned out, was launched in the 1920s by the Nicaraguan avant-garde (*Vanguardistas*) in Granada. As Cardenal has written, for the *Vanguar-distas* "the struggle was not against Darío, but against the falsifiers of Darío. *They* were...the true continuators of his work" (Cardenal 1982d [1948]).

This mission was reflected in daring poems, blazing manifestoes, and eccentric public displays. The clarion call was clearly José Coronel Urtecho's "Oda a Rubén Darío," published shortly after the author's return to Nicaragua from California in 1927.[8] The poem's final stanza (to be accompanied by a whistle — *con pito*!) called the *Vanguardistas* to action:

En fin, Rubén,	And so, Rubén
paisano inevitable, te saludo	my inevitable countryman, I greet you
con mi bombín,	with a flip of my derby
que se comieron los ratones en	that the rats ate in
mil novecientos veinte y	nineteen hundred and twenty
cinco. Amén. (El Diario	five. Amen. (Anderson-Imbert 1969, 582)
Nicaragüense, May 29, 1927)[9]	

A "Short Version of the Permanent Manifesto" (September 1932) called urgently for: "poets, narrators, historians, painters, geographers, public defenders (*apologistas*), botanists, architects, musicians, artisans, farmers, photographers, actors, film-makers, librarians, printers and a sovereign Nicaraguan people. We want to see all informed and impartial persons in the service of the country" (Cuadra 1979b, 31). But there was also a consistent emphasis on recovering the "true Nicaraguan culture" from invading forces. "We are intervening on behalf of a special race. We want to preserve intellectually what is ours. Not to permit the evaporation of our Latin spirit: Indo-Spanish. To preserve our traditions, our traditional customs, our language. To preserve our nationality" (Cuadra's "Dos Perspectivas," [1931] in Cuadra 1979b, 27). A poster in the *Vanguardia* office read: "We distrust: copies, rhetoric, rules, academicism, linguistic purism, baggie eyes at dusk, the dead who write to the dead. We promote: originality, creativity, innovative work that makes its own rules, linguistic invention, naughty words, youthful and spirited poetry, the dawn of a national literature" (Cuadra 1979b, 173). These angry young writers were not afraid to state just what parts of Nicaragua's poetic legacy they would support and what parts they would ignore or condemn.

The avant-garde of the late 1920s and early 1930s was a brilliant, experimental, iconoclastic movement that gave all subsequent Nicaraguan poetry a language of the native land, of open protest and provocation, of play. Cardenal has called Coronel Urtecho, the acknowledged leader of the movement, "the master of his generation and...the master of all succeeding generations up to the present" (Stansifer 1981, 2). And Cardenal's claim is made in the face of the well-known antidemocratic political inclinations of many of the active *Vanguardista* writers. In response to a 1932 questionnaire on the youth's views on the potential of a democratic system, Coronel Urtecho said: "I believe that democratic and liberal ideas, along with democratic institutions, have brought about the ruin of Nicaragua in all areas of human activity" (Cuadra 1979b, 69). Indeed, in a 1975 poem Cardenal wrote: "You were a reactionary before / and now you are 'uncomfortable' in the left / but in the extreme left, / without having changed anything inside you; / the reality around you has changed" ("Epistle to José Coronel Urtecho," in Walsh 1980, 95).[10] Today, a vigorous supporter of the Sandinista revolution, Coronel is a contributor to Cardenal's Culture Ministry magazine *Nicaráuac*. Still, he finds himself in a kind of cultural no-man's-land, burdened by a pro-Somoza past and yet reenergized artistically by the victory of the Sandinistas.[11]

A special feature of the *Vanguardista* movement in Nicaragua was its focus in Granada, a provincial bourgeois city, the traditional political home of the Conservatives, on Lake Nicaragua at the foot of Mount Mombacho (Cardenal 1982d [1948], 73; Tirado 1983, 65). Although engaged in constant innovation, the group had a cohesiveness that was not characteristic of avant-garde movements elsewhere in Latin America at the time. They were less fragmented by the competing "ismos" that were rampant in Buenos Aires/Montevideo, Santiago de Chile, Mexico City, Lima, Rio/Sâo Paulo, and other cultural centers of the day (Forster 1975, 12-50; Paz 1974, 102-64). The Nicaraguan *Vanguardistas* were, in fact, a kind of artistic extended family in Granada.

The *Vanguardistas* were placed uniquely in time as well. There is a striking coincidence between the timing of this literary revolt and the revolt of Sandino (1927-1933) (See Sandino's July 1927 proclamation in Macaulay 1967, chap. 4; and Booth 1982, 41-46). Indeed, the active period of the *Vanguardistas* and of the first Sandinistas overlapped almost perfectly. And this fact was not lost on the *Vanguardista* poets. One of the questionnaires they distributed to "the older generation" in 1931 included the following item: "What is your view of the American intervention in Nicaragua?" And some of the editorials of their papers addressed the revolt in the Segovias (See, e.g., Cuadra 1979b, 75-77). A 1932 *Vanguardia* editorial, in response to a published attack on the rebel leader, asked: "What does Sandino represent? Despite *Diario Nicaragüense*, Sandino is the one who speaks for Nicaragua today. He is the only one with a national conscience to raise his cry of shame, because shame is what we must call it when a foreign country tires to play tutor in the foolishness of such an unimportant and valueless thing as is [this] election" (Cuadra 1979b, 76). And in an appeal against the deeper cultural attacks of the North Americans, another editorial stated: "Under the weight of the uncultured yankee, foreign to the heart and to the mind of the Nicaraguan people, our nationalist vigor is succumbing to both political and moral prostitution" ("La Fratria Nicaragüense," in Cuadra 1979b, 77). Coronel recalls the "duality" that Sandino's cause represented to the Granadan group:

> We were supporters of Sandino because he was anti-yankee and so were we. Although we took some fundamentals of yankee culture for our readings in North American poetry, we were against North American domination over America and the things they wanted to impose on us: commercialism, capitalist industrialism, capitalism. This did not appear to us to be a good thing. Something like that—without much analysis. (Tirado 1983, 113, 119)

Nor was the historical contemporaneity of the two events lost on the later participant-historians of the movement. In 1979 Pablo Antonio Cuadra's *El Pez y la Serpiente* hinted at the parallel between the Sandinista victory and fifty years of literary struggle (Cuadra 1979b, 189).

Although it is appropriate to speak of a literary revolt in the case of the *Vanguardistas*, it is virtually impossible to generalize in any other way on their writings. The streams that flowed through Coronel were many and diverse — Cortés, de la Selva, the North American poetry of Rachel Lindsay and Ezra Pound, Edith Sitwell, and the surrealists of Europe. Thus, whereas some of the *Vanguardistas* spoke with a sharply political voice regarding the suffering and death of their countrymen, Coronel treated death more philosophically. "They all die," he said recently, referring to other writers of his generation. "The strange thing is that I don't seem to die" (Tirado 1983, 105). "What projects are you working on now?" Steven White recently asked the aging poet. Coronel answered: "I'm working, as always, at trying to work—and preparing myself to die properly" (White 1986, 13). In "Hipotesis de tu Cuerpo," for example, the poet works images of life and death into a powerfully erotic and surrealist language:

... ...	
Vida muerte.	Deathly life.

Cuánto camino da a tu ombligo	How many paths lead to your navel
si hecho raíces ánclote a fond	if turned to roots I anchor deeply
puerto de tierra	in you, oh earthly port
puerta a mi tierra tuya a cerrojo	door to my land, yours under sacred
sagrada.	bolt.

Tesómosme, Mesómoste.	Tesomosme, Mesomoste.

Cávote sepultura en mi otro sexo	I dig a grave for you in my other sex,
Cávame sepultura en tu otro sexo.	Dig a grave for me in your other sex,too.
Muéreme Vívote Víveme Muérote	Die for me and I live for you;
	Live for me and I die for you
No nos distingo.	I can't tell us apart.

Sésamo....	Sesame...(Gutiérrez 1970, 106-9).

"Hipotesis" is full of neologisms favored by the *Vanguardistas*. "Tesómosme, Mesómoste," which appear to be nonsense derivatives of some indigenous incantation, also suggest the persistent linkages of *yo* and *tu* throughout the poem. (A possible translation would be: "For-you-we-are-for-me, For-me-we-are-for-you.") Likewise, the final line/word *Sésamo* might, on this approach, be rendered something like: "Open up to me. I know (sé), I love (amo) you." This may, of course, be an inappropriate play with the text. But the point is that the repetition and transpositions within "Tesómosme, Mesómoste" and "Sésamo" invite the reader to break up and rearrange the poet's words — only to put them back together, embarrassed by the obvious trick.[12]

In "To a Late-Blooming Oak," Coronel Urtecho expresses surprise at the force of renewal in the cycle of life. The aging, scraggly oak, "the next victim of the woodcutter / who was like an unloved maiden / languishing in her barrenness, / who, with last night's rain — oh what joy! — / awoke this morning in full bloom. / I became somewhat perplexed / as I contemplated that blooming oak / with so much of spring's tenderness...." (Gutiérrez 1970, 90). Coronel offered a new idiom through which to present images of death — he was largely responsible for introducing Poundian *exteriorismo*, later popularized by Cardenal — but his own vision remained irreverent, surrealistic, fatalistic, that is, still within the field of the first pole of death imagery.

Not so several other avant-garde writers. Often mixing Spanish and English as a comment on the cultural invasion of the North Americans, several poets spoke directly with a political voice. In his "Desocupación pronta, y si es necesario violenta," Joaquín Pasos called out:

> Yankees, go home,
> go home, go home, yankees.
> Go home, go home, go home,
> go home, go home, yankees.
> This land's perfume is only for us.
> . . .
> Go home, go home, go home.
> GO HOME!
> In these environs is the soul of a people
> whose essential beauty cannot attract you
>   with a *ticket* like some tourist trinket (Cuadra 1979b, 115-16).

Pasos' call was echoed by Manolo Cuadra, José Román, and Luis Alberto Cabrales (Cuadra 1979b, 119-28). Images of death — in concrete, everyday language — were now mingling with the theme of national humiliation.

Pablo Antonio Cuadra: The Double Vision and the Revolution

Among these latter voices was a nephew of Coronel Urtecho, Pablo Antonio Cuadra, who took Coronel's experimental lead to develop a language of the Nicaraguan landscape, of indigenous pre-Columbian metaphors, of Christian mysticism and, a broad current throughout, of political protest. For this reason — and because of his sustained, and critically recognized, productivity and editorial leadership over more than fifty years — Cuadra occupies a particularly important position in our discussion. Cardenal has called Cuadra — his current ideological foe — "the most Nicaraguan of all our poets" (White 1982, 45).[13] Another commentator has concluded that, because of the extraordinary breadth of his literary work, Cuadra is "the most complete and representative Nicaraguan intellectual" (Llopesa 1982, 13). Thus Cuadra becomes an intriguing transitional figure.

Cuadra was born in 1912 in Managua. When he was four his family moved to Granada. He was related by blood or marriage to Coronel Urtecho, Cardenal, and Pasos. He spent much of his early life in the Lake Nicaragua area, as a worker on family farms. He also began a university career in law, but soon abandoned it. He joined the *Vanguardistas* in Granada before he was twenty. Ultimately, however, he would combine journalism and poetry, becoming first the literary editor for *La Prensa*, and, following the assassination of Pedro Joaquín Chamorro in 1978, the editor of *La Prensa* until the Sandinista government closed it in July 1986 (Tünnermann-Bernheim 1973; Cuadra 1979a, xiii-xix; Yepes Boscán 1980, 7-22; Zavala Cuadra 1982).

Cuadra's early poetry often invoked images of death close to the Nicaraguan countryside he had come to know well. Thus, in "The Dead Cow," he wrote:

It was she, dead.
Isolated in the rough and barren highlands,
under the eternal parenthesis of her defenseless horns,
between the four lids of her vacant eyes. (Cuadra 1934; Cuadra 1983-
1985, 1:165)

This was truly Nicaraguan poetry, the poetry of the land, of campesino life. Ernesto Cardenal subsequently observed that *Poemas nicaragüenses* (1933) was "the first book of Nicaraguan poetry published in Nicaragua. More than that...this book *is* Nicaragua" (Cardenal 1968, 123). Cardenal recently recalled, "They had his first book, *Poemas nicaragüenses* at home, and when I learned to read, that was another book I liked going through. It was *Vanguardista...*, but it used a very real language, words from the Nicaraguan countryside, the language of Chontales, 'the dead cow,' all those poems...I didn't understand it all, some of the *Vanguardista* images were lost on me, but I liked a lot of what I found there" (Randall 1984, 93).

Soon Cuadra revealed an unabashed nationalism in the face of intervention by the U.S. Marines. In "Intervención (a poem to stick on the wall)," he wrote"

Here comes the big-footed yankee
and the gringo woman with honey-colored hair.
To the yankee say:
 go on
and to the little gringo girl:
 very well. (Cuadra 1979b, 115; Cuadra 1983-1985, 1:93).

Even more powerful was his 1935 poem "Por los caminos van los campesinos," an eerie foreshadowing of some of his most recent criticisms of the current Sandinista government:

Two by two,
ten by ten,
by hundreds,
by thousands,
the campesinos go barefoot

with their bedrolls and their rifles.

....

Two by two the sons have left,
hundreds of others have cried,
thousands of men have fallen
and turned to dust forever
dreaming on their bedrolls
about the life that was their rifle.

Two by two,
ten by ten,
by hundreds
and thousands
the *campesinos* go down the roads
to fight the civil war! (White 1982, 61)[14]

Like Coronel, Cuadra also experimented with Somocista politics but, breaking with the founder of the dynasty following a personal religious experience, he went into "voluntary exile" in the United States and South America from 1946 to 1950. Later, Cuadra's poems combine his growing fascination with indigenous Nicaraguan culture with a contemporary political statement. For example, recounting the Indians' ancient flight from volcanic terror, Cuadra etched his poem of the late 1950s "Written on a Roadside During the First Eruption":

...

They heard the cavernous voice of the monster.
From the high trees they watched the dirty decapitated giant,
the rugged back, only the rugged breast vomiting anger.

We will abandon our country and our kin
because a sterile god has dominated our land.... (Cuadra 1959; Cuadra 1983-1985, 3:97-98; White 1982, 59)

Indeed, death stalks his two major collections of the 1950s and 1960s. In "Urn with Political Profile," Cuadra sketched an epitaph for Somocismo:

El caudillo es silencioso   The chief is silent:
  — (dibujo su rostro silencioso). — (I draw his silent face.)

El caudillo es poderoso   The chief is powerful:
  — (dibujo su mano fuerte).   — (I draw his mighty hand.)

El caudillo es el jefe de los	The chief is leader of
hombres armados	armed men:
— (dibujo las calaveras de los	— (I draw the skulls of
hombres muertos).(Cuadra 1983-	dead men). (Cuadra 1971, 22-23)

1985, 3:89)

And in "Maiden's Lament for the Warrior's Death," Cuadra begins to express the martyr motif — still in a mythical setting — that will characterize so much of the poetry of the 1970s and 1980s:

. . .   . . .

desde tiempos antiguos	Ever since the old days
la muerte ronda.	Death has stalked.
Sin embargo,	And yet
nuevo es tu silencio	your silence is new,
y nuevo es dolor mío.	and new is my pain!
(Cuadra 1983-1985, 3:79)	(Cuadra 1971, 34-35)

In his epical ode to the wonders of Lake Nicaragua (one of which is dedicated to Ernesto Cardenal and his Solentiname community), *Songs of Cifar and the Sweet Sea*, Cuadra returns again and again to the image of the dead bird: "From shore to shore / bones / and skeletons of birds / calcined feathers / stench / of death, / dying / sea birds, / caws / of agony, / sad trills / and a few / quivering skulls / still erect / with beaks / open to the wind" (Cuadra 1979a, 98-99; Cuadra 1983-1985, 4:135). But the possibility of transcending death remained at the edges of Cuadra's poetry, nowhere perhaps as political as in "Interioridad de dos estrellas que arden": "He who fought for liberty / was given a star, right next / to the shining mother who died in childbirth / ... / 'and did you know the fruit of your struggle?' / 'I died too soon.' / 'Do you sleep?' asked the Warrior. / 'I dream,' replied the mother" (Cuadra 1959, 22-24; White 1982, 62-63; Cuadra 1983-1985, 3:83; see also Battle 1965, 111-12; see "El Poeta Muerto," Cuadra 1983-1985, 4:27-28 for an earlier statement of transcendence). Cuadra was building a unity of life and death through the theme of cyclical renewal in all its natural forms.

Throughout the 1960s and 1970s Cuadra extended his literary influence through ambitious editing for *La Prensa*. In 1961, mobilizing the resources of Nicaragua's conservative elite during a period of relative cultural liberalization, Cuadra launched the literary journal *El Pez y la Serpiente*, the title joining symbols of the indigenous and Hispanic sources of Nicaraguan culture as well as the struggle between good and evil "and the agony of the con-temporary writer" (*El Pez y la Serpiente* 1, Jan. 1961, 6; Stansifer 1981, 4-7). In the colorful pages of *La Prensa*'s literary supplement of the late 1970s, Cuadra published such "political" poets as Julio Cortázar, Roque Dalton, Giaconda Belli, Michele Najlis, and Rosario Murillo, as well as Cardenal's sculpture and commentary on the Solentiname experiment (see, e.g., *La Prensa Literaria* throughout 1976). And he regrouped Granadan *Vanguardistas* and their students for the editorial board of *El Pez*: his original co-editors included Coronel Urtecho, Ernesto Cardenal, Fernando Silva, and Ernesto Gutiérrez. Cuadra, especially following the assassination of *La Prensa*'s owner Pedro Joaquín Chamorro in January 1978, became openly critical of "Tachito" Somoza. The central symbol of his poetry of the late 1970s was the tree, a metaphor for both crucifixion and resurrection. In particular, the last of the series, "El Jícaro" (dedicated "to the memory of Pedro Joaquín Chamorro, whose blood gave life to a Nicaragua of liberty") employed indigenous myths from the *Popol-Vuh* account to address contemporary political developments (Yepes 1980, 79-85, 91).[15] Thus, the vision, although more lyrical and historically conscious than that of Coronel Urtecho, and more tied to Nicaraguan realities than that of Darío, was still a double vision of esthetic sensibility and political engagement.

But Cuadra was moving increasingly out of the field of the first pole into that of the second. Or, perhaps more accurate to the rhythm of his artistic/poetical development, Cuadra had recovered the political activism of his youth. Recalling Cuadra's literary roots among the *Vanguardistas* of the early 1930s, Marc Zimmerman has pointed out: "[There is] a somewhat paradoxical fact about the Nicaraguan avante-garde (but not without precedent in other countries): constructing a poetics relying on an almost feudal and utopian reaction to the advance of capitalist and imperialist penetration, they created a body of poetry that [even] writers of a Marxist bent could use and transform" (Zimmerman 1980, 57).

With the Sandinista victory, Cuadra initially celebrated the overthrow of Somoza as an extension of earlier literary revolts.[16] Still, he rejected a Sandinista offer to assume the prestigious diplomatic post of ambassador to Spain (Stansifer 1981, 14). And with the withdrawal of Violeta Barrios de Chamorro, widow of the slain editor of *La Prensa*, from the Governing Junta of National Reconstruction in early 1980, Cuadra, too, became more critical of the Sandinista-dominated junta. Over the next few years, the U.S.-backed Contra attacks in the countryside having provoked a declaration of national emergency (March 1982) and its censorship of newspapers and the church, Cuadra adopted an increasingly hostile stance to the government. By 1984 his condemnation of Sandinista cultural policy was sharp and polemical. In a volume published outside Nicaragua invoking Orwellian images of the Sandinista state, Cuadra spoke of a "dramatic struggle between an ideology and a culture" (Zavala et al. 1985, 237). Stung by Sandinista Jaime Wheelock's labeling of the earlier literary avant-garde as "decadent," Cuadra claimed that the Sandinistas had turned a "tradition of democratic aspiration" into a cultural dictatorship—creating "'slogans' but no poems, propaganda but no life" (Zavala et al. 1985, 238-39; Johnson 1985a, 24; White 1986, 23-24). Cuadra's poem "1984 Nicaragua" recalls the author's earlier "Por los caminos...":

My country is occupied by soldiers! My country,
which seethed with poetry,
is now repeating slogans! My country,
with its streams of children
condemned to death.
. . .
. . . We call out names
in the void: Manuel!
Ramon! Felix! Federico!
But our sons
      have departed...! (Zavala et al. 1985, 9)

Cuadra's original editorial board for *El Pez y la Serpiente* had departed as well. Ernesto Cardenal, now Nicaraguan Minister of Culture, was editing his own journals of poetry—in the name of a new vision for a new Nicaragua. Thus, Cuadra, the student of Coronel and the teacher of Cardenal, was now ranged against both in an increasingly ideological struggle to shape cultural renewal in post-Somoza Nicaragua.

Cardenal and the Revolutionary Vision: Death as History-Making Martyrdom

In a real sense, the double vision of which we have spoken is closed into a single vision in the work of Ernesto Cardenal. "I now see," Cardenal told Margaret Randall recently, "that my entire life, my initial commitment to God, my time with Merton in Kentucky, the years at Solentiname, the poetry, everything, was part of a single road to the revolution" (Randall 1984, 90). Cardenal thus breaks out of the field of the first pole of contemplating death as ineffable, at once beautiful and terrible, and places it in real life in all its grittiness, amidst the gunfire, mud, and official proclamations. His Christian voice requires a profound sense of resurrection, of victory over death; his political voice raises that death to the status of history-making martyrdom. If Cuadra's death imagery increasingly tied the past to the present, Cardenal's ties the present to the future.

Nephew of Coronel Urtecho and younger cousin to Pablo Antonio Cuadra, Ernesto Cardenal was born into a wealthy Granadan family in 1925 (Smith 1979a; Borgeson 1984, 183-97). Cardenal thus belongs to the literary "Generation of 1940" in Nicaragua. Currently Minister of Culture, Cardenal's background brought him into contact with North American poetry (especially that of Ezra Pound, Walt Whitman, and William Carlos Williams) during study at Columbia University in 1947-1949. A religious conversion experience led him to enter the Trappist monastery in Gethsemane, Kentucky, where he was novitiate to Thomas Merton. Although he left Gethsemane for health reasons, he continued his religious studies in Mexico and Colombia, was ordained a Roman Catholic priest in 1965, and began his famous religious commune among the campesinos on the islands of Solentiname in Lake Nicaragua the following year.

By the time he began the Solentiname experiment, Cardenal had already been deeply involved in anti-Somoza politics. He had participated in an abortive 1954 attempt on the dictator's life and had to flee the country following the assassination of Somoza García in 1956. His early published poetry reflects a drive toward an ever more explicit political statement in a style accessible to the widest possible audience. He (with Coronel Urtecho) would term this style *exteriorismo* and define it as follows:

> *Exteriorismo* is a poetry created with images of the exterior world, the world we see and sense....*Exteriorismo* is objective poetry: narrative and anecdote, made with elements of real life and with concrete things, with proper names and precise details and exact data, statistics, facts, and quotations....In contrast, interiorist poetry is a subjectivist poetry made only with abstract or symbolic words: rose, skin, ash, lips, absence, bitterness, dream, touch, foam, desire, shade, time, blood, stone, tears, night....
>
> I think that the only poetry which can express Latin American reality and reach the people and be revolutionary is exteriorist....Poetry can serve a function: to construct a country and create a new humanity, change society, make the future Nicaragua as part of the future great country that is Latin America. (Zimmerman 1985a, x; Cardenal 1974, 9-11)

Already by 1954 Cardenal had linked images of death to political struggle. His "In the Tomb of the Guerrilla Fighter," written during his participation in the ill-fated conspiracy to assassinate Somoza García, lends a cosmic significance to rebellion:

> And afterwards?
> Afterwards we'll fall apart more, we'll fly, atoms in the cosmos.
> And perhaps matter is eternal, brother,
> without beginning or end or it has an end and starts again each time.
> Your love surely had a beginning but has no end.
> And your atoms that were in the soil of Nicaragua,
> your loving atoms, that gave their life for love,
> you'll see, they'll be light.
> I imagine your particles in the vastness of the cosmos like signs
> like living posters....(Zimmerman 1985a, 118-19; see also Randall 1984, 97-98)

And in his classic epic of revolt, "Hora 0" [Zero Hour], Cardenal juxtaposed, collage-like, Sandino's murder in 1934 and the death of one of his own co-conspirators in 1954, Adolfo Báez Bone. Here the natural cycle of rebirth in spring is cruelly broken by concrete historical events: "But April in Nicaragua is the month of death. / They killed them in April. / I was with them in the April rebellion / and I learned to handle a Rising machine gun. / And

Adolfo Báez Bone was my friend." Cardenal interjects a conversation to
prepare for the dominant theme of resurrection:

> "If they asked me to choose my fate"
> (Báez Bone had said to me three days before)
> "to choose between dying murdered like Sandino
> or being President like Sandino's murderer
> I'd choose Sandino's fate."
> > And he did choose his fate.
> Glory isn't what the history books teach:
> It's a flock of buzzards in a field and a great stink.
> > But when a hero dies
> > > he doesn't die:
> > > for that hero is reborn
> > > in a Nation. (Walsh 1980, 12)[17]

Cardenal's poetry employs the theme of death, then, as a contingent, historical experience. Except for his earliest work, there is none of Darío's private
anguish over the terror of death, none of Coronel Urtecho's dreamlike scenes
of foam and stone, none of Cuadra's symbolic trees against the evening sky.
And yet there are links from the past.[18] Following the "April Conspiracy" and
his religious conversion two years later, Cardenal entered a period of extended
contemplation that drew him to the pacifist Trappist monk Thomas Merton.
In this period a more cosmic voice appears, as in "The Marmots are not dead,"
in which the poet affirms the promise of new life in the depths of winter:

> The marmots in their burrows are not dead,
> they sleep. Nor are the chipmunks dead,
> nor have they gone away: curled up
> they lie asleep beneath the earth.
> ...life is asleep.
> in caves, cracks, hollows, secret galleries,
> eggs, silk cocoons, seeds, buds
> all wait for spring....(Cardenal 1975b, 59)

One recalls Coronel Urtecho's surprise at the "vast tenderness of spring" as
the ragged old oak regains its youth. Or in more immediate, human terms,
Cardenal's "Coplas on the Death of Merton" (1968-1969) speaks of a cosmic
process: "Our lives are rivers / that go to empty into the death / that is life."
This is a turn on Jorge Manrique's classic fifteenth-century elegy to his father
(Cardenal 1975b, 31-32). But one also recalls Darío's "Del Otoño": "In us,
Life becomes force, Life becomes fire. / Let us travel to the land of Death by
the path of Love!"

Somoza's destruction of the Solentiname community in 1977, however,
threw Cardenal decisively behind the FSLN armed struggle. Cardenal now
became an international ambassador for revolution in Nicaragua and the

recorder of the cost of the final bloody struggle with the National Guard. Perhaps the most powerful treatment of that cost is "Landing with Epitaph," which records a return by plane to Managua after the victory in July 1979:

> I think, I don't know why, of the dead ones,
> not all of them, but *those*,
>   our dead ones,
> in the mountains, in common ditches, in a solitary tomb,
> in cemeteries, on the roadsides,
> near this airport, all over the country,
> the ones with monuments, the anonymous ones without any monument,
> all transformed into this soil, making this soil more sacred,
> Sandino, Carlos Fonseca, Julio Buitrago, Oscar Turcios,
> . . .
> and so many more, and so many more, and so many more:
> May I be buried in this soil together with you Comrades,
>   Death's Comrades.
> The wheels now only a few meters off the ground.
> And a voice over the microphone should say: Ladies and Gentlemen
> the ground we're about to touch is very sacred.
> . . . the wheels have just landed, passengers,
> on a great tomb of martyrs. (Zimmerman 1985a, 36-37).

Finally, Cardenal sings of the martyr's death, of the struggle, as Darío said, for "the triumph of life on earth." His imagery of death is filled with the gritty historicity of revolutionary comradeship. More than that, it is dominated by the certain prophecy of reconstruction, of the building of the new society (Christ 1974, 191; Valdés 1983).[19] As Robert Pring-Mill has written of the documentary form in Cardenal: "Poets and cameras can both affect what they record, but whereas a documentary camera's presence conditions the 'ongoing situation,' Cardenal's recording of the present or the past is aimed at helping to shape the future — involving the reader in the poetic process in order to provoke him into full political commitment, thus fostering the translation of the poet's more prophetic visions into sociopolitical fact" ("The Redemption of Reality Through Documentary Poetry," in Walsh 1980, x; see also Alstrum 1980).

It will not be surprising, then, that Sandinista cultural policy under Cardenal has emphasized both the content of political themes and the style of "popular" poetry in constructing the new Nicaragua. Cardenal has thus again selected some themes from Nicaragua's past and rejected others. "Literature for literature's sake," he has said, "is worthless...poetry also must be political, not political propaganda but political poetry" (Stansifer 1981, 12).[20] Thus, although there is a strong strain of official Sandinista admiration for *nuestro* Rubén, as well as for certain aspects of the avant-garde (in spirit if not in content), much of the poetic legacy lacking social consciousness is rejected. Sandinista cultural policy is based on conscious choices against: abstract art, elitist literature, "meaningless" poetry, and cultural influences from the United States and Western Europe. On the other hand, Sandinista cultural policy affirms primitive painting, folk art, popular struggle and martyrdom, the "people's voice" in theater and literature, and poster and mural art (Stansifer 1981, 9-10; See also Instituto de Estudio del Sandinismo 1982.).[21]

Conclusion: Devaluing and Reclaiming the Poet's Vision

Focusing on death imagery in the poetry of Darío, Coronel Urtecho, Cuadra, and Cardenal has revealed not only an important reality in Central American life; it has also revealed different artistic and political approaches to that reality. Through a process of literary selection, the twentieth century in Nicaraguan poetry has come to reject strictly philosophical and surrealistic treatments of death. The press of events—of history—has driven poets of diverse ideological positions to affirm a socially conscious poetry, with strong political content. At the same time that the process of revolution has given poetic voice to many who had been silenced by the Somoza dictatorship, it has also forced others to sacrifice their double vision of the artist's role, to choose to be for or against "the process." Political, military, and economic pressure from outside has only narrowed the lines of poetic practice, thus devaluing the one resource of cultural expression that has been the special pride of Nicaragua.

But despite the pressures of the historical process itself, a vigorous debate over the shape of Nicarauga's poetry of the future continues—both within pro- and anti-Sandinista camps. New poets, young poets, especially women, black and indigenous poets, will make their own contribution to the rich heritage of this "republic of poets." May the Nicaraguan people reclaim its full voice to speak on the pain and death of the past—and of the life in its future.

NOTES

1. For a broader perspective on Nicaraguan cultural policies since 1979, see chapter 9 below. Other revolutions, of course, have inspired "cultural revolutions." Mao's "Great Proletarian Cultural Revolution" of the late 1960s and Khomeini's Islamic "cultural revolution" of the 1980s come to mind. Most recently, on cultural developments within the relatively bloodless revolution in the Philippines, see Seth Mydans, "Aquino Inspires Artistic Renaissance," *New York Times*, Aug. 31, 1986. The Nicaraguan case, however, presents features that distinguish it sharply from these other examples.

2. Sandino read this natural catastrophe as a clear sign that God was on his side in his rebellion against the government and Yankee interventionists (see Macaualy 1967, 191).

3. Feierabend et al. 1972, 399, reports the following 1965 homicide and suicide rates per 100,000 population:

Country	Homicide	Suicide
Denmark	0.8	19.1
West Germany	1.2	19.3
Japan	1.5	14.9
Costa Rica	3.5	3.0
United States	5.1	10.8
Guatemala	14.0	3.0
Mexico	22.0	1.8
Nicaragua	26.0	1.0

Government figures for crude death rates in Nicaragua during the mid-1960s were so suspect that the United Nations Population Division estimated a rate more than twice the official rate, which ranked Nicaragua behind only Haiti and Honduras among North and Central American countries (*Demographic Yearbook* 1970 1971, 655, 659, 662).

4. No attempt will be made here to suggest an evolution of this theme *within* Darío's work. Our main interest is on the evolution from Darío through twentieth-century Nicaraguan poetry. Thus, the range of his death imagery should suffice to identify the national poetic legacy on which subsequent writers had to draw. (I emphasize the *national* poetic legacy because, needless to say, all the poets discussed here were also shaped by important foreign literary influences and encounters.) A different, but helpful, framework for interpreting death imagery is offered by Valdés 1966. On the Pythagorean themes in Darío's poetry, see Jrade 1980; Jrade 1983, 25-53; and Skyrme 1975.

5. "Rarely has a poet violated logical, grammatical, rhythmical, and stanzaic patterns with greater expressiveness. The power of the emotion and feeling reigns supreme in the final unwritten line of the unfinished sonnet" (Predmore 1971, 437-38; see also Ellis 1974, 61-64) The English translations used here are in Darío 1965, 90; the Spanish text is in Darío 1967, 688.

6. Soto 1977, 229, says that Darío proclaims here "a kind of stoically resigned epicureanism."

7. On the "immense isolation" of de la Selva, the first Hispanic American to be nominated for a Nobel Prize in literature, see Arellano 1982, 170-71. White 1982, 23, writes: "De la Selva's actions are significant in that they signal the first attempt on the part of Nicaraguan intellectuals to reverse the flow of culture from the United States by working outside Nicaragua."

8. A brief chronology of events central to the *Vanguardista* movement may be found in Cuadra 1979b.

9. On the background to "Oda a Rubén Darío," see Tirado 1983, 51-56. For another example of homage to/parody of Darío by Coronel, see "Contrarrima" (1925), in Gutiérrez 1970, 22.

10. This poem also appears with several others commemorating Coronel's seventieth birthday in *El Pez y la Serpiente* 17 (Summer 1976), 9-21. Cardenal's more charitable comments on Coronel and the *Vanguardistas* are in Johnson 1985a, 14-16.

11. Coronel told José Miguel Oviedo, "They [Sandinista officials] haven't offered me anything, and they won't. I don't think it would be

appropriate" (Oviedo 1982, 22). Coronel has accounted for his early support of Somoza García (which was rewarded with a diplomatic appointment in Madrid and brief membership in the National Assembly) by citing the seductive influence of Charles Maurras, the philosopher of French fascism. "La disputa por el poder y la división del pueblo por quién debía tener el poder se resolvía mediante la implantación de la monarquía. El asunto del poder no hay que discutirlo, porque si lo discutimos, nos matamos, y siguen las disputas. El lo argumentaba con mucha sutileza, o nos parecía a nosotros. Pero no se aplicaba a nuestra situación. Nosotros creíamos que Nicaragua necesitaba un gobierno fuerte, apoyado en un ejército vencedor, para que se estableciera un gobierno estable que pudiera trabajar en pro del pueblo. Esa era la teoría mas o menos." (Tirado 1983, 118-19). On Maurras, see Weber 1962. In fact, says Coronel, "It was an exceedingly confused time....It was a difficult and dangerous time....We were all boys. I was 20 and the others were even younger" (Tirado 1983, 66, 81; see also Stansifer 1981, 2-3). For a sampling of Coronel Urtecho's recent political poetry, see Zimmerman 1985b, 167, 171-72, 183, 188-89, 223-24, 293-96, 298, 300, 302-3. See also his pro-FSLN/anti-Yankee "prose poem" (Coronel 1981).

12. For much of this analysis of "Hipotesis," I am grateful to James J. Alstrum and Marina E. Kaplan. Both offered helpful readings of this difficult and previously untranslated poem.

13. Cardenal has also called Cuadra's poetry "grandes sueños políticos, poesía, tradición, pueblo y comunión con la tierra" (Guardia de Alfaro 1971, 21).

14. This poem was later adapted by Cuadra into a short play, first performed in 1937 (Cuadra 1981).

15. "El Jícaro" may be the only Cuadra poem to be published by a Sandinista government-sponsored journal; see *Nicaráuac* 1 (May-June 1980), 107-9.

16. An editorial afterward to the first post-Somoza issue of *El Pez y la Serpiente* (1979) acknowledged the connection between the Sandinista-led victory and the anniversary of the *Vanguardistas*.

17. On the "resurrection motif," see Schaefer 1982, 171-79; see also Borgeson 1984, 154-55, for the view that the vision of hope in "Zero Hour" is "unconvincing."

18. On earlier poems, including "Immortal amor" (1943-1945), in which the image of death is linked to the sea, see Borgeson 1984, 21-25. Some passages in "Inmortal amor" reminders of Coronel Urtecho's "Hipotesis de tu Cuerpo, " for example: "Tu cuerpo es otro cuerpo mío más lejano /..." (Your body is my other more distant body /...). See Borgeson 1984, 24.

19. Michele Najlis, a Granadan influenced in her earliest poetry by Cardenal, may have been the first woman to publish militant anti-Somoza poetry. See Randall's interview with her in Randall 1984, 109-17. For Najlis' use of the theme of death as martyrdom, see "To the Martyrs of Bocay" in Zimmerman 1985b, 41-42. On the importance of martyrdom in Cardenal's poetry, see Schopf 1985, 188-89.

20. This selecting out from the past has gone even to the point of suppressing his own earlier poetry that does not speak with a properly revolutionary voice. See Pring-Mill in Cardenal 1975b, 14; and Borgeson 1977, 5, n. 7. Coronel Urtecho has taken up Cardenal's call in his "The Past Will Not Return," a poem that plays with past, present, and future in deadly earnest:

Ya el pasado realmente es pasado.	Now the past is really the past.
El presente presente el futuro	The present present the future
futuro	future
Antes era el pasado el presente	Before the past was the present
el presente el pasado	and the present the past
Era imposible separar el presente	It was impossible to separate the
del pasado	present from the past
El pasado el presente el futuro	The past present and future
eran solo el pasado	were only the past
Pero el pasado ya ha cambiado	But now even the past has changed
aun de significado	its meaning
Todo el pasado ha sido juzgado	All the past has been tried and
y condenado	condemned
No volvera el pasado.	The past will not return.

(Nicaráuac 1, July-June 1980, 131) (Murguía & Paschke 1983, 153-59)

Coronel recently told Steven White: "Because of the Revolution, now we can write history as we make it — and that's the true history. This history identifies itself with truth and poetry. The three things are *one* in the Revolution: history, truth, poetry. By making poetry, now we are making history" (White 1986, 12).

21. The first several volumes of *Nicaráuac*, the Culture Ministry's literary journal, featured a department commemorating "heroe y martir." See also Instituto de Estudio del Sandinismo 1982, and Johnson 1985a, for selections from the "poetry workshops," most emphasizing themes of love and sex rather than death and politics. For a comment on the continuing debate within the Sandinista cultural leadership over the value of the poetry workshops, see Bennett 1987.

CHAPTER 9

Sandinista Cultural Policy: Notes Toward an Analysis in Historical Context

David E. Whisnant

Among the themes that regularly emerge when Sandinista leaders speak of the role of culture in the revolution, two are particularly salient: the revolution's deep cultural roots, and the crucial involvement of Nicaragua's creative artists at every stage of the revolutionary process. Nearly fifteen years after leaving as a swaggering high school graduate to join the FSLN in the mountains, Omar Cabezas recalled the transforming power of his first political work in Subtiava, an Indian barrio of his native León:

> The Subtiavans were there even before there was a León, even before the Spanish conquest....I left for the mountains confident mainly because I felt that Subtiava was behind me....*Subtiava*, that was power....
>
> Before the Subtiavans started marching, they beat their *atabales*....And you felt a unity in the beat of the drums....For this was the Indian awakening....I realized at that moment they were marching not only in Subtiava but over all of Latin America—over history, over the future (Cabezas 1982; Cabezas 1985b, 40).[1]

Speaking at the Casa de las Américas in Havana almost simultaneously with Cabezas' recollections, novelist Sergio Ramírez, member of the Governing Junta of National Reconstruction and later vice president of Nicaragua, made a statement frequently quoted by other Sandinista leaders: "The revolution has been a most important cultural fact of our history not only because the people wove its multiple warp with imagination and creative capacity, invented new forms of war and methods of fighting, [and] resorted to their best traditions," he declared, "but also because their poets, their musicians, and their painters took their places in the trenches and assaulted the enemy's position" (Ramírez Mercado 1982).

Thus at every stage the Sandinistas have portrayed the origins, development, and aims of the revolution as complexly interwoven with the dynamics of Nicaraguan cultural history. Commander Henry Ruíz has told how in its early days the FSLN was able to build "chains" of support by using the

cherished family and godparent links within Nicaraguan campesino culture
(Booth 1985, 141). Culture later became a central concern in the structuring
of the new government and in initial policy formulation: the decree establishing the Ministry of Culture was one of the first half-dozen issued by the
ruling junta the day after they entered Managua. Six months later, Culture
Minister Ernesto Cardenal asserted that "the revolution is culture, and our
culture now is revolution; there is no distinction between revolution and culture" (Cardenal 1982e, 175) Early reports of the Sandinistas' apparent success
with cultural programs, especially the widely acclaimed literacy crusade and
the poetry workshops, led many outside Nicaragua to make a similar equation
(Stansifer 1981; Craven & Ryder [1983?]; Dore 1985; White 1982; Hirshon &
Butler 1983; Randall 1984).

Within Nicaragua itself, a consensus account of the relationship between
the political, social, and cultural aspects of the revolution took shape rather
quickly after 1979, and has been repeated on many occasions by Sandinista
leaders. It goes something like this: Through the agony of the Spanish conquest, the years of internal strife and new foreign domination following independence, and particularly the recent decades of U.S. cultural imperialism
facilitated by the puppet Somoza dictatorship, the authentic culture of
Nicaragua survived. Although fragmented and suppressed, it maintained its
integrity, its vigor, and its genius for resistance. At length it formed the
strongest and most durable substratum of the Sandinista movement—an in-
exhaustible reservoir of will and strength, a referential reality against which
the movement's directions could be checked. The victory of the Sandinistas
in 1979 was thus among other things a warrant of the ancient legitimacy and
resurgent vitality of that culture, whose honoring and nurturing therefore
necessarily had to be provided for legally and institutionally within the new
government. Responsive to their cultural mandate, the Sandinistas began immediately to build an entirely new cultural apparatus within the country—in-
sistently independent of foreign domination, democratic, decentralized, and
deeply respectful and supportive of national cultural traditions (Cardenal
1980; Cortázar 1983; Galeano 1981).

Like many consensus reports, this one contains substantial, of easily
documentable truth. Of the history of cultural imperialism, for example, there
can be no doubt. But like all national cultural histories, that of Nicaragua is
also more complex than can be comprehended within such a paradigm. Perennial factional strife among local elites, for example, has frequently not only
proved brutally insensitive to the cultural identity and interests of the majority
of ordinary people (as when vast numbers of campesinos were dispossessed
of their land in the elite-controlled conversion from subsistence agriculture
to the production of coffee and cotton for export), but also acted upon many
occasions to welcome and facilitate foreign economic and cultural intervention and domination (Booth 1985, 11-26).

This chapter therefore sketches an analytical framework within which
the cultural dimensions of the Sandinista revolution may be more adequately comprehended in relation to the complex histories of both the revolution

and Nicaragua itself: the cultural development of Nicaragua prior to the revolution; the sources of and influences upon the formation of the Sandinistas' cultural ideas and assumptions; the actual role of culture in the revolution, both as an enabling and empowering resource and as a confusing and frustrating impediment; and the Sandinistas' successes and failures in embodying their cultural ideas and policies in actual operating programs.

Beyond that, however, we shall also try to comprehend the more fundamental relationship between culture and revolutionary ideology, insofar as the perils peculiar to it emerge in particular forms in the Nicaraguan context: the intractabilities (social or intrapsychic) of historical cultural formation; the tension between the need for postrevolutionary stability and an ideological commitment to artistic freedom (which may lead in practice to destabilizing criticism of the emergent state); the seductive tendency — perhaps especially prominent among an internationally oriented (and thus to some degree culturally *dis*oriented) intellectual elite in a state undergoing decolonization — to romanticize and sanitize the national cultural past; and the perennially problematic linking of state-sponsored cultural programming (informed by whatever ideology) with national power and prestige. Hence central to our analysis is the contention that conceptions of culture are inseparable from both power and ideology, and therefore inevitably interactive with each. This is an essay on some aspects of the politics of culture as they may be seen in the recent history of Nicaragua.[2]

Culture as Preamble

When, in 1979, the Sandinistas finally entered Managua triumphantly, they faced a task of cultural reconstruction burdened by a tragic national cultural history four-and-a-half centuries long and many layers deep. Indeed, as the Sandinistas began to reach backward toward their remotest cultural origins, even the pre-colonial experience of Nicaragua presented to them not a tranquil and reassuring panorama of cultural unity to be recovered and celebrated, but a turbulent and disquieting diversity, disunity, and conflict reinforced by geography and other factors. As both Helms and Radell have outlined, eastern Nicaragua prior to the conquest was peopled by hunting and gathering Indian groups culturally related to South America. The salubrious climate and rich volcanic soils of the Pacific coast, on the other hand, supported more sedentary agricultural Indians culturally related to Mesoamerica. Moreover, a generally low and uneven population density created sectors of relatively autonomous cultural development even within the eastern and western regions, as well as differentials of political power and cultural influence (Radell 1969, 32-38; Helms 1975).

The conquest further complicated the situation, in some respects extending existing cleavages and disparities, and in others clearing the slate and starting anew. Radell has pointed out that "the Indian culture regions of pre-Columbian Nicaragua coincide closely to the later colonial administrative areas" (1969, 32). Granada was at the center of a large existing Indian population, for example, and most upper-class Spaniards settled there; the earliest nonindigenous residents of León, on the other hand, were mostly low-ranking Spanish foot soldiers stationed to forestall Cortés' threatened move southward from Mexico.

Even more important culturally than any of these factors, however, was the genocidal destruction of the native population and the irremediable reorganization of the cultural map of the country. As the sixteenth century began, Nicaragua had approximately one million native inhabitants. Nearly half were sold into slavery in the single decade between 1527 and 1536. Tens of thousands more died of epidemic disease or were exterminated by the Spanish. By the 1570s, a mere remnant of something like eight thousand remained (Radell 1969, 66-80).[3]

The impact of the culturally genocidal conquest did not fall equally upon the country, however; it was less severe as one moved eastward from the Pacific coast through the central highlands and toward the Atlantic coast. Indeed in the period between the conquest and independence, western Nicaragua was progressively Hispanicized and homogenized culturally, while the Atlantic coast, increasingly isolated from that dynamic, maintained more racial, cultural, and linguistic diversity and autonomy which in turn led much later (along with other factors) to an enduring Atlantic coast hostility to the "Spanish" Nicaraguans of the opposite coast.

The arrival of political independence in 1838 had considerably less meaning within the cultural sector than one might at first assume. Most of the indigenous population was gone, their communities, languages, lifestyles, and expressive practices forever erased. The majority of the population (concentrated along the Pacific watershed) had long since become mestizo, Catholic, and Spanish-speaking. The separation of the Atlantic coast had been exacerbated by English buccaneers, who for a century and a half manipulated the remnants of the local indigenous population as pawns in their struggle against the Spanish for military and commercial control of the area. Hence the dominant language of the Atlantic coast was English, and the dominant religious orientation Protestant, especially after Moravian missionaries arrived in 1849 (Dennis 1981). Thus what is now known as Nicaragua was—as it began its "independence"—in fact two countries, as it would remain for another century and a half.

On the west coast, where national identity was focused, and the major urban centers, most of the population, and virtually all national institutions were concentrated, two dynamics with profound cultural implications operated from the earliest days of independence: the rise of Positivism and Liberalism, and the United States' persistent intervention in Nicaragua's internal affairs.[4]

Throughout Latin America, Positivist thought gained its strongest adherents among the agricultural, commercial, and professional elites. Woodward has distilled the essence of Positivistic values and assumptions as they manifested themselves in Liberal regimes throughout Central America: obsession with material development; anticlericalism; faith in scientific and technical education; willingness to subordinate political democracy to economic growth and prosperity; emulation of European and North American values, capital, and leadership; and insensitivity to the desires and needs of the working classes (Woodward 1985, 156).

Culturally speaking, the implications of such a perspective were disastrous for the few scattered surviving remnants of indigenous cultural forms and practices, and even for the widespread mestizo, Hispanicized, Catholic working class culture that had developed following the conquest. The vernacular cultures of the urban working class and the subsistence agriculture-based campesinos alike were arrogantly depreciated by the modernizing Europeanizing elites of León, Granada, and Managua. Virtually no aspect of those cultural systems — land tenure patterns, family and community structure, diet, customs and ceremonies, economic relationships — escaped transformation under the Liberal agenda (Booth 1985, 11-14, 20-21).

Such patterns of transformation were exacerbated by the growing intervention of the United States, beginning with the struggles for control of a Nicaraguan interoceanic route. The episode with the most dramatic cultural implications was, of course, the William Walker intervention of the mid-1850s. According to a popular U.S. newsweekly of the period, Walker and his troops were "shedding their blood and sacrificing their lives" in Nicaragua not only to establish progressive government, but also to bring cultural enlightenment. One article accompanied by an elegant engraving envisioned "a future Venice in Nicaragua." As for the natives, it harbored no "mawkish sympathy" for "the miserable, hybrid, wretched creatures that form the mass of the population of the Central American states." "The only way to purify and enlighten such people," they judged, "was with powder and ball" (*Frank Leslie's Illustrated Newspaper*, Feb. 7, 1856, and June 6, 1857, 146-47, 158, 182-84; Bermann 1986).

Practically speaking, as soon as he managed to have himself elected president of the country, Walker declared English an official language, legalized slavery, and instituted vagrancy laws to force peasants to work for large landowners. For its part, the United States immediately recognized Walker's as the legitimate government of Nicaragua, inaugurating an era of direct intervention in the country's cultural (and other) affairs that was to last more than a century.

Although the Walker episode itself was short-lived, the broader and more durable patterns of Liberal subservience to North American and European culture can be glimpsed in, for example, the musical culture of Nicaragua's urban centers in the late nineteenth century. In a series of biographical sketches of about forty prominent Nicaraguan musicians and composers born between 1811 and 1911, Gilbert Vega Miranda noted the essential details: trained for the most part by European-educated teachers (or their Nicaraguan students), most composed within the dominant European forms (symphonies, operas, concertos, oratorios), and performed on European instruments (strings, winds, piano) within the bounds of established European performance practices. Miranda's lone reference to the popular song "Zopilote" by Luis Felipe Urroz (1857-1915) ("who knew how to extract the general sentiment from a folkloric melody") evokes the cultural conflict and loss: In the song an Indian, baptized against his will, is converted into a vulture which sings and dances at night on the outskirts of the "colonia indígena" (Vega Miranda 1982).[5]

Thus, as the nineteenth century closed, the outlines of two-and-a-half centuries of cultural loss and tragedy were clear: any culture that could reasonably have been called indigenously Nicaraguan was practically extinct; the replacement postconquest, preindependence, subsistence agriculture-based, Hispanicized vernacular culture itself had been decimated and dispersed by the Liberal-Positivist drive toward agro-export "modernization"; urban Liberal elites were fully in control of cultural norms and institutions, in which European and North American forms were dominant; culture itself (of whatever complexion) was subordinate to the the perennial factional political struggles over the direction of economic development and the division of spoils; a major east-west cleavage divided the country culturally as well as in many other respects; and the relatively sparse population (barely a half million at the turn of the century, or an average of fewer than ten per square mile) was concentrated principally in the three urban areas of León, Managua, and Granada.

Such a cultural tragedy was not greeted with passive acquiescence on the part of the entire populace, however. As Jaime Wheelock Román has demonstrated, instances of resistance can be documented all the way back to the conquest. A major episode of what may in some respects be termed "cultural resistance" emerged, for example, at the turn of the century during the presidency of José S. Zelaya (1894-1909). Although Zelaya was a classic Liberal whose major policies (infrastructure development, stimulation of agro-exports, expropriation of communal lands, forced labor drafts, and increased foreign investment) were beneficial to the elite and disastrous for campesinos, his nationalism and expansionism led him to oppose U.S. intervention and to end once and for all British control of the Atlantic coast.[6]

Zelaya's opposition to Yankee imperialism led to his replacement (with the help of U.S. Marines) by the successive, short-lived , U.S.-approved regimes of José Madriz, Juan Estrada, and Adolfo Díaz. Rebel general Benjamín Zeledón (*el indio*), who was killed leading an armed insurrection of peasants and poor artisans against Díaz, became—paradoxically, since he was backed by Liberal coffee growers—a cultural martyr. When his body was paraded before the public, it was viewed by seventeen-year-old Augusto Sandino (Booth 1985, 30; Black 1981, 9; "Nuestro pueblo, dueño de su historia," *Barricada*, Sep. 27, 1981, 3).

A full analysis of the cultural significance of Sandino in the Sandinista revolution lies far beyond the scope of this chapter, but several points are essential. Sandino was first of all the illegitimate son of a coffee grower and a peasant woman and was conscious of carrying within himself both Indian blood and some of the fundamental cultural conflicts of Nicaragua's national history (Bermann 1986, 192-94; Booth 1985; Ramírez Mercado 1984). "I am

Nicaraguan," he insisted, "and I am proud that in my veins flows, more than any other, the blood of the American Indian, whose regeneration contains the secret of being a loyal and sincere patriot." Hence Sandino's anti-imperialist challenge had a strong racial and cultural — as well as political and economic — basis. "The Yankees *say* according to the Monroe Doctrine," he observed, "'America for the Americans'" but "they *interpret* the Doctrine as 'America for the Yankes.' But so that the blond beasts will not continue in their deception, I recast the phrase as follows: the United States of North America for the Yankees. Latin America for the Indolatinos" (Marcus 1985, 396; Ramírez Mercado 1984, 1:259, 270).

Thus Sandino's fundamental importance as the focal cultural hero and the center of the emergent legitimizing cultural myth of the Sandinist revolution is beyond question. More than any other single figure in Nicaraguan history except the nationally venerated poet Rubén Darío, Sandino collected and focused the national cultural history for *los muchachos* of the 1960s and 1970s. The seeds he planted had to lie mostly dormant, however, during the long Somoza night to come. Like the children of Israel, Sandino's children faced forty years in the wilderness before their deliverance.

The cultural landscape of Nicaragua during the Somoza dynasty has yet to be mapped in detail, but the image projected by both the Sandinistas themselves and by many independent observers is not attractive: the accelerated decimation of vernacular culture (especially in rural areas) as a result of the regime's economic policies; the emergence of Managua as the center of "national" culture; the manipulative exacerbation of tensions between the east and west coast areas; increasing hegemony of U.S. culture; the starvation of national cultural institutions; and the repression of free cultural expression.

From 1934 through 1979 public policy in Nicaragua was shaped principally by the Somoza dynasty's brutal drive for personal wealth (Millett 1977; Diederich 1981; LaFeber 1983; Booth 1985, 51-95). In that process, the lives and culture of the majority of Nicaragua's ordinary people were on the one hand neglected, and on the other hand ground up by the regime as the increasingly concentrated ownership of agricultural lands drove hundreds of thousands of campesinos into poverty-ridden urban barrios, and the few public services and institutions that had been available deteriorated. Such a pattern of national "development" made the entire country one vast underdeveloped periphery feeding the insatiable maw of the Managua metropole.

Viewed from a cultural perspective, both the metropole-periphery polarization and the particular character of metropole cultural development were disastrous. Compounding the losses attendant upon the cultural neglect and destruction evident elsewhere in the country, Managua itself was a veritable wonderland of cultural skewings, ironies, and contradictions. As Nicaraguan intellectual Mariano Fiallos Gil lamented in the 1960s, a respectable system of national cultural institutions had for the most part never been built. During the early years of the Somoza regime, Cristiana Chaves described in a personal letter how she was continuing without pay the work of her father, who for a salary of sixteen córdobas a month had labored for years to nurture the tiny National Museum, which lacked even a building of its own. Chaves noted that such institutional starvation had been compounded by earthquake, fire, and systematic private and commercial looting of archaeological sites (Fiallos 1965, 59; Cristiana Chaves to Erwin P. Dieseldorf, July 18 and Sep. 19, 1939, Dieseldorf Collection, Box 152, Folders 3 and 4, Latin American Library, Tulane University).

Thus the domination of the cultural metropole by the United States occurred at once actively (both prior to the Somoza regime and later in collaboration with it) and by default. The U.S. hold on the country began in earnest with the toppling of Zelaya. By the late 1920s the intrusion of North American commercial culture was clearly evident as advertisements for Yankee automobiles, toothpaste, cigarettes, patent medicines (including Adalina sleeping pills for children), foods, appliances, tools, and office machines proliferated in Nicaraguan newspapers.

In subsequent decades the avalanche continued, until by the 1950s most of products advertised were of U.S. origin. The media were also saturated with the creations of North American mass culture. The issue of *La Prensa* that published lavish reports of the funeral of Anastasio Somoza García in 1956 also offered its readers Mutt and Jeff and Buck Rogers comics, reports of U.S. major league athletics, and their choice of a half-dozen Hollywood movies at Managua theaters (*El Diario Nicaragüense*, July 1929, and Jan.-Mar. 1931; *La Noticia*, Sep. 22, 1934, and Nov. 8, 1940; *El Centroamericano*, July and Aug., 1937; *La Prensa*, Oct. 2, 1956).[7] During the early days of July 1979, just before the Sandinistas entered Managua, seventeen of the city's thirty-one movie theaters were showing U.S. films, seven out of eight of *La Prensa*'s comics were from the U.S., and the Somoza-owned television system (linked to the Chase Manhattan Bank through the Banco Nicaragüense) was offering a regular diet of U.S. major league baseball, Hollywood films, Disney cartoons, and the fundamentalist Christian PTL Club (Black 1981, 38; *La Prensa*, July 1, 1979, 21).

The leftover scraps of support the Somozas threw to national cultural development were aimed very selectively, and frequently combined with rigorous cultural repression. Sandinista leaders (a number of them intellectuals, novelists, and poets) have recalled repeatedly, for example, the Somoza regime's attempts to censor books they wanted to read, or wrote and tried to publish (See, e.g., Carrión 1982, 54, and Ernesto Cardenal's interview in Zwerling & Martin, 1985, 45).

One of the most dramatic and widely known events of cultural repression was the destruction of Ernesto Cardenal's peasant community at Solentiname in 1977 by Somoza's National Guard. Cardenal's imaginative attempts to encourage local people to examine their lives, express themselves, and develop a heightened political consciousness through poetry, graphic art, Bible study, economic cooperation, and intense political reading (of Marx, Mao, Castro, and others) began in 1966 and attracted worldwide attention. As Cardenal himself indicated when he later referred to Solentiname as "a little pilot plan for certain things that the revolution is now doing on a larger scale," the experiment was both complexly cultural and intensely political. "The most important thing we learned in our dialogues with Ernesto," said one member of the community, "was that the system had to be changed. The only way forward was to take up arms." Thus some members went to Costa Rica to receive military training. Somoza, of course, found such developments intolerable, and National Guard troops therefore laid waste the whole enterprise: buildings, library and archaeological collections, studios, workshops, and exhibits (Cardenal 1981b, 3; Randall 1983a, 85. On Solentiname, see Cardenal 1975a; Cardenal 1982a, 3-5; Cardenal 1982c; and several articles by Cardenal in Arce et al. 1982, 169-75, 217-44, and 267-73).

Thus in the same sense that the destruction of Solentiname was an apt metaphor for much of the tragic pre-1979 cultural experience of Nicaragua, so was the task of national cultural reconstruction prefigured in many aspects of the Solentiname experiment itself: its relationship to the complexly layered national cultural history; its stock of cultural ideas and assumptions (especially its perhaps somewhat romantic conceptions of and preference for working-class culture); its choice of culturally reconstructive approaches; and its conception of the role of culture in the larger revolutionary process.

The Revolution and Ideas of Culture

Comprehending fully the Sandinistas' cultural ideas and assumptions — and the process through which they were formed — would require far more complete biographical information and analyses than is thus far available for any of them, with the possible exception of Ernesto Cardenal.[8] Yet a few tentative inferences may be drawn.

It is clear, for example, that the radical student movement in Nicaragua was an important formative influence upon many Sandinistas, and that certain cultural assumptions, ideas, and activities figured importantly in that movement. The interests of students and indigenous people came together as early as 1822, when a group of students joined some artisans of León's Indian barrio of Subtiava to attack a militia headquarters. But organized student activity of such a variety was infrequent until the present century. In the early 1930s students tried to establish a student federation, and in the 1940s they mounted their first tentative moves against the Somoza regime. In the early 1950s they agitated in favor of university autonomy, and at the end of the decade several of them died and more than eighty were wounded when the National Guard fired on a demonstration (Wheelock 1974, 28, 49, 88 ff., 90 ff., 115, 146; Ortega Saavedra 1979, 75-93, 115; Cabezas 1985b, 21 ff.).

A pivotal figure in infusing the student movement with a sense of Nicaraguan culture as a source of strength and direction was Mariano Fiallos Gil, who became rector of the National University at León in 1957. Having been neglected, starved, manipulated, and repressed for years by the government, the university was a pathetic shell when Fiallos took over. But he envisioned a major role for the institution in a national "resurrection," and turned it into a forum for the open discussion of national issues and experimentation with new educational and social programs. He created an experimental theater group, instituted a series of courses and conferences on the arts, started a museum of popular art, and attached the long dormant national schools of music and art to the university. Sergio Ramírez later called Fiallos' work "a vital experiment with Nicaraguan culture" (Ramírez Mercado 1971, 15, 94-109, 186).

Much of the cultural activity at the university was organized by a group of radical students (including Sergio Ramírez) who were publishing a new literary journal called *Ventana*, which directly addressed social, political, and cultural issues. The journal drew political energy from a series of radical student activities of the late 1950s, and literary models from among writers and literary movements linked to progressive social change: a number of North American writers, including Langston Hughes, Thomas Merton, the Beats, and Faulkner; Chinese poetry; Quechua poetry; and Nicaraguan poets Rubén Darío, Ernesto Cardenal, Salomón de la Selva, and others. An "anti-editorial" in the October 1960 issue declared that literature "is no pastime or diversion; it is a vehicle of culture, a way to life and truth." A year later, the group — which Ramírez later described as "the cultural counterpart to the Frente Sandinista" — organized a "culture week" at the university, featuring musical and theatrical presentations, and discussions of the relationship between the poet and society, between indigenous culture and Nicaraguan poetry, and related topics (*Ventana* 5 (Oct. 1960), 1-2; 9 (n.d. [before June 12, 1961]), 8-11; 10 (n.d. [before Oct. 1961]), 1, 6; 11 (n.d. [early 1962?]), 4).[9]

The student movement of the 1960s — at least the *Ventana* wing of it — aroused and focused several of what were to become central cultural elements of the Sandinista movement: the preeminence of poet Rubén Darío (1867-1916) as the intellectual fountainhead for a resurgent cultural nationalism, and of Sandino as its charismatic hero; and an emphasis on the creative revolutionary potential of (what was regarded as) Nicaraguan culture.

Despite the fact that Darío was most famous for his role in the birth of the Modernist movement in Spanish poetry, which emphasized form over content, and despite his having spent most of his life outside Nicaragua and having produced a corpus of work much of which had little to do with Nicaragua, he came to be regarded — as he was called when the Sandinistas established the Order of Rubén Darío prize in poetry — "the highest exponent of Nicaraguan culture" (Decree No. 927, *Nicaráuac* 2(7) 1982, 99). As a champion of indigenism, Darío had proclaimed in his *Prosas profanas* (1896) that "if there is poetry in our [Latin] America, it is to be found in the old things: in Palenké and Utatlán, in the legendary Indian and the refined Inca," and he understood resistance to cultural conquest as a permanent feature of that culture. That perspective naturally made him especially wary of *los norteamericanos* — indeed somewhat precociously so, since he died before the period of the most pervasive and brutal North American intervention (Vanden 1982, 42).

Current Minister of Culture Ernesto Cardenal has characterized all later Nicaraguan poetry as proceeding from Darío, and Darío himself as the "precursor of the Revolution." Cardenal traces a direct line from Darío through Sandino to FSLN founder Carlos Fonseca Amador. The revolution, Cardenal says, "was a dream of Darío. And a decision of Sandino. And a strategy of Carlos Fonseca" (Arce et al. 1982, 235-38). The point here is not that the complex cultural history matches such an elegant paradigm, but that the paradigm itself arose and functioned as part of the conceptual ground on which the Sandinistas launched and guided the revolution.

With the advent of the FSLN, Darío's emphasis upon the creatively resistant strains within indigenous culture flourished as never before, but it had never been entirely absent since the poet's death almost a half-century earlier. It persisted as a major concern of the *Vanguardia* poets in the late 1920s and 1930s, and Mariano Fiallos Gil picked up the theme in the late 1950s and urged a whole generation of young radical students to explore it.[10]

The nature and importance of specifically Marxist ideas about culture in the Sandinista analysis of Nicaraguan cultural history and their formulation of cultural policy is difficult to assess, both because detailed analysis of the political development of individual Sandinista leaders for the most part remains to be done, and because the little that has been done already makes it clear that their commitment to Marxist ideology varies both in intensity and in emphasis, and derives from widely differing cultural as well as political experiences.

Both Tomás Borge and Carlos Fonseca joined Nicaragua's own communist movement as early as the mid-1950s, but it is unlikely that the particular involvement supplied any of the cultural ideas later characteristic of the FSLN, since at the time the communist PSN (Partido Socialista Nicaragüense) was so Stalinist in orientation that it viewed even Sandino himself contemptuously. As a young man Fonseca traveled and studied in Russia, but Ernesto Cardenal first became enamored of Marxist thought fairly late in life through a process he insists had more to do with the time he spent with Thomas Merton living "the communist life" at the Gethsemane monastery and studying Scripture than it did with studying the usual sources. "I came to the revolution through the Gospel," he has said. "It was not by reading Marx, but through Christ. It can be said that the Gospel made me a Marxist." The younger Sandinista theorist Ricardo Morales Avilés (b. 1939) takes a relatively hard Marxist view of cultural matters—so much so that he is strongly critical of Cardenal and of what he sees as the well-intentioned but misguided romanticism of Cardenal's Solentiname experiment (Vanden 1982, 48; Booth 1985, 138; Diederich 1981, 68; Borgeson 1977), 63).[11]

An analytical tack potentially more useful than simply trying to measure Sandinista cultural ideas and practice against some established version of Marxist cultural theory is suggested in Harry Vanden's recent cultural assessment of the broader ideology of the Sandinista insurrection. Sandinista ideology, Vanden observed, is "a very flexible and non-sectarian Third World Marxism...carefully applied to the specific conditions of Nicaragua." More specifically, it is the Marxism of Ché, Fidel, and Ho Chi Minh—the Marxism of the postcolonial Third World, one persistent element of which has been a resurgence of cultural nationalism and independence (Vanden 1982).[12]

Certainly one aspect of older Marxist formulations which the Sandinistas substantially modified was the characteristic depreciation (indeed intolerance) of indigenous culture and cultural difference within the body politic. In this respect they were in agreement with some other Latin American Marxists (especially in Peru, Bolivia, and Mexico) who at least since the 1920s had been arguing that progressive social change had to be linked to (perhaps even based primarily upon) the cultural heritage, thought systems, and practices of indigenous peoples (Vanden 1982, 57; Liss 1984, 35, 129-40, 177-81, 207, 219-23, 274, 288).

Both their emerging understanding of the prerevolutionary cultural experience of the nation and the more urgent postrevolutionary necessity to formulate policy and programs demanded that from such a many-stranded complex of sources, influences, and ideas the Sandinistas construct a coherent analytical perspective, select some guiding principles, and mark out directions for cultural development in the new Nicaragua.

Nicaragua's prerevolutionary history impelled them to emphasize first of all that, from the earliest days of Spanish colonialism to the most recent PTL Club television broadcast, their cultural past was marked by cultural imperialism and what they came to call "ethnocide." "The most important characteristic of the Nicaraguan's bourgeoisie's cultural attitude," Sergio Ramírez has said, "has been its desire to import a model." Linked in a fatal symbiosis with that desire has been the United States' insistence upon "denationalizing" Nicaragua, turning its citizens into cultural copies of Díaz and Somoza, and sending them Air Force Band concerts and crates of *Reader's Digest* (See, e.g., Cardenal 1982c, and 1981a; Ramírez' remarks are in White 1986, 83).

The Sandinistas emphasize, however, that parallel to that colonial-imperial history there has been a countervailing dynamic of cultural resistance which was coeval with the conquest itself, and reached unbroken through Zeledón and Sandino to the spontaneous uprising in the Indian barrio of Monimbó in February 1978.[13] Hence for the Sandinistas the inescapable logic of the cultural past demanded that a central aim of cultural policy and programming be anti-imperialist cultural liberation (Cardenal 1980, 163-67).

Fortunately, in that process the colonially and imperialistically enforced syncretism of Nicaraguan culture has proven in some instances to be a strength rather than an impediment. A dramatic demonstration of the utility of cultural syncretism in resisting domination occurs in the fiesta of *el torovenado*, for example. Blending the most salient attributes of the Spanish bull — strength, haughtiness, brutishness — with the Indian stag — alertness, sagacity, agility — *el torovenado* is an emblem of cultural syncretism. The fiesta shows how in acts of agile cultural resistance indigenous people are perennially able to incorporate as new sources of strength those repeated efforts at cultural domination. The fiesta of *el torovenado* is intended, Carlos Alemán suggests, "to protest, to denounce, and to explain to people how things are." It limns "the cultural stance against conquest, cultural penetration and political opportunism" (Alemán Ocampo 1981).

The particular character of the postrevolutionary challenge — flowing substantially, but not completely, out of national cultural history — evokes certain additional emphases. Perhaps the most important are cultural revitalization and democratization. Culture Minister Cardenal has commented repeatedly on the former: "[Our] revolutionary culture has been a re-encounter with origins. And this re-encounter, the re-creation of a new life....Our patrimony, which before was unseen, has been made present." Likewise, democratization has been conceptually central, perhaps sharing with anti-imperialism the honor of being emphasized most strongly. "If before [the revolution] culture was the closed preserve of a minority," Cardenal declared, "now it will be...the right of the masses" (Cardenal 1982c, 10-12, 17; Cardenal interview in Zwerling & Martin 1985, 44; Arce et al. 1982, 272).

Finally, Nicaragua's principal theoreticians of culture view cultural change and development as both conceptually inseparable from and practically essential to development in other sectors. "To political development and the immense effort to move beyond economic underdevelopment," Cardenal observed, "we have joined cultural transformation," so that the restructuring of a new society is a "political duty" of the new culture (Cardenal 1982c, 12, 26; see also Tomás Borge, "La Cultura es el Pueblo," in Arce et al. 1982, 25-33).

The Policy Challenge

Within the cultural arena, therefore, the Sandinistas have met many aspects of the analytical and conceptual challenge in an impressive fashion. Among the Sandinista leadership the level of conceptualization of the whole issue of culture is very high in comparison with many wealthier, larger, and supposedly more "advanced" nations. Only during the New Deal years, for example, did the United States approach the task of conceiving and implementing a democratic cultural policy with comparable vision, imagination, and enthusiasm, and its successes were modest and in most cases of rather limited duration. The more recent flourish of cultural programming at the federal level has on the whole been conceptually timid, elitist, and funded at barely a pilot level.[14]

By contrast, the Sandinistas have articulated (as sketched briefly above) a highly conscious set of analytical and programmatic concepts, directed toward correcting the cultural distortions of the past, building upon the cultural givens of the present, and looking toward a vital and democratic cultural future.

Nor is an awareness of a commitment to those concepts by any means limited to Ernesto Cardenal and other Ministry of Culture officials; it is generally evident in the thought of most members of the junta. Virtually every member of the FSLN National Directorate has spoken and written of the role of culture in social reconstruction with sensitivity and sophistication only rarely encountered among political leaders in the United States (Representative samples of their statements on culture are in Arce et al. 1982).

As a consequence of the high general level of awareness of the importance of culture as a base and guide for change in all areas of public policy,
cultural concepts, policies, institutions and programs have been projected as
playing an important role in social, economic, and political reconstruction.
More specifically, the Sandinistas have made extensive and fundamental changes in cultural policy itself, and consequently in cultural institutions and
programs. For certain institutions and programs, the initial results have been
substantial, and have consequently been written about rather extensively: the
literacy campaign, the poetry workshops, the Centers for Popular Cul-
ture(CPCs), and (to a lesser extent) graphic arts and experimental theater.[15]

These efforts constitute only a small part, however, of the much more
extensive developments that were projected in the cultural arena. In view of
the fact that the country was so bereft of public cultural institutions of any consequence prior to 1979, the task facing the new Ministry of Culture was formidable. Although hampered by the war's drain on the economy and thus
reduced in most cases to relying on volunteers rather than a paid professional
staff, the ministry has initiated an impressive array of efforts to construct an
infrastructure of cultural institutions and inaugurate cultural programs
throughout the country. At their best they have not only effectively used
limited available resources, but have even managed to turn calamity to advantage. In response to the Reagan administration's grain embargo, for example, the Ministry of Culture staged a corn festival (Feria del Maíz) in May
1981, celebrating the historical and mythic importance of corn in the culture
in order to raise people's spirits, direct their energies, and rally their support
for national survival and reconstruction (*Nicaráuac* 2 [Dec. 1981], 55, 61-75).

However energizing at a moment of crisis, such events are of limited use
in the broader restructuring of cultural institutions, which both requires
longer-term strategy and may not produce results which are as dramatic from
a public relations standpoint. Prior to 1979 there was, for example, almost no
book or journal publishing going on in the country outside of the relatively
small amount being done by the universities and the large private banks which
during the Somoza period had to some degree filled the void created by the
regime's default in the area of cultural institutions and programming (Stansifer 1981, 6-8). Since the revolution, both the Ministry of Culture and
Editorial Nueva Nicaragua have established publication programs, oriented
rather directly, as one would expect, toward encouraging and supporting the
revolution. Some of the earliest books to appear under the new regime's im-
primatur were those by Sergio Ramírez and Carlos Fonseca on Sandino, Jorge
Eduardo Arellano on Darío, Cardenal on Solentiname, several collections of
eulogies of the heroes and martyrs of the popular uprisings in Monimbó and
Subtiava, volumes of poetry by Daisy Zamora and Rosario Murillo (both
respected poets prior to the revolution), and speeches and policy statements
on culture by Sandinista leaders.

Archives, libraries, and museums also received substantially increased
attention and a level of public support which, although limited by required expenditures for arms, they had never before enjoyed. The overall aim was to

establish them securely, to disperse them widely throughout the country in order to make their collections and services easily available, and to make them useful instruments of renewed national pride, identity, and social-political reconstruction. Corollary efforts were directed toward the conservation and restoration of historical buildings (such as Sandino's birthplace and Darío's home), and the collection of folk and popular culture — ranging from foodways and herbal remedies to slogans painted on walls during the revolution.[16]

Prior to 1979 music and film were practically virgin territory with respect to policy (hence funding as well), but the Sandinistas addressed them with vigor and imagination. As already indicated, musical production in Nicaragua before 1979 had been dominated (at least so far as official legitimation was concerned) by western European and North American popular music forms; formal presentation was focused on the principal west coast cities. But from the 1960s onward new politically progressive currents such as *nueva canción* appeared in Latin American music, and were eventually felt in Nicaragua. Two years before the Sandinistas entered Managua, a crowd of more than three thousand at a human rights festival in the city responded enthusiastically to themes rarely heard before in Nicaraguan music. A few months after the triumph, Tomás Borge observed that "with such songs as these [it is] impossible not to have a revolution, and...with a revolution such as ours, it would be impossible not to have songs such as those we have." Hence there were encouraging new developments in music: the National School of Music reopened; the Nicaraguan Symphony Orchestra reorganized; a National Chorus and a musical journal were started; and phonograph record production was inaugurated with compositions such as Carlos Mejía Godoy's *Misa campesina nicaragüense*. More recently such performers as Salvador Bustos and Salvador and Katia Cardenal have helped to energize the new *volcanto* (from *volcán* = volcano and *canto* = song) musical movement (*Gaceta Sandinista* 2 [May 1977], 9; Cardenal 1982e, 172; Arce et al. 1982, 27).[17]

A parallel development has occurred in film. The task was no less than to create a national film industry from the ground up, initially using the meager production facilities of PRODUCINE — which had made public relations films for the National Guard, and the like — and the skills gained by the small War Correspondents Corps in the FSLN. The new Nicaraguan Institute of Cinema (INCINE) was structured into the Ministry of Culture from the beginning. Assisted by politically oriented film-makers from other countries, INCINE began to produce both historically based fictional films (such as *Alsino y el cóndor*), news programs, and documentaries (J. Ramírez 1984; Abelleira 1981; Gumucio Dragón 1982). Pertinent interviews with foreign film makers involved in the Nicaraguan film industry are published in *Nicaráuac* 2 (Jan. 1981), 165-68, and *Barricada Cultural*, June 4, 1983, 2-3).

Thus by any reasonable measure — especially if one defines that measure to be the sophistication of current cultural programming in most countries, which after all is not that high — the Sandinistas have made remarkable strides both conceptually and programatically. And yet the endemic hazards of making cultural policy in a revolutionary context are both numerous and well

known, and there are signs that the Sandinistas have not escaped them entirely.

The Hazards of Cultural Policy Making in a Revolutionary Context

Recent history provides numerous examples of the ways in which nation-states in situations of revolution or convulsive sociopolitical change (as
well as, of course, those which are not) manipulate culture in terms of their
ideologies, unique histories, and the pressure they encounter in various international arenas. Those that come most readily to mind are the American and
French revolutions of the late eighteenth century, the Russian and Mexican
ones of the early twentieth, fascist Italy and Nazi Germany of a quarter-cen-
tury later, the United States during the Great Depression, a long list of former
imperial colonies that have emerged as new nations since World War II, Cuba
and China in the 1960s, and most recently Nicaragua itself.

Since substantial comparative analysis is not possible here, these other
cases must serve in a merely suggestive way to contextualize more broadly a
sense of the inescapable complexity of cultural policy within a revolutionary
context — and perhaps therefore to soften any impulse to blame the Sandinistas for not "solving" problems that have proved so resistant to solution (Cannistrano 1971; Fitzpatrick 1970; Wurgraft 1971; Hagopian 1974, 240-42;
Turner 1968, 254-306).[18] Nevertheless, the Sandinistas have in fact encountered substantial difficulties in the process of forming cultural policy and
constructing cultural institutions and programs in the midst of their own particular historical circumstances, and those difficulties must be taken into account in the present analysis. Doing so reminds us once again of the complex
linkages between ideology, the realities of power, and conceptions of culture.

In 1972 Ernesto Cardenal visited Cuba's new national school of art,
housed in the facilities of a former Havana country club. The artists he met
seemed refreshingly modest and dedicated to integrating their work into the
larger effort of national reconstruction. "Their preoccupation," Cardenal observed, "is that poets and artists should be one with the people." And yet the
students told him that the director of the school was more interested in the
country's new sports program than in the arts because sports stars won medals
for Cuba in international competition, while artists did not (Cardenal 1972,
73-75).

Several of the inherent pitfalls of forming cultural policy in a revolutionary context are implicit in the incident: the inescapable tension between official ideology and aesthetic values on the one hand, and day to day bureaucratic
practice on the other; the conflict between the needs of individual artists for
creative freedom and support, and the drive of the state for stability and
legitimacy vis-à-vis both its own people and the international community; and
(by no means least) the perdurable limits of frail human beings engaged in
ideologically guided enterprises situated in fragile, socially constructed
realties.

Among the Sandinista leadership, both Bayardo Arce Castaño and Sergio Ramírez have spoken of some of the potential risks of post-1979 cultural development in Nicaragua: ideological dogmatism (and therefore creative narrowness) in the arts, and the temptation to reflect only a narrowly conceived "revolutionary reality" in artistic production (Arce, "El difícil terreno de la lucha: el ideológico," in Arce et al. 1982, 17-24, and "Tanto arte...tanta actividad cultural," *Barricada Cultural*, July 19, 1983, 2-4; Ramírez Mercado, "Cultura de masas y creación individual," in Arce et al. 1982, 157-66). Rosario Murillo has also noted the temptation to institutionalize certain modes of creation (such as Cardenal's *exteriorismo* in the poetry workshops), and to the corollary tendency to engage in self-censorship in the face of the dominance of such modes (White 1986, 100-5).

But the first seven years of the Sandinista government suggest that the risks are even broader than these cautions imply — even if one avoids invoking the usual simple-minded and self-congratulatory cant about cultural freedom and vitality in capitalistic democracies.

In the first place, revolutionary ardor tempts one to project cultural changes on a scale that is not likely to be realized in the short or medium term with available resources. Before the revolution, Cardenal has said, the green uniforms and helmets of the police were "symbols of terror and death," but now the police are writing poetry. The difference, he says, is "between the horror and a smile, between those who tortured and assassinated, and those who now love and write poetry" (Cardenal 1982c, 7-9).

And yet in many areas of cultural activity, the changes have in fact been hesitant and slow. In sports, for example, the Ministry of Culture projected a decisive turn away from the urban-based, elitist, professionalized North American-derived sports of the Somoza era (baseball and boxing in particular), toward a dispersed, egalitarian system geared to mass voluntary participation. Yet two years after the Sandinistas took over, the Sandinista newspaper *Barricada* still regularly carried articles on major-league sports in the United States, and virtually none on local sports events of the kind originally envisioned (Wagner 1982; *Barricada Cultural*, Sept.-Oct., 1981).

More serious, however, than the logistical difficulty of effecting rapid change where such change is easily conceivable are the deeper structural intractabilities of historical cultural formation. It is one thing to speak of forming a culture that is "democratic, anti-imperialist, popular, and national," as Cardenal consistently has, but the cultural system of ideas, practices, values, predispositions, assumptions, and institutions that was in place when the Sandinistas entered Managua was split east-to-west, class-stratified, urban-dominated, complexly amalgamated and factionalized racially, mestizo, macho, and in many respects (e.g., technologically) irreversibly global-villaged.

The psychic and historical residue of these processes emerged in perplexing and painful ways, especially with respect to the Miskito problem and the role of women in the new society. The psychic and institutional strength of the macho ideal makes the latter problem formidable indeed. On the other hand, both the prominent and undeniably crucial role of women in the FSLN and the new government, and the egalitarian thrust of Sandinista ideology, make avoiding the issue virtually unthinkable. Moreover, Nicaraguan women are mobilized, determined to play a central role in shaping the new social order, and linked to the supporting network of the international women's movement. A solution would also appear to be possible — however long and arduous the process may prove to be — largely without external interference or manipulation.[19]

The staggering complexity of the Miskito problem, by contrast, makes it difficult even to conceive of a workable approach to the problem.[20] The poignancy of the Sandinistas' initial naive hopes for national cultural unity has been noted as repeatedly as the tortuous problem itself has been outlined: the ancient geophysical and cultural divisions of the country; the manipulation and exacerbation of that division by successive external and internal groups (the British, North American corporations, Moravian missionaries, the Somozas, the U.S. government acting in concert with Contra mercenaries); factionalisms and conflicts among racially and culturally distinct Atlantic coast groups themselves; and the Sandinistas' own bumbling efforts to deal with the problem under the dual pressures of a broad need for national reconstruction and U.S. efforts at destabilization. Philippe Bourgois has crystallized the problem as follows:

> By the end of the fifth year, tensions with ethnic minorities had become an Achilles heel of the Nicaraguan Revolution: militarily, the Atlantic Coast region where the minorities lived had exploded into an arena of bitter fighting; politically, accusations of human rights violations against the indigenous population had damaged the Revolution's internal image; and morally, the inability to incorporate minorities...into a full participation in the revolutionary process had contradicted Sandinista political principles. (Bourgois 1985b, 201)

Thus the Atlantic coast dilemma has put Sandinista cultural theory and practice to a more severe test than any other single problem, and has revealed that the road to national cultural unity, independence, and vitality will be long and arduous.

There are also suggestions that — like the leaders of every revisionist enterprise (those who have led the black power, native American, and feminist movements in the United States, for example) — the Sandinistas have sometimes been romantically selective in their characterization of Nicaraguan cultural history. For a revolution that so strongly emphasizes the culture of common (and especially rural) people, it is important to bear in mind that the Sandinista leadership is drawn heavily from the urban bourgeoisie. Perhaps deriving partially from needs induced by their own inevitable cultural dislocation and alienation, the tendency to idealize lower-class culture is ever present and tempting. To distinguish between the relative importance of objective reality and inner need as sources of Omar Cabezas' excitement upon hearing the drums of Subtiava would be a daunting endeavor.

Equally troublesome is the corollary danger of sanitizing national cultural history in order to make "national" culture more serviceable as an energizing and legitimizing resource. Thus patterns of internal factional strife and collaboration (León Liberals with William Walker, Miskitos with Somoza), no less present in Nicaraguan than in any other national history, are rarely mentioned.

Similarly, it is one thing for Cardenal to assert that Rubén Darío is the father of all Nicaraguan poetry—which consequently is characteristically proud, nationalistic, and resistant to external domination from whatever quarter. It is another thing, however, to deal with the actual literary record, which is quite mixed. It is true, on the one hand, that Salomón de la Selva (1893-1958) was implacably opposed to Somoza, and that his spirit and that of Darío flourished later in the Grupo Gradas poets of the 1960s, the *Ventana* group that proclaimed itself the generation that would not betray Nicaragua, and the still younger soldier- and brigadista-poets of the poetry workshops. But it is also true, on the other hand, that the *Ventana* group's "we will not betray" declaration had such force partly because it was a response to the whining plaint of the "Betrayed Generation" of Nicaraguan poets who found their heroes among the Beat poets of the United States, and proclaimed that "we don't belong to any country."

Thus Nicaraguan poets have in fact been strongly divided in their political ideas and alignments. Within the *Vanguardia* movement, Pablo Antonio Cuadra wrote poems against the U.S. Marine occupation and was twice imprisoned for anti-Somoza activity, but the movement on the whole was elitist, pro-Somoza, and enamored of European-style fascism. Ernesto Mejía Sánchez was forced into exile for ten years because of his opposition to Somoza, and Ernesto Cardenal participated in the April rebellion (1954) against him. But another of the generation, the romantic dandy Carlos Martínez Rivas, tried to help shore up Somoza's image at the very time of the April rebellion by organizing a celebratory cultural event for the Somocista newspaper *Novedades*, and much later insisted to interviewer Steven White that "I have no ideas, no ideals, and no ideology."[21]

Moreover, the very notion of "revolutionary culture" is problematic. Among the Sandinistas, characterizations of the relationship between culture and the revolution range from Bayardo Arce's rather commonsensical assertion that "cultural activity is an inherent part of the revolution itself" (Arce, "Tanto arte...tanta actividad cultural," *Barricada Cultural*, July 19, 1983) to Cardenal's categorical but nonetheless romantic equation of revolution and culture, to Ricardo Avilés' more instrumental assertion that "cultural struggle is...one front of the revolutionary struggle" (Cardenal 1982e, 175). In a more nuanced way, Sergio Ramírez, while admitting that revolution is in some practical ways costly to a person who wants to be "just" a writer, maintains that it is more importantly an event of enormous creative potential. It is, he says, "first and foremost a great human event that completely transforms lives, creates multiple new histories, events, heroisms, villainies, happiness and sorrow," all of which become the stuff of new literature (Ramírez interview in White 1986).

Even if some or all of that is true, however, the notion of revolutionary culture – like all such global notions, of whatever theoretical construction or ideological stripe – in its insistence upon total congruence between theory and reality carries a potential both for misapprehension of cultural complexity and contradiction, and for preferential skewing of institutions and programs. Poet and newspaper editor Pablo Antonio Cuadra – first a supporter and then an opponent of the Sandinistas – has spoken of the dangers of cultural *dirigismo* and of throwing off one cultural imperialism only to fall prey to another one emanating from the "culturally gray" countries of the communist bloc (Cuadra interview in White 1986).

Although Cuadra's view begs the whole question of whether culture in contemporary socialist or communist countries can legitimately be characterized by such a sweepingly pejorative term as "gray," and whether state-derived *dirigismo* is either essentially different from or worse than the usual modes of cultural legitimation and control under advanced corporate capitalism, the danger he fears cannot be lightly dismissed: that as culture is wedded to (and conceived specifically in terms of) nationalism, a new national cultural myth – partly clarifying and energizing, partly obfuscating and stultifying – will be created and placed in the service of both abstract political ideology and all too concrete political power. Eric Hobsbawm and Terrence Ranger's recent collection of essays on the British penchant for inventing cultural "traditions" and using them in the service of British imperialism – in highland Scotland and Wales, in Victorian India and colonial Africa (and on the Miskito Coast of Nicaragua, although Hobsbawm and Ranger do not treat this case) – shows the usefulness of cultural manipulation in establishing political hegemony (Hobsbawm & Ranger 1983).[22]

Thus the cultural agenda facing the Sandinistas is daunting: (1) to throw off the historical-cultural imperialisms without encouraging new ones in the essential task of forming supportive political relationships, establishing legitimacy on the international scene, and seeking economic and military aid; (2) to maximize the positive aspects of their authentic cultural past without ignoring its contradictions; (3) to forge a functional national culture that bridges historical hostilities and distrust without riding roughshod over legitimate and durable differences; (4) to create a sensitive and stable array of national cultural institutions and programs that will be serviceable in all of these ways, at the same time that the country is burdened by the necessity to defend itself against a powerful enemy with a hundred times its population and thousands of times its economic and military power; (5) and not least to tolerate, amidst its drive for order and stability, the irreducibly messy and potentially disloyal and destabilizing unpredictability of the individual and collective creative process.

To guard against impatience as well as critical arrogance and intolerance, it is well to remind oneself – as Rosario Murillo did in an interview three years after the Sandinistas entered Managua – not only of the perplexity, fear, vacillation, nostalgia, and suffering that are inescapable amidst such circumstances, but also that if the Sandinistas accomplish even a modest portion of such an agenda, they will not only have worked a near miracle in terms of analytical sophistication, institutional structure, and actual programs, but will also have done what no nation in the world, "advanced" or otherwise, has yet demonstrated a reliable ability to do. As Murillo reflected, discussing what the Ministry of Culture was to be and do in the revolution "was like talking about the creation of a world" (Murillo interview in White 1986, 96, 105).

NOTES

1. A revealing collection of statements by Sandinista leaders Bayardo Arce, Tomás Borge, Carlos Núñez, Luis Carrión, Daisy Zamora, and Daniel Ortega on cultural aspects of the revolution may be found in Arce et al., 1982. I have employed several terms to refer to various manifestations of Nicaraguan culture: *traditional culture*, *national culture*, *indigenous culture*, and *vernacular culture*. In view of the enormously complicated cultural history of the country, each of these terms (as well as any other conceivable term) is problematic in some respects. Acutely aware of the inadequacy of all such terms, I have alternated their use as one or the other seemed less inadequate or misleading in a particular context.

2. I am grateful to Julie Franks for helping me sharpen my sense of this connection. The approach I apply here has emerged neither in the broader scholarly analyses of the revolution, nor in the few existing detailed analyses of specific cultural programs. Stansifer 1981 begins with Rubén Darío; Walker 1982 and 1985 has four brief essays on selected cultural programs; Booth 1985 devotes fewer than three pages to cultural policy; Vilas 1986 does not mention culture at all; Craven & Ryder [1983?] is prefaced by a précis of Nicaraguan social and political history from the mid-nineteenth century on, but the cultural strand of that history is curiously absent.

3. Radell's figures are based on a meticulous and rigorous analysis of the best available contemporary records.

4. On Liberalism and Positivism's impact throughout Latin America in the nineteenth century, see Burns 1980, especially 5-17; Woodward 1971, especially ix-xiii and 12-14; on agro-export monoculture, see Wheelock 1975.

5. Originally published ca. 1945. Vega was apparently a co-conductor of the National Guard band, which he said was "the only band that we have in Nicaragua."

6. For a more extensive discussion of the Zelaya regime, see Teplitz 1973. For a comprehensive history of U.S. imperialism in Nicaragua, see Bermann 1986. The long history of Nicaraguan resistance to foreign intervention is chronicled in Wheelock 1974.

7. For a broader analysis of the importance of comic strips and other forms of popular culture within larger patterns of economic imperialism in Latin America, see Dorfman 1972, which by 1983 had gone through twenty-

four printings, and Dorfman 1983. Still broader in its treatment of the problem is McPhail 1981, especially 189-97.

8. Biographical information on Sandinista political and cultural leaders is scattered through their speeches, interviews, and articles. See, for example, Randall 1983b, 7-12; Randall 1984; the documents and interviews in White 1986; and Marcus 1982. For Cardenal, see Arellano 1979.

9. On the founding and purposes of the journal, see Ramírez' comments in *Barricada Cultural*, Jan. 30, 1982, 3; in Arce et al. 1982, 157-66; and in White 1986, 75, 78-81.

10. A few of Pablo Antonio Cuadra's remarks on the *Vanguardista*'s interests in indigenous culture may be found in White 1986, 20, 23. See Fiallos' discussion in his "Introducción al estudio del proceso cultural centroamericano," *Ventana* 1 (2a trimestre, 1964), 3-63. Evidence of sustained interest can be seen in Arellano 1977.

11. Pablo Antonio Cuadra noted the PSN's hostility toward Nicaraguan nationalism (cultural and otherwise) in White 1986, 20. On the differences between Morales and Cardenal, see "Ernesto Cardenal: la misión libertadora de la poesía," in Morales 1981, 114-20.

12. The emerging cultural politics of the Third World in the period immediately before the Sandinista triumph were adumbrated in a series of conferences on cultural policy organized by UNESCO in the 1970s. See Whisnant 1983b. The conference for Latin America and the Caribbean took place in Bogotá in January 1978. UNESCO published a summary of its proceedings in 1978.

13. Wheelock 1974 covers the period to 1881. References to the Monimbó episode abound in Sandinista commentary on the revolution. See, for example, Instituto de Estudio del Sandinismo 1982.

14. The literature on New Deal culture programs is vast. On the centrally important issue of their egalitarian character, see Mathews 1975. For a survey of the pre-New Deal period, see Overmyer 1939. An useful overview of more recent U.S. cultural policy conceptualization and administration is available in Mulcahy & Swaim 1982. Useful comparisons are available in Girard 1972; Nilsson 1980; and E. White 1975.

15. See, for example, Hirshon & Butler 1983; Jiménez 1983, and her interview in White 1986, 106-13. See also Ernesto Cardenal, "Talleres de poesía: socialización de los medios de producción poéticos," in Arce et al. 1982, 225-32; Kidd 1983; Bravo 1983; and Kunzle 1983. Additional details on the CPCs are available in the first three numbers of *La Chacalaca* (Apr.-Dec. 1982). For the poetry itself see Johnson 1985.

16. On museums see Cardenal 1982c, 19-20, and 1982b; and *La Chacalaca* 1 (Apr. 1982), 6, and 2 (July 1982), 71. On libraries see Cardenal 1982e, 173; and *Barricada Cultural*, Oct. 4, 1981, 4. On cultural conservation, see Torres 1982, 5-8; Cardenal 1982e, 173-75; and Arce et al. 1982, 271. In 1985 the Ministry of Culture published *Cocina nica*, brief selections from Angélica Vivas' earlier treatment of Nicaraguan foodways, *50 años de cocina*.

17. On *nueva canción* see Morris 1986. Albums released by Luis Enrique and/or Carlos Mejía Godoy include *La nueva milpa* and *El son nuestro de cada día* (Madrid: CBS Records, 1978), *Amando en tiempo de guerra* (San José, 1979), *Convertiendo la oscuridad en claridad* (Managua: Ministry of Culture, 1980), *La misa campesina nicaragüense* (Managua: Ministerio de Cultura, 1981); *Un son para mi pueblo* (San Francisco: Paredon, 1983), *La tapisca* (Enigrac, Pantagrama, 1985). Performed in less traditional style but thematically related are Guardabarranco (Salvador and Katia Cardenal), *Si buscabas*; and Salvador Bustos, *Tragaluz* (Oakland, Calif.: Redwood Records, 1985).

18. Walk 1981 has commented perceptively, if briefly, on the American Left's perennial difficulty in explaining the connections between politics and culture.

19. Pre-1979 FSLN statements on women's needs and rights may be found in "The Historic Program of the FSLN" (1969), reprinted in Marcus 1982, 13-22, and *Gaceta Sandinista*, Oct., 1976, 3, 10. Brief overviews are available in Maier 1980; Ramírez-Horton 1982, 147-60; and Molyneux 1985. Testimonies of Nicaraguan women are collected in Randall 1981; and several women writers are in Randall 1984.

20. The Miskito question is dealt with elsewhere in this volume by George P. Castile. Titles 89 and 90 of Article 4 of the new Nicaraguan Constitution adopted in November 1986 grant broad cultural recognition and rights, as well as considerable social and political autonomy, to Atlantic coast groups. On the new constitution, see *Envio* 6 (Jan. 1987), 14-31.

21. This discussion is based almost exclusively on White 1986. On the political conservatism of the *Vanguardistas* see Arellano 1977, 57ff.

22. The dynamic is not limited to conservative political perspectives; my own recent study of systematic cultural intervention in the southern mountains of the United States examines the well-meaning cultural manipulations indulged in by liberal cultural missionaries as the region opened to capitalist economic "development" (and concurrently, to an intense popular interest in its purportedly unsullied "native" culture). See Whisnant 1983a. Twenty-five years ago, Fanon (1961) warned of similar dangers in his essay "On National Culture."

CHAPTER 10

Belize and Revolutionary Grenada: A Partnership in the Caribbean, 1979-1983

Kai Schoenhals

At first glance, an examination of the relationship between Belize and revolutionary Grenada might seem like a rather quixotic undertaking. What could these relatively new nations possibly have in common?

Belize, the size of Massachusetts, is on the Central American mainland, whereas Grenada, whose three islands could all fit into the area of Washington, D.C., lies thousands of miles to the southeast, almost at the end of the string of Caribbean islands that run in an arch from Cuba to Trinidad near Venezuela. The former British Honduras' approximately 150,000 Creoles, Mestizos, Garifuna (Black Caribs), and Maya Indians as well as Caucasians, Chinese, and East Indians constitute one of the most heterogeneous populations anywhere on this continent. Grenada, in contrast, has a very homogeneous population. Its 110,000 inhabitants are, for the most part, the descendants of black slaves. Belize shares with Honduras the distinction of being the most sparsely populated region in Central America. Grenada, on the other hand, is the most densely populated island of the Anglophone Caribbean.

Since it obtained self-government in 1964, Belize was ruled by the deeply religious Roman Catholic Prime Minister, George Price, who had studied for the priesthood in both the United States and Guatemala. Grenada's Prime Minister, "Comrade Leader" Maurice Bishop, on the other hand, was rumored to be an atheist. He found himself embroiled in frequent conflicts with Grenada's Roman Catholic Church as well as other religious faiths during his four-and-a-half year reign.[1] These religious groups feared that Bishop envisaged the formation of a Marxist state which would severely curtail, if not abolish, their activities. Finally, Belize's two political parties, the People's United party (PUP) and the United Democratic party (UDP) firmly upheld the British Westminster model of parliamentary democracy, whereas the New Jewel Movement in Grenada was determined to make a radical break with the British parliamentary heritage that Grenada shared with Belize. Maurice

Bishop and his iconoclastic followers viewed parliamentary rule as a sham and a relic of British colonialism. A "People's Power" scheme, based on Castro's Cuba, was to replace it.

A closer examination of the relationship between the two countries reveals that they also had much in common as they faced the difficult 1980s. Two centuries of British colonial rule left a strong British legal and constitutional tradition in both. The ruling elites of both Belize and Grenada consisted of the descendants of black slaves (known as Creoles in Belize). In spite of its location as an Anglophone enclave in an otherwise Hispanic Central America, Belize is much more closely connected to the English-speaking Caribbean, an area with which it shares its political and cultural values. Both countries have experienced a huge exodus of their populations to Anglophone metropolitan centers. It is estimated that between 75,000 and 100,000 Belizeans have permanently moved abroad. In Grenada the number of emigrants is even more startling. While 110,000 Grenadians still live in their homeland, there are close to 300,000 Grenadians residing in the United States, Canada, Great Britain, and Trinidad.[2] The finance ministries of Belize and Grenada welcome the remittances sent home by these expatriates, but the "brain drain" created by their exodus reduces even further the development of their native lands. Finally, Belize and Grenada were both hit by that devastating crunch which affected practically all third world countries during the period under discussion. Whereas under the impact of rising oil prices they were forced to pay more for imports from the developed world, the prices which they received for their primary exports (sugar in the case of Belize and spices in that of Grenada) were falling precipitously (Everitt 1984).

The year 1979 was a particularly momentous one in the history of the Caribbean and Central America. For the first time since Fidel Castro marched victoriously into Havana in January 1959, revolutionary forces were able to gain control in two countries in these regions. In Grenada, on March 13, 1979, about forty armed insurgents toppled the corrupt, repressive, and bizarre regime of Eric Gairy who, during his reign of three decades, had lectured at the United Nations on flying saucers and the Bermuda Triangle. The seizure of power by Marxist-oriented rebels in a black Anglophone country in the Caribbean came as a shock to many governments which had assumed that the deeply ingrained British tradition of parliamentary democracy had immunized the English-speaking Caribbean against coup d'états.

Four months later in Nicaragua, the Sandinistas terminated the reign of the Somoza dynasty which had lasted for more than four decades. The Sandinista victory clearly lent encouragement to the revolutionary forces battling in El Salvador and Guatemala, and in Washington there were fears that all of Central America, including heretofore tranquil countries such as Belize, Honduras, and Costa Rica, might eventually be engulfed by this revolutionary conflagration. In contrast to the Carter administration, which viewed the events in Grenada and Nicaragua with apprehension, the Price government regarded the two revolutionary victories with equanimity, if not outright joy (*The Belize Times*, June 20, 1979, 1; Aug. 8, 1979, 10; Aug. 15, 1979, 8; Dec. 2, 1979,

3).[3] Why was the rather conservative, Bible-quoting Price not disturbed by these two radical revolutions?

Belizean politics cannot be understood without taking into account the menacing presence of its powerful neighbor, Guatemala, whose population (8,000,000) and armed forces (20,000) dwarf the 150,000 Belizeans and their tiny Belizean Defense Force (BDF) of 600 soldiers. This is not the place to trace the convoluted course of the British-Guatemalan controversy over Belize which has been done elsewhere (Bloomfield 1953; Calvert 1976, 7-12; Menon 1979, 343-71). Suffice it to say that in 1859 Great Britain and Guatemala signed a treaty in which Guatemala recognized England's sovereignty over Belize, provided that the United Kingdom would build a road from Guatemala City to the Caribbean coast. Since the British never constructed the promised road, various Guatemalan governments have regarded the 1859 treaty as null and void and considered Belize as an integral part of Guatemala. It seems that the more repressive a Guatemalan government acted at home, the more vociferously it advocated the annexation of Belize, perhaps in order to deflect the population's grievances. Perhaps the reverse could also be applied. At any rate, the Arbenz government (1950-1954), which happened to be one of the few democratically elected and least repressive governments since the turn of the century, remained silent on Guatemala's claim to Belize. Instead, it called for the withdrawal of England from British Honduras and vigorously supported the Belizean nationalist movement which had arisen under the leadership of Price in 1950.

Price met frequently with Guatemalan officials and there is evidence that the Arbenz government supplied financial and material assistance to the PUP.[4] In 1951, one of Price's closest associates, Philip Goldson, paid a week's visit to Guatemala and then proceeded to write an article ("Seven Days of Freedom") about Arbenz' Guatemala, which he contrasted in glowing terms to "this stinking, little, oversized village of ours."[5]

During the 1950s, the British government was as determined as the Eisenhower administration to prevent the establishment of Marxist governments in this hemisphere. It viewed the Arbenz presidency in Guatemala with as much distaste as Washington, and suspected that Price and his followers were becoming subversive agents of Guatemala's leftist government. British fears were exacerbated by the contemporaneous specter of a possible Marxist takeover in Guyana, where Great Britain intervened in 1953 to prevent the Marxist Cheddi Jagan from becoming prime minister.

In addition to British fears about the PUP's Guatemalan connection, the United Kingdom's future plans for British Honduras were diametrically opposed to Price's vision of an independent Belize. The British government saw such a nation intimately connected to a West Indian Federation and the British Commonwealth. Price, whose mother was a Mayan Indian, did not belong to the old Belizean Creole elite which felt that their future prosperity depended on close ties with England. Between 1950 and 1968, Price asserted repeatedly that Belize's future was linked to the other Central American states. No doubt influenced by his pro - American employer, the Belizean multimillionaire, R. S. Turton, who held huge investments in several American companies competing with the British-controlled Belize Estate and Produce Company (BEC), Price regarded the United States as the future protector of his country. PUP rallies during this period were marked by the waving of American flags and the singing of "God Bless America" (*The Belize Billboard*, Feb. 5, 1950, 1).

Price's efforts at a close relationship with Guatemala and the rest of Central America met with a positive response only during the short-lived Arbenz regime which was toppled in 1954. The subsequent Guatemalan military regimes resurrected the claim that Belize was an integral part of their country, thereby nullifying all of Price's efforts to establish a cordial relationship with his western neighbor. In solidarity with Guatemala, other Central American countries, too, rejected Price's repeated efforts to form closer economic and political ties with the the region. The final straw came in 1968 when the Central American Common Market rejected Belize's application for membership (Grant 1976, 128-38, 235-41).

The United States also disappointed Price. When a hurricane devastated Belize in 1961, U.S. aid fell below expectations and the meager U.S. sugar quota (an annual ten thousand tons) for Belize shattered the country's hope that North America would purchase most of its sugar. Politically, the United States seemed to be largely supportive of Guatemala. The Castillo Armas regime (1954-1957), after all, owed its very existence to Washington. The United States, in turn, was indebted to Miguel Ydígoras Fuentes (1958-1963), the conservative president who had permitted the United States to launch part of the Bay of Pigs invasion from Guatemalan soil. When, in 1968, the U.S.-sponsored Webster Proposals suggested future Guatemalan control over the foreign policy, defense, and economy of Belize after that country's attainment of independence, Belizeans of all political shades had little doubt on whose side Washington stood in their conflict with Guatemala.[6]

Constantly rebuffed by Guatemala (except during the Arbenz regime) and the rest of Central America and disillusioned with the United States, Price's outlook on Belize's future underwent an agonizing reappraisal in 1968. From then on, PUP began to look primarily to the Commonwealth of Nations, the Non-Aligned Movement, and especially the Caribbean for political and economic succor. These efforts were already rewarded in 1968 when Belize obtained membership in the Caribbean Area Free Trade Association (CARIFTA). Seven years later, Belize could rely on its newly found friends for support at the United Nations' General Assembly, where a resolution favoring independence for Belize passed by a vote of 110 to 9, with 16 abstentions.[7]

The opposition party, however, continued to view Price as a Guatemalan stooge who wanted Belize annexed by its larger Hispanic neighbor. In all fairness, it must be pointed out that Price's PUP flung equally absurd accusations at former UDP leader, Dean Lindo, who was portrayed in *The Belize Times* as a simultaneous agent of Guatemala, the KGB, Jim Jones, and the Mafia.[8]

When Bishop and his followers seized power in Grenada, *The Belize Times* displayed an old photograph from the *San Francisco Chronicle* that showed Sir Eric Gairy, flanked by Jim Jones and California's Lieutenant Governor Mervyn Dymally, watching a karate demonstration at Jones' People's Temple in San Francisco. The text underneath the photograph read: "Bad things continue to happen to people who once associated with Jim Jones and Mervyn Dymally. Standing between these two above is Eric Gairy, Prime Minister of Grenada, who lost his country to a Communist-led takeover last week." The PUP's organ obviously hoped that Lindo's former association with Jones and Dymally would have an equally disastrous effect (*The Belize Times*, Mar. 18, 1979, 2).

Remembering that the leftist Arbenz government (1950-1954) had been the only post-World War II regime in Central America to embrace the cause of Belizean independence, Price was convinced that the two revolutionary victories of 1979 in this hemisphere could only redound to Belize's benefit. The Belizean leader was not to be disappointed. From their very inception, the Sandinista government in Managua and the People's Revolutionary government in St. George's, fervently advocated Belize's total independence. After the achievement of that goal on September 21, 1981, both Nicaragua and Grenada urged the world community to protect the newest nation of Central America from the annexationist designs of its western neighbor.

At practically every international meeting which he attended, from the time that he seized power until his murder in October 1983, Bishop took up the cause of Belize's independence and security. These meetings included the Sixth Summit Conference of the Non-Aligned Countries at Havana, Cuba (summer 1979), the Third Heads of Government of CARICOM Meeting at Ocho Rios, Jamaica (November 1982), the Seventh Summit Conference of the Non-Aligned Countries at New Delhi, India (March 1983), the Protocolary Session of the Organization of American States (June 1983), and the Fourth Heads of Government of CARICOM Meeting at Port-of-Spain, Trinidad (July 1983), which was the last major international gathering that Bishop attended before his death (GDC, Microfiche DSI-83-C-006946, DSI-83-L-005807, DSI-83-C-006944, and DSI-83-C-005481).

Typical of Bishop's rhetoric in support of Belize were his remarks on February 24, 1980, at Managua, Nicaragua, on the occasion of the commemoration of the forty-sixth anniversary of Augusto Sandino's assassination:

> Our common struggle must free the region of all attempts to seize territory from other people. Right here in Central America, the bestial Guatemalan dictatorship aims to deny the people of Belize their national territory, thus delaying their just right to independence and full sovereign control over all their present land.

> We welcome your decision since the revolution to join us, other sister Caribbean nations, and the vast majority of peoples and states throughout the world in condemning Guatemala's claims and rendering full support to the Belizean people. (GDC, Microfiche DSI-83-C-005805)

Given its miniscule size and the wide range of issues it had to deal with, it is truly remarkable that the Grenadian Ministry of Foreign Affairs composed at least three major position papers which were designed to guide Grenadian officials in dealing with their Belizean counterparts. The first of these papers, entitled *Guatemala's Claim to Belize*, traces in minute detail the long and complicated course of British-Guatemalan negotiations over Belize from the Anglo-Guatemalan Treaty of 1859 until the end of 1978 (GDC, Microfiche DSI-83-C-006138). The second one, *The Belize Question*, questions the wisdom of entrusting Belize's future security solely to Great Britain because "too great reliance by Belize on one country for its very survival will jeopardize its sovereignty." Instead, the paper suggested that the commonwealth countries should set up a combined defense force to protect an independent Belize from Guatemalan incursions (GDC, Microfiche DSI-83-C-005716). The third position paper, which was written in the fall of 1982, examined the internal situation in Belize and lamented the lack of a "progressive movement" in that country. Both PUP and UDP were described as "traditional bourgeois parties which are anti-Communist and pro-imperialist," with the UDP standing to the right of the PUP in the political spectrum of Belize (GDC, Microfiche DSI-83-C-005716).

Yet in some respects at least, the PUP hardly resembled this description by the Grenadian Foreign Ministry. It did not even become disturbed by the prospect of a possible takeover by leftist insurgents in Guatemala, even though the nature of a rebel-controlled government there in the 1980s would be infinitely more radical than the reformist Arbenz government of the early 1950s with which the PUP had had such cordial contacts. When in November 1979 the Belizean black nationalist newspaper *Amandala* printed a release by the Guatemalan Guerrilla Army of the Poor (EGP) which discussed Belizean-Guatemalan relations, the PUP reprinted it with approval in its newspaper. The EGP statement read in part:

> The Guatemalan landowners of the past as well as the new finqueros of today who have evicted tens of thousands of Kekchi Indians from their lands, forcing them to take refuge in Belize, now seek in the name of an alleged Guatemalan sovereignty over the territory of Belize, which was never real, to extend their voracity to the British colony that is about to attain independence.
>
> The people of Belize and Guatemala share no common historical, economic or cultural heritage. But today they have common social and political interests. Both struggle against imperialism and for real independence, for justice and social well-being, for a society without exploited and exploiters. The Guatemalan and Belizean people could live happily content and in fraternal neighborhood in their countries, if they could freely marshal their own destinies. The Belizean people's struggle for independence is part of the general struggle of the Central American people against imperialism, ethnic oppression, repression and class exploitation. (*The Belize Times*, Dec. 16, 1979, 10; *Brukdown*, No. 1 1980, 5)

The year 1979 was not only significant for Belize because of the important external events that were transpiring, but because of the general elections held on November 21. The opposition United Democratic party ran under the slogan "Time for a Change," but it was actually Price's People's United party which promised to bring about the greatest change: full independence for Belize within five years. In contrast, the UDP, holding meetings which were decked out with the Union Jack, called for a moratorium on Belizean independence for at least ten years during which time the country's economy and defense would be significantly strengthened.

The 1979 elections became a referendum on the policies which George Price had pursued over the previous two decades, policies which came under heavy attack by Lindo, the leader of the opposition since 1974. Accusing Price of "looking to Cuba and the East," Lindo predicted that Belize's independence would be followed by the rapid occupation of either Cuba or Guatemala which could only be prevented by the stationing of American, British, Mexican, and Canadian troops on Belizean soil. Lindo ridiculed Price's reliance on the Caribbean Community and the Non-Aligned Movement (which the UDP leader viewed as communist-controlled since Fidel Castro had been elected its chairperson for 1979-1983). Instead of "taking any guarantees from Jamaica, Barbados or Trinidad" or "going to Yugoslavia, Panama and Czechoslovakia," Lindo vowed that upon a UDP victory, he would form a close alliance with the United States, the only country which, in his opinion, had the power to tame both Cuban and Guatemalan designs upon Belize. Expressing his doubts about Carter, whom he mistrusted, Lindo promised to build a strong pro-Belizean lobby in the U.S. Congress (Interview with Lindo in *Brukdown*, No. 9, 1978, 15-17).

Price felt much more positive about the policies of the Carter administration than did Lindo. The Belizean leader welcomed Carter's elimination of military aid to the Guatemalan military rulers who happened to be among the worst violators of human rights in Latin America. The PUP government also approved of Carter's cordial relations with the Manley government of Jamaica as well as the initial improvement of relations between Washington and Havana. But Price and most Belizeans were quite disappointed when in November 1979 the United States, along with six other countries, abstained from voting at the United Nations in favor of a resolution supporting Belize's independence which was backed by 123 countries (*The Belize Times*, Nov. 11, 1979).[9] The disappointment was all the more intense because Belize's Olympic Association had chosen to heed Carter's appeal to the nations of the world not to send any athletes to the Moscow Summer Olympics because of Soviet intervention in Afghanistan. The Belizean people's bitterness, however, turned to joy during the following year, when the United States, along with 129 other countries, including the Central American states of Costa Rica, Panama, and Nicaragua, voted in favor of a UN resolution calling for Belize's independence before the end of 1981 (*The Belize Times*, Nov. 8, 1980).

In contrast to its rather pleasant dealings with Belize, the Carter Administration's relations with the Bishop regime in Grenada proved to be anything but cordial. About a month after the PRG's seizure of power, then U.S. Ambassador to the Eastern Caribbean, Frank Ortiz, visited Grenada and warned its government not to establish relations with Cuba. Ortiz' warning was perceived by Bishop as an insulting threat. Ignoring the U.S. government's concern, the PRG from its very beginning established close diplomatic, cultural, economic, and military ties with Cuba, ties which were to persist and grow until Bishop's murder in October 1983.[10]

The Carter administration became particularly annoyed in early 1980, when Grenada was the only country in this hemisphere besides Cuba to vote with the USSR when the question of the Soviet intervention in Afghanistan came before the United Nations. As signals of his continual displeasure with the PRG, Carter refused to accept the credentials of the Grenadian Ambassadress-designate, Dessima Williams; ordered Ortiz's successor, Sally Shelton, not to visit Grenada in the future; attempted to exclude the island nation from some U.S. aid programs to the Caribbean; and ordered the holding of the "Solid Shield 80" Maneuver. This sea and air exercise slated for the Caribbean was, however, canceled when Panama protested this apparent militarization of the Caribbean. What must be remembered is the fact that the Carter administration, which was beset by larger crises, such as Afghanistan and the Iranian hostage situation, never regarded developments in Grenada as more than a nuisance which could be handled at the assistant secretary level (Schoenhals & Melanson 1985, 35-39, 56-59, 111-16, 130-77).

Belize's relations with Grenada and Nicaragua might well have taken a turn for the worse if Lindo's UDP had come to power in November 1979. The polls, most of the press, and even many PUP supporters, were predicting a UDP victory; but in a stunning upset, Price's PUP was able to achieve its seventh successive electoral victory, winning thirteen of the eighteen parliamentary seats. Soon after this amazing feat, which in the Belizean press was compared to Truman's 1948 victory over Dewey, Price formed a new eleven-member cabinet which was to run the country for the next five years (King 1980). This cabinet, which encompassed the entire political spectrum of the PUP, was divided into three factions. There was the right wing, which in its outlook on domestic and foreign matters was practically indistinguishable from the UDP. It consisted of the Minister of Energy and Communications, Louis Sylvestre, and the Minister of Works, Fred Hunter.[11] The large centrist part of the cabinet included, among others, the Deputy Prime Minister and Minister of Home Affairs, C. L. B. Rogers, the Minister of State, V. H. Courtney, and George Price himself, who, in addition to being prime minister, retained control over the Ministry of Finance. Finally, there was the left wing, represented by the Attorney-General and Minister of Education and Sports, Said Musa, and Minister of Health, Cooperatives and Housing, Assad Shoman.

The inclusion of Musa and Shoman in Price's cabinet evoked uneasiness among the PUP's conservative faction and a storm of protest from the opposition party, whose new leader, Theodore Aranda, hinted darkly that the election results were not a triumph for the PUP, but a victory for its Communists, who had been arming themselves with weapons allegedly smuggled into Belize by the Soviet Union years before under the guise of hurricane relief shipments of clothing (see conversation with Theodore Aranda in *Brukdown* 1980, No. 1, 28). During the general elections, the UDP candidate, who was running against Shoman in the Cayo District, had labeled his opponent a card-carrying Communist, atheist, and racist.[12] The fact that during the coming years, Musa and Shoman turned out to be revolutionary Grenada's and Nicaragua's best friends within the Price cabinet only served to heighten the suspicions which many conservative Belizeans expressed about these two young politicians. Given their importance in the Price government and the amount of controversy which has always swirled around them, it might be appropriate to look at their backgrounds in an attempt to sort out fact from fiction.

Both Shoman and Musa were offsprings of prosperous Palestinian Arabs who had settled in British Honduras in the 1930s and married local women. Shoman was raised at San Ignacio, the largest town of the Cayo District, while Musa grew up in Belize City. Both excelled as students and won scholarships that enabled them to obtain law degrees in Great Britain. Instead of joining some of their Belizean contemporaries who used their education as a springboard for seeking their fortune abroad, Shoman and Musa returned to work for Belizean independence. By independence, however, they not only meant the formal relinquishment by Great Britain of her residual power, but the reduction in Belize of the overwhelming British and North American economic and cultural influence which, in their opinion, threatened to transform that country into a neocolonial entity.

Disillusioned with Belize's conventional political parties, which they accused of excluding the masses, Shoman and Musa, influenced by the writings of Frantz Fanon and Che Guevara, formed a Belizean national liberation movement that differed from the standard political party of the Anglophone Caribbean. In May 1969, they organized the People's Action Committee (PAC) which by October of that year united with the black nationalist movement known as the United Black Association for Development (UBAD) in order to form the Revolitical Action Movement (RAM) (Interview with Assad Shoman at St. George's, Grenada, Nov. 1982; Grant 1976, 268-75). This organization turned out to be short-lived for several reasons. In the first place, the diverse aims of its two main components, PAC and UBAD, proved quite incompatible. Second, and more importantly, the British system of parliamentary democracy was deeply entrenched in Belize and the majority of its population was unwilling to abandon its political tradition for the experiment of a new-fangled national liberation movement. Nobody realized that more quickly than Shoman and Musa, who by early 1970 had resigned from RAM, which, for all purposes, signaled the end of this transitory organization.

What is interesting, however, is that the founding of PAC and RAM roughly coincided with Price's major shift from a policy which had been turned toward Central America and the United States, to one that was directed toward the Caribbean, the nonaligned world, and the Commonwealth. In making this change, Price was in need of bright young advisers who were atuned to the mood and spirit of the emerging Third World. Shoman and Musa probably filled this need more adequately than any other individuals in Belize and by the mid-1970s, both of them had been co-opted into the PUP. Beginning in 1974, Shoman was serving as Minister of State in the prime minister's office at Belmopan. When, a year later, Price began to undertake his successful lobbying effort for Belize's total independence to the United Nations, it was Shoman who spearheaded this campaign among the third world countries, which by then constituted a majority among the nations of the world organization. Both Shoman and Musa ran unsuccessfully as PUP candidates during the general elections of 1974. Thereafter, Shoman was appointed attorney general, a position which he held until 1978, while Musa served as a PUP senator.

About the same time that Shoman and Musa were establishing PAC and RAM, a young Grenadian by the name of Maurice Bishop was returning to his homeland after obtaining a law degree in England. Like his two contemporaries in Belize, Bishop had also been influenced by the ideas of Frantz Fanon and Che Guevara. In addition, he was attracted to the writings of Kwame Nkrumah, Walter Rodney, and Malcolm X and found himself drawn to the Black Power Movement that had penetrated the English-speaking Caribbean ("Maurice Bishop — Premier in the Spotlight" 1979).

Like his Belizean counterparts, Bishop had become dissatisfied with the British system of parliamentary democracy, which, in the case of Grenada, had been subverted by the vote-rigging and repression of Eric Gairy. When Bishop returned to Grenada in 1970, the only opposition to Gairy consisted of the conservative plantocracy and business elite, which was contemptuous of the Grenadian agro-proletariat that had been drawn into Gairy's party, only to be exploited by him. Thus, when Bishop and other radical Grenadian professionals formed a national liberation organization called the New Jewel Movement (NJM) in 1973, they filled a real need. In contrast to Belize, where a relatively healthy parliamentary system kept RAM confined to the status of an ephemeral oddity, Gairy's perversion of the Grenadian parliament allowed the NJM to gather mass support so that by 1979, Bishop was able to seize power with the overwhelming backing of the Grenadian people. In spite of the different developments of their liberation movements and the divergent paths of their political careers, Shoman and Musa retained many ideas which corresponded to Bishop's concepts. They shared, for example, the fear that the cultural identity of their respective countries was gravely threatened by the inundation of North American values which were flooding the entire Caribbean, if not the world.

A Grenadian delegation, visiting Belize during the early 1980s, reported back to St. George's that television had arrived there with a vengeance. At that time, television programs in Belize were pirated from U.S. satellites and, for some reason, transmissions from the Chicago area came in best. Thus the Belizeans were treated to television fare which consisted primarily of local Chicago news, the Chicago Cubs baseball games, situation comedies, "Dallas," and the evangelist Jimmy Swaggart. The Grenadian report quoted Musa as saying: "The way it's going, the next prime minister of Belize may be Chicago Mayor Jane Byrne" (GDC, Microfiche DSI-83-C-007600). The above-mentioned example of North American influence could well be dismissed with a smile, but Professor Milton Jamail has listed a much more serious effect of U.S. television in Belize: "U.S. network news are the main source of information on international events. So while their government did not support the U.S. invasion of Grenada in October 1983, Belizeans formed opinions, for the most part, from what they saw on U.S. television" (Jamail 1984, 16).

When Shoman attended the First Conference on Culture and Sovereignty in the Caribbean in November 1982, which was held in Grenada in order to rally Caribbean artists, writers, intellectuals, and politicians against the negative aspects of foreign cultural penetration of the area, he was shocked to see that revolutionary Grenada, far from setting an example for the rest of the region, had apparently made little effort to improve the quality of the nation's cultural life. The two shabby theaters at St. George's were showing the same selection of fourth-rate foreign films that could be viewed in Belize at any time, and the only licensed Grenadian newspaper, the *Free West Indian*, ranked below most Belizean publications in quality. During his speech to the assembled delegates, Shoman pointed out that Grenada's only two book stores presented an equally dismal picture. While visiting these stores, which were filled with cheap novels and religious tracts, Shoman had been unable to discover a single book by George Lamming, the noted Barbadian novelist who had actually organized the very conference that the delegates were attending (Notes taken by the author at Shoman's speech and in a subsequent interview with him).

At the time that Prime Minister Price appointed Shoman as head of the Ministries of Health, Cooperatives and Housing, the former editor of *The Belize Sunday Times*, Emory King, commented that all of these ministries were considered safe ones "where the ideologically tainted Shoman can work 24 hours a day doing only good deeds" while "his opponents will find it difficult to call the improvement of the nation's health a Communist plot" (King 1980, 7).[13] The fact of the matter, however, was that Shoman and Musa by no means restricted their activities to the realm of their respective ministries, but continued to represent Belize on diplomatic missions to third world countries. In early 1980, Said Musa was appointed Ambassador to the Caribbean Community. He attended the Fifth Meeting of CARICOM Foreign Ministers on the island of St. Lucia. In April of the same year, Shoman and Musa traveled to Jamaica, Panama, and Nicaragua. They responded positively to a request from Nicaraguan Education Minister Carlos Tünnermann for Belizean volunteers to help with the Sandinista Literacy Crusade among the hundred thousand illiterates who could be found among the English-speaking population of Nicaragua's Atlantic coast (*The Belize Times* Apr. 27, 1980, 12).

As a token of his gratitude for the Sandinistas' unswerving support for Belize's independence, Price visited Nicaragua himself in July 1980 to attend the celebration of first anniversary of the final victory over Somoza. While representatives of twenty-five nations and international organizations attended the festivities at Managua, only three heads of state put in an appearance: Fidel Castro, Maurice Bishop, and George Price. His visit enabled the Belizean prime minister to meet for the first time with Bishop.

With the pro-PUP press hailing the Sandinista victory as "a triumph of human rights" and "a cause for celebration," the opposition UDP doubted the benefits of the Sandinista takeover for the Nicaraguan people and severely criticized Price for appearing on the same platform with the top leaders of the Cuban, Grenadian, and Nicaraguan revolution (*The Belize Times*, July 20, 1980, 2). Pushed into the defensive by the vehement and seemingly interminable UDP attacks on Price's Nicaraguan journey, an editorial in the PUP's organ, *The Belize Sunday Times*, as late as December 1980, pointed out that whereas Fidel Castro had spoken for two hours and Maurice Bishop for half an hour, Price's comments, consisting mostly of biblical quotations, had taken only three minutes. The editorial went on to imply the necessity of having had a man of religion standing next to such godless Communists as Castro and Bishop: "Here was this great but humble leader of a small struggling nation standing up before about half a million people,...before Fidel Castro, the self-proclaimed Communist, before Maurice Bishop, who reports say is leaning towards Communism....Here was this man of faith, calling on the Almighty and Eternal God to be the guiding force in rebuilding Nicaragua" (*The Belize Times*, Dec. 7, 1980).

This fearful editorial, still attempting to justify Price's July visit to Nicaragua five months after its occurrence, was not only written to deflect UDP's criticism, but also to appease Ronald Reagan, who had been elected president one month prior to its appearance. Although Reagan would not be inaugurated until January 1981, Price recognized that his electoral victory foreshadowed a profound change in U.S. policy toward Central America and the Caribbean.

In contrast to the Carter administration, which had viewed the revolutionary outbursts in Central America and the Caribbean as primarily the results of local repression and exploitation, Reagan and his advisers looked at this revolutionary conflagration through "the constricting prism of East/West confrontational struggle for global power and influence" (Barrow 1982, 23).[14] According to Reagan, Carter had helped to undermine staunchly pro-American governments in the region in order to further his naive human rights campaign. The Reagan administration made it clear that it was not only determined to prevent any further revolutionary victories in the region, but that it would attempt to ostracize and, if possible, strangle the new revolutionary governments in Nicaragua and Grenada. Such a policy not only entailed the increased militarization of Central America and the eastern Caribbean, but also the application of great pressure upon such countries as Belize, Costa Rica, and Panama that had viewed the 1979 revolutionary victories in Nicaragua and Grenada as positive developments.

Pressures on Belize by the Reagan administration were not long in coming. On June 1, 1981, an item appeared in the "Washington Whispers" column of *U.S. News and World Report* stating that according to U.S. intelligence reports, Guatemala and Belize had replaced Nicaragua as conduits for Cuban arms shipments to the guerrillas of El Salvador (June 1, 1981, 5). In Belize it was held that the Reagan administration had deliberately planted this totally unfounded allegation as "a warning shot across the bow" in order to make sure that once Belize had obtained full independence in September 1981, Shoman and Said Musa would no longer be allowed to influence Belize's foreign policy. The news item concerning the alleged Cuban arms shipments was not appreciated in Belize. The politically independent Belizean magazine *Brukdown* declared "that the United States of America is dead set against a truly non-aligned Belize should come as no surprise. But to carry out its foreign policy goals by using the media to create a false impression about what is happening here," it continued, "is to do a great disservice to the people of Belize, many of whose livelihoods are dependent upon the attitude of U.S. tourists and investors" (1981, No. 2, 30).

As a further sign of its displeasure with the Price government, the Reagan administration appointed an obscure Florida congressman, Dan Mica, to head the official U.S. delegation to the Belizean independence ceremony on September 21, 1981. Congressman Mica, who did not even belong to Reagan's own political party, was so little known in Belize that he was addressed at one point as "Mr. Formica" (*Brukdown* 1981, no. 5, 9). In contrast, the Nicaraguan delegation was headed by such prominent members of the Sandinista government as Sergio Ramírez, Ernesto Cardenal, and Miguel D'Escoto.

On September 2, 1981, Bishop sent a warm message to Price which read in part: "The occasion of your country's independence is a signal achievement not only for the peoples of Belize and the Caribbean region but, indeed, for all non-independent peoples who are at present struggling for their liberation. For the Caribbean region in particular, it represents an additional step forward in our mutual quest to have the Caribbean declared a Zone of Peace." Bishop thanked Price "for the firm message of solidarity which you sent to us as a result of the recent aggressive military maneuvers in the region," and announced that he would personally lead the Grenadian delegation which would also include the Minister of Agriculture and Acting Foreign Minister, George Louison, the Chief of Protocol, Shahiba Strong, and four body guards, two of whom, Cletus St. Paul and Errol George, were to play a fateful part in the bloody denouement of the Grenadian revolution during October 1983 (GDC, Microfiche DSI-83-C-011752 and DSI-83-C-011755). The Grenadian body guards constantly surrounding Bishop caused a sensation in Belize, where people were used to seeing their own prime minister walk the streets without any protection whatsoever. Besides Bishop, Prime Minister Edward Seaga of Jamaica and President Rodrigo Carazo of Costa Rica were the only other heads of state to attend Belize's independence celebrations (*The Belize Times*, Oct. 4, 1981, 7, 10).

The Cuban government, which had also sent a high-level delegation headed by Deputy Foreign Minister Ricardo Alarcón, brought along an "independence gift" of twenty-five university scholarships for Belizean students. This offer triggered a grave crisis in Price's cabinet, where Shoman and Musa advocated its acceptance while Sylvestre and Fuller put up a vehement resistance to it. Price, who realized that the acceptance of these scholarships would antagonize the Reagan administration, sided with the PUP's right wing and the offer was declined. The Cubans then renewed the offer outside of government channels and, within a short period of time, six Belizeans were on their way to Cuba in order to study medicine, veterinary science, and electronics. Even though Cuba had staunchly backed Belize in its disputes with Guatemala, Price, fearful of incurring the Reagan's wrath, postponed indefinitely the establishment of diplomatic relations with Cuba (*Brukdown* 1982, no. 1, 24).

By early 1982, Price seemed to have moved Belize even closer to the United States and further away from his avowed policy of nonalignment. In January an agreement between Belmopan and Washington provided for the training of members of the Belizean Defense Force by U.S. military advisers in the United States, Panama, and in Belize itself (*Brukdown* 1982, no. 1, 24). Heretofore, Belize had relied solely upon Great Britain for its defense against a possible Guatemalan invasion. Even after Belize had obtained full independence, the United Kingdom had agreed to leave behind 1300 British troops to protect Central America's newest nation. By 1982 it had become apparent that the United States would gradually replace Great Britain as guarantor of Belizean sovereignty.[15]

Since the late 1970s, the Price government had been under pressure from Washington to do something about the export of Belizean marijuana to the United States. By 1985 Belize was the fourth largest exporter of cannabis after Mexico, Colombia, and Jamaica. When the Reagan administration took over in March 1981, pressure on Belmopan over marijuana cultivation increased. The U.S. Drug Enforcement Agency (DEA) asked for permission to eradicate the marijuana crop in Belize by aerial spraying of the herbicide Paraquat, which was rumored to be harmful to human health. This request created a dilemma for the Price administration. On the one hand, the PUP government realized that any drastic action against marijuana cultivation would thoroughly antagonize the population of the northern districts (particularly Corozal) where, after the collapse of the world sugar prices, marijuana had become the lifeblood of the economy. On the other hand, Price was eager to placate the Reagan administration, whose ire it had previously aroused by its sympathetic attitude toward the Nicaraguan and Grenadian revolutions.

Thus in early 1982, the Price government reluctantly agreed to an all-out campaign to eliminate marijuana from Belize. DEA helicopters, flying at first from Mexico but, later on, from Belizean soil, destroyed, in conjunction with Belizean ground forces, two hundred million dollars worth of marijuana, especially in the northern districts. Over three hundred persons, half of them foreigners, were arrested in connection with this campaign. The DEA even kidnapped an alleged Belizean drug dealer in Guatemala and flew him to

Texas where he was lingering in jail as late as 1986 (*The Belize Times*, Jan. 1, 1983, 4).

Price's increased cooperation with the Reagan administration to be rewarded in a variety of ways. Reagan's Caribbean Basin Initiative (CBI) allocated Belize a $10 million dollar, 25-year loan at 2 percent for the first 10 years and 3 percent thereafter. Half the loan was for public projects, with the remainder to aid the private sector. In addition, Price was able to sign a $4 million agreement for housing improvement with the U.S. Agency for International Development (AID) (*The Belize Times*, Sept. 19, 1982, 27).

In spite of these successful overtures to the Reagan administration, Price did not entirely abandon his long-standing interest in nonalignment. This became apparent in March 1982, when the CARICOM foreign ministers (including Grenada's Foreign Minister Unison Whiteman) met at Belmopan. In his address to the conference, Price stressed the necessity of including all Caribbean and Central American countries in the Caribbean Basin Initiative, an idea which ran counter to Reagan's intention to exclude Cuba, Grenada, and Nicaragua. The People's Revolutionary Government of Grenada appreciated Price's attitude. In a special report entitled *The Political Situation in the Caribbean and Grenada's Present Situation Within That Scenario*, the Director of the Political and Economic Division of the Ministry of Foreign Affairs, Merle Collins, observed in May 1982:

> Belize with all of its caution and conservatism could be regarded as Grenada's most dependable partner in CARICOM today.
>
> This simply serves to show the gravity of the situation and the depth of isolation, for Belize's representatives at international meetings are not renowned for being articulate or certain of their political direction. The overall picture then, is that if we look closely for friends of convenience within CARICOM, there may be Belize, Guyana and possibly Antigua. Trinidad will abstain. The rest of the Caribbean is unequivocally on the other side. (GDC, Microfiche DSI-83-C-007)

The almost total isolation of Grenada to which Merle Collins' report referred was at least partially caused by the Falklands (Malvinas) crisis of 1982. When Argentina seized these islands from Great Britain in April, thereby inviting a British counterattack and reconquest, the Anglophone Caribbean countries (except for Grenada) found themselves on opposite sides of this hemisphere's Spanish-speaking lands, which lined up solidly behind Argentina.

Belize stood with Great Britain from the very beginning of the crisis for a variety of reasons. In the first place, there was a genuine feeling of outrage against the actions of Argentina's military dictators who, previous to their assault on the Falklands, had sent military advisers to Central America to bolster the military regimes of that region. Second, Belize was indebted to Great Britain for providing the troops which were protecting her from Guatemalan aggression. Finally, Belize, along with Guyana, was strongly opposed to the use of force in solving territorial disputes. If Argentina should get away with seizing the Falklands, Guatemala might be encouraged to grab Belize, and

Venezuela might follow suit in seizing Guyana's Essequibo territory, which it had claimed for many decades. It is hard to say why Grenada, in a break with all other Anglophone countries, backed Argentina, thereby increasing her isolation, which her enemies had long desired. She could well have abstained from voting in the United Nations just as Nicaragua had done on the Afghanistan issue. In all probability, the PRG wanted to demonstrate once again its utter loyalty to Cuba and the Soviet Union, who were both backing Argentina on the Falklands issue.

Concerned about the rift which had arisen between revolutionary Grenada and the rest of the Anglophone Caribbean over the Falklands War, the PRG was eager to mend at least some fences by being represented at a meeting of thirteen Central American and Caribbean political parties which convened between October 26 and 29, 1982 at Belize City in order to discuss how independent Belize related to Central America and the Caribbean. With the exception of the Frente Sandinista of Nicaragua and the Movimiento Nacional Revolucionario of El Salvador, most of the attending parties were either center or left-of-center (e.g., Mexico's PRI, Belize's PUP, the Dominican Republic's PRD, Costa Rica's PLN, etc.). In spite of this fact, the Belizean opposition press described the conference as a meeting of Communists convoked by Assad Shoman and Said Musa.

Aware of this criticism, West Germany's Friedrich Ebert Foundation and Belize's PUP, the two co-sponsors of this conference, had not at first included Grenada's New Jewel Movement among the list of invited parties. But exhortations by Jamaica's People's National party (PNP) resulted in a last-minute invitation to the NJM which was represented at the conference by none other than Merle Collins. The report which this leading official of Grenada's Ministry of Foreign Affairs sent home about the general atmosphere surrounding the conference could hardly have been reassuring to superiors back at St. George's. Collins stated that the conference was regarded within Belize "as a Musa/Shoman Communist show" which was boycotted by the right wing of the PUP. As a matter of fact, when a power black-out threw the conference into darkness, many people expressed their suspicion that the black-out was a deliberate act of sabotage by the right-wing PUP Minister of Energy, Louis Sylvestre. In front of the Fort George Hotel where the conference was being held, thirteen youths marched with placards reading: "Communists Go Home," "Manley and Castro Destroyed Jamaica," and "Three Blind Mice: Musa, Shoman, Price." About Price's brief appearance at the conference, Collins had these sarcastic comments: "Prime Minister Price opened the conference with a presentation the high point of which was: 'Commit your works to the Lord and your plans will be fulfilled.' The Prime Minister kept a very low profile at the reception which followed and thereafter disappeared" (GDC, Microfiche DSI-83-C-600).

The NJM delegate described Price as being caught in a tug-of-war between the PUP's two factions, with the right wing gaining. She went on to warn that this situation boded ill for Grenada's position at the upcoming CARICOM Heads of Government Summit Meeting at Ocho Ríos, where she expected Price "to be less likely to support Grenada's position" at a time when Grenada was likely to come under fierce assault from the prime ministers of Barbados and Jamaica. Musa and Shoman tried to be as helpful to Collins as they could be under the circumstances and aided her in setting up a Belizean-Grenadian Friendship Society. There was also a discussion of setting up a Belizean youth organization patterned upon Grenada's National Youth Organization (NYO).

At the end of the conference, the representatives of the thirteen attending parties issued the "Declaration of Belize," in which they announced "unconditional support for the sovereignty and territorial integrity of Belize" and called "for absolute respect for its demarcated borders." The declaration also "expressed support for the people of Grenada in their struggle to build a just society and attain meaningful development" and "condemned any attempt to isolate Grenada or threaten the process of development in that country" (*The Belize Times*, Nov. 7, 1982, 7).

In the meantime, preparations had been underway for the Third Heads of Government of CARICOM Meeting at Ocho Rios, Jamaica, in November 1982. It was common knowledge that the chairman of this meeting, Edward Seaga, along with the prime minister of Barbados, Tom Adams, would be using the occasion to try to expel both Grenada and Guyana from CARICOM on the grounds that these two countries had been ignoring the principles of parliamentary democracy and violating human rights. In a special directive to the Grenadian delegation, Bishop outlined his strategy for blocking the expected move to ostracize his country. The Grenadian delegation was "to struggle to defeat steps to isolate or discredit Grenada at the conference or afterwards; propose and support steps that will strengthen practical cooperation and the overall regional integration movement; hold bilateral [talks] with a number of governments at three parallel levels: head, foreign, and other ministers and officials; hold discussions (and participate in other activities) with progressive forces in Jamaica and support Surinam's application for associate membership in the organization" (GDC, Microfiche DSI-83-C-600) Bishop, furthermore, stated that the Grenadian delegation must "reject any proposals to amend the Chaguaramas Treaty,[16] to make provisions for 'human rights' and 'parliamentary democracy'" and "reject attempts to 'try' Grenada and interfere in its internal affairs." Full use was to be made of the media "to influence the climate of the conference and, therefore, the conference itself." The Grenadian delegation was urged "to establish intelligence gathering machinery in order to get to know and to plan to counter the tactics of Grenada's opponents at the conference." Bishop himself planned "to hold bilateral meetings with Chambers, Burnham, Price, Pindling, Simmonds and Compton with a view of getting them not to support any anti-Grenada amendments or positions."[17]

Since he regarded Belize as Grenada's most reliable partner at the conference, Bishop ordered that the Grenadian delegates approach their Belizean counterparts "at all three levels." Revolutionary Grenada was fortunate in having one of its staunchest Belizean friends, the ambassador to

CARICOM, Said Musa, constitute part of the Belizean delegation which, otherwise, consisted of Prime Minister George Price, Minister of State V. H. Courtnay, and the Permanent Secretary for Foreign Affairs, Everal Waight.

According to Bishop's instructions, the Grenadian officials at Ocho Rios were to approach their Belizean counterparts in the following manner: gratitude was to be expressed to the Belizean government for "correcting the Friedrich Ebert Foundation's error" in neglecting to invite Grenada to the recently held Conference of Political Parties of Central America and the Caribbean. Belize was to be reassured that she had Grenada's total support in the defense of her territorial integrity and the Grenadian delegates were to inquire "how concretely Grenada could further demonstrate its solidarity with Belize's just cause." In return, Grenada expected Belize to reject "any anti-Grenadian amendments under the guise of human rights or parliamentary democracy." The Belizean delegates were also to be to support Grenada's proposal to transform the Caribbean into a "Zone of Peace." Finally, Price was to be invited to make a state visit to Grenada (GDC, Microfiche DSI-83-C-007041).

As expected, the delegations of Barbados, Jamaica, St. Vincent, and Dominica advanced an amendment whose acceptance would have meant the exclusion of both Grenada and Guyana from further participation in CARICOM. Ironically, it was Vere Bird, Sr., the conservative prime minister of Antigua and Barbuda, who had not even been on Bishop's list of Caribbean heads of state that were to be cultivated before the start of the conference, who first assailed the attempt to oust Grenada and Guyana from the organization. Bird called for "a stop to all this preaching" and remarked that even though "some may accept the Westminster Model as their Bible, others may not." The Antiguan prime minister stated that it was wrong to apply pressure to fellow Caribbean nations and to interfere in their political systems. He warned that by the endorsement of such conduct, CARICOM would share the fate of the abortive West Indian Federation. The gathered heads of state, according to Bird, should explore every avenue to keep the people of the Caribbean together instead of "rocking the boat and creating a bad atmosphere."

Bird's remarks were enthusiastically seconded by Price, who also counseled his colleagues to refrain from any action that would lead to the break-up of the Caribbean Community. Price declared that Bishop had already partially remedied the situation by agreeing to a definite time table for the holding of free elections in Grenada. The prime minister of Trinidad and Tobago, George Chambers, joined his Antiguan and Belizean counterparts in a plea not to exclude Grenada and Guyana from CARICOM while, at the same time, urging the holding of free elections and an end to the detention of political prisoners on Grenada (GDC, Microfiche DSI-83-C-002634). The attempt by Seaga and Adams to expel Grenada and Guyana from CARICOM had turned out to be a failure and an exhausted but triumphant Bishop returned to his country on the very same day the CARICOM meeting had ended. In a virulent speech at Sea Moon, Grenada, he rubbed salt into the wounds of his two antagonists by denouncing them as "cretins," "yard fowl" and "Uncle Toms" (Author's notes during Bishop's speech at Sean Moon, Grenada). The Ocho Ríos meeting certainly represented a high-water mark in the amiable relationship between Belize and revolutionary Grenada, and the differences between the two countries, which had arisen earlier in the year over their attitudes toward the Falkland (Malvinas) crisis, seemed to be all but forgotten.

The Reagan administration, however, could hardly have been pleased by Price's support for Grenada during the Ocho Rios Meeting. At any rate, it showed little consideration for Belize when it announced in January 1983 that it would terminate the five-year-old arms embargo against Guatemala and supply that country with $6,368,600 worth of military spare parts because the Efraín Ríos Montt regime there had supposedly eased up on political repression. Perhaps in order to ease somewhat the shock of this announcement for the Belizeans, Reagan announced simultaneously that he had nominated Malcolm Barnabey, a career foreign service officer, as the first U.S. Ambassador to Belize.

The situation was aggravated by the fact that, although dropping his country's previous claim to all of Belize, Rios Montt demanded during January 1983 a Guatemalan outlet to the Atlantic which would run through Belize's Toledo District. This claim was immediately rejected by the Belizean government, and on January 10, Price made use of one of his first meetings with the newly appointed Barnabey to lodge a formal protest over renewed U.S. military aid to Belize's enemy. In his protest, Price remarked that any North American military assistance to Guatemala would eventually be used for that nation's designs upon Belize (*The Belize Times*, Jan. 16, 1983, 1, 4, 13).

The events of January 1983 must have convinced the Belizean prime minister more than ever that, although his country had moved much closer to the United States during 1982, it must never abandon its close ties with the Caribbean Community and the nonaligned world. Consequently, when the Seventh Non-Aligned Summit took place at New Delhi, India, during March 1983, Price dispatched a high-powered Belizean delegation to India which was headed by the Deputy Prime Minister, C. L. B. Rogers. In the course of his March 11, 1983, address to the Non-Aligned meeting, Rogers expressed his gratitude for Cuba's past leadership of the nonaligned world: "Our movement has been enriched by Cuba's dynamic and positive role as chairman of the Movement over the past three-and-a-half years and by the personal commitment of President Fidel Castro to the ideals of peace, justice and development. His sensitive and enlightened chairmanship helped steer our movement through a very difficult period. We all owe him a sincere debt of gratitude." Rogers went on to point out the continuing threat posed by Guatemala to the independence, territorial integrity, and nonaligned status of Belize. The Belizean deputy prime minister observed that Guatemala was attempting to fool the world by its feigned "reasonableness" of demanding now only one-third of Belize instead of its previous claim to the entire country. He exclaimed that Belize was determined to preserve its sovereignty and territorial integrity and that he was convinced that the nonaligned movement would back Belize now just as it had done in the past. Rogers was not to be disappointed; the New Delhi conference passed a strong resolution supporting the territorial integrity of both Belize and Guyana (GDC, Microfiche DSI-83-C-005477).

Just as at previous international gatherings, the Grenadian prime minister at New Delhi pledged his country's support for Belize's struggle against its powerful western neighbor. Unlike Rogers, however, Bishop did not hesitate to bring up the resumption of U.S. arms shipments to Guatemala: "We condemn and reject the U.S. decision to restore the supply of arms to the blood-thirsty Guatemalan dictatorship. The arming of Guatemala increases the direct threat which that country poses to the security and territorial integrity of Belize" (GDC, Microfiche DSI-83-L-005807).

In spite of the tensions which had developed between Washington and Belmopan over the resumption of U.S. military aid to Guatemala and Belize's stance at the Non-Aligned Conference at New Delhi, the Reagan administration, aware of Belize's strategic importance in Central America, decided to improve relations with that country by inviting Price for a state visit to the United States. On May 12, 1983, the Belizean prime minister, accompanied by four of his cabinet ministers, was received by Reagan at the White House. In a typical balancing act, Price had included his right-wing Minister of Works, Fred Hunter, as well as his leftist Minister of Education, Sports and Culture, Said Musa, among the delegation.

During his conversations with Price, Reagan tried to convince him of the great danger which a Sandinista-led Nicaragua constituted to all of Central America, including Belize. The Belizean prime minister, however, seemed to be much more concerned about the Guatemalan threat and pleaded with Reagan to use his influence with Great Britain to persuade that country to leave its troops in Belize in order to prevent a Guatemalan invasion. The request met with no response from the president. Reagan, who was aware of how reluctant Price had been to wage an eradication campaign against marijuana, urged the prime minister to continue his cooperation with the United States to curtail the growing of cannabis in Belize. The two heads of state also discussed trade questions as well as an increase in U.S. aid.

After the White House meeting, Reagan stated that "in contrast to the war and turmoil of the region, Belize, Central America's newest independent democracy, serves as a model of peace and stability." He also commented that he had been "impressed and encouraged by the efforts of prime minister Price's Government [!] to suppress the cultivation of cannabis, a drug which threatens both of our societies." In his reply, the Belizean prime minister stressed "the basic values of a common heritage" shared by the United States and Belize, and thanked Reagan for the help his country had received as a result of the Caribbean Basin Initiative (*The New Belize* 1983, no. 5, 1-5).

The Belizean prime minister concluded his visit to the United States by traveling to New York, Chicago, Los Angeles, Houston, and New Orleans, all cities with large Belizean communities. During Price's sojourn, the Agency for International Development announced that it would assist Belize in the construction of much needed housing as well as the training of Belizean citizens for public service jobs. Although not all obstacles between the United States and Belize had been removed, the Reagan-Price meeting had certainly brought the two countries closer together.

Just the opposite process was taking place as far as the U.S. dealings with Grenada were concerned. The long-standing Reagan hostility toward the Bishop regime reached an apogee during the first half of 1983. In contrast to Carter's policy of regarding developments on Grenada as a minor nuisance which could be handled at the assistant secretary stratum, the Reagan administration coordinated its policy towards Grenada at the highest government level. Between March and May 1983, Reagan delivered three major speeches that dealt in part with Grenada. In the course of these orations, Reagan claimed that Grenada had become a threat to the security of the United States because of the ongoing construction of an air field and a naval base (?) on that island which would threaten the vital sea lanes of the United States (*Miami Herald*, Mar. 17, 1983). Already in February 1983, Nestor D. Sánchez, the Deputy Assistant Secretary of State for Inter-American Affairs, had claimed that the existing military installations on Grenada "would provide air and naval bases...for the recovery of Soviet aircraft after strategic missions. It might also furnish missile sites for launching attacks against the United States with short and intermediate range missiles" (*Washington Post*, June 8, 1983, A-10).

This massive U.S. onslaught contributed considerably to the grave internal crisis on Grenada which began during the summer of 1983 and ended with the self-immolation of the Grenadian revolution by October of that year. A substantial faction within the central committee of the NJM demanded that the extraordinary crisis demanded extraordinary measures which would include a total reorganization of the government, the transformation of the NJM into a genuine Marxist-Leninist party, and the establishment of a joint leadership consisting of Bishop and his Deputy Prime Minister, Bernard Coard.

It was during the initial stages of this crisis that Bishop had to leave his country in order to attend his last major international gathering before his death. In early July 1983, the leaders of the thirteen member countries of the Caribbean Community convened for the Fourth Meeting of the Heads of CARICOM at Trinidad and Tobago, where ten years before the organization had been founded by the Treaty of Chaguaramas. In contrast to the 1982 CARICOM Summit at Ocho Ríos, where the attempt had been made to oust Grenada from the organization, Bishop at Trinidad found himself not only being accepted, but actually courted by everyone except Edward Seaga of Jamaica, who engaged him in some acerbic exchanges.

As always during CARICOM gatherings, Bishop was the champion of Caribbean unity and an advocate of Belize's interests. One of the main issues arising at the Trinidad meeting was the continued availability of the University of the West Indies to those Caribbean territories which do not possess institutes of higher learning. There were powerful elements in all of the host countries of this university (Barbados, Jamaica, and Trinidad and Tobago) that questioned the future use of their campuses by students from other

Caribbean locations. Since both Belize and Grenada lacked university-level institutions, they closely cooperated during the conference to insure the survival of the UWI's services to their respective nations.

An agreement was reached at Trinidad which met the demands of the noncampus territories by the establishment of two Offices of University Service, one at the Cave Hill Campus in Barbados for the eastern Caribbean, and one at the Mona Campus on Jamaica, for Belize, the Bahamas, the Cayman Islands, and the Turks and Caicos. These offices were to be opened by October 1, 1984. Not only had Price and Bishop secured the continuation of university services for their own countries, but they had succeeded in improving the conditions under which these services would be offered to the students of all those Caribbean locations which did not possess university facilities. During the conference, Bishop also once again spoke up for the preservation of Belizean independence in the face of continued Guatemalan territorial claims. The conference's final communique did, indeed, uphold the sovereignty and territorial integrity of both Belize and Guyana (GDC, Microfiche DSI-83-C-006946; *The New Belize* 1983, no. 7, 6-8).

Little did Bishop and Price realize at Trinidad that they would never see each other again. It was ironic that at the very moment that Bishop was able to enhance Grenada's role in the region, his own position at home was being rapidly undermined, a process that was to reach its bloody denouement when the Grenadian leader, along with three of his ministers and many ordinary Grenadians, were murdered on October 19, at Fort Rupert. This massacre evoked an almost unanimous condemnation from Caribbean leaders — from Fidel Castro and Michael Manley to Edward Seaga and Tom Adams. For Price, Bishop's death was a deep personal loss since the Grenadian leader had been a firm advocate of Belizean independence. In a special statement, Price condemned "the senseless killing of Prime Minister Bishop" and declared "that Belize mourns the loss of the CARICOM leader and the suffering of the Grenadian people" (*The New Belize* 1983, no. 10, 11).

The Belizean prime minister attended the special emergency meeting of the CARICOM Heads of Government which convened on October 22 and 23 at Port-of-Spain, Trinidad in order to discuss the unsettled situation in Grenada. When it became apparent that a number of CARICOM leaders had already made up their minds that a military intervention in Grenada was all but inevitable, Price, as well as the prime ministers of Trinidad and Tobago, Guyana, and the Bahamas made it clear that they did not favor such an action.

What Adams and a number of OECS (Organization of East Caribbean States) leaders did not tell their CARICOM colleagues was the fact that they had already decided at an OECS meeting in Barbados on October 21, to launch an attack against the Revolutionary Military Council that had been ruling Grenada since the October 19 massacre. They also failed to inform their colleagues that they had appealed to the Reagan administration to aid them in this endeavor. When the U.S. military, along with token forces from Jamaica, Barbados, and four smaller East Caribbean countries, invaded Grenada on October 25, the Belizean government opposed this action by stating that "our government remains firmly committed to the principles of non-intervention in the internal affairs of other states, the non-use of force and respect for the right of self-determination" (*The New Belize* 1983, no. 10, 11).

The Price government survived the collapse of the Grenadian revolution by only one year, during which time relations between Belmopan and Washington once again deteriorated. The Reagan administration was, of course, annoyed by the Belizean government's open disapproval of the U.S. armed intervention in Grenada. It was equally disturbed by Price's decision in early 1984 to suspend, in view of the up-coming general elections, the aerial eradication campaign against marijuana in Belize's northern districts (U.S. Congress 1985, 7).

As a result of the Reagan administration's open sympathies for the UDP, the current prime minister of Belize, Manuel Esquivel, and the veteran UDP politician, Lindo, found themselves as honored guests at the 1984 Republican Convention in Dallas, Texas, where Lindo, in an obvious reference to Shoman and Musa, informed some Republican delegates that Price's PUP contained "communist elements" (Merida 1985). The reckoning came during the December 1984 general elections which resulted in a landslide victory for the UDP whose candidates emerged victorious in twenty-one out of twenty-eight constituencies. The UDP triumph brought to an end the more than two-decade predominance of Belizean politics by Price and the PUP. The main reason for Price's defeat was undoubtedly the poor state of Belize's economy, which had been battered by the falling prices for sugar and other commodities. Yet the conservative wave which swept the Caribbean in the aftermath of the bloody events on Grenada should not be underestimated in any assessment of the PUP's electoral defeat in 1984.

Belize and revolutionary Grenada, while different in many aspects, also had much in common, which furthered their Caribbean partnership. The Price government was grateful for revolutionary Grenada's unswerving support for Belize's independence and the assurance of her territorial integrity in the face of Guatemala'a annexationist designs. The Bishop regime, in turn, valued Belize's help in defeating the attempts to ostracize revolutionary Grenada from the Caribbean Community. During his four and a half years in power, Bishop was a staunch champion of Caribbean unity which was constantly threatened by the political and cultural heterogeneity of the region as well as outside influences. As part of his advocacy of Caribbean unity, Bishop fought hard to preserve the availability of the University of the West Indies to all parts of the Caribbean, an effort which was appreciated by Belize.

Where the two governments parted company, was in their attitude toward their historical past as well as their assessment of the power relationships in the region. The Bishop regime espoused a radical break with the Westminster System of parliamentary democracy by the establishment of a Marxist-Leninist state in Grenada. In foreign affairs, Bishop and his young, iconoclastic disciples attempted to imitate Castro's Cuba in defying the North

American giant while at the same time allying themselves with the Soviet Union, a country far removed geographically, politically, and culturally from the Anglophone Caribbean. But Grenada's miniscule population, resources, and geopolitical significance proved inadequate for this task. In the end, the pressures exerted by the most powerful nation on earth upon the smallest political entity of this hemisphere proved to be too much for Grenada's revolutionary government to bear.

In stark contrast to revolutionary Grenada, the Price government, as far as domestic policies were concerned, never made any radical break with Belize's political, religious, and cultural heritage. In regard to foreign policy, the former Belizean prime minister was constantly aware of the overwhelming power of the United States in both the Caribbean and Central America. While attempting to maintain a modicum of independence by his close links with the Commonwealth, CARICOM, and the Non-Aligned Movement, Price avoided any act (such as establishing diplomatic relations with Cuba) that might have seriously alienated the Colossus of the North which was rapidly replacing Great Britain's influence in both Belize and the eastern Caribbean.

NOTES

1. Roman Catholicism is the predominant faith in both Belize and Grenada. For a discussion of the relationship between the Bishop regime and the various religious denominations on Grenada, see Schoenhals & Melanson 1985, 61.

2. According to the 1980 Belizean census, the Creoles constitute 37.7 percent of the population. The next largest ethnic group are the Mestizos (Latinos) who make up 33.1 percent of the populace. Since the Creoles are heavily concentrated in and around the largest urban center (Belize City) and have long monopolized the government bureaucracy, they have been regarded as the most important ethnic group. The recent influx of over ten thousand Spanish-speaking refugees from Guatemala, El Salvador, and Honduras, as well as the large-scale emigration of Creoles to the United States, Canada, and Great Britain, threaten to erode the Creoles' predominant position. For an excellent discussion of the recent influx of refugees into Belize, see Palacio 1985. The number of Belizeans in the United States is estimated to be between thirty-five thousand and fifty thousand. There are large Belizean communities in New York, Chicago, Los Angeles, and New Orleans.

3. *The Belize Times* is the official newspaper of the People's United party (PUP). The opposition United Democratic party (UDP) publishes *The Beacon*.

4. For a superb account of the development of Belizean nationalism as well as the PUP's relations with the Arbenz government, see Grant 1976.

5. Goldson was managing editor of *The Belize Billboard*, a newspaper which supported the PUP. As a result of his article on Guatemala, Goldson, along with news editor Leigh Richardson, was accused of treason by the British

colonial government and given a jail term of eighteen months. Goldson and Richardson broke with Price in 1956 because they opposed his (then) Central American orientation. Goldson eventually ended up in the ranks of the conservative opposition party. After the UDP's landslide of 1984, Goldson was appointed Minister of Local Government, Social Services and Community Development in the cabinet of Manuel Esquivel. In order to irritate Goldson, the PUP reprinted in full Goldson's 1951 article, "Seven Days of Freedom," in *The Belize Times* during the 1979 general election campaign.

6. The Webster Proposals were the work of New York lawyer, Bethuel M. Webster, Lyndon Johnson's appointee to mediate the Belize-Guatemala dispute (Webster 1968).

7. After Belize gained self-government in 1964, Great Britain still kept control of her foreign affairs and defense. For a detailed account of Belize's turning away from her Central American orientation toward one of closeness with the Caribbean and the nonaligned countries, see Young & Young 1983.

8. See, for example, *The Belize Times*, March 3 and Oct. 28, 1979. Jim Jones had indeed met with Lindo in San Francisco in 1977. Jones went to Belize to inspect the Corozal District as a possible site for a settlement of his followers. To Belize's great fortune, Jones selected Guyana instead, where he committed suicide along with over nine hundred followers (including two Belizeans) in November 1978. The former Lieutenant Governor of California and present (1986) Congressman, Mervyn Dymally, allegedly gave Lindo $5000 for the UDP's campaign chest. Since Dymally was later accused of having allegedly accepted a campaign contribution from a Las Vegas casino owner who had ties to the Mob, the PUP reached the rather far-fetched conclusion that Lindo had been paid off by the Mafia. After his disastrous electoral defeat in 1979, Lindo ceased to be the UDP's political leader, but after the UDP's landslide victory in December 1984, Lindo became Minister of Natural Resources in the cabinet of Manuel Esquivel.

9. The other six countries were Spain, Morocco, Mauritania, Israel, Chile, and the Dominican Republic.

10. Shortly after his visit to Grenada, Ortiz became U.S. Ambassador to Guatemala. His efforts to improve the strained relations between the Carter administration and the Guatemalan military regime evoked trepidations in Belize. When Ortiz lauded the Lucas administration for decreasing the number of political murders, the Price government pointed out that "this decline may simply indicate that the effective opposition has, in fact, already been killed or gone into hiding or exile." When Ortiz said that he hoped "to create a dialogue between the government and the opposition," the PUP newspaper characterized such a dialogue as "one between sharks and sardines" (*The Belize Times*, Feb. 17, 1980, 1).

11. After the PUP's disastrous electoral defeat in 1984, both Sylvestre and Hunter broke away from the PUP in order to form their own political party, known as the Belize Popular party (BPP).

12. For the bitter exchange of letters between the UDP candidate, Joseph Andrews, and Assad Shoman, see *The Belize Times*, July 4, 1979, 5.

13. For a sampling of the tirades against the alleged "Communists" Shoman and Musa, see *The Reporter*, July 15, Aug. 12, and Nov. 18, 1979.

14. Upon the UDP's victory in 1984, Barrow became foreign minister.

15. By 1986, U.S. military assistance to Belize amounted to $1.1 million. (U.S. Department of State 1985).

16. CARICOM was founded in 1973 by the Treaty of Chaguaramas which was drawn up at Chaguaramas, Trinidad.

17. Bishop was referring here to Prime Minister George C. Chambers of Trinidad and Tobago, Prime Minister Forbes Burnham of Guyana, Prime Minister George Price of Belize, Prime Minister Lynden Pindling of the Bahamas, Prime Minister Dr. Kennedy A. Simmonds of St. Kitts-Nevis, and Prime Minister John Compton of St. Lucia.

CHAPTER 11

Mexico and Central America:
The Continuity of Policy

Hugh G. Campbell

> *What would become of Mexico if the Yanquis succeeded in their dastardly designs to colonize Central America? With all their virility the heroic Mexican people could do nothing, because Uncle Sam's monkey wrench would promptly tighten around their necks....They would have to fight the Yanqui imperium in isolation from the other Latin American nations and with their own resources, as is happening to us now.*
>
> Letter from Augusto César Sandino to the Presidents of Latin America, January 19,1929 (Selser 1981, 124).

Since 1979 Mexico has played an active role in the events on the isthmus (Herrera Zúñiga & Ojeda 1983; Williams 1984; Bagley 1984). Although interpretations of Mexico's motives for being actively involved in Central America vary, a common observation is that this activism represents a new departure in Mexican foreign policy.[1] This represents a rather narrow historical perspective, however, for followers of Mexican foreign policy have traced a "new" activist policy vis à vis Central America back at least twenty-five years, to the administration of Adolfo López Mateos (Guillén 1966; Hamilton 1975; Kaye 1975; Poitras 1974). Indeed, an even broader historical approach reveals that Mexico has followed an active and expanding role in Central America whenever the circumstances permitted, at least since the early twentieth century.

This chapter examines Mexico's involvement in Central America since 1979 and places it in historical perspective by reviewing Mexican ambitions in the isthmus since the early twentieth century. The review will focus on two other periods when Mexico became involved in Central America and which also centered around Nicaragua: the Zelaya affair of 1909 and the Nicaraguan civil war of 1926-1927. This analysis seeks to provide insight into the motivations for Mexico's continual involvement in Central American affairs.

Mexico's active contribution to the Sandinista victory in Nicaragua began in early 1978, well over a year before the ouster of Anastasio Somoza Debayle, the last member of the dynasty that had ruled for forty-five years. In January 1978 Pedro Joaquín Chamorro Cardenal, the widely respected critic of the Somozas, was assassinated in Managua. Although the dictator was not directly implicated, the murder placed a large blot on his government, and touched off widespread and violent opposition. Political factions with little or nothing in common ideologically now cooperated closely to achieve the common goal of overthrowing the hated president. Most of his opponents paid little heed to who or what might replace him. Thus members of the traditional Conservative party, of which Chamorro had been a member, were willing to ally with such radical elements as the Marxist-Leninist Frente Sandinista de Liberación Nacional (FSLN).

Presciently, Mexico could see the decay of the Somoza regime and could perceive its ultimate demise. Fortuitously, at this particular time, tremendous oil discoveries were being made in southern Mexico, in the Tabasco-Chiapas region and off the Campeche coast. With the skyrocketing price of petroleum in the late 1970s, Mexico was enjoying windfall wealth, putting the administration of José López Portillo in an expansive mood. Central America became an object of this expansiveness. Since the early 1960s Mexico had tried, without too much success, to expand its commercial and diplomatic relations with Central America (Medina Luna 1974). The flow of petro dollars offered new opportunities for Mexico to realize her Central American ambitions. In addition, the hapless Carter administration in the United States was abdicating the traditional U.S. leadership role in Central America, providing an opportunity for Mexico to move into the vacuum.[2]

Beginning in early 1978, Mexico provided small amounts of money to the Sandinistas and allowed them to open propaganda offices in Mexico City (Riding 1986, 510; Castañeda 1985, 80). In addition, the Mexican embassy in Managua became a refuge for hundreds of Nicaraguan rebels, especially after the abortive offensive of September 1978. Many of those refugees subsequently held top positions in the Sandinista government (*New York Times*, Aug. 20, 1980). A severe blow was dealt the reeling Somoza regime when, on May 20, 1979, Mexico severed diplomatic relations with Nicaragua. After the triumph of the Sandinistas on July 19, 1979, the leaders of the new government arrived in Managua aboard the Mexican presidential jet, *Quetzalcoatl*.

Having established itself as a patron of the new Sandinista government in its rise to power, Mexico continued to ingratiate itself by being one of its staunchest supporters. Between 1979 and 1981 Mexico donated a total of $39.5 million in cash and goods, an amount exceeded only by Cuba. In addition, it extended $72.9 million in loans (Pellicer 1983, 121). In the summer of 1980 Mexico cooperated with Venezuela in the San José Agreement, which permitted the oil-importing countries of Central America and the Caribbean, including Nicaragua, to purchase oil on very favorable terms. The *New York Times* summed up Mexico's material aid to the Sandinista government when it reported on May 8, 1981, a new $200 million aid agreement between Mexico and Nicaragua and noted that since "July 1979, Mexico has responded positively to almost every request for assistance made by Nicaragua."

President López Portillo supplemented Mexico's material aid to the Sandinistas with a vigorous campaign of personal diplomacy in the region. He visited several Central American and Caribbean capitals and hosted visits to Mexico from various regional heads-of-state. He established a close personal rapport with Cuban dictator Fidel Castro, as well as with the Sandinista leaders. Beginning in early 1981, he took it on himself to act as mediator between the revolutionary government and the incoming Reagan administration. Thus Central American affairs were high on the agenda at the January 1981 meeting between López Portillo and President-elect Reagan in Ciudad Juárez, and during López Portillo's visit to Washington the following June. Mexico's pivotal role in North-South relations was emphasized when it hosted a conference of the heads-of-state of twenty-two developed and underdeveloped nations at Cancún in October 1981. López Portillo's ability to induce Reagan to attend the conference gave the meeting increased significance and, by implication, enhanced Mexico's prestige. Mexico's key role was emphasized the following month when U.S. Secretary of State Alexander Haig paid a quick visit to Mexico City to discuss U.S. differences in regard to Nicaragua. Again Mexico offered to act as an intermediary, and summoned Nicaraguan Foreign Minister Miguel D'Escoto, who promptly arrived in Mexico three days later.

The high water-mark of López Portillo's vigorous campaign to place Mexico at the center of events in Central America came in February 1982, when he visited Managua to receive the Augusto César Sandino medal from a grateful Sandinista government. In accepting the award, López proposed an elaborate and ambitious plan to bring harmonious relations to the Caribbean and Central America, which would involve Mexico acting as an intermediary between the United States and its antagonists in Nicaragua, El Salvador, and Cuba (López Portillo 1982). The Mexican president hoped that by taking the "initial step in setting up a new framework for international relations in the area and in offering its services as a mediator among the United States, Cuba, and Nicaragua, Mexico clearly established its status as a nation with with regional influence" (Pellicer 1983, 125-26). López dispatched his foreign minister, Jorge Castañeda, to Washington to discuss implementation of the grandiose proposal. The U.S. reaction was not negative, but decidedly cool; no provision was included to stop Nicaraguan aid to the Salvadoran rebels.

Soon after the Managua proposal, a variety of circumstances persuaded Mexico to follow a more subdued policy in Central America. Declining oil prices, combined with government corruption and mismanagement, were having a disastrous effect on the Mexican economy. During 1982 the Mexican GDP fell for the first time since 1929. Inflation rose from 30 percent to 150 percent. The peso was devalued by 600 percent, while the foreign debt climbed to an astronomical $77 billion (Madrid 1984, 66).

As a result of these developments, Mexico cut back its strong financial support of the Sandinistas. Several ongoing assistance programs were suspended. Finally, Mexico withheld oil shipments to pressure the Sandinistas to renegotiate their debt. By August 1983 Nicaragua owed Mexico $480 million and was told that it would have to start paying the debt before oil shipments would be resumed (Riding 1986, 523; Kohan 1983).

Another factor was the temperament of the new Mexican president, Miguel de la Madrid, who was inaugurated on December 1, 1982. He did not inherit López Portillo's strong emotional ties to the Nicaraguan and Salvadoran revolutionary movements. Moreover, given Mexico's growing financial crisis, he had sound economic reasons for not alienating the United States. Also, business and other conservative elements within the Mexican governing coalition were becoming increasingly critical of the support being tendered to the revolutionary Left in Central America and the threat to Mexican stability which the spread of the revolutionary conflagration portended. Thus de la Madrid followed a middle-of-the-road policy in Central America, involving cooperation with other Latin American countries rather than taking a unilateral approach. This new tack contrasted with López Portillo's "rhetorically confrontational approach which had isolated Mexico within Latin America" and had done little to restrain Reagan. It was under these circumstances that, in early 1983, Mexico took the initiative in setting up the Contadora group (Colombia, Mexico, Panama, and Venezuela) as a multilateral approach to mediating conflicting interests in Central America. In the process, Mexico softened its rhetoric, but continued to maintain familiar positions. Thus, it has continued to criticize outside intervention in the region, that is, by the United States, and "to treat both Cuba and Nicaragua with special warmth." The Contadora group reached its peak of influence in September 1984, when it presented a draft treaty which Nicaragua immediately accepted. However, U.S. ability to mobilize Central American opposition undercut Contadora's triumph (Purcell 1985; Farer 1985. See also Riding 1986, 520-21).

There are two fundamental obstacles which preclude the resolution of conflict in Central America. First is the refusal of the Marxist-Leninist Sandinista regime to permit a truly pluralistic political process in Nicaragua and the Reagan administration's insistence that this is a sine qua non for a settlement. The second obstacle is Reagan's insistence that the Sandinistas disavow any intent to export their revolution, and the latter's unwillingness to accept this restraint, at least publicly. The inability of the Contadora group to solve the conundrum of these two obstacles has left the process adrift. Although efforts to overcome the impasse have continued through 1986, no breakthroughs have emerged. And although Mexico on occasion did revert to unilateral efforts at mediation, as in the Manzanillo talks in 1984 between representatives of Mexico, the United States, and Nicaragua, these direct negotiations foundered on the same rocks as the multilateral negotiations (Purcell 1985, 79; Farer 1985, 71; "Contadora Collapse" 1986; Valero 1985, 141).

After the triumph of the Sandinistas in July 1979, the focus of the armed revolutionary struggle shifted from Nicaragua to El Salvador. The scenario unfolding there seemed to be a clone of the Nicaraguan revolution. Following the successful model of the Nicaraguan revolution, the Frente Farabundo Martí de Liberación Nacional (FMLN) stepped up armed opposition to the Salvadoran government. A civilian political-front organization, the Frente Democrático Revolucionario (FDR) was formed in April 1980, similar to what had been done in Nicaragua with the participation of leading moderates, such as Social Democrat leader Guillermo Ungo.

Just as Mexico had given impetus to toppling Somoza by withdrawing recognition in May 1979, so in mid-1980 it took a similar step in regard to El Salvador by withdrawing its ambassador, although diplomatic relations were not completely severed. In the summer of 1980, top Mexican officials began to hold secret meetings with Salvadoran opposition leaders, including comandantes of the FMLN, just as they had done with the Sandinistas. Also following the Nicaraguan pattern, the Salvadoran rebels were allowed to set up offices in Mexico (Bagley 1984, 268).

As the insurrection in El Salvador gained momentum in late 1980, the Carter administration belatedly began to perceive a similarity between the events which had taken place in Nicaragua, where the true nature of the Marxist-Leninist dictatorship was becoming evident, and those which were unfolding in El Salvador. Thus, in his final week in office, on January 17, 1981, Carter resumed military aid to the Salvadoran government, which he had suspended in 1977.

Almost immediately upon taking office, the Reagan administration announced that it would step up aid to the Salvadoran government and would start sending U.S. military advisers to assist the Salvadoran army. López Portillo immediately criticized these steps (*New York Times*, Feb. 25, 1981).

Mexico's boldest move toward playing a leading role in events in El Salvador came later in 1981. On August 28, Mexico and the socialist government of France issued a joint communique to the United Nations Security Council, proposing that the FDR/FMLN be recognized as a legitimate political entity in El Salvador, and calling for negotiations between the rebels and the Salvadoran government to settle the conflict. If accepted, this proposal would have in effect granted equal standing to the Salvadoran government and the leftist rebels (Bagley et al. 1985).

Mexico's support of the Salvadoran rebels, however, received much less collaboration from other Latin American countries than had its earlier support for the Sandinistas. José Napoleón Duarte was a far cry from Anastasio Somoza. The Venezuelan government, which had cooperated closely with Mexico and Cuba in aiding the Sandinista rise to power, was by 1981 under the presidency of Luis Herrera Campín, who had a natural sympathy for his fellow Christian Democrat, Duarte. Costa Rica, especially after Luis Alberto Monge replaced Rodrigo Carazo as president in 1982, was decidedly anticommunist and thus unsympathetic to FMLN (Ojeda 1983, 145). Panama, one of the prime supporters of the Sandinistas, after the death of the charismatic Omar Torrijos, was also less inclined toward foreign adventurism. Thus Mexico found itself alone among the noncommunist countries of the region in its support of the Salvadoran rebels. Further, Mexico received criticism from several Latin American countries for bringing an extrahemispheric power into the Central American situation through the Franco-Mexican communique of August 1981.

Despite its isolation, Mexico continued to lend moral support to the Salvadoran rebels during the remainder of the López Portillo administration. In December, together with Nicaragua and several extrahemispheric countries, it sponsored a United Nations General Assembly resolution that attempted to discredit the upcoming March 1982 Salvadoran elections by contending that conditions for free elections did not exist in El Salvador.

After the inauguration of President de la Madrid, in keeping with his generally less overt support for Central American revolutions, Mexican support for the FDR/FMLN became more subdued. Indeed, Mexican Foreign Minister Sepúlveda flew to San Salvador to attend Duarte's inauguration as constitutional president of El Salvador on June 1, 1984, even though the two countries had not had full diplomatic relations for four years (*New York Times*, Aug. 8, 1984). When the Duarte government opened talks with the FDR/FMLN in October 1984, the Mexican government felt vindicated in its efforts to gain some form of recognition for the rebels (Valero 1985, 141).

Mexican support for Central American leftists had its limits even under López Portillo. Guatemala is the only Central American state, aside from Belize, that borders on Mexico. As a result, Mexico's relationship with Guatemala has historically been different than with the rest of Central America. Just as Mexico has traditionally looked upon the United States as the "Colossus of the North," so Guatemala has considered Mexico to be its own Colossus. Guatemalans regarded Mexican acquisition of Chiapas, soon after independence, in a manner similar to Mexican attitudes toward their loss of Texas to the United States. The blatant seizure of Soconusco by Mexico in 1842 rubbed salt into the wound. Thus, "historically, relations between Mexico and Guatemala have been characterized by mutual tension and suspicion" (Aguilar Zinser 1983, 161). Mexican apologists have played down the parallel between Guatemalan-Mexican relations and Mexican-U.S. relations: "The case of Mexico is distinct [from the United States], its [Mexico's] interests are concentrated in Guatemala because of geographical and economic reasons and by the existence [in Guatemala] of a large Mexican population; in the others [Central American countries], on the other hand, our interests are minimal" (Statement by Mexican Foreign Minister Ignacio Mariscal in 1909 in Cosío Villegas 1960, 702).

Other Mexican apologists have contended that the "Colossus of the North" concept has been fabricated by the ruling classes of Guatemala, who "for reasons of their own...want to view us as a threat. Faced with the lack of secular legitimacy and their isolation from the most numerous sectors of society, they have frequently attempted to gain legitimacy and support by citing supposed Mexican aggressions" (Aguilar 1983, 162). Nonetheless, there has been constant strain in Guatemalan-Mexican relations, with a few exceptions, since independence. During the present century there has been considerable hostility, especially during the Estrada Cabrera rule in Guatemala (1898-1920) and the Ubico regime (1931-1944). Uncharacteristic cordiality existed during the social reform era of 1944-1954 in Guatemala, but a severe rupture of relations took place in early 1959, when Guatemalan warplanes sank some Mexican fishing vessels (Wolff 1981).

From the early 1960s until the late 1970s Mexican-Guatemalan relations were relatively trouble free. During these years sporadic leftist guerrilla activity was efficiently suppressed by the Guatemalan army, with the help of U.S. military aid and technical assistance. Due to human rights violations in Guatemala, the Carter administration withheld military aid after 1977. By the late 1970s three Guatemalan guerrilla groups were active in Guatemala, all along the Mexican border. These included the Guerrilla Army of the Poor (EGP), the Organization of People at Arms (ORPA), and the Rebel Armed Forces (FAR). In 1980, despite the absence of U.S. aid, the Guatemalan army undertook a bloody counterinsurgency campaign in the highlands and in October 1981 launched a scorched earth policy. As a result of this campaign of terror, as many as 150,000 Guatemalans, mostly Indian campesinos, fled across the border seeking refuge in Mexico (Sereseres 1984, 204-6; Aguilar 1983, 167; Barry & Preusch 1986, 203-35).

The influx of refugees into Mexico caused a strain in Mexican-Guatemalan relations and multifaceted problems for Mexico internally. López Portillo and Guatemalan president Romeo Lucas García held a cordial meeting in Tapachula, near the border, in September 1979. Post-1979 border incidents, however, forced postponement and cancellation of scheduled future meetings. Also, Guatemala reacted harshly to the 1981 Franco-Mexican communique in support of the Salvadoran rebels, as well as to Mexico's announcement that it would recognize the Belize government and back its entry into the United Nations.

Within Mexico Guatemalan refugees created problems both in terms of dealing with them per se, and in the threat of revolutionary activity spreading to Mexico. After 1980 the number of refugees entering Chiapas increased steadily. Of the estimated one hundred thousand who remained there, about half were settled in refugee camps and half became vagrants. Although the Guatemalan government encouraged the refugees to return and even set up model villages to accommodate them, few refugees did so. Reports began to filter out of the refugee zone that local Mexican officials were beating, raping, and extorting bribes from the hapless refugees ("Borderline" 1984). In July 1981 the Guatemalan ambassador to Mexico complained that Guatemalan refugees in Mexico were being systematically mistreated by their employers and that "when the time comes to be paid, they are reported to the migratory officials and deported without getting the pay they are owed" (Aguilar 1983, 180). Not all the refugees were innocent victims, however; some were

Guatemalan guerrillas seeking respite from pursuit by the Guatemalan army. Inevitably there were instances of Guatemalan army penetration into Mexican territory when in "hot pursuit" of guerrillas, resulting in rising diplomatic tension between Mexico and Guatemala (Williams 1984, 321).

Of even greater concern to Mexico than the need to care for the Guatemalan refugees was the fear that successful revolutionary activity in Guatemala might well spill over into Mexico. Southern Chiapas is among the poorest areas in Mexico. Not only did the area's poverty make Chiapas a matter of concern to the Mexican government, but the presence of Mexico's richest oil deposits, less than one hundred miles from the frontier, caused apprehension about national security. In addition, the transisthmian railway and the close ethnic ties between the indigenous population of the Chiapan and Guatemalan highlands also caused Mexican apprehension (Williams 1984, 313-14).

All these worries contributed to Mexico's "double standard" when considering the armed guerrillas in Guatemala as compared to those in the rest of Central America. As already discussed, Mexico was unstinting in trying to occupy the moral high ground and in projecting the image that it was carrying on the tradition of the Mexican revolution by championing the interests of the downtrodden in Central America. This policy was fine for Nicaragua and El Salvador, but in the case of Guatemala, right on Mexico's border, a more pragmatic policy seemed in order. Thus, a policy debate developed within the Mexican leadership. On the one hand were those, particularly in the Foreign Ministry, who wanted Mexico to show greater support for the Guatemalan refugees and, tacitly at least, greater solidarity with the Guatemalan rebels. On the other hand were those, particularly in the Defense and Gobernación ministries, who were more concerned with the internal security of Mexico than with its international image, and thus took a harder line against the refugees. They were willing to cooperate with the Guatemalan army to force the refugees back into Guatemala and thus prevent the Guatemalan rebels from using Mexico as a sanctuary (Riding 1986, 518-19).

The policy debate was won by those determined to place primacy on internal security over international prestige. As early as December 1980, Mexico conducted a forty-thousand-man military exercise in Chiapas, a massive undertaking by Mexican standards, involving nearly half the nation's standing army. These maneuvers sent the message that Mexico would not permit highland Chiapas to become a haven for Marxist guerrillas from neighboring Guatemala (Sanders 1981).

Thus, in contrast to its support of the Sandinistas and the Salvadoran rebels, Mexico withheld even moral support from the Guatemalan guerrillas. Although Mexico was unwilling to mar its international image to the extent of openly condemning the Guatemalan rebels, it was clear they could find no succor from Mexico to the repression by the Guatemalan army. López Portillo put it succinctly: "We have neither sympathies nor antipathies [for the Guatemalan rebels]. We do not judge what is happening there." At the same time, in an NBC television interview, he put it another way, as he distinguished between the situation in El Salvador, where "we want the solution to this situation to be a political one so that the violence can end," and Guatemala, where "we are totally detached from this problem and we simply lament that they have it." Of Guatemala, he added, "As we say in bullfighting language, leave them alone in the ring" (Aguilar 1983, 174; see also *New York Times*, Nov. 29, 1981).

In practice, however, the Mexican government went beyond mere passivity, actively cooperating with Guatemala to cope with the frontier area guerrilla activity. In March 1982 the Mexican and Guatemalan defense ministers met and discussed plans for dealing with the border problems (Aguilar 1983, 169). Later in the year, when the new de la Madrid government took office, a more comprehensive plan to deal with the southern border problem was formulated. This was the Chiapas Plan, designed to undermine the potential for unrest in the area and to provide tighter security (Riding 1986, 425). In 1983 an unprecedented $900 million was spent on new schools, health facilities, and nutrition. A 278-mile strategic highway running through the Lacandon jungle was completed along the Guatemalan border. An integrated development plan was subsequently set forth for the entire southeast. To prevent the border refugee camps from being used as havens and staging areas by the Guatemalan guerrillas, 46,000 refugees were relocated to the state of Campeche in 1984. Also during this period, Mexico undertook to build up its military capability. It projected doubling the size of the military, improving its quality, and updating its hardware (Riding 1986, 425-26; *New York Times*, Jan. 4, 1981).

Thus Mexico reacted sharply to the perceived threat to its internal security caused by the influx of a large number of refugees and the presence of armed revolutionary bands along her southern border. This reaction gives some insight into the motives behind Mexico's activist policy toward Central America since the late 1970s. One explanation, favored by some ultra-leftists in the United States, contends that proleftist activism reflects Mexican "understanding" that revolutionary leftist regimes "mean more stability" in the area than rightist ones (*New York Times*, Jan. 4, 1981). Such an explanation, of course, requires a leap of faith and is based on a blind credulity in the peacefulness and noninterventionism of Marxist-Leninist regimes. Its acceptance by Mexico is belied by Mexico's decidedly cool reaction to the potential of a revolutionary leftist regime rising on its own border. If Mexico did indeed believe revolutionary leftist regimes portended stability it would not be cooperating with the Guatemalan army.

A more plausible and commonly repeated explanation for Mexico's active Central American policy is one summed up by Carlos Fuentes: "Mexico always sounds like the Soviets, but always acts like the Americans" (Nissen 1983, 28). This refers to the concept that the political leadership of Mexico purposefully carries on a very prorevolutionary and anti-American foreign policy, in order to distract and undercut its domestic leftist opposition. As one observer summed it up, "Left-leaning diplomacy helps to maintain Mexico's political stability. It strengthens the government's hand in its dealings with the country's left wing opposition, whose demands are occasionally pre-empted by government action" (Pellicer 1981, 91; see also Thorup & Ayres 1982, 9). Indeed, some observers have perceived that the desire to distract the Mexican Left internally has dominated Mexican foreign policy so greatly that foreign policy appears to be merely an extension of internal politics (Grabendorff 1978).

Validity for this assessment of Mexico's motivation for following an activist, pro-leftist, anti-American policy in Central America (except for Guatemala) was provided by Foreign Minister Sepúlveda. After some observers noted a decrease in Mexican support of Central American leftists, one and one-half years into the de la Madrid administration, Sepúlveda issued a blunt declaration of Mexico's independence and its continuing support for leftist causes at odds with the United States (*New York Times*, Aug. 8, 1984).

Although the practice of using their left hand abroad and their right hand within Mexico does have some efficacy for the ruling coalition, this does not entirely explain Mexico's active Central American policy in recent years. A comprehensive overview of possible motives for recent activism in Central America must include the sociocultural affinities between Mexico and Central America, the historical bonds, the ideological affinities, possible economic advantages to Mexico, political concerns, and strategic and national security interests (Williams 1982). Of these explanations, the one which seems most valid is that dealing with political concerns. Although the other explanations have varying degrees of validity, Mexico seems to have been, especially between 1979 and 1982, primarily motivated by its desire to establish Central America as a Mexican "sphere of influence." This assessment is based on the testimony of a primary architect of Mexican foreign policy from 1979 to 1982, Foreign Minister Jorge Castañeda, and to the historical evidence that this consideration has continually motivated Mexico at least since the beginning of this century.

Castañeda contends that "from mid-1978 on Mexico's actions sprang from a general ideal of goals in the region and how to achieve them. Mexican policy aimed to carve out a sphere of influence in the only areas where such an ambition was feasible: Central America and the Caribbean Basin." He contends that Mexico realized it could never replace the United States in the hearts and minds of the rightist regimes of the area, so Mexico purposefully followed a policy of encouraging the rise of leftist regimes. It was thought that Mexico's surging economy was building a large and diverse industrial base and that its "economy increasingly complemented that of most Central American and Caribbean countries." Mexico's bonanza oil discoveries between 1976 and 1979, with the prospect of tremendous oil export income, seemed to provide the resources for its program of making Central America and the Caribbean its own sphere of influence (Castañeda 1985, 76).

As we have seen above, after 1982 this policy ran afoul of a more determined and assertive U.S. response, declining oil revenues, and a potentially dangerous proximity of radicalism in Guatemala. Thus Mexico moderated its policy and turned to Contadora as an alternative means of achieving its some-what reduced goals.

On two other occasions in this century, Mexico has taken an active ap-proach in its relations with Central America, and, just as it has done since 1979, became deeply involved in area affairs. Both of these twentieth-century- in-volvements reflected an ongoing desire by Mexico to establish a sphere of in-fluence in the area. This desire represented a paternalistic and possessive attitude on the part of Mexico which emanated from the historic relationship between Mexico and Central America.

During the colonial period the Audiencia of Guatemala, including the areas which encompass the five Central American provinces, had been part of the Viceroyalty of New Spain, headquartered in Mexico City. At the time of independence, Central America remained part of the Mexican Empire under Agustín Iturbide. When in 1823 Central America declared its inde-pendence of Mexico, one of the Central American provinces, Chiapas, was retained as part of Mexico. The chaotic internal conditions of Mexico during the early decades after independence precluded it from pursuing its ambitions for influence in Central America. However, during the *Reforma* in the 1860s and 1870s there was considerable Mexican meddling in Guatemalan politics in an effort to ensure the establishment of an ideologically congenial govern-ment in the largest of the Central American countries. But it was only toward the end of the long reign of Porfirio Díaz (1876-1911) that a degree of politi-cal stability and international prestige was achieved which would permit Mexico to proejct itself more broadly into Central American affairs and un-dertake to reestablish its historic influence there.

In the early years of this century, relations between the Central American nations were dominated by the rivalry between the area's two lead-ing Liberals of the era, José Santos Zelaya, who had ruled Nicaragua since 1893, and Manuel Estrada Cabrera, dictator of Guatemala since 1898. Both of these strongmen habitually meddled in the internal affairs of their neigh-bors, most notably harboring dissidents from bordering countries and aiding those exiles in invading and toppling the regimes in the neighboring countries. Thus, Zelaya and Estrada Cabrera hoped to establish friendly, subordinate governments in the surrounding states and, by doing so, eventually emerge as dominant over the entire isthmus. Mexico, hoping to establish Central America as its own sphere of influence, became involved in these machina-tions.

Traditionally, Mexico had followed a practice of opposing any Guatemalan government which sought to unify Central America. This was be-cause Mexico and Guatemala were constant antagonists, especially over bor-der disputes. A Guatemala with a unified Central America behind it would be a much more formidable foe. Therefore, Porfirian Mexico was happy to sup-port Zelaya in his rivalry with Estrada Cabrera. As the *New York Times* put it, "The Mexican government feels the strong need in Central America of a strong man to hold him [Estrada] in check, and the strong man they see is Zelaya" (Dec. 12, 1909). At one point, according to U.S. Ambassador to

Mexico Thompson, Zelaya offered ten thousand men to Díaz if Mexico should go to war against Guatemala" (Scholes 1960, 620). In 1906 Mexico permitted anti-Estrada exiles to use Chiapas as a staging area to invade Guatemala, and at the same time aided El Salvador in its sporadic warfare with Guatemala (Munro [1964] 1980, 145; Cosío Villegas 1960, 628 ff.).

In addition to trying to carve out a sphere of influence through its bilateral relations with the Central American states during these years, Mexico also manifested its growing international stature by cooperating, on an equal basis, with the United States. Thus, it participated in the Marblehead Pact of 1906, which led to the Mexican and American presidents being designated as arbitrators of Central American disputes, and the Washington Conference of 1907, which resulted in the establishment of a Central American Court of Justice (Woodward 1985, 192-93).

U.S. and Mexican policies began to diverge after the inauguration of Taft in March 1909. Taft directed a more aggressive policy in Central America, proposing armed intervention, if necessary, to maintain peace on the isthmus. His Secretary of State, Philander Knox, also proposed that the chronic fiscal mismanagement of Honduras be rectified by placing it in receivership, as the United States had already done with the Dominican Republic. Mexico, with its traditional repugnance of U.S. armed intervention, disassociated itself from the new policy (Munro [1964] 1980, 166). Its interests could better be served through diplomatic means than by acquiescence to U.S. armed intervention in the region, which Mexico knew it could not match.

The new, assertive U.S. policy focused especially on Zelaya. He had now become *persona non grata* from the U.S. perspective. Since coming to power, he had granted several monopolies to family members and cronies, frequently at the expense of U.S. entrepreneurs. He had negotiated with Mexico to build a railroad from Mexico across the isthmus, but negotiations had broken down. Most unpardonably, he had sought help from Germany, to build a transisthmian canal through Nicaragua which would be Nicaraguan-controlled. For the United States, he was obviously a dangerous man (Munro [1964] 1980, 177; Selser 1981, 26).

Just as it would do several decades later with the Sandinistas, Mexico used Nicaragua as a surrogate in confronting U.S. hegemony on the isthmus. In the spring of 1909, Mexico appointed an ambassador to Nicaragua after a two-year vacancy in the position. In March 1909 Mexico made it a condition of its cooperation in a peace conference proposed by the United States that Zelaya be included.

In October 1909 Juan J. Estrada, a member of Zelaya's own Liberal party and governor of the eastern part of the country, defected and started an insurrection. The United States was initially neutral in this uprising, although the U.S. Consul at Bluefields, Thomas P. Moffat, gave it his enthusiastic personal support. Moreover, funds to support the revolt came from local American businessmen and from Zelaya's rival in Guatemala, Estrada Cabrera. The official U.S. attitude became openly hostile to Zelaya when, in early November, he ordered the execution of two American soldiers of fortune who had been captured while serving in the rebel army (Munro 1958, 215). Shortly thereafter, U.S. troops landed on the Caribbean shore of Nicaragua, ostensibly to protect American lives and property. This intervention alarmed Mexico. Zelaya's overthrow and his replacement by a government friendly to the United States would mean the unfettered rise of Estrada Cabrera as the dominant figure in Central America. Mexico would be surrounded by U.S. power. Just as it was to do later with the Contadora process, Mexico attempted to save its position in Central America by following a diplomatic avenue in an effort to protect its surrogate, Nicaragua.

On November 27 Porfirio Díaz, relying on the rapport which had been established in a meeting at El Paso, Texas, the previous month, sent a personal note to Taft saying that he would persuade Zelaya to resign and leave the government in the hands of another member of Zelaya's Liberal party. Díaz suggested that the United States quit landing troops and, once Zelaya left, that it help disarm the rebels. U.S. response to this proposal was cool, and avoided a direct answer (*New York Times*, Dec. 1, 1909; Scholes 1960, 622; Zelaya 1910, 110-11).

On December 1, without informing Mexico in advance, U.S. Secretary of State Knox publicly described Zelaya's regime as a "blot on the history of Nicaragua" and openly expressed sympathy for the rebels. At the same time, the United States severed diplomatic ties with Nicaragua. Mexico expressed surprise at the break in U.S.-Nicaraguan relations, and was dismayed at not being consulted by the United States before the action was taken (U.S. Department of State 1909, III, 455; *New York Times*, Dec. 3, 1909).

Hurried consultation between Mexican Foreign Minister Mariscal and President Díaz resulted in a new approach. They decided to send Enrique Creel to the United States as Díaz' personal envoy to deal with the Nicaraguan situation. The choice of Creel indicated the importance which Díaz attached to maintaining a pro-Mexican government in Nicaragua. Creel had formerly been a successful Mexican ambassador to Washington. A few months later, upon Mariscal's death, Creel was to be made Mexico's foreign minister. He was one of Díaz' closest confidants, and it was even rumored that he was the aging dictator's choice to succeed him.

Creel arrived in Washington on December 13. On the following day he proposed to Knox that the two governments cooperate in the pacification, first, of Nicaragua, and then of all Central America. Specifically, Creel submitted a list of ten precise suggestions, in the form of questions, to the American secretary of state. If accepted, these suggestions would, in effect, make Nicaragua a joint protectorate of the United States and Mexico. However, Creel made it clear that, because of Mexico's cultural affinity, it better understood the points of view and sentiments of Latin Americans. Therefore, it should play the main role in the protectorate. Even more specifically, he proposed that Zelaya be removed as president, to be succeeded by José Madriz, another Liberal. Madriz had formerly been at odds with Zelaya, but more recently he had been appointed by Zelaya as Nicaragua's representative on the Central American Court of Justice (Scholes 1960, 622-24).

The United States flatly rejected not only Mexico's proposal to place Madriz in the presidency, but the entire plan. It seemed clear that the plan was designed to make Mexico the leading power in Nicaragua, and in Central America as a whole over the long term (*New York Times*, Dec. 15, 1909). One can imagine, therefore, the State Department's chagrin when, two days later, on December 16, Zelaya announced his intention to resign and indicated that Madriz would be his successor. Mexico intended to implement its plan even without U.S. approval, in effect challenging the United States as the dominant power in Central America.

On December 21, Zelaya formally resigned the presidency. Three days later he left the country, accompanied to the port of Corinto by Mexican Minister Carvajal y Rosas. There Zelaya was picked up by a Mexican warship and transported to Mexico, where he was President Díaz' guest for a month before he went on to exile in Europe (Zelaya 1910, 115-16).

During the next several months the United States and Mexico, through their surrogates, continued to vie for dominance in Nicaragua. The United States supported the rebels under Estrada and Mexico backed the Madriz government. At times, when rebel forces were on the point of being defeated, the United States sent in troops, ostensibly to protect U.S. lives and property. In reality, the time and locations of these landings were clearly designed to lend succor to the beleaguered rebels. During the same period, Mexico was supplying arms and financial support to the Madriz government (Munro [1964] 1980, 181; Munro 1958, 216).

Ultimately, the United States won the contest and the Estrada rebels entered Managua triumphantly in August 1910. Shortly thereafter, in October, U.S. special envoy Thomas Dawson arrived to work out an agreement among the rival factions which was to provide the foundations for making Nicaragua unilaterally a U.S. protectorate.

Within a few months of the "Dawson Pact," Mexico was plunged into its own civil war. For the next several years it was to be preoccupied with the chaos of the Mexican revolution, unable to follow any coherent policy in regard to Central America. These were the years when "dollar diplomacy" was at its zenith, and the United States was unchallenged in its domination of Central America and the Caribbean.

Mexican interest in Central America revived briefly and tepidly during 1916-1917, when the Carranza government in Mexico, allegedly with German aid, attempted to implement the "Carranza Doctrine." This involved Mexico encouraging "the spread of the principles of revolutionary nationalism," and acting as the "leader of the underdeveloped nations' quest for development, economic independence, and equality of treatment in international relations" (Smith 1972, 79-80; Salisbury 1986, 323).

During the period 1912-1924, the Conservative party dominated Nicaraguan politics. Emiliano Chamorro, president from 1916 to 1920, because the Constitution precluded immediate reelection, turned over the presidency to his uncle, Diego Chamorro, for the 1920-1924 term. Unfortunately for Emiliano Chamorro's plans, his uncle died in October 1923. This disruption provided an opportunity for a dissident branch of the Conservative party to ascend to power. In the 1924 election, a coalition between the anti-Chamorro Conservatives and the rival Liberal party resulted in the election of anti-Chamorro Conservative Carlos Solórzano, with Liberal Juan B. Sacasa as vice president.

At about the same time, a new government took office in Mexico. In December 1924 Plutarco Elías Calles succeeded to the Mexican presidency. In the early years of his administration, he followed a vigorous policy intended to consolidate political control of the new revolutionary elite and to foster the development of a national consciousness based upon the "emergent mythology of the Mexican Revolution" (Smith 1972, 229). This growing nationalistic fervor found expression not only in an active program for the industrial and financial development of the country, but also in the revival of the Carranza Doctrine. Thus, economic development and political independence, especially from the United States, were encouraged in other underdeveloped countries. Nicaragua seemed a particularly propitious country in which to assert the doctrine of exporting Mexican revolutionary ideals. Therefore, in late 1924 and early 1925, cordial relations developed between the Calles government and the Solórzano-Sacasa government. Representatives for the labor union affiliated with the Mexican government, the *Confederación Regional de Obreros Mexicanos* (CROM), visited Nicaragua and helped organize the Nicaraguan Confederation of Labor, encouraging it to support the Nicaraguan government (Salisbury 1986, 324).

Mexican designs of influence in the Nicaraguan government seemed propitious in 1925, especially after the withdrawal of U.S. Marines on August 1. For thirteen years this small but intimidating garrison had had a stultifying effect on any anti-American political development in Nicaragua. The withdrawal of the Marines appeared to open the way for Mexico to play a greater role in Nicaragua, and perhaps, to supplant the United States as the dominant foreign power there.

However, Mexican plans suffered a setback when, on October 25, 1925, Emiliano Chamorro effected a coup d'état against the Solórzano-Sacasa government. Although Solórzano was permitted to continue as president for a few months, he became a mere figurehead. All Liberals were removed from the cabinet, and Chamorro assumed the key Minister of War portfolio. Sacasa fled the country. Chamorro promptly moved to consolidate his power and maneuvered to ease Solórzano out completely. He was successful in January 1926, when Chamorro had Congress declare him president. This situation presented the United States with a dilemma to which it reacted with vacillation and indecision. The resulting political vacuum plunged Nicaragua into a bloody civil war (D'Alba 1927).

The United States refused to recognize the Chamorro government, on the grounds that it was a usurper and that its treaty obligations to the Central American nations prevented the United States from recognizing governments which came to power by force. At the same time, however, having recently, and with great fanfare, withdrawn the Marines, it was loath to send them back to rectify the situation.

The exiled Sacasa paid visits to the State Department in early 1926 and sought U.S. support for his claim to the presidency of Nicaragua. He contended that, with the resignation of Solórzano, he (Sacasa) should constitutionally ascend to the presidency. Although the State Department conceded the legitimacy of his cause, Sacasa was told that the United States would not countenance a revolution to support his claim, and that the United States would disapprove the intervention into Nicaragua of any other country in support of Sacasa's claim. Sacasa was counseled to have patience, that moral pressure would ultimately right the situation.

As the months passed, Sacasa became increasingly frustrated. Therefore, when a Liberal rebellion broke out in eastern Nicaragua on May 2, 1926, he accepted leadership of the movement with alacrity, although he did not go to Nicaragua. The uprising was short-lived, squashed by the Chamorro government by the end of the month. Although the United States maintained an air of neutrality in regard to it, it was the new U.S.-trained and -officered constabulary which was primarily responsible for suppressing the rebellion (Munro 1974,187-54).[3]

Failing to get any support from the United States, and unable to challenge Chamorro by themselves, the Liberals sought help elsewhere. In late May Sacasa took up residence in Mexico City. Through personal meetings and detailed correspondence, Sacasa and President Calles worked out a formal, written agreement whereby Calles agreed to furnish the Nicaraguan Liberals with arms, supplies, and logistical support so that they could overthrow Chamorro. Once in power, Sacasa agreed that he would abrogate the Nicaraguan canal treaty with the United States and "would also cooperate in plans to set up a Central American union which would be dominated by Mexico" (Munro 1974, 200). Sacasa also agreed that Nicaragua would "adopt in its constitution the principles of international defense and nationalization of the sister Mexican republic, following a social and political program that was developed by Mexico" (Salisbury 1986, 328).

Had the Liberals been successful in regaining power under Sacasa at this time, and had they fulfilled their promises under the Calles-Sacasa Pact, Nicaragua would have become a client state of Mexico and, through Nicaragua, Mexico would have had a wedge to realize its continuing ambition to exert dominance over the isthmus.

Mexico certainly fulfilled its commitments under the pact. In August 1926 the Liberal field commander, General José María Moncada, initiated the attempt to overthrow Chamorro by seizing Puerto Cabezas, on the east coast of Nicaragua. Immediately, Mexican aid began pouring in to the rebels. Numerous ships cleared Mexican ports bearing arms and supplies, and soon a new front was opened in western Nicaragua. The Chamorro government denounced the Mexican aid and appealed to the League of Nations, complaining that Mexico was violating Nicaraguan sovereignty.[4]

As the fighting spread and grew more intense, the United States decided to step in to try to mediate between the antagonists. Therefore, in October 1926, the new U.S. envoy, Lawrence Dennis, brought the Conservatives and Liberals together aboard the USS *Denver* in Corinto harbor to negotiate a settlement. The Conservatives seemed more willing to compromise than did the Liberals. Perhaps the Liberals felt that with their strong Mexican support and the refusal of the United States to back the Chamorro government, they were in the commanding position (Kamman 1968, 64-65).

After the Corinto Conference, the U.S. sentiment clearly shifted to the more accommodating Conservatives. A few days later, the unacceptable Emiliano Chamorro was finally induced to resign the presidency. Within two weeks, on November 14, he was succeeded by Adolfo Díaz, the same Conservative leader who had restored order and U.S. hegemony in Nicaragua in 1912. The United States immediately recognized the Díaz government, but before the month was out, Sacasa landed in rebel-controlled eastern Nicaragua. On December 8 Mexico granted him official recognition. Thus again, Mexico and the United States were working through surrogates in vying for dominance in Nicaragua.

Arriving from Mexico at Puerto Cabezas with Sacasa were seven hundred tons of war supplies. In December 1926 and January 1927, as the rebels made significant gains in the field, President Díaz complained bitterly about Mexican support for the Liberals and demanded help from the United States. Díaz threatened to resign if the United States did not do something. Some European nations were demanding that the United States take steps to protect their nationals or, it was hinted, they might be forced to take action themselves, thus challenging the Monroe Doctrine (Selser 1980, 154; Kamman 1968, 68-71; Selser 1981, 57-58; Munro 1974, 215).

Pressure was building up for the United States to respond effectively to the Mexican challenge. A memorandum dated December 2, 1926, from Assistant Director of the State Department's Latin American Division, Stokely Morgan, summed up the American position: "The evidence before the Department shows an unmistakable attempt on the part of Mexico to extend Mexican influence over Central America with the unquestionable aims of ultimately achieving a Mexican primacy over the Central American countries..." and setting up a government in Central America "which will be not only friendly but subservient to Mexico and completely under Mexican domination" (Wood 1961, 15).

Decisive action by the United States finally came on January 6, 1927, when 160 U.S. Marines were sent to Managua, thus reestablishing the "Legation Guard" whose calming influence had been absent for more than a year. On January 10 President Coolidge issued a statement justifying the return of the Marines to Nicaragua, citing Mexican intervention as being responsible for it. On January 27 Secretary of State Kellogg made it explicit that the United States would not recognize a government headed by Sacasa or anyone imposed by revolution (Munro 1974, 215; U.S. Department of State 1927, 3:288-98; Kamman 1968, 90-91).

U.S. presence in Nicaragua became pervasive during the early months of 1927. Aside from the beefed-up, so-called Legation Guard, sizable fleets of U.S. warships patrolled both coasts. Marines landed and "neutralized" the Caribbean ports previously held by the rebels. Calles, as Díaz had before him, realized that Mexico could not win in a direct confrontation with the United States. Thus there is little evidence of continued Mexican arms shipments to Nicaragua after January 1927, when the United States moved in.

Also contributing to Calles' more moderate stance in 1927 was Mexico's financial exigency. One of Mexico's primary sources of income was oil revenue. Oil production declined from 193 million barrels in 1921 to 64 million barrels in 1927. In 1926 alone, production declined 21 percent. Duties on the production and export of oil had declined from 86 million pesos in 1922 to 19 million in 1927. Not only were some oil companies pulling out because of the the the threat of nationalization by the government, but production elsewhere was driving down the price of oil. In the early 1920s there were several oil discoveries in the United States as well as in Colombia and Venezuela. Thus, just as was to recur in the early 1980s, declining oil revenues were to force Mexico to curtail an aggressive policy of intervention in Central America (Horn 1973, 466-67).

The civil war ground on in Nicaragua in the early months of 1927, with neither side making decisive gains. In April 1927, in an effort to negotiate a settlement, the United States sent special envoy Henry Stimson. He successfully concluded an agreement, signed at Tipitapa in early May by General Moncada, in which the Liberal forces agreed to lay down their arms. They agreed that Adolfo Díaz would be permitted to finish the 1924-1928 presidential term, but that a fair and honest election would be conducted under U.S. supervision in 1928. The Stimson Agreement accomplished the same ends as had the Dawson Pact earlier.

However, one of the Liberal generals, the ultranationalist Augusto César Sandino, refused to accept the Tipitapa accord and demanded immediate and complete U.S. withdrawal from Nicaragua and, presumably, a bloody fight to the finish between the two factions. Sandino took refuge in the rugged terrain of northern Nicaragua and, beginning in June 1927, carried out hit-and-run raids against towns in the area. The United States increased its Marine brigade gradually until it reached a peak strength of five thousand in January 1929. When the Liberal General Moncada became president in late 1928, he declared martial law in the four departments where the Sandinistas were most active. Being an experienced guerrilla fighter himself, Moncada was able to curtail Sandino's activity considerably (Kamman 1968, 185-86). The only funds for support Sandino received during this period were forced loans from businesses in the area where he operated, especially wood-cutting businesses, and funds from volunteer support organizations abroad (Selser 1980, 290-91).

In August 1928 the Honduran government closed down the periodical *Ariel*, the main conduit of Sandinista propaganda. In December 1928, that paper's editor and the Sandinistas' chief spokesman, Froylan Turcios, quit the

Sandinista cause when he was offered the position of Nicaraguan Consul in Paris (Selser 1980, 389).

Thus, by early 1929 Sandino's fortunes were at a low ebb. He wrote the Mexican president, Emilio Portes Gil, on January 6, asking that he might be permitted to enter Mexico. U.S.-Mexican relations at this time were more cordial than they had been in years, mostly the result of the shrewd diplomacy of U.S. Ambassador Dwight Morrow (Hackett 1928, 727-29). Portes consulted with Morrow about the U.S. reaction to Sandino's entering Mexico. The ambassador recommended that Sandino be accepted, adding that the United States would do what it could to let Sandino leave Nicaragua safely (Kamman 1968, 125-26).

Why Sandino wanted to go to Mexico is unclear. Portes Gil contends that Sandino requested asylum in Mexico due to his military reverses and because he feared he was suffering from malaria (Portes Gil 1954, 365-68). Sandino later contended that he was not giving up the fight at all but was merely seeking Mexican aid. Circumstantial evidence supports Portes Gil's version, for Sandino stayed in Mexico almost a year, from mid-1929 until May 1930, an unseemingly long time to present his case for aid (Selser 1981, 130-34; Alemán Bolaños 1932, 46). Moreover, Mexican Marxists, who had previously strongly supported Sandino and gathered funds for him through such front groups as *Manos Fuera de Nicaragua* [Hands Off Nicaragua], turned against him after he entered Mexico. They accused him of selling out to the United States and of accepting a $60,000 bribe to give up the fight in Nicaragua (*New York Times*, Dec. 26, 1929; Baylen 1951, 412; Kamman 1968, 140-41).

In April 1929 Morrow asked Portes Gil to recognize the Moncada government in Nicaragua. Portes replied that he could not do that as long as American troops occupied Nicaragua, but suggested that if U.S. troops withdrew, then he could promise that Sandino would lay down his arms. With Morrow's encouragement, Portes instructed his minister in Costa Rica, Antonio Mediz Bolio, to send an unofficial representative to Moncada seeking his agreement to ask the U.S. to withdraw its troops, with the understanding that Portes Gil would promise that Sandino would lay down his arms. Moncada rejected the offer (Portes Gil 1954, 353-62).

For whatever reason he took up residence in Mexico, Sandino returned to Nicaragua in May 1930 empty-handed. He resumed·the fight against the government and the U.S. Marines until 1933, when the Marines were withdrawn. Mexico maintained its position of no aid for Sandino, but nonrecognition of the Nicaraguan government as long as U.S. troops remained. When the Marines left, in January 1933, Mexico recognized the newly elected Sacasa government.

For the next thirty years Mexico's relations with Central America were relatively uneventful, as Mexico carefully refrained from intrusion into Central America. The Cárdenas administration (1934-1940) was primarily concerned with internal matters. For the first time, great strides were made toward effecting the social changes necessary to bring the ideals of the revolution to fruition. Rather than trying to distract the Mexican people from the failure to achieve the goals of the revolution within Mexico by trying to export the revolution, as Calles had done, Cárdenas occupied himself with truly implementing the revolution's ideals within Mexico. During World War II, the overriding need for inter-American cooperation seemed to preempt any Mexican adventurism in Central America. After the war, the probusiness and internal development orientation of Miguel Alemán (1946-1952) and Adolfo Ruiz Cortines (1952-1958) maintained cordial relations with the United States and manifested little desire to contest U.S. hegemony in Central America. To be sure, there were sources of conflict between the socially progressive, reformist-oriented governments of Mexico and the repressive, right-wing dictatorships that dominated much of Central America, but Mexico refrained from active involvement in Central America during these years (Guillén 1956; Grieb 1979, chaps. 14 & 15).

Revived Mexican interest in Central America came in the late 1950s and early 1960s, and had nothing to do with exporting revolutionary ideas. Instead, it had to do with the capitalistic concern of exporting Mexican products. Trade between Mexico and Central America had increased somewhat during World War II, out of necessity, but after the war returned to prewar levels. With the formation of the Central American Common Market (CACM) in 1958, Mexico became interested in expanding its trade with Central America. President López Mateos took several trips to Latin American countries to support greater trade. In 1960 Mexico joined the Latin American Free Trade Association (LAFTA) and offered to act as an intermediary or bridge between CACM and LAFTA. This trend continued under President Gustavo Díaz Ordaz (1964-1970). In 1965-1966 commercial missions traveled back and forth between Mexico and Central America. In January 1966 Mexico signed a Reciprocal Technical Assistance Treaty with Nicaragua; also in early 1966 Díaz Ordaz launched the first goodwill tour of the Central American nations ever undertaken by a Mexican chief-of-state. Central American chiefs-of-state were invited to reciprocate and many visited Mexico in the late 1960s. Mexican interest in Central America grew so rapidly during these years that there was even talk of Mexican imperialism in Central America and in Guatemala, always sensitive to Mexican intentions, *La Prensa* warned against the new "Aztec imperialism" (Medina Luna 1974, 445, 469; Castañeda 1969, 158; Kaye 1975, 88-92; Rubio Sánchez & López Ryder 1979, 1295-1296; Williams 1982, 27-28).

President Luis Echeverría (1970-1976) was motivated to continue Mexico's activist foreign policy for a variety of reasons, including his own personal ambitions, the need to diversify Mexico's exports due to a recession, and the need for a more nationalistic foreign policy to placate Mexico's leftists and intellectuals, after the Tlatelolco massacre of 1968. His policies went beyond Central America, however, and were aimed more grandiosely at Latin America, and indeed third world countries as a whole. Thus the stage was set for the active and expansive policy of José López Portillo in Central America in the late 1970s (Riding 1986, 500; Poitras 1974; Pellicer de Brody 1972, 139 ff.).

From the forgoing survey of Mexican-Central American relations in the twentieth century, some insight can be gained into Mexico's motivations during those periods when it became actively involved in Central America. The most frequently repeated explanation for Mexican involvement in Central America is the "Two Handed Thesis," which contends that Mexico follows a progressive, anti-U.S.-imperialism foreign policy, aggressively asserting the principles of nonintervention and the right of self-determination, in order to assuage and placate leftist elements in Mexico and thereby distract them from the social conditions in Mexico and the politically repressive regime which rules it. It conducts its foreign policy with its left hand and its domestic policy with its right hand.

Obviously, this thesis cannot explain the Díaz interventions of 1909. It appears to have some validity in regard to the Calles intervention in 1925-1926 and that of López Portillo between 1978 and 1982. However, this seems to have been more of a side benefit for the Mexican government, in these latter two episodes, than a prime motivating cause.

The "Monkey Wrench Thesis" is another explanation advocated by many observers to explain the periods of active Mexican intervention in Central America. This thesis contends that Mexico becomes more assertive in Central America only as a defensive measure in reaction to direct U.S. intervention there. As General Sandino indicates in the quotation at the head of this chapter, U.S. control of Central America places Mexico in the jaws of a monkey wrench, between the United States to the north, and a hostile, U.S.-dominated Central America to the south (Riding 1986, 507). Although it appears that this thesis also has some validity in explaining the episodes of heightened Mexican interest in Central America, it appears secondary to a more compelling explanation.

The most pervasive common factor in these episodes is a conviction on Mexico's part, similar to the "Manifest Destiny" concept of the United States in the nineteenth century, that Central America is a right and proper area for Mexico to realize its expansive tendencies. Due to Mexico's cultural affinity with the people of the isthmus, its historical bonds with the region, and its geographical proximity, it has assumed a "big brother" attitude toward Central America and has considered it as a natural sphere of influence.

Of course, Mexico has only been able to follow this policy when two conditions have obtained. The first prerequisite is that Mexico must not be too preoccupied with domestic political instability or economic problems, to the extent that it cannot carry out a coherent and aggressive foreign policy. The second condition is that Mexico must find an opportunity, an opening, which will permit it maneuvering room within the context of the overall U.S. dominance in the region. Each of these conditions obtained at the beginning of the three episode described here. In 1909, following thirty-three years of the Porfiriato, Mexico appeared to be the epitome of political and economic stability. In March 1909 a new administration took over in Washington and the Díaz regime took advantage of the initial tentativeness of the new administration in regard to Central America to move in and become an important actor in the events which were unfolding in Nicaragua. In 1925 the new Calles government in Mexico took office, with the benefit of succeeding Alvaro Obregón, the first Mexican president since Díaz to serve out his term. This political stability in Mexico provided an opportunity to take advantage of the restrained attitude of the Coolidge administration in regard to Central America. The U.S. withdrawal of the Marines from Nicaragua in August 1925 was the go-ahead sign to Mexico to move into the power vacuum there. Finally, the Carter administration's firm commitment to avoid U.S. intervention in Central America, and to undermine any regime which did not meet its lofty human rights standards, also created an opening for Mexico. With its new-found oil income, Mexico saw a great opportunity to project itself into Central America. In each of these episodes, then, when Mexico was provided with the means and the opportunity, it chose to follow an aggressive and active role in Central America.

NOTES

1. For instance, Pellicer 1981, 89, observes: "Until recently, Mexico was indifferent to the political destiny of Central America. Despite its economic development, natural wealth, and large population, Mexico did not nurture grand schemes for regional leadership." Similar observations are made by Williams 1984, 304-5; Ojeda 1983, 158-59; and Pellicer 1983, 133.

2. The *New York Times*, Jan. 24 and Sep. 28, 1979, discusses Carter's problems in Nicaragua and his administration's "tunnel vision emphasis on one issue, human rights."

3. Munro was a State Department officer who participated in these events. He explains the situation in detail from the U.S. perspective.

4. There are several accounts providing the details of Mexican support of the Liberal rebels, including a relatively contemporary account by Alemán Bolaños 1927. More recent reconstructions are given by Kamman 1968, 60-62; and Salisbury 1986, 328 ff.

CHAPTER 12

The Nonmilitary Neutrality of Costa Rica

Frank J. Kendrick

In 1982 Dr. Oscar Arias Sánchez summarized much of what has characterized Costa Rican development for decades:

> The Costa Rican society is characterized, among other virtues, by its high grade of civility and its great confidence in peace and liberty. Even when it seems commonplace, we will never tire of mentioning that we are a country of more teachers than soldiers, or more schools than cannons, of more books than rifles, and of more libraries than barracks. And these sentiments and this manner of being have formed a basic part of our national character for many generations. They are, as a result, the fruitful seed of the gains that we have realized until now, and will undoubtedly determine the construction of our society in the future. (Arias Sánchez 1982, 1:197)

Although there have been notable interruptions in the peaceful, progressive evolution of Costa Rican society, there is enough truth in Arias' claims to describe Costa Rican development as truly unique in Central America.

There are two facets to the peaceful development of Costa Rica over the past decades that are presently receiving greater emphasis than ever before: the nonmilitary approach to defense and neutrality in foreign relations. Both have resulted from deliberate policy choices, and have contributed to the creation of one of the more democratic and prosperous states in the Western Hemisphere. But these extremely important policies are now threatened by events and pressures that seriously challenge Costa Rica.

History has been kind to Costa Rica (Vega 1981).[1] That is, a variety of special circumstances have permitted it to exist in relative isolation and peace. In recent years these have included the policies of nonmilitarism and neutrality which have special significance when considered in relation to the present crises on the isthmus.

Under Article 12 of the 1949 Constitution of Costa Rica, "the army is proscribed as a permanent institution," although "for the vigilance and conservation of public order, there will be necessary police forces"; "only by international agreement or for the national defense may military forces be organized." Moreover, "both will always be subordinate to civil power" and "they will not be able to deliberate nor hold demonstrations nor make declarations in individual or collective form" (Arguedas 1981, 44).

Although there is some disagreement about the origin of this constitutional provision, it doubtless was intended to institutionalize the ceremonial act of December 1, 1948, by which the government disbanded the army and turned over the keys of the Bella Vista barracks to the minister of education, an act that demonstrated a significant shift of emphasis from military training to public education. Moreover, the leader of the 1948 revolution, José ("Don Pepe") Figueres Ferrer, intended to do away with any potential military threat to his Second Republic.

Only a few days after disbanding the army, the new nonmilitary policy of Costa Rica was tested when an invading force backed by ex-President Rafael Calderón Guardia attacked from the north with the alleged support of Nicaragua. The Costa Rican Junta immediately appealed to the Organization of American States and began to reassemble Figueres' revolutionary Caribbean Legion. Prompt action by the OAS brought an end to the hostilities within fourteen days, and thereby also ended the threat of a Nicaraguan-Costa Rican war. The peaceful resolution of this conflict thus added substance to the claim that demilitarization was a wise course for the future. The precedent was established for Costa Rica to rely on the OAS, the Rio Pact of 1947, and existing international peace-keeping machinery to guarantee its sovereignty and security. As the U.S. ambassador commented at the time, "Costa Rica simply decided to take all these defensive agreements at their word" (Bird 1984, 101).

Another legacy of the 1948 revolution that is related to the proscription of the army, and which has also had important effects upon the development of Costa Rican democracy, is the strong tradition of anticommunism. President Calderón Guardia and his successor Teodoro Picado Michalski had developed a working relationship with the Communist party of Costa Rica during the 1940s. The nature of this seemingly paradoxical alliance between groups that had previously been strongly opposed has been explained by John Bell and other writers. Cooperation between the two groups enabled Calderón and Picado to enact reformist programs that included the first social security system in Central America, collective bargaining, revisions of the land law to help squatters, and encouragement of cooperatives. Moreover, Calderón created the first national university in Costa Rica. Picado followed with a much needed program to tax incomes in the country (Bell 1971, 41-61).

But events after World War II, particularly the emergence of the Cold War, provided opponents of the alliance with an excellent issue to use against the government. Although the Communist party (or *Vanguardia Popular*, as it renamed itself during the war) cooperated with the government and did not engage in violence, intimidation, or efforts to seize the government by force, its presence was characterized by the opposition as a dire threat. Allegations were made that Calderón himself was a Communist, and that Costa Rica was about to become the first Western Hemisphere state to fall to the Communists. The United States and its allies were pictured as the "good people," while the Russians and their allies in the West (including all kinds of Communist parties everywhere) were pictured as the "bad people." There were certainly many other issues for which the government could have been legitimately attacked, including corruption, mismanagement, and electoral fraud. But the communist issue was widely used, although it exaggerated the situation and obscured the real issues.

Another result of the use of the communist issue was that the United States came to be involved in the 1948 revolution, as well as in events of later years. Fearing that the Communists might win in Costa Rica, the United States placed its troops on alert in the Panama Canal Zone and hinted strongly at direct intervention in Costa Rica in April 1948, if it appeared that the *Vanguardia Popular* might be able to consolidate its power. The United States, therefore, indirectly helped the anticommunist revolutionaries to succeed in 1948 and thereby established a precedent for similar intervention in the years to follow.

Another important military incident like that of December 1948, occurred in 1955, when an invading force, led by the son of former President Picado, entered the country from Nicaragua for the purpose of attacking Figueres. The invaders also had a small air force that bombed San José and several other towns. This led to an appeal to the OAS, which followed its 1948 agenda of intervention. Volunteers were called up to work with the Civil Guard, and the United States, with OAS approval, sold Costa Rica four fighter planes for one dollar apiece. Hostilities rapidly came to a close with the invaders' retreat into Nicaragua, thus again convincing the Costa Ricans that they could count on existing defensive arrangements to preserve their independence, and that they did not need a permanent standing army. Costa Rica's position was summed up in the statement of one local government official, that "even if we had an army it would be so small it could not defend us – so why have one?" (Bird 1984, 103).

Although Costa Rica has no permanent standing army, it does maintain Civil and Rural Guards. One critical biographer of Figueres has suggested that all he really did was to change the military's name from "army" to "Civil Guard," in "keeping with his desire to impress the world with his democratic tendencies" (Bonilla 1975, 152). Indeed, the army had numbered only a few hundred men when it was "abolished," but by 1974 the Civil Guard included several thousand troops. The invasion of 1955 demonstrated that along with its appeal to the OAS, Costa Rica could mobilize a defense force of nearly ten thousand Civil Guardsmen to fight the invaders. Once hostilities ended, however, the guard was reduced in size and no effort was made to rebuild the army.

The Civil and Rural Guards are presently far from being the equivalent of an army, although the Civil Guard does have distinctively military features. Together the two Guards number about eight thousand, slightly more than one percent of eligible Costa Rican males. The Civil Guard's five thousand members are under the direction of the the Minister of Public Security, while the Rural Guard is under the Ministry of Government and Police, thus insuring the security forces' subordination to civil authority. In 1983 President Luis Alberto Monge directed that all security forces be coordinated by the National Security Council, chaired by the second vice president of the Republic. At the same time Monge assured the public that this improved coordination in no way implied that the armed forces were being militarized.

A further check on the political pretensions of the security forces developed in the 1950s, when it became customary to appoint officers of the two Guards on a political patronage basis. Thus with each new president, especially when there was a change in party leadership, many Guard personnel are changed. This feature precludes the possibility of either of the Guards becoming highly professionalized military forces. Moreover, service in the Guards is not highly paid, and it has been estimated that attrition of Guardsmen was as high as 10 percent per month until the unemployment problems of the 1980s (Nelson 1983, 257-76).

The Civil Guard is the most effective law enforcement agency in the country. About half its strength is in San José where it is organized into a Metropolitan Police Company, while the remainder of the Guard operates in the six provincial capitals and in several area commands in rural areas. It includes detective forces, traffic police, a radio patrol unit, the Presidential Guard, and several special Guard companies. Two new units, the Condor and Cobra Battalions, were created in 1981 and 1982, with Panamanian National Guard training, to patrol the area near the Nicaraguan border. Finally, U.S. special forces trained a new Lightning Battalion in 1985. The United States has also provided enough weapons during the past several years to give each Guardsman the firepower capability of a U.S. infantryman.

The Rural Guard, as its name implies, is concerned with law enforcement in rural areas. It also performs various "public service" functions such as carrying mail, local public works, distribution of information and food, and so on. It is not counted upon to perform defensive duties, and in some remote areas it has been subordinated to Civil Guard commands.

A special unit of several hundred members attached to the Civil Guard is the Intelligence and Security Directorate (DIS), an internal intelligence-gathering agency that has as its main duty the investigation of "security incidents." Another unit, called OPEN (Organismo Popular de Emergencias Nacionales), was created in 1982 to improve the country's security. Reports vary concerning the nature of OPEN, but it appears to be a replacement for the volunteer reserve that existed earlier with several thousand members who met on weekends for drill and instruction. OPEN is said to have some ten thousand members and has been called "the backbone that will enable us to smash any attempt to destabilize the democratic regime" (Nelson 1983, 269).

Thus the question of whether or not Costa Rica has an army depends on one's definition of military organization. In 1978 the U.S. Congress decided that the Civil Guard had primarily "military responsibilities" and could, therefore, receive certain assistance. However, as long as it maintains its patronage method of appointment, performs primarily civil functions, and remains under civil control, its potential role as a professional army will remain limited, and it should not pose a threat to the maintenance of a democratic political system. Yet the latter possibility remains an ever present concern to many Costa Ricans, as demonstrated by a 1983 poll in which 83 percent of those surveyed opposed the creation of an army, 80 percent opposed the draft, and 77 percent opposed the purchase of arms (Partido Socialista Costarricense 1984, 1). Fear of the military is so much a part of the Costa Rican mentality that any extensive professionalization or institutionalization of the Civil Guard would probably meet with strong opposition.

Costa Rica's policy of neutrality is not incorporated in its constitution, although attempts have been made in recent years to do so. It is instead a result of executive policies rooted in a strong sense of ethnic homogeneity and an apparent aloofness in regard to the turmoil that has characterized its Central American neighbors. Costa Rica has also not been victimized by foreign invasion, since it repelled William Walker in 1856. Finally, it can be said that its neutrality policy is in a real sense an expression of the country's uniquely democratic foreign policy.

One critic has listed several factors that have led to Costa Rica's self-image as a nation among nations. First, Costa Ricans pride themselves on the stability of their government. It has suffered only three coups in the past century, and Costa Ricans proudly boast that their first president was a teacher, not a soldier. Second, Costa Ricans consider themselves to be on a different cultural level than their neighbors. This, along with their characteristic ethnic homogeneity, has tended to lessen internal strife. Third, foreign investments in Costa Rica have tended to serve the best interests of the nation "without substantial loss of political self-determination...since Costa Rica seemed able to turn foreign investment into national projects rather than seeing the exploitation of all profits from such investments" (O'Connor 1976, 6). This has contributed to the maintenance of relatively high levels of economic and political independence from other nations.

These elements have contributed to a foreign policy that emphasizes Costa Rica's neutrality, although it has not in fact always been strictly neutral. Costa Rica was an ally of the United States in both World Wars and has frequently backed or endorsed U.S. actions in hemispheric affairs. It supported the U.S. embargo of Castro's Cuba, sent a small number of Guard personnel to participate in the occupation of the Dominican Republic in 1965, and even offered to send volunteers to the Korean War. Thus, Costa Rica's neutrality has been "flexible," or "selective," at times. In fact, Costa Rica has sometimes been aggressively interventionist, as after the revolution of 1948 when it pursued an antidictatorship policy in Central America and the Caribbean. José Figueres, in planning his revolution, had sought and received the support of a variety of revolutionary and exile groups from several Central American and Caribbean countries. The Caribbean Legion, providing crucial military support to the 1948 rebellion, was based at Figueres' ranch, *La Lucha Sin Fin* (The Endless Struggle). The "Caribbean Pact" of December 1947 had committed Figueres to assist political exile groups in Costa Rica in return for their help in his fight against Calderón Guardia. Costa Rica, therefore, actively supported revolutionary attempts against the governments of the Dominican Republic in 1949, Venezuela in 1954, Nicaragua in 1954, Cuba in 1959, and Nicaragua again in the 1970s. Indeed, Costa Rican support of the Sandinistas against the Somoza dynasty probably was crucial to the outcome of that revolution. In essence, therefore, a "flexible" neutrality permits Costa Rica to follow a course of strict neutrality when it is expedient to do so (as with the Grenada invasion), and to alter that course when it is expedient to do that. It is also a neutrality that has generally been pro-U.S.

One of the clearest statements of the policy is found in President Monge's Neutrality Proclamation of November 17, 1983:

> I. The neutrality of Costa Rica will be perpetual and not transitory. It will be practiced in the face of all the warlike conflicts that affect other states.
>
> II. The neutrality of Costa Rica will be active. It does not signify impartiality in the ideological or political field. Consequently, Costa Rica affirms its faith in the social and political conception that it has shared and shares with the western democracies. This active neutrality is fully compatible with the rights of Costa Rica as a member of the United Nations, of the Organization of American States, and of the Inter-American Treaty of Reciprocal Assistance. (Bagley et al. 1985, 149)

As Monge explained a year later, "We are not ideologically neutral; we support democracy and oppose all dictatorships. Costa Rican neutrality reflects the special circumstances of our history" (Bird 1984, 150).

The neutrality policy is now integrated with the policy of not supporting a military so that the two are, in effect, one policy. According to Monge's neutrality proclamation:

> III. The neutrality of Costa Rica will not be armed. Its external security will continue founded on the free will of its people, on the norms of international law, and on the systems of collective security to which it is party, which neither require the maintenance of armies as permanent institutions, nor the employment of armed force on the part of Costa Rica in the solution of the warlike conflicts that confront other states (Bagley et al. 1985, 150).

As he elaborated a year later, "We remained convinced — as we have been over thirty-five years since we disbanded our armed forces — that poor countries do not have resources for education and an army. We choose education, health and the welfare of our people. There is no alternative, we do not have resources for both those and an army. We intend to maintain our position" (Bird 1984, 185).

Central to the thinking of most of the political leadership of Costa Rica since 1948 has been the ideology of the party of National Liberation. Although the PLN has not elected all the presidents of the country, its thinking about governmental and economic matters have left an impression on Costa Rican society. The social democratic model would probably be the best way to characterize Costa Rican development since the 1940s. Social democracy was deliberately chosen as the road to follow with the goal of creating a "society attentive to the well-being of all its members under a capitalist economic system within a framework of state regulation and selective state involvement" (Blachman & Hellman 1986, 160).

The welfare state with its commitment to political democracy has worked relatively well. The electoral system it has perfected since 1948 stands as a model to the Third World. In recent years, the Communist party (*Vanguardia Popular*) has been permitted to return to electoral politics, although elections have been monopolized by two-party competition between the PLN and various opposition party coalitions (in 1986 the opposition was the Social Christian Unity party). Moreover, Costa Rica has been an island of sanctuary for groups and individuals from other Latin American countries. Cubans, Nicaraguans, Venezuelans, and Chileans, among others, have sought and found refuge in an extremely tolerant society. The United States, in fact, has held up Costa Rica as a model of democracy for all of Central America.

Within the context of social democracy, Costa Rica has attained the highest and most equitable standard of living in Central America. The state also has invested heavily in its infrastructure, creating adequate roads, hydroelectric projects that supply Nicaragua as well as Costa Rica with energy, and a good public school system. Indeed, education has long been emphasized and Costa Rica has one of the most literate and school-going populations in the hemisphere.

The government's direct involvement in economic development has also been high since 1948. Following the precepts of a "mixed economy" model, the large majority of the population now receive free health care and hospitalization, and social security reaches everyone. Government subsidies provide basic foods and services to virtually the entire population, although there is still poverty. Moreover, banks were nationalized in 1949, and the government channeled credits and resources from the banks to diversify the economy. The result has been that Costa Rica has also attained levels of employment and economic diversification unprecedented in Central America.

The relationship between the relatively favorable political and economic situation of Costa Rica since 1948 and the country's nonmilitary neutrality is that the latter has definitely contributed to the realization and perpetuation of the former. By maintaining a neutral position toward its neighbors with whom it trades, and by not spending more than a tiny fraction of its budget on the military, Costa Rica has been able to devote the great bulk of its resources and energy to domestic pursuits. In so doing, the democratic system and high living standard have been greatly augmented and the population has developed a broad consensus of support for the policy of nonmilitary neutrality.

Yet Costa Rica has serious problems. Its economy is highly dependent on agro-exports sensitive to fluctuations in world prices of a few cash crops. On the other hand, nearly 30 percent of consumer goods and services, as well as all petroleum, are imported. The resultant vulnerability of the economy is related to the debt situation of Costa Rica. For many years, successive governments financed a great portion of the country's economic and social development by borrowing from abroad. The result of this is that by the 1980s the country had acquired one of the highest per capita debts in the world. By 1981, the foreign debt was 80 percent of the GNP. Thus the debt, coupled with the vulnerability of the agro-export economy and the rising prices of imported petroleum, led eventually to the financial crisis of the 1980s.

Costa Rica entered the decade of the 1980s as a bankrupt democracy. It was unable to pay either the principal or the interest on the large foreign debt that had grown so rapidly during the late 1970s. The great drop in coffee prices in 1978, followed by the worldwide economic recession of the 1980s and the impact of regional war on the Central American Common Market, shrank the markets for Costa Rican exports. When these problems struck Costa Rica, the effects were immediate and nearly disastrous. The GDP dropped between 1979 and 1982 by 1.4 percent annually; inflation rose to almost 40 percent annually after 1979; the trade deficit rose from $97 million in 1977 to more than $360 million in 1980; the external debt more than doubled from 1979 to 1982; and the national currency was devalued by nearly 500 percent from 1980 to 1983. Thus, Costa Rica was forced to sell its gold reserves and to suspend debt payments. Of all the issues, the debt crisis was, and is, the worst, both for its long-term effects and as a symptom of other problems. Considered along with private debt, by 1981 the total debt of the country had reached a level 4 times greater than earnings from exports and about 80 percent of the GDP. Indeed, service of the external debt alone required nearly 50 percent of all export earnings for 1980 (Blachman & Hellman 1986, 163).

Within Costa Rica, these happenings brought about a collapse of the internal productive capacity, a drop in real wages by more than 40 percent, a doubling of unemployment, and an increase in poverty. Beggars began to appear on the street and the danger of polarization between rich and poor, so prevalent in the rest of Central America, seemed imminent.

President Rodrigo Carazo's National Unity government (1978-1982) reacted by printing more money to pay the debts, reforming taxes, and reducing public spending. The government also negotiated two successive loans with the International Monetary Fund. However, failure to meet the conditions imposed by the IMF — in the opinion of the Carazo government these conditions would have produced "social regression to an intolerable degree" — led to breakdowns in the agreements (Trejos 1985, 21). By the end of 1981, on the eve of national elections, the economic situation was so desperate that some critics warned that Costa Rica could eventually follow the tragic example of Uruguay, where a similar kind of social welfare state under great economic stress had been taken over by a military dictatorship (Edelman 1985, 173). Thus, the Monge government, elected by a decisive majority of almost 60 percent, inherited a situation in 1982 that demanded immediate remedies. And Monge knew that he would have to secure immediate help from two outside sources: the IMF and the United States.

Another crisis — increasing internal political tension — was related to the deteriorating relations between Costa Rica and Nicaragua. Conflicts between these two countries have been common for many decades, so common that a local saying is that there are three seasons in Costa Rica: the rainy season, the dry season, and the season for fighting Nicaragua (Blachman & Hellman 1986, 173). When the old enemy, Somoza, was overthrown, a victory parade for the Sandinistas was held in San José and for a time it appeared that relations between the two governments were improving.

By the end of 1979, however, the situation had begun to change rapidly. There were several crucial resignations from Nicaragua's Junta of National Reconstruction, including that of Alfonso Robelo, who later moved to San José after accusing the Sandinistas of betraying the revolution. Also, the Costa Rican press, noted for its conservatism, began to attack the "communist" Sandinistas almost daily. Edén Pastora, the dashing and bold Comandante Zero, broke with the Sandinistas and began his efforts to use Costa Rican territory as a base of operations against the Sandinistas. Although opposed by the Carazo government, he and another exile, Fernando Chamorro, continued their counter-revolution. Finally, the election of Ronald Reagan in 1980 immediately introduced a new and more aggressive U.S. position toward the Sandinistas. The significance of this event to Costa Rica became apparent when Jeanne Kirkpatrick, U.S. Ambassador to the United Nations, said late in 1981 that Costa Rica should accept U.S. "security assistance" as part of future economic aid. Although this statement has been interpreted as anything from a subtle hint to an outright threat, the idea of U.S. pressure was enough to prompt Carazo to demand an apology. When it was not forthcoming, relations with the United States notably cooled for a time.

It was at this time that the old fears of communism and the tendency to seek help from the United States again began to coincide in Costa Rica, laying the groundwork for the present situation in which Costa Rica has come to be considered as a base for U.S. efforts to destabilize the Sandinista government. The problem now is that a policy of anticommunism with U.S. support also poses a grave challenge to the policy of nonmilitary neutrality.

Although the present situation in Costa Rica is complex and controversial, several developments stand out: the temporary resolution of the economic crisis by President Monge; the great increase in economic aid from the United States; the increased activities of the anti-Sandinista Contras; the increases in internal political turmoil; and the subtle (and not always so subtle) U.S. pressures on Costa Rica to become an active ally in the war against Nicaragua.

Monge came to office with a "Hundred Day Plan" designed to rebuild confidence in the Costa Rican economy by checking inflation and currency devaluation. His government reopened negotiations with the IMF and was able to secure a short-term loan of $100 million after agreeing to meet stringent conditions that would have long-term effects on the Costa Rican economy. As Monge admitted, "To deal with the IMF is bad, but not to deal with it is catastrophic" (Blachman & Hellman 1986, 167). The conditions included reducing public expenditures, increasing taxes, raising prices on certain commodities such as gasoline, ending price subsidies for basic foods, and reducing social service programs. Naturally, these cutbacks were felt most by the poor and middle classes.

Along with the IMF agreements came a great increase in U.S. aid for which Costa Rica had to meet a variety of similar conditions. U.S. aid had never amounted to much before 1981. From 1962 to 1979, it totaled only about $200 million and consisted mainly of loans and grants. With the approval of the IMF agreement, U.S. aid began to increase rapidly in the 1980s to total more than $200 million per year by 1984, and to a grand total of nearly a billion by 1987. Moreover, Economic Support Funds used to subsidize imports from the United States, went from zero in 1980 to more than 75 percent of the total aid package by 1985. The impact of U.S. aid on the economy can be illustrated by comparing it to the country's budget which totals about $700 million this year. Therefore, U.S. aid amounts to a figure nearly one-third of the government's operating expenses and about 10 percent of the entire GNP of the country. When added to aid from other sources, the total almost equals the entire budget of the country.

Security assistance from the United States has also greatly increased during the past five years. From 1952 to 1968, the United States provided only about $1 million worth of weapons to Costa Rica along with training for a small number of Civil Guardsmen. After 1968 the United States ceased providing weapons or training altogether. But since 1980, the United States has sought to professionalize the Civil Guard, to equip its members with U.S. infantry weapons, and to train special units in counterinsurgency tactics. Security aid has totaled over $30 million over the past six years, and has been tied to a strong suggestion that Costa Rica maintain a permanent, trained officer corps in the Civil Guard. U.S. troops and trainers have been limited, although U.S. Special Forces did train more than 700 Civil Guardsmen in counterinsurgency tactics at a special camp near the Nicaraguan border in 1985. U.S. assistance has also contributed a communications system, helicopters, boats, light airplanes, trucks, jeeps, antitank weapons, uniforms, and so on. Although it is often pointed out that nothing is transferred to Costa Rica except on direct request from its own National Security Council, the fact is there has been a real move toward professionalization of the Guard, with the result that the population is now becoming accustomed to the presence of a military-like force.

At least as significant as the creation of a professionalized Civil Guard is the Contra activity that has been going on in Costa Rica since the early 1980s, in particular that of Edén Pastora's Democratic Revolutionary Alliance (ARDE). Contra leaders have also included Alfonso Robelo, Miskito Indian leader Brooklyn Rivera (who organized Indian refugees into a group called MISURASTA), and Fernando Chamorro from the Nicaraguan Democratic Front (FDN) that is based in Honduras. Estimates are that the Contra forces in Costa Rica have trained between 1000 and 1500 individuals to engage in attacks across the border into Nicaragua. Much of this activity has been conducted with the knowledge and help of the Civil and Rural Guards, although officially the government has denied any support for the Contras.

Contra activities in Costa Rica have reportedly diminished greatly within the past three years for several reasons. For one thing, Edén Pastora fell out with the leadership of ARDE and the FDN. An attempt to assassinate Pastora in 1984 at a press conference is still shrouded in mystery, but he later requested political asylum in Costa Rica and apparently stopped leading the resistance movement. Meanwhile, the Costa Rican government has assumed a militant, anti-Contra position, threatening to arrest individuals and groups that use Costa Rica as a base for anti-Nicaragua activities. All of these events have thus reduced direct threats to neutrality from the Contra forces.

Internal political turmoil within Costa Rica has been another great contributor to the present situation. Terrorist activities, including kidnappings, bombings, and so forth, that occurred mainly in 1982 and 1983 contributed to a feeling of insecurity and fear that the country was on the verge of being drawn into a conflict that would endanger the maintenance of its democratic institutions. While Sandinistas were not implicated in most of the incidents, there were enough involving Nicaraguans to cause great concern and to feed the latent anticommunist feelings that are ever present in Costa Rican thinking.

Border clashes between Costa Rica and Nicaragua occurred a number of times and added to the anti-Sandinista sentiment growing in Costa Rica. By mid-1985 Costa Rica had issued sixty-eight notes to Nicaragua concerning "acts of aggression" and Nicaragua had issued thirty-six such notes to Costa Rica. Among the more serious incidents was an attack in September 1983 on the Pan-American Highway which destroyed the Nicaraguan border post at Peñas Blancas. Although the attack had been committed by Pastora's ARDE forces, the Costa Rican press interpreted the event as an attack by Nicaraguans on Costa Rica. Subsequent investigation only inflamed the dispute between the two states. But the most serious border incident was a 1985 shoot-out at Las Crucitas, which resulted in the deaths of two Civil Guardsmen. Each side accused the other of starting the shooting, although it was quite possible that Contra forces were responsible. Nonetheless, the incident seriously impeded efforts at peaceful resolution of border disputes. With the current and apparently successful policy of ending Contra activities within Costa Rica, the border incidents have also diminished during the past two years.

Within Costa Rica, too, there are a number of militant, right-wing groups that have been encouraged by the hostilities between Costa Rica and Nicaragua. The leading group is the Movement for a Free Costa Rica (MCRL) that has claimed to have "several thousand" soldiers and connections with the World Anti-Communist League. As a paramilitary organization it has been responsible for, among other things, a violent demonstration at the Nicaraguan embassy, and an attack on a group of peace marchers who were visiting Costa Rica in December 1985. During the latter, the police were said to have watched the attack for four hours before intervening to protect the marchers.

One of the MCRL's founders, Benjamin Piza Carranza, was appointed Minister of Public Security in 1984 following a crisis-provoked cabinet shakeup instigated by the chamber of commerce (which Piza also headed). The chamber had approached President Monge with a claim of having discovered a communist plot to destabilize the country, and implied that the incumbent Public Security Minister Angel Edmundo Solano might be involved along with other high officials. A cabinet turnover followed in which two ministers were removed, an action that demonstrated the power of the right. Piza remained as head of public security until his dismissal in 1986 by newly inaugurated President Oscar Arias.

Something should also be said here concerning the role of the press in Costa Rica. Regarded as one of the leading institutions of Costa Rican society that the 1948 revolution had not changed, it has tended since the beginning of the 1980s to be extremely anti-Sandinista and concerned about communist and other left-wing insurgency threats to Costa Rica. The misinterpretations of the Peñas Blancas incident was typical of the largely anti-Sandinista press and its willingness to fan the flames of controversy.

Currently, there is also evidence that the U.S. Central Intelligence Agency has been funding an intense propaganda campaign through the Costa Rican mass media with the intent of portraying Nicaragua as a threat to the Western Hemisphere. The CIA is alleged to have funded the purchase of a San José radio station. Also, *Nicaragua Hoy*, a weekly, four-page newspaper supplement produced by a public relations official of the FDN, Pedro Joaquín Chamorro, Jr., is another particularly ambitious CIA project. The supplement has been carried by the influential *La Nación*, and is distributed to seven-hundred-and-fifty-thousand readers. Obviously, all of this represents a serious U.S. attempt to mold public opinion in Costa Rica (Sharkey 1986).

In summary, the clashes with Nicaragua, the acts of terrorism, the operation of the Contras who are drawn mainly from the ranks of the thousands of Nicaraguan refugees now living in Costa Rica, the activities of militantly anticommunist, right-wing groups, and the attitude of the press, have all contributed to creating a volatile domestic political atmosphere that is open to anticommunist hysteria much like that which existed in the country in 1948. Add to this U.S. efforts to enlist the country in its anti-Sandinista war, and one finds the roots of a serious threat to the continuation of Costa Rica's policy of nonmilitary neutrality.

There are several facets to Costa Rican relations with the United States at the present time. First, the U.S. has encouraged Costa Rica to professionalize the Civil and Rural Guards and to permit training in counterinsurgency methods. The statement that arms and training are always requested by the Central American government is technically true, but there has no doubt been plenty of "friendly persuasion" to induce the requests, as well as direct appeals to certain important officials within the Costa Rican government who favor militarization. For example, the training of Civil Guardsmen by U.S. Special Forces in 1985 resulted from an agreement between the U.S. embassy and Public Security Minister Benjamin Piza Carranza, during President Monge's visit to Europe. Monge did nothing to reverse the agreement upon his return. Moreover, U.S. aid has been linked to the issue of securing the north border with Nicaragua. Border incidents and the terrorist attacks of 1982 and 1983 have no doubt heightened the apprehensions of Costa Ricans, so that they are conscious of their vulnerability from the north. They have, therefore, sought to improve their frontier security with better equipment and trained person- nel. Whether or not the potential threat of Nicaraguan intervention is real is less important than the fear of leaving the border area open to military activity or infiltration, whether by Contra forces, Sandinista soldiers, or anyone else. Costa Rica may still be some distance from creating an army, but there is no doubt that it is now better prepared defensively than it has ever been since 1948.

Another facet of the situation is that the Contra activity that has taken place within Costa Rica has been supported, indirectly at least, by the United States. Besides receiving help from Civil and Rural Guardsmen, ARDE received both the encouragement and the help of the United States which also attempted, through the CIA, to bring about an alliance between ARDE and the Honduran-based FDN. Logically, because encouragement of Contra ac- tivity is part of U.S. policy to "destabilize" the Sandinistas, Costa Rican neutrality would not be considered an insurmountable barrier to such support. Indeed, allegations have been made that the CIA was implicated in the at- tempt to kill Edén Pastora in 1984 because of his refusal to become allied with the CIA-backed FDN's war against Nicaragua.

Another facet of U.S.-Costa Rican relations is the manipulation of U.S. aid money to make Costa Rica more dependent on the United States and to develop policies more conducive to U.S. interests. According to a secret State Department document of May 1984, a military aid request of $7.6 million by Costa Rica was regarded as a way to draw the Central American republic away from its "neutralist tightrope act." The request was called "potentially an im- portant milestone in our relations" with Costa Rica which could lead it to take a harder line toward Nicaragua and make it more hospitable to the Contras. "It provides an opportunity to help shift the political balance in our favor on Nicaragua's flank," the report said, according to the *Washington Post*, and "it could lead to a significant shift from the neutralist tightrope act and push it more explicitly and publicly into the anti-Sandinista camp. This could pay im- portant political and diplomatic dividends for us." The report also said that approval of the request is the "only way to stiffen their resolve and prevent a backsliding into neutrality" (May 10, 1984, A-1, A-23). Although a State Department official later said the report was written by "junior people" who had been succeeded by "more balanced and relaxed thinking," it indicates an attitude of the U.S. government.

In particular, the expressions of Ambassador Curtin Winsor, who was U.S. representative in San José from July 1983, to February 1985, demonstrate an impatience with Costa Rica's neutralist and antimilitary attitude. Ambas- sador Winsor is reported to have called Costa Rica's democratic system "in- efficient" and "ineffective" in dealing with the threats posed by Nicaragua. In asserting his own country's security interests, the ambassador said in 1983 that the United States "does not discard the possibility of invading Nicaragua, as it cannot live with an active subversive, Marxist-Leninist regime in the region." After Monge issued his Neutrality Proclamation in November 1983, the ambassador is said to have denounced it as "bullshit" (although the embassy denied this). In an interview in August 1984, he lauded the proposed merger between the FDN and ARDE Contra forces, and commented that "this strengthens the U.S. interests in the region." In fact, just before leaving Costa Rica, he said that he had conferred with General Paul Gorman, then head of the U.S. Southern Command, about the possibility of assembling U.S. defense parts in Costa Rica. His successor, Arthur Lewis Tambs, was at least more restrained in his public statements ("Costa Rica: Neutrality vs. Militarization" 1985, 1).

Other U.S. officials also demonstrated incredible arrogance toward Costa Rica, including Undersecretary of Defense Fred Ikle, who in 1983 suggested the installation in Costa Rica of a U.S. force of about 1000 men, and General Paul Gorman, who talked about the virtues of sending U.S. National-al Guardsmen to Costa Rica to get a "realistic opportunity" for training in a third world country. Such assertions have been too many and too consistent to be dismissed as anything but a reflection of a U.S. government attitude that would welcome a military, nonneutralist position on the part of Costa Rica. There were also more subtle pressures to secure a response favorable to U.S. interests. Invitations to participate in military and naval maneuvers in the Caribbean and to be an observer in the reactivated regional defense pact, CONDECA (Central American Defense Council), have been turned down by Costa Rica. More controversial was an announcement that came only ten days after the the Neutrality Proclamation that 1000 U.S. "combat engineers" would be coming to Costa Rica to build highways and bridges in the northern border area. This generated a great deal of controversy within the country, and the offer was eventually formally refused by the legislative assembly. It is noteworthy that at that time even the normally conservative press expressed dismay over the offer. However, some 180 U.S. Army engineers did actually arrive in Costa Rica in 1985 to work on upgrading and constructing bridges along a coastal highway in the southwest. They were unarmed, and Nicaraguan protests over their presence were dismissed by saying that these personnel were there to work only on civil projects. Nevertheless, their arrival was also followed by the visit to Costa Rica of two U.S. warships, the USS *Iowa* and the USS *Hull*. Because the U.S. Navy refused to disclose whether or not the ships carried nuclear weapons, their visit aroused more controversy within the assembly, although it did grant permission for the docking in Limón of the "good will mission."

In 1983, the Committee on Foreign Affairs of the U.S. House of Representatives expressed the view that "Costa Ricans seem very pleased with the bipartisan understanding that Costa Rica has gotten from the United States." However the house report also stated that "the only major factor clouding this picture is the continuing attempts by some in the Reagan

Administration to undermine Costa Rican neutrality." It added that "these unfortunate efforts threaten to undermine the otherwise good relations that the United States and Costa Rica now enjoy" (U. S. Congress 1984, 11). Moreover, both houses of Congress have passed resolutions supporting Costa Rican neutrality. As Senator Dodd (D-Ct.) explained, "Costa Rica is different because it chose the democratic route...and it is different because it has refused to be anyone's pawn in the conflicts that rage throughout the region" ("Costa Rica: Neutrality vs. Militarization" 1985, 2). Nonetheless, the official U.S. attitude is best summed up by a recent statement of the political affairs officer of the U.S. embassy in San José, who said, "Given the current situation, we don't think the neutrality proclamation clearly distinguishes between ideological and military neutrality" (Adams 1985, 3).

The Neutrality Proclamation is probably an attempt to reassert the policy of nonmilitary neutrality on the one hand, and to answer U.S. pressures to narrow the effect of the policy on the other. As some have described the policy, it represents a kind of "military neutrality v. ideological belligerence." In announcing the policy, Monge hoped to maintain the independence and security of his country in the face of a threat of armed intervention from Nicaragua, as well as pressure to support the U.S. anti-Sandinista campaign in return for much needed U.S. economic aid. Concerning the public's attitude, a recent Costa Rican opinion poll indicates that strong disapproval of the Sandinistas had risen from 84 percent in 1985 to 87 percent in 1986. Moreover, some 89 percent of the public considered the Sandinistas to be a real threat to Costa Rica. Finally, although over half of those polled had "positive" feelings about U.S. aid, many were also of the opinion that the U.S. merely uses aid to "serve its own interests," and were thus concerned about the aid's effects (*Times of the Americas*, Sep. 3, 1986, 4).

The elections of 1986 demonstrated much of the internal dissension that exists in Costa Rica. The party of Social Christian Unity (PUSC) and its candidate, Rafael Angel Calderón, Jr. (son of the president of the 1940s), asserted a highly anti-Sandinista position, while also strongly criticizing the policy of neutrality and urging a domestic military build-up. Although Calderón was opposed to establishing an army or intervening in the internal affairs of other states, he did indicate that in the event of a war between Honduras and Nicaragua, Costa Rica should "send a Civil Guard company to fight on the Honduran side" (*Mesoamérica*, Jan. 1986, 1). The PLN and its candidate, Oscar Arias, asserted, after some early vacillation, a strongly proneutrality position similar to that of President Carazo. Indeed, Arias became known as a "peace candidate" for his pledge to restrict activities of the Contras and by his emphasis on peace with all of Costa Rica's neighbors. Regarding the Contras, he was quoted as saying "we don't want our land, liberty, or hospitality used [by them]." Concerning neutrality, he said, "We reaffirm our belief in neutrality." But he also expressed his belief that an "expansionist" Nicaragua is a threat to his country's stability (*Akron Beacon Journal*, Feb. 3, 1986, D-6).

The February 1986, election gave Arias 52.3 percent of the 1,200,000 votes cast, or a margin of about 80,000. The PLN also won 29 of 57 seats in the legislative assembly, giving the party the barest of majorities. According to some analysts, Arias received his majority from the 10 to 20 percent of voters concerned about peace, because most voting followed party lines. Since the peace issue had such a crucial effect on the outcome of the elections, one could say that the election of the new president could be called a narrow mandate for neutrality.

On May 8, 1986, Oscar Arias was inaugurated as Costa Rica's forty-seventh president. Attending the inauguration were presidents from all the Central American republics except Nicaragua. (President Daniel Ortega said he feared demonstrations by Nicaraguan exiles and Contras living in Costa Rica.) Arias declared in his inaugural address that the Contadora draft treaty for Central America "must be signed" by June 6, 1986, and he called for a number of specific steps to be followed, including "national reconciliation talks in the countries beset by violence" (*Latin American Monitor* 1986, 299). He made no mention of the Contras in his speech, or of U.S. support of the Contras, but he reasserted that Costa Rica's pledge to neutrality should be given more than just lip service. As for Nicaragua, he called for a campaign to "democratize" that country. Finally, concerning relations with the United States, he is reported to have said later that "We are as happy as a recently married couple" (*CANN*, June 1986, 9).

Economically, Costa Rica has continued to be as dependent on North American and IMF beneficence as ever. Confronted with another financial crisis caused by a shortage of foreign exchange, and the possibility of default-ing on its debt, the country has moved again to satisfy conditions for new loans from IMF, U.S.-AID, and the World Bank. Figures from 1985 showed a GDP growth rate of only 1.2 percent (as compared with 7.3 percent in the previous year), another devaluation of the currency, a reduction in exports, and an in-crease in the unfavorable trade balance. So, some of the 1984 gains of the Monge administration were seriously muted the following year, and in 1986 also. In all, Costa Rica's economic picture indicates a continuing and growing dependence upon the United States, with the latter supplying the equivalent of about one-third of the total operating budget.

In his actions, Arias apparently has followed his pledge "not to tolerate the utilization of our territory by Contras" (*Latin American Monitor* 1986, 299). Rebels have been arrested, a clandestine hospital for Contras was closed, a U.S.-funded Contra airstrip near the Nicaraguan border was closed, and Arias has strongly criticized U.S. aid to the Contras saying, "The more you give the Contras, the more Ortega gets from the Soviets" (Cleveland *Plain Dealer*, Sep. 11, 1986, 2-A). He also did not reappoint the notoriously right-wing Benjamin Piza as Minister of Public Security, and has backed a neutrality bill in the legislative assembly that would convert the Neutrality Proclamation into law.

As an indication of the public response to the president's actions and commitments, the opposition party's leaders oppose the neutrality bill on the grounds that Costa Rica should not attempt to be neutral while its survival depends on good relations with the United States. The press, as represented by the leading dailies, *La Nación*, *La República*, and *La Prensa Libre*, has strongly criticized Arias. As *La Nación* has editorialized, "Don Oscar should have avoided making these declarations in the name of the Fatherland he has always seemed so willing to defend" (Myers 1986, 1).

At least some of the Costa Rican government's current concern about neutrality is based on a suit filed by Nicaragua in the International Court of Justice, claiming that Costa Rica has harbored U.S.-sponsored terrorists. After accepting the jurisdiction of the court (Honduras rejected the jurisdiction of the court in a similar suit), Costa Rica is now obliged to present a sincere position of noninvolvement in the U.S.-backed war against Nicaragua. If it fails to do so, its manifested neutrality would appear to be a very hollow claim.

President Arias presently faces a difficult task: how to remain politically independent while being economically dependent on the United States. Perhaps his own statement could be considered an appropriate response to this predicament: "Friendship should not mean being servile. A friend who does everything you want is not a friend, but a slave" (*New York Times*, Sep. 10, 1986, A-3).

Several concluding observations are in order concerning the general dilemma within which Costa Rica now finds itself. Foremost, it should be stressed that the policy of nonmilitarism is in essence a state of mind among the people—a state of mind that overlooks the reality of a developing Civil Guard with more weapons, troops, and professionalized leadership, and that has recently received a large amount of U.S. training. In other words, while the populace is opposed to having an army, it also seems ambivalent about accepting the best military force that ever existed in Costa Rica's history. Former President Pepe Figueres warned that the new Guardsmen are "dangerous goosesteppers": "The army in Latin America is the traditional arbiter of all political disputes. It nullifies the results of an election when its leading officers do not like them and exercises power to promote its own interests. If the army returns to Costa Rica, we will be served no better than our Latin American brothers who labor and suffer under its authoritarian yoke" (*Mesoamérica*, Sep. 1985, 1). In saying this, Figueres touches a sensitive nerve in the population that so far has reacted negatively to reviving a permanent army.

Yet the Guard continues to be augmented in strength, and the public appears inclined to accept this as a fact of life. Apparently, the perceived threat of a militarized Nicaragua has provided the rationale for the kind of "remilitarization" that is not called "remilitarization." These days, one sees more armed Guardsmen riding around in jeeps as well as Guardsmen training and doing calisthenics at a center only a few blocks from the old Bella Vista barracks. This is truly remarkable in a country that has for almost forty years prided itself on not having an army. As for neutrality, this is obviously a highly flexible concept, the Arias administration's views to the contrary notwithstanding. Flexibility has permitted Costa Rica to react to foreign involvements in various ways depending on its particular interests at any one time. Called "neutrality Costa Rican style" by one author, it permits an ambivalence based upon a distinction between political neutrality and ideological neutrality. Thus, Costa Rica can "maintain an image of being separated from the crisis in Central America, an image it desperately needs to attract foreign investment and foreign economic assistance and to improve trade relations with nations within and beyond the region" (Lincoln 1985, 332). This can be done while also demonstrating a hatred of communism and a strong anti-Sandinista position. As a state of mind, neutrality is also an effective (at least to those anti-Sandinista Costa Ricans who voted for Oscar Arias) way of maintaining good relations with both the United States *and* Nicaragua, while at the same time feeling morally unique in the world.

Together, nonmilitarism and neutrality have blended into the official policy of nonmilitary neutrality that is perceived as a guarantor of peace, security, democracy, and a relatively high standard of living. This is probably a sound assumption, as is seen in economic and political developments since the revolution of 1948. Nonetheless, the policy must be regarded as a success only insofar as Costa Rica has been able to rely upon international organizations and assistance from the United States at crucial times. Assistance has been military in the past and is mainly economic now—but whatever its character, Costa Rica has depended upon the United States for its development into the most prosperous and democratic regime in Central America. The unique Neutrality Proclamation is seen, therefore, as both an answer to this dependence, and as an attempt to assert a degree of independence in a dangerous world.

Costa Rica's real dilemma is that it wishes to continue to remain both neutral in Central America and to receive extensive assistance from the United States. This would not be such a problem if it were not for the unrelenting pressure to support the U.S. war against Nicaragua. From the evidence presented here as well as from abundant evidence elsewhere, it is clear that the United States wants Costa Rica to assume a more aggressively anti-Nicaragua stance as well as permit the operation of the Contras on the "southern front." Although the United States claims to respect Costa Rica's neutrality and sovereignty, its actions of the last seven years indicate otherwise. There is no question that the United States has blatantly attempted to manipulate Costa Rica, and to use economic dependency as a lever to change its policy toward Nicaragua. Thus, it is not surprising to hear in Costa Rica the phrase, "Beware of gringos bearing gifts."

The United States and Costa Rica have been friends for many years and have enjoyed a special, noninterventionist relationship from the beginning. However, the directions of the past seven years have been well described by Rodrigo Carazo Ochoa, former president, who said in a recent interview:

> We Costa Ricans are good friends of the United States because we have never been invaded. But the countries that have suffered the presence of the Marines are not your friends. Why is Costa Rica the United States' best friend in Latin America? Because you have never failed to respect us. But recently, I've felt that you've begun to stop respecting us. When did you begin doing so? When you began to think

that the security of this country could be maintained through military training of our police forces. This country is worth much more than that; it's worth more than the money you can give our government and worth more than the defense potential of the Lightning Brigades. This country is a better friend of the United States...to the extent that you leave us alone. (Reding 1986b, 332)

This statement expresses the anxiety and concerns felt by numerous Costa Ricans of all political affiliations.

With all that is said by Costa Rican leaders, however, the United States continues to press its position, as exemplified in the commonly heard statement that Central America is the "backyard" of the United States. President Carazo had this to say about the "backyard" concept: "The difference between how U.S. policy makers see Costa Rica and how I see it is very easy to explain in your own language. To them, this is their 'backyard.' For me, this is my 'living room,' my heart, my way of life. If by reason of so-called defense of national security, they decide to mine the 'backyard' in order to keep certain people out, they are mining my 'living room'" (Reding 1986b, 332). José Figueres has put the issue even more emphatically: "If the U.S. wishes to change the government of Nicaragua, let its own troops do it instead of asking farmers from Costa Rica and Honduras to go and die on its borders. To us it seems wrong that a great power should financially contribute to the slaughter now taking place; it also seems wrong that the U.S. should not respect the way of thinking of the governments of other nations" (*Mesoamérica*, Sep. 1985, 1).

Both the United States and Costa Rica stand to gain from a policy of mutual respect for each other's foreign policies and sovereignty. Also, Costa Rica is a country that the United States needs very much to hold up as a model of independence in an area of the world in which intervention by great powers has been commonplace for four centuries. As Andrew Reding of the World Policy Institute so aptly describes the situation: "To the extent that we in the United States truly believe our own accolades of Costa Rican democracy as the 'model' in Latin America, and our own public pronouncements of respect for the self-determination of our continental neighbors, we need to begin listening to our Costa Rican friends themselves, who would have us act much differently toward them and other countries of the region" (Reding 1986a, 314).

NOTES

1. For a superb review of Costa Rican historiography and discussion of the myth of Costa Rican egalitarianism, see Gudmundson 1986.

References and Abbreviations
Cited in Notes

AA. Archiv des Auswärtigen Amts, Bonn.

AAM. Archive de l'Armée de la Mer, Paris.

AAT. Archive de l'Armée de la Terre, Paris.

Abelleira, Jorge. 1981. Entrevista paralela con el cine y la TV nicaragüense, *Barricada Cultural: Ventana*, December 12:2-4.

Acción Social Cristiana. 1945-1950. Guatemala.

Adams, Abigail. 1985. U.S. Pressure Erodes Costa Rican Neutrality. *Latinamerica Press* 17(16) (May 2, 1985):3-4.

Adams, Richard N., ed. 1957. *Political Changes in Guatemalan Communities*. New Orleans: Middle American Research Institute, Tulane Univ.

— — —. 1970. *Crucifixion by Power: Essays on Guatemalan National Social Structure, 1944-1966*. Austin: Univ. of Texas Press.

— — —. 1981a. The Dynamics of Societal Diversity: Notes from Nicaragua for a Sociology of Survival. *American Ethnologist* 8:6-19.

— — —. 1981b. The Sandinistas and the Indians, the "problem" of the Indians in Nicaragua. *Caribbean Review* 10:23-25, 55-56.

Aguilar Zinser, Adolfo. 1983. Mexico and the Guatemalan Crisis. In *The Future of Central America: Policy Choices for the U.S. and Mexico*, eds. R. Fagen and O. Pellicer, 161-86. Stanford: Stanford Univ. Press.

Aguirre-Beltrán, Gonzalo. 1967. *Regiones de Refugio*. Mexico: Instituto Indigenista Interamericano.

Akron Beacon Journal. February 3, 1986.

Alba, Victor. 1965. *Alliance Without Allies: The Mythology of Progress in Latin America*. Trans. John Pearson. New York: Praeger.

Aldaraca, Bridget, et al., eds. 1980. *Nicaragua in Revolution: The Poets Speak*. Minneapolis: Marxist Educ. Press.

Alemán Bolaños, Gustavo. 1927. *El país de los irredentes*. Guatemala: Tipografía Sánchez y DeGuise.

— — —. 1932. *Sandino, estudio completo de heroe de las Segovias*. México.

Alemán Ocampo, Carlos. 1981. El torovenado y la resistencia cultural. *Barricada Cultural: Ventana*, October 31:2-3.

Alexander, Robert J. 1967. *Communism in Latin America*. New Brunswick, N.J.: Rutgers Univ. Press.

Allen, Cyril. 1967. *France in Central America: Felix Belly and the Nicaraguan Canal*. New York: Pageant.

Alstrum, James J. 1980. Typology and Narrative Techniques in Cardenal's *El Estrecho Dudoso. Journal of Spanish Studies: Twentieth Century* 8(1/2):9-27.

Alvarez, Víctor Hugo. 1986. Celebradores de la Palabra: de Choluteca a Latinoamerica. *La Tribuna* (Tegucigalpa), November 22:12.

Amador Amador, Jorge Reynaldo. 1975. Los sucesos de la Talanquera enfocados por la prensa hondureña. Thesis, Universidad Nacional Autónoma de Honduras, Tegucigalpa.

AMAE. Archive du Ministère des Affaires Etrangères, Paris.

AMEF. Archive de Ministère de l'Economie et des Finances, Paris.

Americas Watch. 1982. *On Human Rights in Nicaragua*. New York: Americas Watch Committee.

— — —. 1984a. *Guatemala: A Nation of Prisoners*. New York: Americas Watch Committee.

— — —. 1984b. *The Miskitos in Nicaragua, 1981-1984*. New York: Americas Watch Committee.

AN. Archives Nationales, Paris.

Anderson-Imbert, Enrique. 1969. *Spanish-American Literature: A History*. 2d ed., vol. 1. Detroit: Wayne State Univ. Press.

Arce, Bayardo, Tomás Borge, Carlos Núñez, Luis Carrión, Daisy Zamora, and Daniel Ortega. 1982. *Hacia una política cultural de la revolución popular sandinista*. Managua: Ministerio de Cultura.

Arce Castaño, Bayardo. 1983. Tanto arte...tanta actividad cultural. *Barricada Cultural: Ventana*, July 19:2-4.

Arellano, Jorge Eduardo, ed. 1977. *25 poemas indígenas de Nicaragua*. Managua: Universidad Centroameriana.

— — —. 1979. Ernesto Cardenal: de Granada a Gethsemany (1925-1957). *Boletín Nicaragüense de Bibliografía y Documentación* 31 (September):25-43.

— — —. 1982. *Panorama de la literatura nicaragüense*. Managua: Editorial Nueva Nicaragua.

Arévalo, Juan José. 1945a. *Discurso al asumir la presidencia de la república*. Guatemala: Tipografía Nacional.

— — —. 1945b. *El presidente electo a los pueblos de la república*. Guatemala: Tipografía Nacional.

— — —. 1945c. *Escritos pedagógicos y filosóficos*. Guatemala: Tipografía Nacional.

— — —. 1945d. *Escritos políticos*. Guatemala: Tipografía Nacional.

— — —. 1946. *La filosofía de los valores en la pedagogia*. 2d ed. Guatemala: Tipografía Nacional.

— — —. 1951. *Homenaje al presidente constitucional de la república y a la señora Elisa Martínez de Arévalo: 10 de enero de 1951. Discurso del Dr. Arévalo*. Guatemala: Depto. de Publicidad de la Presidencia de la República.

— — —. 1963a. *Anti-Kommunism in Latin America*. New York: Lyle Stuart.

— — —. 1963b. *Carta política: pueblo de Guatemala, con motivo de haber aceptado la candidatura presidencial*. México: Costa Amic.

— — —. 1963c. *Memorias de aldea*. México: Editorial Orión.

– – –. 1970. *Inquietud normalista; estampas de adolescencia y juventud, 1921-1927.* San Salvador: Editorial Universitaria de El Salvador.

– – –. 1974. *La personalidad, la adolesencia, los valores, y otros escritos de pedagogia y filosofía.* Guatemala: Editorial José de Pineda Ibarra.

Arguedas, Carlos Manuel, ed. 1981. *Constitución política de la República de Costa Rica.* San José: Editorial Costa Rica.

Arias Sánchez, Oscar. 1982. Desarrollo económico y social, in Chester Zelaya, ed., *Costa Rica contemporánea.* 2d ed. San José: Editorial Costa Rica.

Ashby, Timothy. 1987. *Bear in the Backyard: Soviet Strategy in the Caribbean.* Lexington, Mass.: Lexington Books.

Asociación de Abogados de Guatemala. 1945. *Anteprojecto de constitución presentado a la Asociación de Abogados por la subcomisión entregado de la manera siguiente, licenciados: Francisco Villagrán, José Rolz Bennett [y otros] y presentado a la comisión de projectos de la asamblea constituyente por los tres primeros nombrados.* Guatemala: Tipografía Nacional.

Asselain, Jean-Charles. 1984. *Histoire économique de la France du XVIII < e > siècle è nos jours.* 2 vols. Paris: Seuil.

Astilla, Carmelo F. 1976. The Martinez Era: Salvadoran-American Relations. Ph.D. diss., Louisiana State Univ., Baton Rouge.

Bacigalupo, Leonard. 1980. *The American Franciscan Missions in Central America: Three Decades of Christian Service.* Andover, Mass.: Charisma Press.

Bagley, Bruce M. 1984. Mexico in Central America: The Limits of Regional Power. In *Political Change in Central America: Internal and External Dimensions,* ed. Wolfe Grabendorff, 261-84. Boulder: Westview.

Bagley, Bruce M., Roberto Alvarez, and Katherine J. Hagedorn, eds. 1985. *Contadora and the Central American Peace Process: Selected Documents.* Boulder: Westview.

Bailey, Norman A. 1967. *Latin America in World Politics.* New York: Walker and Co.

Bailey, Thomas A. 1936. Interest in a Nicaraguan Canal, 1903-1931. *Hispanic American Historical Review* 16:2-28.

Baker, George W. 1961. The Caribbean Policy of Woodrow Wilson. Ph.D. diss., Univ. of Colorado, Boulder.

– – –. 1964. Ideals and Realities in the Wilson Administration's Relations with Honduras. *The Americas* 21:3-19.

Balladares, José Emilio. 1982. Rubén Darío y lo nacional: temas darianos vistos a la luz de la "vasta llama tropical." *Nicaráuc* 3(7):89-98.

Barber, Willard F., and C. Neale Ronning. 1966. *Internal Security and Military Power: Counterinsurgency and Civic Action in Latin America.* Athens, Ohio: Ohio State Univ. Press.

Barcos Archilla, Jaime. 1985. *Biografía mínima del doctor Juan José Arévalo Bermejo.* Guatemala: Departamento de Producción de Material Didáctico, adscrito a la Misión de Asistencia Técnica de la UNESCO.

Barricada. 1981. Managua.

Barricada Cultural: Ventana. 1981-1984. Managua.

Barricada Internacional. 1986. Managua.

Barrow, Dean. 1982. Independent Foreign Policy? Between a Rock and a Hard Place. *Brukdown* (1):23-25.

Barry, Tom, and Deb Preusch. 1986. *The Central American Fact Book*. New York: Grove.

Battle, John. 1965. Pablo Antonio Cuadra's *El jaguar y la luna. Romance Notes* 6(2):111-12.

Baylen, Joseph O. 1951. Sandino: Patriot or Bandit? *Hispanic American Historical Review* 31:394-419.

Beale, Howard K. 1956. *Theodore Roosevelt and the Rise of America to a World Power*. Baltimore: Johns Hopkins Univ. Press.

Becerra, Longino. 1982. *Evolución histórica de Honduras*. Tegucigalpa: Baktun Editorial.

Beisner, Robert L. 1975. *From Old Diplomacy to the New, 1865-1900*. New York: Thomas Y. Crowell.

Bell, John P. 1971. *Crisis in Costa Rica: The 1948 Revolution*. Austin: Univ. of Texas Press.

Belly, Félix. 1858. *Percement de l'isthme de Panama par le canal de Nicaragua*. Paris: Librairie Nouvelle.

Bemis, Samuel Flagg. 1943. *The Latin American Policy of the United States*. New York: Harcourt, Brace and World.

Bennett, Philip. 1987. Poetry of the Sandinista Revolution: Some Questions Mix of Politics and Art. *Boston Globe*, May 15:49-50.

Berle, Adolf A. 1961. Alliance for Progress vs. Communism. *U.S. State Department Bulletin*, June 24:763-64.

Bermann, Karl. 1986. *Under the Big Stick: Nicaragua and the United States Since 1848*. Boston: South End.

Bird, Leonard. 1984. *Costa Rica: The Unarmed Democracy*. London: Sheppard Press.

BK. Bundesarchiv Koblenz.

BLAC. Benson Latin American Collection, Univ. of Texas, Austin.

Blachman, Morris J., et. al. 1986. *Confronting Revolution: Security Through Diplomacy in Central America*. New York: Pantheon.

Blachman, Morris J., and Ronald G. Hellman. 1986. Costa Rica. In *Confronting Revolution: Security Through Diplomacy in Central America*, ed. M. J. Blachman, 156-82. New York: Pantheon.

Black, George. 1981. *Triumph of the People: The Sandinista Revolution in Nicaragua*. London: Zed.

Blaufarb, Douglas. 1977. *The Counterinsurgency Era: US Doctrine and Performance, 1950 to the Present*. New York: Free Press.

Blom, Franz, and Oliver LaFarge. 1926. *Tribes and Temples: A Record of the Expedition to Middle America*. New Orleans: Middle American Research Institute, Tulane Univ.

Bloomfield, L. M. 1953. *The British Honduras-Guatemalan Dispute*. Toronto: Carswell.

BMF. Bundesarchiv, Militärarchiv Freiburg, Freiburg.

Bollinger, William, and Daniel Manny Lund. 1982. Minority Oppression: Toward Analyses That Clarify and Strategies That Liberate. *Latin American Perspectives* 9(2):2-28.

Bonilla, H. H. 1975. *Figueres and Costa Rica: An Unauthorized Political Biography*. San José: Editorial Texto Limitada.

Booth, John A. 1982. *The End and the Beginning: The Nicaraguan Revolution*. Boulder: Westview.

– – –. 1985. *The End and the Beginning: The Nicaraguan Revolution*. 2d ed. Boulder: Westview.

Borderline. 1984. *Time* 123 (June 18):50.

Borge, Tomás. 1985. We Had Difficulty in Grasping the Ethnic Character of the Miskito Problem. In *Sandinistas Speak: Speeches, Writings, and Interviews with Leaders of Nicaragua's Revolutions*, ed. B. Marcus, 348-51. New York: Pathfinder.

Borgeson, Paul W., Jr. 1977. The Poetry of Ernesto Cardenal. Ph.D. diss., Vanderbilt Univ., Nashville, Tenn.

– – –. 1984. *Hacia el hombre nuevo: poesía y pensamiento de Ernesto Cardenal*. London: Tamesis.

Bossen, Laurel Herbenar. 1984. *The Redivision of Labor: Women and Economic Choice in Four Guatemalan Communities*. Albany: State Univ. of New York Press.

Bourgois, Phillipe. 1985a. Class, Ethnicity and State Among the Miskitu Amerindians of Northeastern Nicaragua. *Latin American Perspectives* 8(2):22-39.

– – –. 1985b. Ethnic Minorities. In *Nicaragua in Revolution*, ed. T. W. Walker, 201-16. New York: Praeger.

Bourne, Kenneth. 1967. *Britain and the Balance of Power in North America, 1815-1908*. Berkeley: Univ. of California Press.

Bouvier, Jean.1974. Les traits majeurs de l'impérialisme francais avant 1914. *Le mouvement social* 86 (January-March):3-24.

Bowman, Stephen Lee. 1985. The Evolution of United States Army Doctrine for Counterinsurgency Warfare: From World War II to the Commitment of Combat Units in Vietnam. Ph.D. diss., Duke Univ., Durham, N.C.

Braudel, Fernand. 1979. *Civilization and Capitalism*. 3 vols. New York: Harper & Row.

Braun, Rudolf, Wolfram Fischer, Helmut Grosskreutz, and Heinrich Volkmann, eds. 1972. *Industrielle Revolution: wirtschaftliche Aspekte*. Cologne: Kiepenheuer & Witsch.

Bravo, Alejandro. 1983. Cultura popular en León: CPC Antenor Sandino. *Barricada Cultural: Ventana*, July 19.

Brett, Donna, and Edward Brett. 1988. *Murdered in Central America*. Maryknoll, N.Y.: Orbis.

Brintnall, Douglas. 1979. *Revolt Against the Dead*. London: Gordon & Breach.

Brotherston, Gordon. 1975. *Latin American Poetry: Origins & Presence*. Cambridge: Cambridge Univ. Press.

Brown, Peter, and Douglas MacLean, eds. 1979. *Human Rights and U.S. Foreign Policy: Principles and Application*. Lexington, Mass.: D. C. Heath.

Brufau, Jaime. 1959. *La formación sacerdotal en Honduras: notas históricas*. Tegucigalpa: Seminario Interdiocesano San José.

Brukdown. 1978-1980. Belize.

Bunzel, Ruth. 1972. *Chichicastenango: A Guatemalan Indian Village*. Seattle: Univ. of Washington Press.

Burgos-Debray, Elisabeth, ed. 1984. *I, Rigoberta Menchu: An Indian Woman in Guatemala*. London: Verso.

Burnett, Virginia Garrard. 1986. A History of Protestantism in Guatemala. Ph.D. diss., Tulane Univ., New Orleans.

Burns, E. Bradford. 1980. *The Poverty of Progress: Latin America in the Nineteenth Century*. Berkeley: Univ. of California Press.

Burr, Robert N. 1967. *Our Troubled Hemisphere: Perspectives on United States-Latin American Relations*. Washington, D.C.: Brookings Institution.

Bush, Archer C. 1950. *Organized Labor in Guatemala, 1944-1949: A Case Study of an Adolescent Labor Movement in an Underdeveloped Country*. Hamilton, N.Y.: Colgate Univ. Bookstore.

Cabezas, Omar. 1982. *La montaña es algo más que un inmensa estepa verde*. Managua: Editorial Nuevo.

― ― ―. 1985a. Agreements Signed with Indian Organization. *Barricada Internacional* 157 (May 2):3.

― ― ―. 1985b. *Fire from the Mountain: The Making of a Sandinista*. Trans. Kathleen Weaver. New York: New American Library.

Calcott, George C. 1942. *The Caribbean Policy of the United States 1890-1920*. Baltimore: Johns Hopkins Univ. Press.

Calder, Bruce Johnson. 1970. *Crecimiento y cambio de la iglesia católica guatemalteca 1944-1966*. Guatemala: Editorial José de Pineda Ibarra.

Calvert, Peter. 1976. Guatemala and Belize. *Contemporary Review* (January):7-12

CANN: Central American Network Newsletter. 1986. 4 (June).

Cannistrano, Philip V. 1971. The Organization of Totalitarian Culture: Cultural Policy and the Mass Media in Fascist Italy, 1922-1945. Ph.D. diss., New York Univ., New York.

Cardenal, Ernesto. 1968. La Poesía Nicaragüense de Pablo Antonio Cuadra. *El Pez y la Serpiente* 9:121-27.

― ― ―. 1972. *En Cuba*. Buenos Aires: Ediciones Carlos Lohlé.

― ― ―, ed. 1974. *Poesía nueva de Nicaragua*. Buenos Aires: Lohle.

― ― ―. 1975a. *El evangelio en Solentiname, Volumen primero*. Salamanca: Sígueme.

― ― ―. 1975b. *Marilyn Monroe and Other Poems*. Trans. Robert Pring-Mill. London: Search Press.

― ― ―. 1980. Cultura revolucionaria, popular, nacional, antimperialista. *Nicaráuac* 1 (May-June):163-68.

— — —. 1981a. La unidad contra el imperialismo. *Nicaráuac* 2 (December):103-7.

— — —. 1981b. Revolution and Peace: The Nicaraguan Road. *Journal of Peace Research* 18:201-7.

— — —. 1982a. Aprender la revolución. *Barricada Cultural: Ventana*, October 10:3-5.

— — —. 1982b. Defendiendo la cultura, el hombre, y el planeta. *Nicaráuac* 3 (January):149-52.

— — —. 1982c. La democratización de la cultura. In *Colección popular de literatura nicaragüense*. Managua: Ministerio de Cultura.

— — —. 1982d [1948]. El grupo de vanguardia en Nicaragua. *Revista de crítica literaria latinoamericana* 8(15):71-76.

— — —. 1982e. La cultura : primeros seis meses de revolución. In Bayardo Arce, et al. *Hacia una política cultural de la revolución popular sandinista*, 169-75. Managua: Ministerio de Cultura.

Cardenal, Rodolfo. 1974. *Acontecimientos sobresalientes de la iglesia de Honduras, 1900-1962*. Tegucigalpa: Instituto Socio-religioso Juan XXIII.

Cardoso, Ciro, and Hector Pérez Brignoli. 1977. *Centro América y la economía occidental, 1520-1930*. San José: Universidad de Costa Rica.

Cardoso, Fernando H., and Enzo Faletto. 1979. *Dependency and Development in Latin America*. Berkeley: Univ. of California Press.

Carney, J. Guadalupe. 1985. *To Be a Revolutionary: An Autobiography*. San Francisco: Harper & Row.

Caron, François. 1979. *An Economic History of Modern France*. New York: Columbia.

Carrère d'Encausse, Hélène. 1978. Determinants and Parameters of Soviet Nationality Policy. In *Soviet Nationality Policies and Practices*, ed. Jeremy R. Azrael, 39-59. New York: Praeger.

Carrión, Luis. 1982. El arte en las fuerzas amardas. In Bayardo Arce, et al. *Hacia una política cultural de la revolución popular sandinista*, 51-59. Managua: Ministerio de Cultura.
51-59.

— — —. 1983. The Truth About the Atlantic Coast. In *National Revolution and Indigenous Identity: The Conflict Between Sandinistas and Miskito Indians on Nicaragua's Atlantic Coast* (WGIA Document No 47), ed. K. Ohland and R. Schneider 1983, 235-68. Copenhagen: International Work Group for Indigenous Affairs.

Carter, William. 1969. *New Lands and Old Traditions: Kekchi Cultivators in the Guatemalan Lowlands*. Gainesville: Univ. of Florida Press.

Castañeda, Jorge. 1969. Revolution and Foreign Policy: Mexico's Experience. In *Latin American International Politics: Ambitions, Capabilities, and the National Interest of Mexico, Brazil and Argentina*, ed. Carlos A. Astiz, 137-65. Notre Dame: Notre Dame Univ. Press.

— — —. 1985. Don't Corner Mexico. *Foreign Policy* 60 (Fall):75-90.

Castellanos Cambranes, Julio. 1977a. Aspectos del desarrollo socio-económico y político de Guatemala, 1868-1885, en base de materiales de archivos alemanes. *Política y Sociedad* 3 (January-June):7-14.

– – –. 1977b. *El imperialismo alemán en Guatemala: el tratado de comercio de 1887*. Guatemala: Instituto de Investigaciones Económicas y sociales de la Universidad de San Carlos de Guatemala.

– – –. 1985. *Coffee and Peasants in Guatemala*. South Woodstock, Vt.: CIRMA.

Castile, George P. Marxism and Native Americans. Manuscript.

Castile, George P., and Gilbert Kushner, eds. 1981. *Persistent People: Cultural Enclaves in Perspective*. Tucson: Univ. of Arizona Press.

CD. Consular Dispatches.

CDH. *See* Centro de Documentación de Honduras.

CEH. *See* Secretaría Conferencia Episcopal de Honduras.

CENSA. 1962. *Carta pastoral colectiva de los obsisposde Honduras sobre el comunismo y la política de partidos*. Tegucigalpa: CENSA.

Centro de Documentación de Honduras. n.d. *Los refugiados salvadoreños en Honduras*. Tegucigalpa: Centro de Documentación de Honduras.

– – –. 1985. *La iglesia en Honduras (1982-1984)*. Serie Cronologías No. 1. Tegucigalpa: Centro de Documentación de Honduras.

Child, John. 1980. *Unequal Alliance: The Inter-American Military System, 1938-1978*. Boulder: Westview.

Christ, Ronald. 1974. The Poetry of Useful Prophecy. *Commonweal* 100(8) (April 26):89-91.

Clark, J. Rueben. 1930. *Memorandum on the Monroe Doctrine*. Washington: GPO.

Cleary, Edward. 1985. *Crisis and Change: The Church in Latin America Today*. Maryknoll, N.Y.: Orbis.

Cleveland Plain Dealer. September 11, 1986.

CNP. *See* Comisión Nacional de Pastoral.

Cochrane, James D. 1972. U.S. Policy Toward Recognition of Governments and Promotion of Democracy in Latin America Since 1963. *Journal of Latin American Studies* 4(1):275-91;

Colby, Benjamin N., and Pierre van den Berghe. 1969. *Ixil Country: A Plural Society in Highland Guatemala*. Berkeley: Univ. of California Press.

Collazo-Dávila, Vicente. 1980. The Guatemalan Insurrection. In *Insurgency in the Modern World*, ed. Bard E. O'Neill, William R. Heaton, and Donald J. Alberts, 109-34. Boulder: Westview.

Comisión Nacional de Pastoral. 1982. X reunión extraordinaria de la Comisón Nacional de Pastoral. *Boletín eclesial* 32 (October 18-21, 1982):5, 18.

Congressional Record. 1905. 58th Cong., 3rd sess. Vol. 39. Washington: GPO.

Conn, Stetson, and Byron Fairchild. 1960. *United States Army in World War II: The Western Hemisphere*. Washington: GPO.

Contadora Collapse. 1986. *National Review*, May 9:18-19.

Cooper, John M. 1983. *The Warrior and the Priest: Woodrow Wilson and Theodore Roosevelt*. Cambridge: Belknap Press.

Coronel Urtecho, José. 1981. *Paneles de Infierno*. Managua: ENIEC.

Cortázar, Julio. 1983. Discurso en la recepción de la Orden Rubén Darío. *Casa de las Américas* 23(138):130-34.

Cosío Villegas, Daniel. 1960. *Historia moderna de México*. Vol. 5, *El porfiriato, la vida política exterior — Primera Parte*. México: Ed. Hermes.

Costa Rica: Neutrality vs. Militarization. 1985. In *Central America 1985: Basic Information and Legislative History U.S.-Central American Relations*. Washington: Coalition for a New Foreign and Military Policy and the Commission on U.S.-Central American Relations.

Craven, David, and John Ryder. 1983? *Art of the New Nicaragua*. n.p.

Cuadra, Pablo Antonio. 1934. *Poemas Nicaragüenses*. Santiago de Chile: Editorial Nascimento.

– – –. 1959. *El Jaguar y la luna*. Managua: Editorial Artes Gráficas.

– – –. 1971. *The Jaguar and the Moon*. Trans. Thomas Merton. Greensboro: Unicorn Press.

– – –. 1979a. *Songs of Cifar and the Sweet Sea: Selections from "Songs of Cifar, 1967-1977"*. Trans. Grace Schulman and Ann McCarthy de Zavala. New York: Columbia Univ. Press.

– – –, ed. 1979b. 50 años del movimiento de Vanguardia de Nicaragua, 1928-29 - 1978-79. *El Pez y la Serpiente* 22/23 (Summer):3-189.

– – –. 1981. *Por los caminos van los campesinos*. 4th ed. Managua: Ediciones El Pez y la Serpiente.

– – –. 1983-1985. *Obra poética completa*. 3 vols. San José: Libro Libre.

D'Alba, Pedro. 1927. Mexico and Nicaragua. *The Living Age*, February 1:204-6.

D'Antonio, Nicholas. n.d. How Personal Renewal Relates to Church Renewal. Unpublished memoir, photocopy in possession of Donna and Edward Brett.

Dane, Heinrich. 1971. *Die wirtschaftlichen Beziehungen Deutschlands zu Mexiko und Mittelamerika im 19. Jahrhundert*. Cologne: Böhlau.

Darío, Rubén. 1965. *Selected Poems of Rubén Darío*. Trans. Lysander Kemp, prologue by Octavio Paz. Austin: Univ. of Texas Press.

– – –. 1967. *Poesías completas*. 10th ed. Madrid: Aguilar.

– – –. 1977. *Rubén Darío: El mundo de los sueños*, ed. Angel Rama. Caracas: Biblioteca Ayacucho.

Davis, Jim F. 1975. *Decade of Disillusionment: The Kennnedy-Johnson Years*. Bloomington: Indiana Univ. Press.

Davis, Shelton. 1983. The Social Roots of Political Violence in Guatemala. *Cultural Survival Quarterly* 7(1):4-11.

Davis, Shelton, and Julie Hodson. 1982. *Witness to Political Violence in Guatemala: The Suppression of a Rural Development Movement*. Boston: Oxfam America, Impact Audit #2.

DD. Diplomatic Dispatches.

DDRS. 1976-1986. *Declassified Documents Reference System*. Washington: Carrolton Press.

DeConde, Alexander. 1951. *Herbert Hoover's Latin American Policy*. Stanford, Stanford Univ. Press.

Demographic Yearbook 1970. 1971. New York: United Nations.

Denain, A. 1845. *Considérations sur les intérêts politiques et commerciaux qui se rattachent è l'isthme de Panama et aux différents isthmes de l'amérique centrale*. Paris: Marchands.

Denkschrift der ältesten der Kaufmannschaft von Berlin betreffend die Neugestaltung der deutschen Handelspolitik...1900. 1901. Berlin: n.p.

Dennis, Philip A. 1981. The Costeños and the Revolution in Nicaragua. *Journal of Interamerican Studies and World Affairs* 23(3):271-96.

— — —. 1982. Coronation on the Miskito Coast. *Geographical Magazine* 54(1):392-95.

Dennis, Philip A., and Michael D. Olien. 1984. Kingship Among the Miskitos. *American Ethnologist* 11:718-37.

Diario de Centro América. 1945-1950. Guatemala.

Diario de sesiones de la comisión de los quince encargada de elaborar el projecto de constitución de la república. 1953. Guatemala: Tipografía Nacional.

Dickey, Christopher. 1983. Central America: From Quagmire to Cauldron? *Foreign Affairs* 62(3):659-94.

Die Deutschen in Lateinamerika: Schicksal und Leistung. 1979. Ed. Harmut Fröschle. Tübingen: Horst Erdmann Verlag.

Diederich, Bernard. 1981. *Somoza and the Legacy of U.S. Involvement in Central America*. New York: E. P. Dutton.

Dinwoodie, David. 1966. Expedient Diplomacy: The United States and Guatemala, 1898-1920. Ph.D. diss., Univ. of Colorado, Boulder.

Dion, Marie Berthe. 1958. *Las ideas sociales y políticas de Arévalo*, 2d ed. México: América Nueva.

Doerries, Reinhard R. 1973. Amerikanische Aussenpolitik im Karibischen Raum vor dem Ersten Weltkrieg. *Jahrbuch für Amerikastudien* 18:62-77.

Dombrowski, John, et al. 1970. *Area Handbook for Guatemala*. Washington: GPO.

Dore, Elizabeth. 1985. Culture. In *Nicaragua in Revolution*, ed. T. W. Walker, 413-22. New York: Praeger.

Dorfman, Ariel. 1972. *Para leer el pato Donald: comunicación de masa y colonialismo*. México: Siglo XXI.

— — —. 1983. *The Empire's Old Clothes: What the Lone Ranger, Babar, and Other Innocent Heroes Do to Our Minds*. New York: Pantheon.

Dozier, Craig L. 1985. *Nicaragua's Mosquito Shore: The Years of British and American Presence*. University, Ala.: Univ. of Alabama Press.

DZM. Deutsches Zentralarchiv, Merseburg.

DZP. Deutsches Zentralarchiv, Potsdam.

Early, John D. 1975. Changing Proportion of Maya Indian and Ladino in Guatemala, 1945-1969. *American Ethnologist* 2:261-69.

— — —. 1982. A Demographic Survey of Contemporary Guatemalan Maya: Some Methodological Implications for Anthropological Research. In

Heritage of Conquest: Thirty Years Later, ed. Carl Kendall and John Hawkins, 73-99. Albuquerque: Univ. of New Mexico Press.

Edelmen, Marc. 1985. Back from the Brink. *NACLA Report on the Americas* 19(6):37-46.

Eighth Special Forces Group (Airborne), 1st Special Forces. n.d. *Special Action Force for Latin America: Historical Report*. Carlisle Barracks, Pa.: U.S. Army Military History Institute.

El Centroamericano. 1937. León, Nicaragua.

El Diario Nicaragüense. 1927-1931. Granada, Nicaragua.

Ellis, Keith. 1974. *Critical Approaches to Rubén Darío*. Toronto: Univ. of Toronto Press.

Engelsing, Rolf. 1973. *Sozial- und Wirtschaftsgeschichte Deutschlands*. Göttingen: Vandenhoeck & Ruprecht.

English, Adrian J. 1984. *Armed Forces of Latin America*. London: Jane's.

English, Burt L. 1971. *Liberación Nacional in Costa Rica*. Gainesville: Univ. of Florida Press.

Enguidanos, Miguel. 1970. "Inner Tensions in the Work of Rubén Darío. In *Rubén Darío Centennial Studies*, ed. M. González-Gerth and G. D. Schade, 13-29. Austin: Univ. of Texas Press.

Envio. 1986-1987. Managua.

Episcopado de Honduras. 1933. *Tercera carta pastoral colectiva del episcopado de Honduras sobre el año santo*. Tegucigalpa.

Etchison, Don L. 1975. *The United States and Militarism in Central America*. New York: Praeger.

Eusebe, Christine. 1972. Les investissements francais en Amérique centrale et dans l'aire des caraïbes. Mémoire de maîtrise, Université de Paris X (Nanterre).

Everitt, John C. 1984. The Recent Migrations of Belize, Central America. *International Migration Review* 18:319-25.

Fagen, Richard, and Olga Pellicer, eds. 1983. *The Future of Central America: Policy Choices for the U.S. and Mexico*. Stanford: Stanford Univ. Press.

Falla, Ricardo. 1980. *Quiché Rebelde*. Guatemala: Editorial Universitaria.

Fanon, Frantz. 1961. On National Culture. In *The Wretched of the Earth*, 206-48. New York: Grove.

Farer, T. J. 1985. Contadora: The Hidden Agenda. *Foreign Policy* 59:59-72.

Feinberg, Richard E., ed. 1982. *Central America: International Dimensions of the Crisis*. New York: Holmes & Meier.

Feierabend, Ivo, et al., eds. 1972. *Anger, Violence, and Politics: Theories and Research*. Englewood Cliffs, N.J.: Prentice-Hall.

Feustle, Joseph A., Jr. 1976. La muerte: la deseada-deseante de Rubén Darío. *Anales de literatura hispanoamericana* 5:493-98.

Fiallos Gil, Mariano. 1965. Los primeros pasos de la Reforma Universitaria en Nicaragua. *Ventana* 2 (July):59.

Findling, John. 1987. *Close Neighbors, Distant Friends: United States-Central American Relations*. Westport, Conn.: Greenwood Press.

Fitzpatrick, Sheila. 1970. *The Commissariat of Enlightenment: Soviet Organization of Education and the Arts Under Lunacharsky, October 1917-1921*. Cambridge: Harvard Univ. Press.

Floyd, Troy S. 1967. *The Anglo-Spanish Struggle for Mosquitia*. Albuquerque: Univ. of New Mexico Press.

Forster, Merlin H. 1975. *Tradition and Renewal: Essays on Twentieth-Century Latin American Literature and Culture*. Urbana: Univ. of Illinois Press.

Fowler, William R. 1985. Ethnohistoric Sources on the Pipil-Nicaro of Central America: A Critical Analysis. *Ethnohistory* 32:37-62.

Francis, Martin. 1985. The Catacomob Honduran Church Now Faces a New Gladiator: U.S. Militarization. *Honduras Update* 3(12):4-5.

Franco, Jean. 1970. *The Modern Culture of Latin America: Society and the Artist*. Rev. ed. Harmondsworth: Penguin.

Frank Leslie's Illustrated Newspaper. 1856-1857. New York.

Frank, André Gunder. 1969. *Essays on the Development of Underdevelopment and the Immediate Enemy*. New York: Monthly Review.

Frank, Luisa, and Philip Wheaton. 1984. *Indian Guatemala: The Path to Liberation*. Washington: EPICA Task Force.

Frankel, Anita. 1969. Political Development in Guatemala, 1944-1954: The Impact of Foreign, Military, and Religious Elites. Ph.D. diss., Univ. of Connecticut, Storrs.

Freye, Alton. 1967. *Nazi Germany and the American Hemisphere, 1933-1941*. New Haven: Yale Univ. Press.

FRUS. *See* U.S. Department of State. *Papers relating to the Foreign Relations of the United States...*

FSLN. 1968. *Poesía Revolucionaria Nicaragüense*. México: Costa-Amic.

Funes de Torres, Lucila. 1984. *Los derechos humanos en Honduras*. Tegucigalpa: Centro de Documentación de Honduras.

Gaddis, John Lewis. 1982. *Strategies of Containment: A Critical Appraisal of Postwar National Security Policy*. New York: Oxford Univ. Press.

Galeano, Eduardo. 1981. La revolulción como revelación. *Nicaráuac* 2(6):109-14.

Galich, Manuel. 1977. *Del pánico al ataque*. 2d ed. Guatemala: Editorial Universitaria.

Gámez, José D. 1939. *Historia de la Costa de Mosquitos*. Managua: Talleres Nacionales.

GDC. Grenada Document Collection, U.S. National Archives, Washington.

Gellman, Irwin. 1979. *Good Neighbor Diplomacy: The United States in Latin America 1933-1945*. Baltimore: Johns Hopkins Univ. Press

Gil, Federico. 1976. United States-Latin American Relations in the Mid-70s. *SECOLAS Annals* 7:5-19.

Gillin, John. 1951. *The Culture of Security in San Carlos*. New Orleans: Middle American Research Institute, Tulane Univ.

– – –. 1957. San Luis Jilotepeque: 1942-55. In *Political Changes in Guatemalan Communities*, ed. R. N. Adams, 23-27. New Orleans: Middle American Research Institute, Tulane Univ.

Gilly, Adolfo. 1965. The Guerrilla Movement in Guatemala. *Monthly Review* 17(1):9-40; 17(2):7-40.

Girard, Augustine. 1972. *Cultural Development: Experience and Politics*. Paris: UNESCO.

González, Pedro. 1949. Review of Salinas 1948. *Hispanic Review* 17:260-63.

González-Gerth, Miguel, and George D. Schade, eds. 1970. *Rubén Darío Centennial Studies*. Austin: Univ. of Texas Press.

Gott, Richard. 1971. *Guerrilla Movements in Latin America*. Garden City: Doubleday.

Grabendorff, Wolfe. 1978. Mexico's Foreign Policy, Indeed a Foreign Policy. *Journal of Interamerican Studies* 20(1):85-92.

Graebner, Norman A. 1985. *Foundations of American Foreign Policy: A Realist Appraisal From Franklin to McKinley*. Wilmington: Scholarly Resources.

Grant, C. H. 1976. *The Making of Modern Belize*. Cambridge: Cambridge Univ. Press.

Great Britain, Foreign Office. 1881. *Nicaragua #1 (Arbitration of the Mosquito Coast)*. London: Foreign Office.

Grieb, Kenneth J. 1970. American Involvement in the Rise of Jorge Ubico. *Caribbean Studies* 10(1):5-21.

— — —. 1971. The United States and the Rise of General Maximiliano Hernandez Martinez. *Journal of Latin American Studies* 3(3):151-72

— — —. 1977. *The Latin American Policy of Warren G. Harding*. Fort Worth, Texas Christian Univ.

— — —. 1979. *Guatemalan Caudillo: The Regime of Jorge Ubico: Guatemala, 1931-1944*. Athens: Ohio Univ. Press.

Grunberg, Georg. 1981. Las Nacionalidades de la coast Atlántica de Nicaragua en la Revolución Sandinista. *Revista Mexicana de Ciencias Políticas y Sociales* 27(103):33-35.

GSPK. Geheims Staatsarchiv Preussischer Kulturbesitz, Berlin.

Guardia de Alfaro, Gloria. 1971. *Estudio sobre el pensamiento poético de Pablo Antonio Cuadra*. Madrid: Editorial Gredos.

Guatemala. Asamblea Nacional Constituyente. 1945. *Constitución de la República de Guatemala decretada y sancionada por la Asamblea Nacional Constituyente el 11 de Marzo de 1945*. Guatemala: El Imparcial.

— — —. Asamblea Nacional Constituyente. 1951. *Asamblea Constituyente 1945. Diario de sesiones*. Guatemala: Comisión de Régimen Interior del Congreso de la República de 1949.

— — —. Junta Revolucionario de Gobierno. 1945a. *Mensaje de la Junta Revolucionaria de Gobierno a la Asamblea Nacional Legislativa al abrir esta sus sesiones ordinarias el 1 de marzo de 1945*. Guatemala: Tipografía Nacional.

— — —. Junta Revolucionario de Gobierno. 1945b. *Legislación revolucionaria: decretos emitidos por la Junta Revolucionaria de Gobierno*. Guatemala: Unión Tipográfica.

— — —. Ministerio de Gobernación. 1947. *Ley de emisión del pensamiento por medios de difusión*. Guatemala: Tipografía Nacional.

Gudmundson, Lowell. 1986. *Costa Rica Before Coffee: Society and Economy on the Eve of the Export Boom*. Baton Rouge: Louisiana State Univ. Press.

Guillén, Pedro. 1966. Las relaciones de México con Centroamérica. *Cuadernos Americanos* 4 (July-August):36-43.

Gumucio Dragón, Alfonso. 1982. Cine obrero sandinista. *Plural* 11 (2a época, July):35-40.

Gutiérrez, Ernesto. 1970. *Pol - la d'anata katanta paranta: imitaciones y traducciones*. León: Universiad Nacional Autónoma de Nicaragua.

Hackett, Charles. 1924. The Background of the Revolution in Honduras. *Review of Reviews* 69(4) (April):390-96.

— — —. 1928. Success of Lindbergh's Good-Will Mission to Mexico. *Current History* 27(5):727-29.

Hagan, Kenneth J. 1973. *American Gunboat Diplomacy, 1877 -1889*. Westport, Conn.: Greenwood Press.

Haglund, David G. 1984. *Latin America and the Transformation of U.S. Strategic Thought, 1936-1940*. Albuquerque: Univ. of New Mexico Press.

Hagopian, Mark N. 1974. *The Phenomenon of Revolution*. New York: Harper & Row.

Halborn, Hajo. 1959-1969. *A History of Modern Germany*. 3 vols. New York: Knopf.

Hamburger Nachrichten. 1925.

Hamilton, William H. 1975. Mexico's *New* Foreign Policy: A Reexamination. *Inter-American Economic Affairs* 29(3):51-58.

Handy, Jim. 1984. *Gift of the Devil: A History of Guatemala*. Boston: South End.

Hausherr, Hans. 1966. Der Zollverein und die Industrialisierung. In *Moderne deutsche Wirtschaftsgeschichte*, ed. Karl E. Born, 55-66. Köln: Kiepenheuer & Witsch.

Hayes, Margaret Daly. 1982. The Crisis in Central America and U.S. Policy Options. *Current* 245(9):73-84.

— — —. 1984. *Latin American and the U.S. National Interest*. Boulder: Westview.

Healy, Paul F. 1980. *Archaeology of the Rivas Region, Nicaragua*. Ontario: Wilfrid Laurier Univ.

Hellman, Ronald G., and H. Jon Rosenbaum, eds. 1975. *Latin America: The Search for a New International Role*. New York: Wiley.

Helms, Mary W. 1969. The Cultural Ecology of a Colonial Tribe. *Ethnology* 8(1):76-84.

— — —. 1971. *Asang: Adaptations to Culture Contact in a Miskito Community*. Gainesville: Univ. of Florida Press.

— — —. 1975. *Middle America: A Culture History of Heartlands and Frontiers*. Englewood Cliffs, N.J.: Prentice-Hall.

– – –. 1977. Negro or Indian? The Changing Identity of a Frontier Population. In *Old Roots in New Lands*, ed. Ann Pescatello, 157-72. Westport, Conn: Greenwood Press.

– – –. 1978. Coastal Adaptations as Contact Phenomena Among the Miskito and Cuna Indians of Lower Central America. In *Prehistoric Coastal Adaptation*, eds. B. Stark and B. Voorhies, 121-49. New York: Academic Press.

– – –. 1983. Misquito Slaving and Culture Contact: Ethnicity and Opportunity in an Expanding Population. *Journal of Anthropological Research* 39(2):179-97.

– – –. 1986. Of Kings and Contexts: Ethnohistorical Interpretations of Miskito Political Structure and Function. *American Ethnologist* 13:506-23.

Henao, Luis A. 1972. Letter to *El Día* (Tegucigalpa), February. In J. R. Amador Amador, Los sucesos de la Talanquera enfocados por la prensa hondureña, 5-11. Thesis, Universidad Nacional Autónoma de Honduras, Tegucigalpa.

Henderson, Galvin B. 1944. German Colonial Projects on the Mosquito Coast, 1844-1848. *The English Historical Review* 56:257-71.

Henderson, W. O. 1975. *The Rise of German Industrial Power, 1834-1914*. Berkeley: Univ. of California Press.

Herrera Zúñiga, René, and Mario Ojeda. 1983. La política de México en la región Centroamérica. *Foro Internacional* 23(4):423-40.

Herwig, H. H., and N. M. Heyman, eds. 1982. *Biographical Dictionary of World War I*. Westport, Conn.: Greenwood Press.

Hinshaw, Robert. 1975. *Panajachel: A Guatemalan Town in Thirty Year Perspective*. Pittsburgh: Univ. of Pittsburgh Press.

Hirshon, Sheryl, and Judy Butler. 1983. *And Also Teach Them to Read*. Westport, Conn.: Lawrence Hill.

Hobsbawm, Eric, and Terrence Ranger, eds. 1983. *The Invention of Tradition*. London: Cambridge Univ. Press.

Hoffer, Eric. 1951. *The True Believer: Thoughts on the Nature of Mass Movements*. New York: Harper & Row.

Hofstadter, Richard. 1959. *Social Darwinism in American Thought*. Rev. ed. New York: G. Braziller.

Holleran, Mary P. 1949. *Church and State in Guatemala*. New York: Columbia Univ. Press.

Holm, John Alexander. 1978. The Creole English of Nicaragua's Miskito Coast: Its Sociolinguistic History and a Comparative Study of Its Lexicon and Syntax. Ph.D. diss., Univ. of London, London.

Hooker, Ray. 1985. Problems of the Atlantic Coast. In *Nicaragua: The Sandinista People's Revolution – Speeches by Sandinista Leaders*, ed. B. Marcus, 86-94. New York: Pathfinder.

Horn, James J. 1973. Did the U.S. Plan an Invasion of Mexico in 1927? *Journal of Inter-American Studies* 15(4):466-77.

Howard, Alan. 1966. With the Guerrillas in Guatemala. *New York Times Magazine*, June 26:8-9.

Howarth, David. 1966. *Panama: 400 Years of Dream and Cruelty*. New York: McGraw-Hill.

Howe, George F. 1937. The Clayton Bulwer Treaty. *American Historical Review* 42:484-90.

Hughes, Charles Evans. n.d. Papers. Period of International Activity, "Latin American Conferences," Library of Congress, Washington, D.C.

Humphries, R. A. 1981. *Latin America and the Second World War*. 2 vols. London: Univ. of London Institute for Latin American Studies.

Immerman, Richard H. 1982. *The CIA in Guatemala: The Foreign Policy of Intervention*. Austin: Univ. of Texas Press.

Instituto de Estudio del Sandinismo. 1982. *Porqué viven siempre entre nosotros: héroes y mártires de la insurreción popular sandinista en Masaya*. Managua: Nueva Nicaragua.

Instituto Histórico Centroamericano. 1986. Miskitos on the Rio Coco: Whose Political Football Are They? *Envio* 5(59):15-27.

Jamail, Milton. 1984. Belize: Will Independence Mean New Dependence? *NACLA Report on the Americas* 18(4):13-16.

James, Daniel. 1954. *Red Design for the Americas: Guatemalan Prelude*. New York: John Day.

Jenkins, Brian, and Caesar Sereseres. 1977. U.S. Military Assistance and the Guatemalan Armed Forces. *Armed Forces and Society* 3(4):575-94.

Jiménez, Marya. 1983. *Poesía de la nueva Nicaragua: talleres populares de poesía*. México: Siglo XXI.

Johnson, Kenneth. 1972. Guatemala: From Terrorism to Terror. *Conflict Studies* (23)(May):8-9.

— — —. 1973. On the Guatemalan Political Violence. *Politics and Society* 4(1):55-82.

Johnson, Kent, ed. 1985a. *A Nation of Poets: Writings from the Poetry Workshops of Nicaragua*. Los Angeles: West End.

— — —, ed. 1985b. *Poems from the Sandinista Workshops in Nicaragua*. San Rafael, Calif.: West End.

Jonas, Susanne, and David Tobis, eds. 1974. *Guatemala*. Berkeley, Calif.: North American Congress on Latin America.

Jones, C. L. 1940. *Guatemala Past and Present*. Minneapolis: Univ. of Minnesota Press.

Jones, Howard. 1985. *The Course of American Diplomacy*. New York: Franklin Watts.

Jones, Wilbur. 1974. *The American Problem in British Diplomacy, 1841-1861*. Athens: Univ. of Georgia Press.

Jrade, Cathy L. 1980. Rubén Darío and the Oneness of the Universe. *Hispania* 63:691-98.

— — —. 1983. *Rubén Darío and the Romantic Search for Unity: The Modern Recourse to Esoteric Tradition*. Austin: Univ. of Texas Press.

Kamman, William. 1968. *A Search for Stability: U.S. Diplomacy toward Nicaragua, 1925-1933*. Notre Dame: Notre Dame Univ. Press.

Kasson, John A. 1881. European Danger to the Americas. *North American Review* (December):523.

Kaye, Harvey. 1975. How *New* Is Mexico's Foreign Policy? *Inter-American Economic Affairs* 28(4):87-92.

Kemp, Tom. 1972. *The French Economy, 1913-1939: The History of Decline.* London: Longman.

Kesaris, Paul L., ed. 1981. *Operation ZAPATA: The "Ultrasensitive" Report and Testimony of the Board of Inquiry on the Bay of Pigs.* Classified Studies in Twentieth-Century Diplomatic and Military History Series. Frederick, Md.: University Publications of America.

Kesaris, Paul L., and Joan Gibson, eds. 1980. *Minutes of Telephone Conversations of John Foster Dulles and Christian Herter.* Frederick, Md.: University Publications of America.

Kidd, Ross. 1983. A Testimony from Nicaragua: An Interview with Nidia Bustos, the Coordinator of MECATE, the Nicaraguan Farm Workers' Theatre Movement. *Studies in Latin American Popular Culture* 2:190-201.

King, Arden. 1974. *Cobán and Verapaz: History and Cultural Process in Northern Guatemala.* New Orleans: Middle American Research Institute, Tulane Univ.

King, Emory. 1980. The Five Percent Solution: How the PUP Committed the Uncommitted. *Brukdown* (1):5-10.

Kinzer, Stephen. 1987. Stranded by Politics and War: Nicaragua's Loved, Neglected Poet. *New York Times Book Review*, January 18:3.

Kohan, J. 1983. Speak Softly or Carry a Big Stick. *Time* 122 (August 29):28-29.

Kortge, Dean. 1973. The Central American Policy of Lord Palmerston, 1855-1865. Ph.D. diss., Univ. of Kansas, Lawrence.

Kossok, Manfred. 1964. *Im Schatten der Heiligen Allianz: Deutschland und Lateinamerika 1815-1830. Zur Politik der Deutschen Staaten gegenüber der Unabhängigkeitsbewegung Mittel- und Südamerikas.* Berlin: Academie Verlag.

Krepinevich, Andrew Krepinevich, Jr. 1986. *The Army and Vietnam.* Baltimore: Johns Hopkins Univ. Press.

Krueger, Chris, and Kjell Enge. 1985. *Security and Development Conditions in the Guatemalan Highlands.* Washington, D.C.: Washington Office on Latin America.

Krueger, Chris, and Carol Smith. 1983. Interim Report of the Advisory Panel on Guatemala. *Anthropology Newsletter* 24(8):20-24.

Kühlmann, Richard. 1948. *Erinnerungen.* Heidelberg: Lambert Schneider.

Kuhn, Joachim. 1969. Napoleon III und der Nicaraguakanal. *Historische Zeitschrift* 208:295-319.

Kunzle, David. 1983. Nationalist, Internationalist and Anti-Imperialist Themes in the Public Revolutionary Art of Cuba, Chile and Nicaragua. *Studies in Latin American Popular Culture* 2:141-57.

La Chacalaca. 1982. Managua.

LaFarge, Oliver, and Douglas Byers. 1931. *The Yearbearer's People*. New Orleans: Middle American Research Institute, Tulane Univ.

— — —. 1947. *Santa Eulalia*. Chicago: Univ. of Chicago Press.

LaFeber, Walter. 1963. *New Empire: An Interpretation of American Expansion, 1860-1898*. Ithaca: Cornell Univ. Press.

— — —. 1978. *The Panama Canal*. New York: Oxford Univ. Press.

— — —. 1982. Inevitable Revolutions. *The Atlantic Monthly*, June:74-83.

— — —. 1983. *Inevitable Revolutions: The United States and Central America*. New York: Norton.

Lafond, Gabriel. 1856. *Notice sur le Golfo Dulce dans l'état de Costa Rica ...et sur un nouveau passage entre les deux océans*. Paris: Fontaine.

La fortune française è l'étranger. 1902. *Bulletin de Statistique et de législation comparée* 26 (October):450-83.

Lange, Frederick W., and Doris Z. Stone. 1984. *The Archaeology of Lower Central America*. Albuquerque: School of American Research, Univ. of New Mexico.

Langley, Lester D. 1976. *Struggle for The American Mediterranean: United States-European Rivalry in the Gulf-Caribbean Region 1776-1904.*. Athens: Univ. of Georgia Press.

— — —. 1980 *The United States and the Caribbean 1900-1970*. Athens: Univ. of Georgia.

La Noticia. 1934, 1940. Managua.

La Prensa. 1956, 1979. Managua.

Latin American Monitor: 2. Central America. 1986. 3(4), May.

Leiken, Robert S., ed. 1984. *Central America: Anatomy of Conflict*. New York: Pergamon.

Lenin, V.I. 1979. *The Right of Nations to Self Determination*. Moscow: Progress Publishers.

Leonard, Thomas M. 1982a. *U.S. Policy and Arms Limitation in Central America: The Washington Conference of 1923*. Occasional Paper Series. Los Angeles: Center for the Study of Armament and Disarmament, California State Univ.

— — —. 1982b. The United States and Costa Rica, 1944-1949: Perceptions of Political Dynamics. *Annals of the Southeastern Council on Latin American Studies* 13:17-31.

— — —. 1984. *The United States and Central America, 1944-1949: Perceptions of Political Dynamics*. University, Ala.: Univ. of Alabama Press.

— — —. 1985. *Decline of the Recognition Policy in United States-Central American Relations, 1933-1949*. Occasional Papers Series. Miami: Latin American and Caribbean Center, Florida International Univ.

Levinson, Jerome, and Juan de Onís. 1972. *The Alliance That Lost Its Way: A Critical Report on the Alliance for Progress*. Chicago: Quadrangle.

Levy, Raphael-Georges. 1897. Les capitaux français è l'étranger. *Revue des Deux Mondes*, March 15:415-45.

Lieuwen, Edwin. 1956. *Arms and Politics in Latin America*. New York: Praeger.

Lincoln, Jackson S. n.d. An Ethnological Study of the Ixil Indians of the Guatemala Highlands. Univ. of Chicago Library, Microfilm Collection on Middle American Cultural Anthropology, No. 1.

Lincoln, Jennie K. 1985. Neutrality Costa Rican Style. *Current History* 84(500):118-36.

Liss, Sheldon B. 1984. *Marxist Thought in Latin America.* Berkeley: Univ. of California Press.

Llopesa, Ricardo. 1982. Sabiduría, profecia y cólera en la poesía de Pablo Antonio Cuadra. *Insula* (Madrid) 37(425):13.

Lockey, Joseph B. 1930. Diplomatic Futility. *Hispanic American Historical Review* 30:265-94.

López Portillo, José. 1982. Discurso del Lic. José López Portillo, presidente de México al ser condecorado por el gobierno de Nicaragua. *Revista del Pensamiento Centroamericano* 37(175):105-8.

Macaulay, Neill. 1967. *The Sandino Affair.* Chicago: Quadrangle.

MacCameron, Robert. 1983. *Bananas, Labor, and Politics in Honduras: 1954-1963.* Syracuse: Maxwell School of Citizenship and Public Affairs, Syracuse Univ.

Mack, Gerstle. 1944. *The Land Divided, A History of the Panama Canal and Other Isthmian Projects.* New York: Knopf.

Madrid, Miguel de la. 1984. Mexico: The New Challenges. *Foreign Affairs* 63(1):62-76.

Magnus, Richard Wener. 1974. The Prehistory of the Miskito Coast of Nicaragua: A Study in Cultural Relationships. Ph.D. Diss., Yale Univ., New Haven, Conn.

Maier, Elizabeth. 1980. Mujeres, contradicciones y revolución. *Estudios Sociales Centroamericanos* 27 (September-December):129-39.

Mann, Thomas C. 1964. Democratic Ideal in Our Policy Toward Latin America. *U.S. State Department Bulletin,* June 29:995-1000.

Manning, William R. 1925. *Diplomatic Correspondence of the United States.* Vol. 2. New York: Oxford Univ. Press.

— — —. 1933. *Diplomatic Correspondence of the United States.* Vol. 3. Washington: Carnegie Endowment for International Peace.

Marchetti, Victor, and John D. Marks. 1974. *The CIA and the Cult of Intelligence.* New York: Knopf.

Marcus, Bruce, ed. 1982. *Sandinistas Speak: Speeches, Writings, and Interviews with Leaders of Nicaragua's Revolutions.* New York: Pathfinder.

— — —, ed. 1985. *Nicaragua: The Sandinista People's Revolution — Speeches by Sandinista Leaders.* New York: Pathfinder.

Marks, Frederick W. 1979. *Velvet on Iron: The Diplomacy of Theodore Roosevelt.* Lincoln: Univ. of Nebraska Press.

Marroquín Rojas, Clemente. 1945. *Crónicas de la Constituyente del 45.* Guatemala: La Hora Dominical.

Martin, Edward E. 1963. U.S. Policy Regarding Military Governments in Latin America. *U.S. State Department Bulletin,* November 4:698-700.

Martin, Percy A. 1925. *Latin America and the War*. 2 vols. Baltimore: Johns Hopkins Univ. Press.

Mathews, Jane DeHart. 1975. Arts and the People: The New Deal Quest for Cultural Democracy. *Journal of American History* 62:316-39.

Maurer, Harry. 1976. The Priests of Honduras. *Nation*, March 6:266-69.

Maurice Bishop — Premier in the Spotlight. 1979. *Caribbean Life and Times* 1(2):11-15.

May, Jacques M., and Donna L. McLellan. 1972. *The Ecology of Malnutrition in Mexico and Central America*. New York: Hafner.

McClintock, Michael. 1985. *The American Connection*. Vol. 2, *State Terror and Popular Resistance in Guatemala*. London: ZED.

McCreery, David J. 1986. "An Odious Feudalism": Mandamiento Labor and Commercial Agriculture in Guatemala, 1858-1920. *Latin American Perspectives* 31(1):99-117.

McCullough, David. 1977. *Path Between the Seas: The Creation of the Panama Canal 1870-1914*. New York: Simon and Schuster.

McNickle, D'Arcy. 1971. *Indian Man*. Bloomington: Indiana Univ. Press.

McPhail, Thomas L. 1981. *Electronic Colonialism: The Future of International Broadcasting and Communications*. Beverly Hills: Sage.

Mecham, J. Lloyd. 1963. *The United States and Inter-American Security, 1889-1960*. Austin: Univ. of Texas Press.

Medina Luna, Ramón. 1974. Proyección de México sobre Centroamérica, *Foro Internacional* (April-June):438-73.

Mejía, Medardo. 1949. *El movimiento obrero en la revolución de Octubre*. Guatemala: Tipografía Nacional.

Mejía Sánchez, Ernesto, ed. 1980. *Nuestro Rubén Darío*. Managua: Ministerio de Cultura.

Melville, Thomas, and Marjorie Melville. 1971. *Whose Heaven, Whose Earth?*. New York: Knopf.

Menon, P. K. 1979. The Anglo-Guatemalan Territorial Dispute over the Colony of Belize (British Honduras). *Journal of Latin American Studies* 2:343-71.

Merida, Kevin. 1985. Ripe for Harvest. *Dallas Morning News*, 7 October.

Mesoamérica. 1985-1986. San José, Costa Rica.

Meza, Bernardo. 1982. *Padre Iván Betancur: Mártir de la Iglesia Latinoamericana*. Tegucigalpa: Editora Cultural.

Meza, Víctor. 1981. *Historia del movimiento obrero hondureño*. Tegucigalpa: Guaymuras.

Miami Herald. 1983.

Miceli, Keith. 1974. Rafael Carrera: Defender and Promoter of Peasant Interests in Guatemala, 1837-1848. *The Americas* 31:72-95.

Millett, Richard. 1977. *Guardians of the Dynasty*. Maryknoll, N.Y.: Orbis.

— — —. 1980. Central American Paralysis. *Foreign Policy* 49(3):99-117.

— — —. 1986. Guatemala's Painful Progress. *Current History* 85(Dec):413-416, 435-36.

Mission Letter. 1986. Parish of St. Ann, Campamento, Olancho, Honduras, February.

Mitchell, John J., Jr. 1985. Embracing a Socialist Vision: The Evolution of Catholic Social Thought, Leo XIII to John Paul II. *Journal of Church and State* 27:465-81.

Molineu, Harold. 1986. *U.S. Policy Toward Latin America*. Boulder: Westview.

Molyneux, Maxine. 1985. Women. In *Nicaragua in Revolution*, ed. T. W. Walker, 145-62. New York: Praeger.

Montgomery, Tommie Sue. 1982. *Revolution in El Salvador: Origins and Evolution*. Boulder: Westview.

Moore, John B., ed. 1911. *The Works of James Buchannan: Comprising His Speeches, State Papers and Private Correspondence*. Vols. 9-10. Philadelphia: Lippincott.

Morales Avilés, Ricardo. 1981. *Obras*. Managua: Nueva Nicaragua.

Morris, Nancy. 1986. Canto porque es necesario cantar: The New Song Movement in Chile, 1973-1983. *Latin American Research Review* 21:117-36.

Morrison, DeLesseps. 1962. The U.S. Position on OAS Consideration of Coups d'Etat. *U.S. State Department Bulletin*, October 6:439-541.

Mulcahy, Kevin V., and C. Richard Swaim, eds. 1982. *Public Policy and the Arts*. Boulder: Westview.

Muller, Gene A. 1981. The Church in Poverty: Bishops, Bourbons, and Tithes in Spanish Honduras, 1700-1821. Ph.D. diss., Univ. of Kansas, Lawrence.

Munro, Dana G. 1958. Dollar Diplomacy in Nicaragua, 1909-1913. *Hispanic American Historical Review* 38:209-34.

— — —. [1964] 1980. *Intervention and Dollar Diplomacy in the Caribbean 1900-1921*. Westport, Conn.: Greenwood Press.

— — —. 1974. *The United States and the Caribbean Republics, 1921-1933*. Princeton: Princeton Univ. Press.

Muravchik, Joshua. 1987. The Nicaragua Debate. *Foreign Affairs* 65(2):366-82.

Murillo-Jiménez, Hugo. 1978. Wilson and Tinoco: The United States and the Policy of Non-Recognition in Costa Rica, 1917-1919. Ph.D. diss., Univ. of California, San Diego.

Murguía, Alejandro, and Barbara Paschke, eds. 1983. *Volcán: Poems from Central America*. San Francisco: City Lights Books.

Myers, David. 1986. Costa Rica: Arias Challenges Reagan's Nicaragua Policy. *Latinamerica Press* 18(17) (May 8):1-2.

Nairn, Allan, and Jean-Marie Simon. 1986. Bureaucracy of Death. *The New Republic*, June 30:13-17.

Nash, Manning. 1967. *Machine Age Maya: Industrialization of a Guatemalan Community*. Chicago: Univ. of Chicago Press.

National Security Council. 1964. Survey of Latin America, April 1. In Lyndon Baines Johnson Presidential Library, Austin, Texas.

Naylor, Robert A. 1960. The British Role in Central America Prior to the Clayton-Bulwer Treaty. *Hispanic American Historical Review* 40:361-82.

Nelson, A. 1980. Central American Powderkeg, What Role for the United States. *Current* 228(12) (December):34-43.

Nelson, Harold D., ed. 1983. *Costa Rica: A Country Study.* Washington: GPO.

New York Times, 1909, 1929, 1960, 1979-1986.

Newbold, Stokes [Richard N. Adams]. 1956. Receptivity to Communist Fomented Agitation in Rural Guatemala. *Economic Development and Cultural Change* 5(4):338-60.

Newson, Linda. 1982. The Depopulation of Nicaragua in the Sixteenth Century. *Journal of Latin American Studies* 14:253-86.

Nicaráuac. 1980-1981. Managua.

Nietschmann, Bernard. 1974. *Caribbean Edge: The Coming of Modern Times to Isolated People and Wildlife.* Indianapolis: Bobbs-Merrill.

— — —. 1980. When the Turtle Collapses, the World Ends. *Caribbean Review* 9(2):14-21.

— — —. 1984. The Unreported War Against the Sandinistas. *Policy Review* 29:32-40.

Nilsson, Nils G. 1980. *Swedish Cultural Policy in the 20th Century.* Stockholm: Swedish Institute.

Nissen, Beth. 1983. The Rhetoric and the Reality. *Newsweek* 102 (August 5):28.

Nouailhat, Yves-Henri. 1982. *Évolution économique des états-unis du milieu du xix<e> siècle á 1914.* Paris: SEDES.

Nyrop, Richard, ed. 1983. *Guatemala: A Country Study.* Washington: Department of the Army.

Oakes, Maud. 1951. *The Two Crosses of Todos Santos.* Princeton: Princeton Univ. Press, Bolligen Series.

O'Connor, Suzanne M. 1976. Costa Rica in the World Community of Nations, 1919-1939: A Case Study in Latin American Internationalism. Ph.D. diss., Loyola Univ. of Chicago.

Ohland, Klaudine, and Robin Schneider, eds. 1983. *National Revolution and Indigenous Identity: The Conflict Between Sandinistas and Miskito Indians on Nicaragua's Atlantic Coast* (WGIA Document No. 47). Copenhagen: International Work Group for Indigenous Affairs.

Ojeda, Mario. 1983. Mexican Policy Toward Central America in the Context of U.S.-Mexican Relations. In *The Future of Central America: Policy Choices for the U.S. and Mexico,* ed. R. Fagen and O. Pellicer, 135-160. Stanford: Stanford Univ. Press.

Olien, Michael D. 1983. The Miskito Kings and the Line of Succession. *Journal of Anthropological Research* 39:198-241.

— — —. 1985. E. G. Squier and the Miskito: Anthropological Scholarship and Political Propaganda. *Ethnohistory* 32(2):111-13.

Ordoñez Argüello, Alberto, ed. 1951. *Arévalo visto por América.* Guatemala: Editorial del Ministerio de Educación Pública.

Organization of American States, Interamerican Commission on Human Rights. 1984. *Report on the Situation of Human Rights of a Segment of the Nicaraguan Population of Miskito Origin.* Washington: OAS.

Ortega Saavedra, Humberto. 1979. *50 años de lucha sandinista*. Managua: Ministerio del Interior.

Ortiz, Roxanne Dunbar. 1984. *Indians of the Americas: Human Rights and Self-Determination*. London: Zed.

— — —. 1986. Autonomy and the Atlantic Coast of Nicaragua. Unpublished paper.

Overmyer, Grace. 1939. *Government and the Arts*. New York: Norton.

Oviedo, José Miguel. 1982. Nicaragua: Voices in Conflict. *Review: Latin American Literature and Arts* 31 (January/April):20-23.

PAAA. Politisches Archiv des Auswärtigen Amts, Bonn.

Palacio, Joseph O. 1985. Recent Immigrants to Belize—A Challenge to Development, *Hemispheric Migration Project ICM and Center for Immigration Policy and Refugee Assistance*. Washington: Georgetown Univ.

Pansini, Jude. 1983. Indian Seasonal Plantation Work in Guatemala. *Cultural Survival Quarterly* 7:17-19.

Parks, E. Taylor. 1935. *Colombia and the United States*. Durham: Duke Univ. Press.

Partido Socialista Costarricense. 1984. *Costa Rica: entre la neutralidad y la guerra*. San José: Partido Socialista Costarricense.

Pastor, Robert A. 1987. *Condemned to Repetition: The United States and Nicaragua*. Princeton: Princeton Univ. Press.

Paz, Octavio. 1974. *Children of the Mire*. Trans. Rachel Philips. Cambridge, Mass.: Harvard Univ. Press.

Pearsall, Priscilla. 1984. *An Art Alienated from Itself: Studies in Spanish American Modernism*. University, Miss.: Romance Monographs.

Peckenham, Nancy, and Annie Street, eds. 1985. *Honduras: Portrait of a Captive Nation*. New York: Praeger.

Pellicer de Brody, Olga. 1972. Cambios recientes en la política exterior mexicana. *Foro internacional* (October-December):139-54.

Pellicer, Olga. 1981. Mexico's position. *Foreign Policy* 41:88-92.

— — —. 1983. Mexico in Central America: The Difficult Exercise of Regional Power. In *The Future of Central America: Policy Choices for the U.S. and Mexico*, ed. R. Fagen and O. Pellicer, 119-33. Stanford: Stanford Univ. Press.

Pincetl, Stanley J. 1968. France and the Clayton Bulwer Treaty of 1850. *Annales* 45:167-94.

Plauchut, Edmond. 1930. La Pénétration des Etats-Unis en Amérique Latine. *Revue des Deux Mondes*, October 15:840-63.

Poitras, Guy E. 1974. Mexico's "New" Foreign Policy. *Inter-American Economic Affairs* 28(3):59-77.

Polakowsky, Helmuth. 1943. Estación naval alemana en Costa Rica, 1883. *Revista de los Archivos Nacionales* 7:56-65.

Portes Gil, Emilio. 1954. *Quince años de política mexicana*. 3d ed. México: Ediciones Botas.

Posas, Mario. 1980. *Lucha ideológica y organización sindical en Honduras (1954-1965)*. Tegucigalpa: Guaymuras.

— — —. 1981a. *El movimiento campesino hondureño*. Tegucigalpa: Guaymuras.

— — —. 1981b. *Luchas del movimiento obrero hondureño*. San José: EDUCA.

Predmore, Michael P. 1971. A Stylistic Analysis of "Lo Fatal." *Hispanic Review* 39:433-38.

Prouty, Fletcher. 1973. *The Secret Team: The CIA and Its Allies in Control of the United States and the World*. Englewood Cliffs, N.J.: Prentice-Hall.

Purcell, Susan K. 1985. Demystifying Contadora. *Foreign Affairs* 64:74-95.

Radell, David R. 1969. An Historical Geography of Western Nicaragua: The Spheres of Influence of León, Granada, and Managua, 1519-1965. Ph.D. diss., Univ. of California, Berkeley.

— — —. 1976. The Indian Slave Trade and Population of Nicaragua During the Sixteenth Century. In *The Native Population of the Americas in 1492*, ed. W. M. Denevan. Madison: Univ. of Wisconsin Press.

Rama, Angel. 1973. *Rubén Darío: el mundo de los sueños*. San Juan: Editorial Universitaria.

Ramírez, John. 1984. Introduction to the Sandinista Documentary Cinema. *Areito* 10(37):18-21.

Ramírez, William. 1985. Today we Speak Naturally of Atlantic Coast Autonomy. In *Nicaragua: The Sandinista People's Revolution — Speeches by Sandinista Leaders*, ed. B. Marcus, 391-95. New York: Pathfinder.

Ramírez-Horton, Susan E. 1982. The Role of Women in the Nicaraguan Revolution. In *Nicaragua in Revolution*, ed. T. W. Walker, 147-60. New York: Praeger.

Ramírez Mercado, Sergio. 1971. *Mariano Fiallos: biografía*. León: Editorial Universitaria.

— — —. 1982. La Revolución: el hecho cultural más grande de nuestra historia. *Barricada Cultural: Ventana*, January 30:15-16.

— — —. 1984. *Augusto C. Sandino: el pensamiento vivo*. 2d ed., 2 vols. Managua: Nueva Nicaragua.

Randall, Margaret. 1981. *Sandino's Daughters*. Vancouver: New Star.

— — —. 1983a. *Christians in the Nicaraguan Revolution*. Vancouver: New Star.

— — —. 1983b. Conversando con Sergio Ramírez: "Hay aquí una fuerza centrífuga." *Barricada Cultural: Ventana*, July 19:7-12.

— — —. 1984. *Risking a Somersault in the Air: Conversations with Nicaraguan Writers*. San Francisco: Solidarity.

Raygada, Jorge. 1951. *Democracia en Guatemala: 20 de octubre de 1944 — 15 de marzo de 1951*. Guatemala: Imprenta Hispania.

Reagan, Ronald. 1983. Central America, Defending Our Vital Interests. In United States State Department, *Current Policy* (482) April 27.

Reding, Andrew. 1986a. Costa Rica: Democratic Model in Jeopardy. *World Policy Journal* 3(2) (Spring):301-15.

— — —. 1986b. Voices from Costa Rica: Interviews by Andrew Reding. *World Policy Journal* 3(2) (Spring):318-45.

Reina, Rubén. 1966. *The Law of the Saints: A Pokoman Pueblo and Its Community Culture*. New York: Bobbs-Merrill.

Reina Valenzuela, José. 1983. *Historia eclesiástica de Honduras, Tomo I: 1502-1600*. Tegucigalpa: Tipografía Nacional.

Revista del Ejército. 1964. Guatemala.

Revista del Pensamiento Centroamericano. 1960-1985. Managua.

Rey, Julio Adolfo. 1958. Revolution and Liberation: A Review of Recent Literature on the Guatemalan Situation. *Hispanic American Historical Review* 38:239-55.

Richards, Michael. 1985. Cosmopolitan World View and Counter-Insurgency in Guatemala. *Anthropological Quarterly* 58:90-107.

Riding, Alan. 1986. *Distant Neighbors: A Portrait of the Mexicans*. New York: Vintage.

Rippy, J. Fred. 1948. French Investments in Latin America. *Inter-American Economic Affairs* 2:52-71.

Rodríguez, Mario. 1964. *A Palmerstonian Diplomat in Central America: Frederick Chatfield, Esq.*. Tucson, Univ. of Arizona.

Rodríguez, Oscar. 1986. The Church and Refugees in Central America. *Social Justice Review* (May/June):91-94, 119.

Rodríguez Beteta, Virgilio. 1963. *La política inglesa en Centro Américan durante el siglo XIX*. Guatemala: Ministerio de Educación Pública.

Roosevelt, Franklin D. 1928. Our Foreign Policy: A Democratic View. *Foreign Affairs* 6:573-86.

Rosenberg, Hans. 1967. *Grosse Depression und Bismarckzeit. Wirtschaftsaublauf, Gesellschaft und Politik in Mitteleuropa*. Berlin: de Gruyter.

Rossell Arellano, Mariano. 1944a. *Carta circular del excelentisimo señor arzobispo de Guatemala a sus sacerdotes y declaración de principios acerca de la presente situación*. Guatemala: Talleres Gutenberg.

— — —. 1944b. *Exhortación pastoral del excmo. señor arzobispo de Guatemala con ocasión de los últimos acontecimientos*. Guatemala: Tipografía Sánchez y De Guise.

— — —. 1945. *Declaraciones de Guatemala sobre la posición de la iglesia: la iglesia no pretende privilegios*. Guatemala: Unión Tipografía.

— — —. 1946a. *Carta pastoral del excelentisimo y reverendisimo señor don Mariano Rossell Arellano, arzobispo de Guatemala, sobre Acción Católica*. Guatemala: Tipografía De Guise.

— — —. 1946b. *A las clases laborante y patronal*. Guatemala: Unión Tipográfica.

— — —. 1948a. *Carta pastoral*. Guatemala: Unión Tipográfica.

— — —. 1948b. *Exhortación de Monseñor Mariano Rossell Arellano, arzobispo de Guatemala, al pueblo católico sobre el deber de la caridad en la práctica del sufragio electoral*. Guatemala: Talleres Gutenberg.

— — —. 1948c. *Instruccion pastoral al pueblo católico de Guatemala sobre el deber y condiciones del sufragio*. Guatemala: Imprenta Sensur.

Rossell Arellano, Mariano, et al. 1945. *Carta pastoral colectiva del episcopado de la provincia eclesiástica de Guatemala sobre la amenaza comunista en nuestra patria*. Guatemala: Tipografía Sánchez y De Guise.

Rowley, Anthony. 1982. *Évolution économique de la France du milieu du xix < e > siècle à 1914*. Paris: SEDES.

Rubinson, Richard. 1978. Political Transformation in Germany and the United States. In *Social Change in the Capitalist World Economy*, ed. Barbara B. Kaplan, 39-71. Beverly Hills, Calif.: Sage.

Rubio Sánchez, Antonio N., and Adolfo López Ryder. 1979. Intercambio comercial México-Nicaragua. *Comercio Exterior* (Banco Nacional de Comercio Exterior de México) (November): 1295-1296.

Ruiz Franco, Arcadio. 1950. *Hambre y miseria*. Guatemala: Tipografía Nacional.

Salinas, Pedro. 1948. *La poesía de Rubén Darío*. Buenos Aires: Editorial Losada.

Salisbury, Richard. 1984. *Costa Rica y el istmo, 1900-1934*. San José: Editorial Costa Rica.

— — —. 1986. Mexico, the United States, and the 1926-1927 Nicaraguan Crisis. *Hispanic American Historical Review* 66:319-39.

Sanders, W. W. 1981. Mexico's Message to Central America. *Business Week*, January 19:53.

Sante Arrocha, Angela delli. 1962. *Juan José Arévalo, pensador contemporáneo*. México: Costa Amic.

SB. Staatsarchiv Bremen. Bremen.

Schaefer, Claudia. 1982. A Search for Utopia on Earth: Toward an Understanding of the Literary Prouction of Ernesto Cardenal. *Crítica Hispánica* 4:171-79.

Scheips, Paul J. 1956. Gabriel Lafond and Ambrose W. Thompson: Neglected Isthmian Promoters. *Hispanic American Historical Review* 36:211-28.

Schlesinger, Arthur M., Jr. 1975. The Alliance for Progress: A Retrospective. In *Latin America: The Search for a New International Role*, ed. R. G. Hellman and H. J. Rosenbaum, eds. 1975, 57-92. New York: Wiley.

— — —. 1978. *Robert Kennedy and His Times*. Boston: Houghton Mifflin.

Schlesinger, Stephen, and Stephen Kinzer. 1982. *Bitter Fruit: The Untold Story of the American Coup in Guatemala*. Garden City: Anchor Books.

Schneider, Ronald M. 1979. *Communism in Guatemala, 1944-1954*. New York: Octagon.

Schoenhals, Kai, and Richard A. Melanson. 1985. *Revolution and Intervention in Grenada*. Boulder: Westview.

Scholes, Walter V. 1960. Los Estados Unidos, México, y América Central en 1909, *Historia Mexicana* 10(4):613-27.

Scholes, Walter V., and Marie V. Scholes. 1970. *The Foreign Policy of the Taft Administration*. Columbia: Univ. of Missouri Press.

Schoonover, Thomas. 1973. Intereres Británicos en Costa Rica cerca 1857. *Estudios Sociales Centroamericanos* 6 (September-December):152-54.

– – –. 1983. Imperialism in Middle America: US Competition with Britain, Germany and France, 1820s-1920s. In *Eagle Against Empire: American Opposition to European Imperialism, 1914-1982*, ed. Rhodri Jeffreys-Jones, 41-58. Aix-en-Provence: Université de Provence.

– – –. 1985. Prussia and the Protection of German Transit Through Middle America, 1848-1851. *Jahrbuch für Geschichte von Staat, Wirtschaft und Gesellschaft Lateinamerikas* 22:393-422.

Schopf, Raquel. 1985. *Zur Genese und Entwicklung der engagierten Dichtung Ernesto Cardenals*. Frankfurt am Main: Peter Lang.

Schottelius, Herbert. 1939. *Mittelamerika als Schauplatz deutscher Kolonisationsversuche, 1840-1865*. Hamburg: Hans Christians.

Schoultz, Lars. 1981. *Human Rights and United States Policy Toward Latin America*. Princeton: Princeton Univ. Press.

Schultz, Johann Heinrich Siegfried. 1843. *Uber Colonisation mit besonderer Rücksicht auf die Colonie zu Santo Thomás, im Staate Guatemala, und die Belgische Colonisations-Compagnie*. Cologne: Dumont-Schauberg.

Secretaría Conferencia Episcopal de Honduras. 1970a. *Boletín de prensa no. 4 de la Conferencia Episcopal*. Tegucigalpa, January 9.

– – –. 1970b. *Carta pastoral colectiva sobre el desarrollo del campesinado en Honduras*. Tegucigalpa, January 8.

– – –. 1971. *Resolución del comité permanente de la Conferencia Episcopal de Honduras*. Tegucigalpa, October 6.

– – –. 1972. *Declaraciones de la Conferencia Episcopal de Honduras.*, Tegucigalpa, April 13.

– – –. 1975a. *Carta de la iglesia Católica de Honduras al Jefe de Estado y Consejo Superior de la Defensa*. Tegucigalpa, July 10.

– – –. 1975b. *Comunicado de la Conferencia Episcopal de Honduras*. Tegucigalpa, July 18.

– – –. 1981. Declaration of Honduran Episcopal Conference Regarding Río Sumpul Incident. *LADOC* 11(3/18a):21-25.

– – –. 1982. *Carta pastoral colectiva sobre algunos aspectos de la realidad nacional de Honduras*. Tegucigalpa, October 22.

– – –. 1984. *Exhortación pastoral de la Conferencia Episcopal de Honduras*, Tegucigalpa, Tegucigalpa, September 4.

– – –. 1985a. *Comunicado de la Conferencia Episcopal de Honduras*. Tegucigalpa, April 15.

– – –. 1985b. *Comunicado de prensa*, Conferencia Episcopal. Tegucigalpa, August 29.

Selser, Gregorio. 1980. *El pequeño ejército loco: operación México-Nicaragua*. México: Brugero Mexicana de Ediciones.

– – –. 1981. *Sandino*. Trans. Cedric Belfrage. New York: Monthly Review Press.

Sereseres, Caesar. 1971. Military Development and the United States Military Assistance Program for Latin America: The Case of Guatemala, 1961-1969. Ph.D. diss. Univ. of California, Riverside.

———. 1984. The Mexican Military Looks South. In *The Modern Mexican Military: A Reassessment,* ed. David Ronfeldt, 201-13. La Jolla: Center for U.S.-Mexican Studies, Univ. of California at San Diego.

———. 1978. Guatemalan Paramilitary Forces, Internal Security, and Politics. In *Supplementary Military Forces: Reserves, Militias, and Auxiliaries,* ed. Louis A. Zurcher and Gwyn Barries-Jenkins, 179-99. Beverly Hills, Calif.: Sage.

Sewell, William H., Jr. 1985. Ideologies and Social Revolution: Reflections on the French Case. *Journal of Modern History* 57:57-85.

SH. Staatsarchiv Hamburg, Hamburg.

Sharkey, Jacqueline. 1986. Back in Control: The CIA's Secret Propaganda Campaign Puts the Agency Exactly Where It Wants to Be. *Common Cause Magazine* 12 (September/October):28-40.

Sheehan, Edward R. F. 1986. The Country of Nada. *New York Review,* March 27:11-16.

Sherman, William. 1979. *Forced Native Labor in Sixteenth Century Central America.* Lincoln: Univ. of Nebraska Press.

Siegal, Morris. 1942. Resistance to Culture Change in Western Guatemala. *Sociology and Social Research* 25:414-30.

Silvert, Kalman H. 1954. *A Study in Government: Guatemala.* New Orleans: Middle American Research Institute, Tulane Univ.

Silvert, Kalman H., et. al. 1975. *Americas for a Changing World: A Report of the Commission on United States-Latin American Relations.* New York: Quadrangle.

Simpson, Charles M., III. 1983. *Inside the Green Berets: The First Thirty Years.* Novato, Calif.: Presidio Press.

Skocpol, Theda. 1985. Cultural Idioms and Political Ideologies in the Revolutionary Reconstruction of State Power: A Rejoinder to Sewell. *Journal of Modern History* 57:86-96.

Skyrme, Raymond. 1975. *Rubén Darío and the Pythagorean Tradition.* Gainesville: Univ. of Florida Press.

Small, Melvin. 1972. The United States and the German "Threat" to the Hemisphere, 1905-1914. *The Americas* 28:252-70.

Smith, Carol. 1984. Local History in a Global Context: Social and Economic Transitions in Western Guatemala. *Comparative Studies in Society and History* 26:193-228.

Smith, Janet L. 1979a. *An Annotated Bibliography of and about Ernesto Cardenal.* Tempe: Center for Latin American Studies, Arizona State Univ.

Smith, Joseph. 1979b. *Illusion of Conflict: Anglo-American Diplomacy Toward Latin America, 1865-1896.* Pittsburgh: Univ. of Pittsburgh Press.

Smith, Robert F. 1972. *The United States and Revolutionary Nationalism in Mexico, 1916-1932.* Chicago: Univ. of Chicago Press.

Smith, Waldemar. 1977. *The Fiesta System and Economic Change.* New York: Columbia Univ. Press.

Soto, Chirinos. 1977. Amor, tiempo y muerte en los poemas de Rubén Darío. *Cuadernos Americanos* 214(5):223-32.

Soustelle, Jacques. 1982. Au Nicaragua: Un Genocide Bien Tranquille. *Revue des Deux Mondes* 10:16-22.

Spicer, Edward H. 1971. Persistent Cultural Systems: A Comparative Study of Identity Systems That Can Adapt to Contrasting Environments. *Science* 174:795-800.

— — —. 1980. *The Yaquis: A Cultural History*. Tucson: Univ. of Arizona Press.

Spree, Reinhard. 1977. *Die Wachstumszyklen der deutschen Wirtschaft von 1840-1880*. Berlin: Duncker und Homblot.

Squier, E. G. 1850. Mr. E. G. Squier, Charge D'Affaires, Central America. *American Review* 6 (October):345-52.

— — —. 1852. *Nicaragua: Its People, Scenery, and Monuments, and the Proposed Interoceanic Canal*. 2 vols. New York: Appleton.

Stalin, Joseph V. 1979. *Marxism and the National Question*. Tirana, Albania: 8 Nentori Publishing House.

Stanislawski, Dan. 1983. *The Transformation of Nicaragua: 1519-1548*. Berkeley: Univ. of California Press.

Stansifer, Charles L. 1981. *Cultural Policy in the Old and the New Nicaragua*. Hanover, N.H.: American Universities Field Staff.

— — —. Forthcoming. United States-Central American Relations, 1824-1850. In *United States-Latin American Relations: The Formative Years*, ed. Ray T. Shurbutt. University, Ala.: Univ. of Alabama Press.

Stephansky, Ben S. 1975. New Dialogue on Latin America: The Cost of Policy Neglect. In *Latin America: The U.S. Search for a New International Role*, ed. Ronald G. Hellman and H. Jon Rosenbaum, 153-66. New York: Wiley.

Steward, Julian H. 1948. The Circum-Caribbean Tribes: An Introduction. In *Handbook of South American Indians*, ed. Julian H. Steward, 4:1-41. Washington: GPO.

Street, Anne, and Nancy Peckenham. 1984. Translated Transcript of an Interview with Bishop Luis Santos, July 30. Unpublished manuscript in Maryknoll Justice and Peace Office, Maryknoll, N.Y.

Tax, Sol. 1937. Municipios of the Midwestern Highlands of Guatemala. *American Anthropology* 39:423-44.

— — —. 1953. *Penny Capitalism: A Guatemalan Indian Economy*. Washington: Smithsonian Institution, Institute of Social Anthropology.

Tenth Inter-American Conference of American States, Caracas, Venezuela, March 1954. 1954. Report of the Delegates. Washington: GPO.

Teplitz, Benjamin I. 1973. The Political and Economic Foundations of Modernization in Nicaragua: The Administration of José Santos Zelaya, 1893-1909. Ph.D. diss., Howard Univ., Washington, D.C.

The Belize Billboard. 1950.

The Belize Times. 1979-1983

The New Belize. 1983.

The Reporter. 1979. Belize.

Thorup, Cathryn, and Robert L. Ayres. 1982. Central America: The Challenge to United States and Mexican Foreign Policy. Washington: Overseas

Development Council, U.S. Mexican Project Series, Working Paper No. 8. *Times of the Americas*. 1986. Washington, D.C..

Tirado, Manlio. 1983. *Conversando con José Coronel Urtecho*. Managua: Nueva Nicaragua.

Tojeira, José María. 1986. *Panorama histórico de la iglesia en Honduras*. Tegucigalpa: Centro de Documentación de Honduras.

[Tojeira, José María]. 1985. Significado político de la penetración protestante. In *Honduras: historias no contadas*, 179-192. Tegucigalpa: Centro de Documentación de Honduras.

Torres, Edelberto. 1952. *La dramática vida de Rubén Darío*. Guatemala: Editorial del Ministerio de Educación Pública.

Torres, Emilio. 1982. Lineas de trabajo para los CPC – 1983. *La Chacalaca* 3:5-8.

Trejos, Juan Diego. 1985. *Costa Rica: Economic Crisis and Public Policy, 1978-1984*. Miami: Latin American and Caribbean Center, Florida International al Univ.

Trueblood, Howard J. 1937. Trade Rivalries in Latin America. *Foreign Policy Reports* 13(13):154-64.

Tucker, Robert C., ed. 1978. *The Marx-Engels Reader*. New York: Norton.

Tumin, Melvin. 1952. *Caste in a Peasant Society: A Case Study in the Dynamics of Caste*. Princeton: Princeton Univ. Press.

Tünnermann-Bernheim, Carlos. 1973. *Pablo Antonio Cuadra y la cultura nacional*. León: UNAN.

Turner, Frederick C. 1968. *The Dynamics of Mexican Nationalism*. Chapel Hill, Univ. of North Carolina Press.

USNA. United States National Archives, Washington.

U.S. Congress. 1901. Senate. *Report of the Isthmian Canal Commission, 1899-1901*. 57th Cong., 1st sess., 1901-1902, Sen. Doc. No. 54.

– – –. 1984. House Committee on Foreign Affairs. *Central America: The Deepening Conflict: Report of a Congressional Study Mission to Honduras, Costa Rica, Nicaragua, and El Salvador, August 27-September 8, 1983*, 98th Cong., 2d sess., August 29.

– – –. 1985. House Committee on Foreign Affairs. *Narcotics Production and Transhipments in Belize and Central America, Hearings Before the Committee on Foreign Affairs, House of Representatives*. 99th Cong., 1st sess.

U.S. Department of State. 1909-1927. *Papers Relating to the Foreign Relations of the United States*. Washington: GPO.

– – –. 1954. *Intervention of International Communism in Guatemala*. Washington, GPO.

– – –. 1981. *Communist Interference in El Salvador*. Special Report No. 80, Feb. 23. Washington: GPO.

– – –. 1985. *Foreign Assistance Program: FY 1986 Budget and 1985 Supplemental Request*. Special Report No. 128. Washington: U.S. Department of State, Bureau of Public Affairs, May.

U.S. News and World Report. 1981.

U.S. Joint Chiefs of Staff. 1977. *Special Historical Study: History of the Unified Command Plan*, 20 December (CONFIDENTIAL study, declassified 1981). Washington: Historical Division, Joint Secretariat.

Valdés, Jorge. 1983. The Evolution of Cardenal's Prophetic Poetry. *Latin American Literary Review* 11(2/3):25-40.

Valdés, Mario J. 1966. *Death in the Literature of Unamuno*. Urbana: Univ. of Illinois.

Valenta, Jiri. 1981. The USSR, Cuba and the Crisis in Central America. *Orbis* 19:715-46.

Valero, Ricardo. 1985. Contadora: la busqueda de la pacificación en Centroamérica. *Foro Internacional* (October-December):125-56.

Van Alstyne, Richard. 1939. British Diplomacy and the Clayton-Bulwer Treaty 1850-1860. *Journal of Modern History* 11:149-83.

Vanden, Harry E. 1982. The Ideology of Insurrection. In *Nicaragua in Revolution*, ed. T. W. Walker, 41-62. New York: Praeger.

Vega Carballo, José Luis. 1981. *Orden y progreso: La formación del estado nacional en Costa Rica*. San José: Instituto Centroamericano de Administración Pública.

Vega Miranda, Gilberto. 1982. Músicos nicaragüenses de ayer. *Boletín Nicaragüense de Bibliografía y Documentación* 48:51-72.

Ventana. 1960-1964. León.

Verbum. 1945-1950. Guatemala.

Vilas, Carlos M. 1986. *The Sandinista Revolution: National Liberation and Social Transformation in Central America*. New York: Monthly Review Press.

Volk, Steven. 1981. Honduras: On the Border of War. *NACLA Report on the Americas* 15(6):2-37.

Wagley, Charles. 1941. *Economics of a Guatemalan Village*. Washington: American Anthropological Association.

Wagner, Eric A. 1982. Sport after Revolution: A Comparative Study of Cuba and Nicaragua. In *Nicaragua in Revolution*, ed. T. W. Walker, 291-302. New York: Praeger.

Walk, Alan. 1981. Remembering the Answers. *The Nation*, December 26:708-10.

Walker, Thomas W., ed. 1982. *Nicaragua in Revolution*. New York: Praeger.

— — —, ed. 1985. *Nicaragua: The First Five Years*. New York: Praeger.

— — —. 1986. *Nicaragua: Land of Sandino*. 2d ed. Boulder: Westview.

Wallerstein, Imanuel. 1974-1980. *The World System*. 2 vols. Orlando, Fla: Academic Press.

Walsh, Donald D., ed. 1980. *Zero Hour and Other Documentary Poems*. Trans. Paul W. Borgeson, Jr., et al. New York: New Directions.

Walton, Richard. 1972. *Cold War and Counter Revolution: The Foreign Policy of John F. Kennedy*. New York: Viking.

Warren, Kay. 1976. *The Symbolism of Subordination: Indian Identity in a Guatemalan Town*. Austin: Univ. of Texas Press.

Washington Post. 1983-1984.

Watanabe, John. 1981. Cambios económicos en Santiago Chimaltenango. *Mesoamérica* 2:21-30.

Watland, Charles D. 1965. *Poet-Errant: A Biography of Rubén Darío*. New York: Philosophical Library.

Weber, Eugene. 1962. *Action Française: Royalism and Reaction in Twentieth-Century France*. Stanford: Stanford Univ. Press.

Webster, Bethuel. 1968. *Draft Treaty Between the United Kingdom of Great Britain and Northern Ireland and the Republic of Guatemala Relating to the Resolution of the Dispute over British Honduras (Belize)*. New York: 1968.

Wehler, Hans-Ulrich. 1972. Industrial Growth and Early German Imperialism. In *Studies in the Theory of Imperialism*, ed. Roger Owen and Bob Sutcliffe, 71-92. London: Longman.

— — —. 1983. *Grundzüge der amerikanischen Aussenpolitik, 1750-1900*. Frankfurt: Suhrkamp.

Westcott, Allan, ed. 1941. *Mahan on Naval Warfare*. Boston: Heath.

Wheelock Román, Jaime. 1974. *Raíces indígenas de la lucha anticolonialista en Nicaragua*. México: Siglo XXI.

— — —. 1975. *Imperialismo y dictadura: crisis de una formación social*. México: Siglo XXI.

Whisnant, David E. 1983a. *All That is Native and Fine: The Politics of Culture in an American Region*. Chapel Hill: Univ. of North Carolina Press.

— — —. 1983b. International Perspectives on Cultural Policy Formation: The UNESCO Conferences. *New Jersey Folklore* 8:21-27.

White, Eric W. 1975. *The Arts Council of Great Britain*. London: Davis = Poynter.

White, Robert A. 1977. Structural Factors in Rural Development: The Church and the Peasant in Honduras. Ph.D. diss., Cornell Univ., Ithaca, N.Y.

White, Steven F., ed. 1982. *Poets of Nicaragua: A Bilingual Anthology, 1918-1979*. Greensboro: Unicorn.

— — —, ed. 1986. *Culture and Politics in Nicaragua: Testimonies of Poets and Writers*. New York: Lumen.

Wiarda, Howard J. 1984. At the Root of the Problem: Conceptual Failures in US-Central American Relations. 1984. In *Central America: Anatomy of Conflict*, ed. R. S. Leiken, 259-78. New York: Pergamon.

Wilde, Margaret D. 1981. The Sandinistas and the Costeños: Reconciliation and Integration. *Caribbean Review* 10(4):8-11.

Wilkins, Mira. 1970. *The Emergence of Multinational Enterprise: American Business Abroad from the Colonial Era to 1914*. Cambridge, Mass.: Harvard Univ. Press.

Williams, Edward J. 1982. Mexico's Central American Policy: Apologies, Motivations, and Principles. *Bulletin of Latin American Research* (October): 21-41.

— — —. 1984. Mexico's Central American Policy. In *Rift and Revolution: The Central American Imbroglio*, ed. Howard J. Wiarda, 303-28. Washington: American Enterprise Institute.

Williams, Robert. 1986. *Export Agriculture and the Crisis in Central America*. Chapel Hill: Univ. of North Carolina Press.

Williams, William Appleman. 1966. *Contours of American History*. Chicago: Quadrangle.

Winckler, Martin. 1964. *Bismarcks Bündnispolitik und das europäische Gleichgewicht*. Stuttgart: Kohlhammer.

Wisdom, Charles. 1940. *The Chorti Indians of Guatemala*. Chicago: Univ. of Chicago Press.

Wise, David, and Thomas B. Ross. 1964. *The Invisible Government*. New York: Random House.

Wolf, Eric. 1957. Closed Corporate Peasant Communities in Mesoamerica and Central Java. *Southwestern Journal of Anthropology* 13:1-18.

Wolff, Thomas. 1981. Mexican-Guatemalan Imbroglio: Fishery Rights and National Honor. *The Americas* 38:235-48.

Wood, Bryce. 1961. *The Making of the Good Neighbor Policy*. New York: Columbia Univ. Press.

Woodward, Ralph Lee, Jr. 1962. *Octubre*: Communist Appeal to the Urban Labor Force of Guatemala, 1950-1953. *Journal of Inter-American Studies* 4:363-74.

― ― ―, ed. 1971. *Positivism in Latin America, 1850-1900: Are Order and Progress Reconcilable?*. Lexington, Mass.: D. C. Heath.

― ― ―. 1976. *Central America: A Nation Divided*. New York: Oxford Univ. Press.

― ― ―. 1979. Liberalism, Conservatism, and the Response of the Peasants of La Montaña to the Government of Guatemala, 1821-1850. *Plantation Society in the Americas* 1:109-29.

― ― ―. 1985. *Central America: A Nation Divided*. 2d ed. New York: Oxford Univ. Press.

WSIGHS. Werner-von-Siemens-Institut für Geschichte des Hauses Siemens, Munich.

Wurgraft, Lewis D. 1971. The Activist Movement: Cultural Politics on the German Left, 1914-1933. Ph.D. diss., Harvard Univ., Cambridge, Mass.

Ycaza Tigerino, Julio. 1961. La muerte en la poesía de Rubén Darío. *El Pez y la Serpiente* 2:131-142.

Yepes Boscán, Guillermo, ed. 1980. *Siete arboles contra el atardecer*. Caracas: Ediciones de la Presidencia de la República.

Young, Alma H., and Dennis Young. 1983. The Impact of the Anglo-Guatemalan Dispute on the Internal Politics of Belize. Unpublished paper presented at the 11th International Congress of the Latin American Studies Association, Mexico City, September 29-October 1.

Zavala Cuadra, Xavier, et al. 1985. *1984 Nicaragua*. San José: Libro Libre.

Zelaya, José Santos. 1910. *La revolución de Nicaragua y los Estados Unidos*. Madrid: B. Rodríguez.

Zimmerman, Marc. 1980. Pablo Antonio Cuadra y Leonel Rugama: dos formas, dos poetas, dos políticas. *Taller* 16/17 (November):44-58.

― ― ―, ed. 1985a. *Flights of Victory/Vuelos de victoria*. New York: Orbis.

— — —, ed. 1985b. *Nicaragua in Reconstruction & at War: The People Speak.* Minneapolis: MEP.

Zwerling, Philip, and Connie Martin, eds. 1985. *Nicaragua: A New Kind of Revolution.* Westport, Conn.: Lawrence Hill.

About the Contributors

EDWARD T. BRETT, Ph.D., Rutgers University, is Associate Professor of Social Sciences at La Roche College. Trained in medieval history, he is the author of *Humbert of Romans: His Life and Views of Thirteenth-Century Society* (1984). Recently he has studied the role of the Catholic clergy in Central America. **DONNA W. BRETT** is a graduate student in Latin American history at the University of Pittsburgh. Together they have co-authored *Murdered in Central America* (1988).

HUGH G. CAMPBELL, Ph.D., University of California, Los Anteles, is Professor of History at California State University, Chico, and is the author of *La derecha radical en México, 1929-1949* (1976).

GEORGE CASTILE, Ph.D., University of Arizona, is Associate Professor of Anthropology at Whitman College. He is the author of *North American Indians: An Introduction to the Chichimeca* (1979), *The Indians of Puget Sound: The Notebooks of Myron Fells, 1894* (1985), and numerous other books and articles in scholarly journals on indigenous peoples.

JOHN D. HEYL, Ph.D., Washington University, is Professor of History at Illinois Wesleyan University and has written numerous articles on revolutionary culture in various historical settings. For their encouragement, critical suggestions, and technical assistance, he wishes to thank Ralph Lee Woodward, Jr., James J. Alstrum, Marina E. Kaplan, David Whisnant, Salvador J. Fajardo, Cecilia Montenegro de Teague, and Thomas Niehaus.

FRANK J. KENDRICK, Ph.D., University of Chicago, is Associate Professor of Urban Studies and Political Science at the University of Akron. He is the co-author of *The New Politics: Mood or Movement* (1971) and *Strategies for Political Participation* (3d ed., 1983), as well as numerous articles on U.S. politics. He has traveled extensively in South and Central America doing research on current social and political change there.

THOMAS M. LEONARD, Ph.D., American University, is Professor of History at the University of North Florida. He is the author of *The United States and Central America, 1944-1949: Perceptions of Political Dynamics* (1984), *Central America and United States Policies, 1820s-1980s* (1985), and several articles. He has served as an officer for the Florida College Teachers of History Association, Society for Historians of American Foreign Relations, and Southeast Council on Latin American Studies.

HUBERT J. MILLER, Ph.D., Loyola University, Chicago, is Professor of Mexican and Central American history at Pan American University, Edinburg, Tex. He is the author of *La Iglesia y el estado en Guatemala, 1871-1885* (1976) and is currently collaborating with Guatemalan historians in writing a five-volume general history of Guatemala. Since 1986 he has served on the editorial board of the *Borderlands Journal*.

MARILYN M. MOORS, M.A., George Washington University, is Associate Professor of Anthropology at Montgomery College, Rockville, Md., and currently serves as the National Coordinator of the Guatemalan Scholars Network. She gratefully acknowledges the assistance and advice of Ralph Lee Woodward, Jr., and Professors Mary Gallagher and Myrna Goldenberg of Montgomery College in the preparation of this essay.

KAI SCHOENHALS, Ph.D., University of Rochester, is Professor of History at Kenyon College. He is co-author of *Grenada: Revolution and Intervention* (1985), numerous articles in *Caribbean Review* and *Caribbean Contact*, and translator of Friedrick Sorge's *History of the American Labor Movement, 1890-1896* (1987).

THOMAS SCHOONOVER, Ph.D., University of Minnesota, is Professor of History at the University of Southwestern Louisiana, and is the author of several books and articles dealing with the Middle American region. He is grateful to his wife, Ebba, for research, editorial, and secretarial support, to Walter LaFeber and R. L. Woodward, Jr. for critical readings, and to the National Endowment for the Humanities, the German Academic Exchange Service (DAAD), the Fritz Thyssen Foundation, the American Philosophical Society, Tulane University's Mellon grant program, and the American Historical Association's Albert Beveridge Fund for aid with research trips.

DAVID WHISNANT, Ph.D., Duke University, is Professor of American Studies at the University of North Carolina, Chapel Hill. He is author of numerous books and articles on traditional and regional culture, the politics of culture, and cultural policy, of which the most recent is *All That Is Native and Fine: The Politics of Culture in an American Region* (1983). For encouragement, technical assistance, and critical suggestions, he is grateful to Ralph Lee Woodward, Jr., John Heyl, Archie Green, John Sinnegen, and Cecilia Montenegro de Teague.

RALPH LEE WOODWARD, JR., Ph.D., Tulane University, is Professor of Latin American History and Chairman of the Department of History at Tulane. He is the author of *Central America, a Nation Divided* (2d ed., 1985), and numerous other books and articles on Central American history, and is an editor of the *Research Guide to Central America and the Caribbean*. He also compiles the Central American history section of the *Handbook of Latin American Studies* and is a member of the boards of editors of *Mesoamérica, The Latin American Research Review*, and the *Revista del Pensamiento Centroamericano*.

LAWRENCE A. YATES, Ph.D., University of Kansas, is currently an historian with the Combat Studies Institute at Fort Leavenworth, Kansas, where he is writing a study of U.S. intervention in the Dominican Republic in 1965. The views expressed in his chapter are those of the author and do not necessarily represent the views of either the Department of the Army or the Department of Defense.

Index